Advanced Progr
Techniques for t
BBC Micro

JIM McGREGOR

ALAN WATT

ADDISON-WESLEY PUBLISHING COMPANY

London · Reading, Massachusetts · Menlo Park, California · Amsterdam
Don Mills, Ontario · Manilla · Singapore · Sydney · Tokyo

Set by the authors in Bookface Academic using SROFF, the text processing system at the University of Sheffield.

Cover illustration by Stuart Hughes.

Printed in Finland by Werner Söderström Osakeyhtiö. Member of Finnprint.

British Library Cataloguing in Publication Data
McGregor, James J.
Advanced programming techniques for the BBC Micro.
1. BBC Microcomputer—Programming
I. Title II. Watt, Alan H.
001.64'24 QA76.8.B3

ISBN 0-201-14059-4

ABCDEF 89876543

Contents

Preface

Ten to fifteen years ago machines with the memory size and processing capability of the BBC micro would have cost many thousands of pounds and were the exclusive domain of computer professionals. Nowadays powerful computers are in the hands of the home user and this book aims to bring the tools of the trade of the computer scientist to the micro user.

The book is a practical introduction to advanced topics in computer science. Rather than adopt the formal approach found in most computer science texts, we have introduced each technique practically, by using simple program modules that act as building blocks. Each topic is covered at sufficient depth so that for a non-professional the waters are neither fathomless nor so shallow as to be trivial

The techniques selected for inclusion in this text form the foundation stone of advanced computer graphics, artificial intelligence, automatic musical composition, databases, arcade game programming, board game programming, adventure game programming, computer assisted learning, computer aided design and language processing.

With the exception of Chapter 3 the book contains no difficult mathematics and perseverance with the material will compensate for a lack of knowledge of the higher echelons of mathematics. Even the mathematics in Chapter 3 can be ignored with impunity and a sound understanding of the material derived from using the procedures.

The text is supported by a considerable number of program fragments, procedures and complete programs together with suggestions on projects that you can undertake yourself.

An essential prerequisite is a knowledge of BASIC, either from our companion volume, 'The BBC Micro, BASIC, Sound and Graphics', or from experience of other BASIC dialects. If your experience is on another machine, you will need access to a BBC Micro 'User Guide'. For the sake of completeness some material from our companion volume is repeated in Chapter 2.

Structured programming techniques are used throughout the text and we have attempted to make the programs readable. The programming style adopted is described in Chapter 1 and it makes extensive use of the BBC BASIC control structures and procedure facilities. Apart from a single unavoidable occurrence there is no use of GOTO or GOSUB anywhere in the text.

A mastery of the material in this book will make you an expert micro-programmer. If you can creatively expand and develop the ideas herein then ring ACORNSOFT and ask for a job.

How to use this book

This book need not be read sequentially, you can if you prefer dip into the topics in any order.

Some chapters are self contained and others can be read only after earlier material has been understood. The following table is a guide to how the book can be used.

Chapter no.	Prerequisite
1	Some knowledge of standard BASIC
2	A knowledge of the basic graphics facilities of the BBC Micro. (See our companion volume)
3	As for Chapter 2
4	Chapter 2
5	A knowledge of the basic sound facilities of the BBC micro. (See our companion volume)
6	Chapter 1
7	Chapter 1
8	Chapters 1 and 7
9	Chapters 1, 7 and 8
10	Chapters 1 and 7

Are you a slow typist?

You can experiment with the programs described in this book without having to type them. All the programs of any length are available on a computer cassette.

Some of the larger programs are useful utilities in their own right and others provide the foundations for fairly elaborate programming projects in sound, graphics, animation and games.

Programs are also available on cassette for the companion volume by the same authors:

The BBC Micro Book: BASIC, Sound and Graphics

Books and cassettes are available from your bookseller or direct from

Addison-Wesley Publishers Ltd.,
53 Bedford Square,
London, WC1B 3DZ.

Chapter 1 Programming style for BBC BASIC

Apart from the powerful graphics and sound facilities, BBC BASIC provides a number of 'control statements' that are not usually available in other dialects of BASIC. A control statement is a statement that is used to control the order in which a program is obeyed and examples of the control statements that are available in standard BASIC are FOR statements, IF-GOTO statements, GOTO statements and GOSUB statements.

It has long been recognised by computer scientists that programs written using combinations of the above statements tend to be difficult to write, difficult to read and difficult to debug. This is because of heavy reliance on the use of GOTO and GOSUB statements. Excessive use of these statements results in programs whose possible execution pathways are so intertwined that the control structure of a program is obscured.

The number of control structures that are needed to cover the majority of programming situations is very small and BBC BASIC provides control statements for implementing most of the common constructions without using GOTOs or GOSUBs. If you are used to programming in 'standard' BASIC it needs a certain amount of self-discipline to learn to use these new statements and abandon old programming habits, but the effort is well worthwhile. The result will be more readable programs. The programmer will also have a much clearer idea of the structure of his programs and will find them easier to debug and alter. Programs are not less efficient as some of the 'GOTO diehards' would have us believe. In many cases, the use of the appropriate control statements instead of a messy combination of GOTO statements results in a more efficient program.

1.1 Control statements in BBC BASIC

In this section, we briefly introduce and illustrate the use of the novel control statements in BBC BASIC, and, in subsequent sections, we discuss ways of using these statements to improve our programming style. Note that there are some dialects of BASIC that provide some, but not all, of the facilities described in this chapter.

Loops

As well as the FOR-NEXT construction available in standard BASIC, BBC BASIC provides a REPEAT-UNTIL construction for use in implementing a so-called 'non-deterministic' loop. A non-deterministic or conditional loop is a loop where the computer cannot calculate in advance how many times to obey the loop and a section of program is to be obeyed repeatedly until some condition has been satisfied. For example, a simple computer-assisted learning program might repeatedly set multiplication questions and input the answers from the keyboard until one of the questions is answered wrongly:

```
10   questions = 0
20   REPEAT
30      questions = questions+1
40      a = RND(11) + 1  :  b = RND(11) + 1
50      PRINT a; "x"; b; "=";
60      INPUT answer
70   UNTIL answer <> a*b
80   PRINT "Wrong!"
90   PRINT "You got "; questions-1; " questions right"
```

The REPEAT statement introduces a section of program that is to be obeyed repeatedly and the UNTIL statement indicates the extent of the loop, and specifies the condition for stopping the repetition. The REPEAT statement and an equivalent construction using a GOTO statement are shown below:

<u>REPEAT loop</u>	<u>Equivalent GOTO loop</u>
20 REPEAT	
.	30 .
.	.
.	.
70 UNTIL condition	70 IF NOT condition GOTO 30

IF statements

The IF statement in BBC BASIC can have the form of the 'standard' logical IF:

```
IF condition THEN   one or more statements
```

The statements after THEN are obeyed only if the condition is TRUE. The other form of IF statement is

```
IF condition THEN   one or more statements
             ELSE   one or more statements
```

In this case, if the condition is TRUE, the statements after THEN are obeyed, otherwise the statements after ELSE are obeyed. A simple example of a program involving an IF-THEN statement is:

```
10  INPUT bankbalance, withdrawal
20  bankbalance = bankbalance - withdrawal
30  IF bankbalance<0 THEN
        bankbalance=bankbalance-0.20 : PRINT "Overdrawn!":
        PRINT "Send this customer a letter from manager"
40  PRINT "Balance is now "; bankbalance
```

Note that an IF statement constitutes a single numbered line of a BBC BASIC program. (A single numbered line can occupy up to 240 characters and may occupy several screen lines.) You must type the complete IF statement without pressing RETURN. The RETURN key is pressed only when a numbered line is complete. If an IF statement does not fit into 240 characters, then it is almost certain that your program would be better structured using procedures (see below).

When more than one statement is typed after THEN, the statements must be separated from each other by colons and these statements are either all obeyed or all ignored. The same rule applies to multiple statements following the ELSE.

To illustrate the use of an IF-THEN-ELSE statement, we could extend our 'multiplication program':

```
100   IF questions>20 THEN
          PRINT "Well done! That was very good."
      ELSE PRINT "You must brush up on your tables."
```

or even

```
100   IF questions>20 THEN
          PRINT "Well done!"
      ELSE IF questions>10 THEN
              PRINT "Room for improvement"
           ELSE PRINT "Learn your tables!"
```

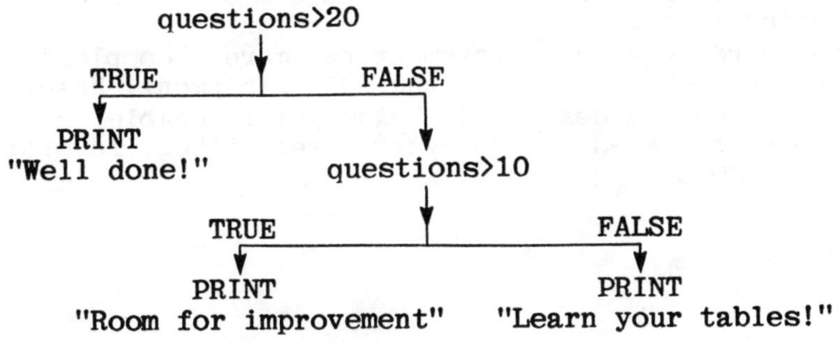

In the second case, the statement after the ELSE is a further IF statement which will be obeyed only if the condition 'questions>20' was FALSE. Only one of the three PRINT statements will be selected and obeyed. The program is selecting one out of three alternative courses of action as illustrated in the tree diagram.

We can compare an IF-THEN statement with an equivalent GOTO construction:

```
10  IF condition THEN            10  IF NOT condition GOTO 20
                                  .
        statements                .      statements (numbered)
                                  .
20  carry on                     20
```

Here is an IF-THEN-ELSE statement together with an equivalent GOTO construction:

```
10  IF condition THEN            10  IF NOT condition GOTO 16
                                  .
       statements                 .      statements (numbered)
                                  .
    ELSE                         15  GOTO 20
                                  .
       statements                 .      statements (numbered)
                                  .
20  carry on                     20  carry on
```

In one of the examples above, we 'nested' one IF statement inside another. Unfortunately, the extent to which we can nest IF-statements in BBC BASIC is limited in several ways. For example, unexpected effects can be obtained if we use an IF-THEN-ELSE after the THEN of another IF statement. (You will find that the computer can not decide to which IF the ELSE belongs.) We are also limited by the restriction that our complete nested IF statement must fit into 240 characters (6 lines in MODE 7). We suggest that the use of nested IF statements is limited to the use of IF after ELSE as illustrated above.

The standard way of implementing more complex IF structures in BASIC is to use the GOTO statement. However, the use of procedures described below will enable us to program complex nested control structures without resorting to the use of GOTO.

Simple procedures
A procedure in BBC BASIC provides a facility for giving a name to a section of program. The programmer can then write the name of the procedure wherever he wants that section of program to be obeyed. This has two main advantages:

Firstly, if the named operation has to be carried out at several different places in a large program, we avoid writing out the same section of program in full at each place.

Secondly, and just as important, careful use of procedures can make a large program easier to write and easier for other people to read.

The first advantage can, of course, be obtained in standard BASIC by using GOSUB statements and the second advantage can be obtained, to a certain extent, by careful annotation of standard BASIC subroutines with REM statements. However, the use of named procedures makes it easier to obtain these advantages and encourages the writing of more readable programs. Here is a short BBC BASIC program that involves a procedure:

```
 10   PRINT "Type first 10 numbers"
 20   PROCaddtennumbers
 30   PRINT "Type next 10 numbers"
 40   PROCaddtennumbers
 50   END

100   DEF PROCaddtennumbers
110   LOCAL i, next, total
120     total = 0
130     FOR i = 1 TO 10
140       INPUT next
150       total = total + next
160     NEXT i
170     PRINT "Total = "; total
180   ENDPROC
```

The section of program from line 100 onwards constitutes a procedure definition and the procedure is referred to or 'called' at line 20, and again at line 40, by writing the name of the procedure. Calling a procedure in this way tells the computer to go and obey the procedure definition and come back when it encounters an ENDPROC statement.

In the program above, we have specified that the variables 'i', 'next', and 'total' are 'local' to the procedure. These variables are available for use only while PROCaddtennumbers is being obeyed. Variables declared at the start of a procedure in this way can <u>not</u> be used after ENDPROC has been obeyed. It is recommended that any variable which is used only within a particular procedure should be declared locally to that procedure. The computer will then ensure that the programmer does not accidentally use the same variable for conflicting purposes in different parts of a large program. A variable with the same name can be used elsewhere in the program and its value will automatically be held in a different storage location, thus eliminating any possibility of confusion. The same program could have been written in standard BASIC using GOSUB statements:

```
 10   PRINT "Type first 10 numbers"
 20   GOSUB 120
 30   PRINT "Type next 10 numbers"
 40   GOSUB 120
 50   END
120   T = 0
130   FOR I = 1 TO 10
140     INPUT N
150     T = T + N
160   NEXT I
170   PRINT "Total = "; T
180   RETURN
```

In the above BBC BASIC program, a section of program was given a name and this name was used (twice) to tell the computer to obey that section of program. As we shall discuss later, it is good programming practice to give a name to any logically separate section of program, even if that section of program is obeyed only once.

Procedures with parameters

A simple procedure can be used to enable a program to carry out the same operation at different points in a program. A common requirement is for similar, but not necessarily identical, operations to be carried out at different points in a program.

As a somewhat contrived example, the procedure of the last section could have been given a 'parameter' indicating how many numbers were to be added up.

```
10   PRINT "Type 5 numbers"
20   PROCaddnumbers(5)
30   PRINT "Now type 10 numbers"
40   PROCaddnumbers(10)
50   END
```

The parameter in brackets after the name of the procedure is a piece of information that is to be transmitted to the procedure that is being called. In this case, the intention is that the number in brackets tells the procedure how many values to add up. The first time the procedure is called it

is to add up 5 numbers and the second time it is to add up 10 numbers.
The procedure must now be defined in terms of a named variable that will be given a value each time the procedure is called:

```
100   DEF PROCaddnumbers(howmany)
110   LOCAL i, next, total
120     total = 0
130     FOR i = 1 TO howmany
140       INPUT next
150       total= total + next
160     NEXT i
170     PRINT "Total = "; total
180   ENDPROC
```

When this procedure is called from line 20, the procedure definition is obeyed with:

```
howmany = 5
```

and when it is called from line 40, the procedure definition is obeyed with:

```
howmany = 10
```

As another example, here is a program that is given a sum of money and which works out how many coins of each available denomination are required to make up that sum of money.

```
 10   INPUT "Change", change

 20   PROChowmany(50) :  PROChowmany(20)
 30   PROChowmany(10) :  PROChowmany( 5)
 40   PROChowmany( 2) :  PROChowmany( 1)
 50   END

100   DEF PROChowmany(denomination)
110   LOCAL noofcoins
120     noofcoins = change DIV denomination
130     change = change MOD denomination
140     PRINT "No of "; denomination; "s "; noofcoins
150   ENDPROC
```

The program first works how many 50p pieces can be fitted into the given sum and works out how much change is left when that has been done. It then does the same, with the remaining change, for 20p pieces, and so on. A procedure is used to work out how many coins of a given denomination fit into the change that is currently left. PROChowmany is the name of a procedure that is used six times. Each time the procedure is called, it is supplied with a parameter in brackets telling it which denomination of coin to deal with next. The operators DIV and MOD are useful in this context. DIV gives the result of dividing two integers or whole numbers, ignoring any remainder. MOD gives the remainder obtained on dividing two integers.

A procedure can have a parameter that is a string and it can also have more than one parameter. These features will be illustrated as and when we need them.

In other programming languages, it is usually possible to pass information out of a procedure by changing the value of one of its parameters while the procedure is being obeyed. In BBC BASIC, parameters can only be used for passing information into a procedure and these parameters are sometimes known as input parameters. If information calculated in a procedure is to be used outside that procedure, the information must be placed in a global variable - any variable that is not a parameter or a local variable. For example, in the program at the beginning of this section the global variable 'change' is altered by each call of the procedure. In fact this global variable is used to transfer information both into and out of the procedure.

Functions

If the result of some process is a single value then a function is sometimes an elegant alternative to a procedure.

First let us look at the ways in which a function differs from a procedure. Certainly, they are both separate modules of program text referred to by name, but they differ in the way in which they are called. Functions are called by using them in expressions - that is the first difference. The second difference is that the result of obeying the function is a single value which replaces the function call in the originating expression. Let us illustrate this by considering the use of one of the standard functions:

```
y = x + SQR(2)
```

When this statement is being obeyed, the computer obeys the definition of the function SQR, and a number - the result of obeying the function - replaces the subexpression SQR(2). In the case of a standard function like SQR, the definition of the function is already stored as part of the BASIC system, but it is also possible for the programmer to define his own functions. In BBC BASIC, the programmer defines a function in a way that is very similar to the way in which a procedure is defined. A function defined in this way can be used in exactly the same way as the standard functions.

This program reads 3 pairs of numbers and adds the larger of the first pair, the larger of the second pair and the larger of the third pair. A function is used to find the larger of two numbers.

```
10    INPUT a,b, p,q, x,y
20    PRINT FNmax(a,b) + FNmax(p,q) + FNmax(x,y)
30    END

40    DEF FNmax(first,second)
50       IF first > second THEN  = first
         ELSE  = second
```

The effect of calling a function is the calculation of a single result. Since calling a function produces a single result, we must indicate, somewhere in the function definition, what this result is to be. Instead of ENDPROC, the function terminates when a statement of the form:

```
= expression
```

is obeyed. The value of this expression is returned as the value of the sub-expression used to call the function.

When the above program is obeyed, evaluation of the sub-expression 'FNmax(a,b)' causes the function definition to be obeyed with 'first' set to the value of 'a' and 'second' set to the value of 'b'. If the function is called when we have the situation

```
a = 4.79
b = 5.64
```

then the function definition is obeyed with

```
first = 4.79
second = 5.64
```

and the statement

```
= second
```

is obeyed as a result of obeying the IF-statement. The value of the sub-expression 'FNmax(a,b)' will therefore be 5.64 and this is the value which will be used in subsequent evaluation of the larger expression:

```
FNmax(a,b) + FNmax(p,q) + FNmax(x,y)
```

Apart from the need to return a particular value as its result, the definition of a function in BBC BASIC is very similar to the definition of a procedure. A function definition can use as many statements as we like in order to calculate the value that is to be the result of the function. More complicated function definitions will be introduced when they are required.

1.2 Stepwise refinement and program design

In the remainder of this chapter, we demonstrate the well-known programming technique called 'stepwise refinement'.

The first step in writing a complex program should be to sketch an outline of what the program is going to do without getting bogged down in the detailed BASIC instructions required. Using procedures for the logically distinct operations in a program allows us to write our initial outline in BASIC where we invent procedure names to describe operations that we have not yet programmed in detail. Only when we have a clear idea of what each named procedure is to do and how it fits into the overall program do we go on to define each procedure in detail.

In a complicated program, writing one of the procedures may itself be a difficult programming task and a procedure can itself be defined in terms of other procedures.

We shall illustrate this approach to programming by writing two moderately complicated programs.

CAL structures - a multiplication competition

The next program is an example of a Computer Assisted Learning program. It could be used to encourage children to learn their multiplication tables by organising a multiplication competition. Once the program is running, the children will take turns to sit at the keyboard and do a tables test. The program will keep a league table of the top ten scores obtained during a run of the program and this table will be printed after each test is completed.

We can outline the process that the program will carry out:

```
10   CLS
20   PRINT "Multiplication Competition"
30   PROCinitialise
40   REPEAT
50     PROCnextcompetitor
60     PROCprinttopten
70     INPUT "Anyone else to play (Y/N)", reply$
80   UNTIL reply$="N"
90   END
```

Note that this outline does not involve any tremendously complicated control structure. It contains only a simple REPEAT loop and writing an outline like this should not present any difficult programming problems.

Now that we have the overall structure of the program clear in our minds, we can introduce a little more detail by defining the procedures used in our outline.

Most programs require variables or arrays to be set to starting values and such 'initialisation' is best tidied away into a special procedure. In this case, PROCinitialise will set up a 'top scores' table to contain ten zero scores. The table will consist of two parallel arrays, one array to contain the names of the top ten players, and the other their scores.

```
100   DEF PROCinitialise
110   LOCAL slot
120     DIM topname$(10), topscore(10)
130     FOR slot = 1 TO 10
140       topscore(slot) = 0
150       topname$(slot) = "--------"
160     NEXT slot
170   ENDPROC
```

We can now concentrate on the problem of defining PROCnextcompetitor which will set a single multiplication test and handle the results. Writing this procedure can be viewed as a separate programming problem that is a little easier than the problem with which we started. We use the same approach to writing PROCnextcompetitor as we used in approaching the original problem - we write an outline description of what the procedure will do using further named procedures to describe operations that will be programmed in detail later. This process can be continued and we can have procedures within procedures within procedures etc. Very complex tasks can be implemented in this way.

```
200   DEF PROCnextcompetitor
210     INPUT "What's your name", name$
220     PRINT "Hello, "; name$
230     PRINT : PRINT "Ready"
240     PRINT : PRINT "Go!" : PRINT
250     PROCgivetest
260     PROCupdatetable(name$, score)
270   ENDPROC
```

We have already written a short program that sets a multiplication test and we use a variation of this program as our definition of PROCgivetest. We introduce a further constraint so that a test is terminated either if a question is answered wrongly or if a time limit is exceeded. The special BBC BASIC variable TIME is automatically increased by 1 every one hundredth of a second and we use this variable to time the test.

```
300   DEF PROCgivetest
310   LOCAL questions, a, b, answer
320     TIME = 0
330     questions = 0
340     REPEAT
350       questions = questions+1
360       a = RND(11) + 1  :  b = RND(11) + 1
370       PRINT a; "x"; b; "=";
380       INPUT answer
390     UNTIL answer<>a*b OR TIME>3000
400     IF answer <>a*b THEN
            PRINT "Wrong!" : score = questions - 1
        ELSE score = questions
410   ENDPROC
```

PROCupdatetable is probably the trickiest procedure to write. We need to check first of all whether the new score should be in the top ten. If it is not, the procedure should terminate immediately. If the new score is in the top ten, then we need to find the position at which it should be inserted, move the other scores and names down to make room and insert the new score and name in the table.

```
500   DEF PROCupdatetable(n$, score)
510   LOCAL slot, position
520     IF score <= topscore(10) THEN ENDPROC

530        REM find slot for new top score
540     slot = 0
550     REPEAT
560       slot = slot + 1
570     UNTIL score>topscore(slot)

580        REM move old scores down
590     FOR position = 9 TO slot STEP -1
600       topscore(position+1) = topscore(position)
610       topname$(position+1) = topname$(position)
620     NEXT position

630     topscore(slot) = score
640     topname$(slot) = n$
650   ENDPROC
```

Finally we define the procedure for displaying the league table on the screen.

```
700   DEF PROCprinttopten
710   LOCAL p
720     CLS
730     PRINT "Last score: "; score  :  PRINT
740     PRINT "TOP TEN" : PRINT : PRINT
750     FOR p = 1 TO 10
760       PRINT topname$(p); TAB(20); topscore(p)
770     NEXT p
780   ENDPROC
```

Exercises

1 If you are familiar with the BBC BASIC SOUND statement, modify the multiplication contest program so that it plays a short 'tension building' tune before each test.

2 We could have applied a further stage of stepwise refinement to PROCupdatetable by defining it in terms of two further procedures, PROCfindslot and PROCinsert. Do this.

3 If a test is terminated because of a wrong answer, the message indicating that the answer was wrong does not remain on the screen long enough for it to be read. Insert a time delay at the appropriate point in the program.

4 As it stands, the program could ask the same question twice during the course of the same test. Modify the program so that it records the questions asked and ensures that the same question is not asked twice.

5 Change the program so that a test is terminated only when a time limit is exceeded. If a wrong answer is typed, the test should continue, but a message should of course be displayed. Only correct answers should be counted towards the score.

Program structure for playing a board game

In Chapters 8 and 9, we shall be looking at some of the techniques needed to write programs that play 'board' games. Examples of the kind of game that we have in mind are NIM, Noughts and Crosses (or Tic-Tac-Toe), Kalah, Go-Moku, Go, Draughts (or Checkers) and Chess.

Programming techniques used for board games are completely different from those required for 'reaction' games like Space Invaders or Pacman where the machine is simply logging the user's reaction speeds and looking for coincidence of objects. In such arcade games, most of the programming effort goes into producing exotic animated displays.

Here we present the outline structure of a program that plays a board game for two players. The obvious possibility is that the computer (or, to be more precise, part of the program) will act as one player and someone seated at the keyboard will act as its opponent. However, as we shall see, this is not the only possibility and the same overall program structure will allow for other useful combinations. The essential requirement for a board game program is that it should repeatedly process one player's move, either its own or its opponent's. The most convenient way of organising this is outlined in the procedure PROCplaygame.

```
 10   PROCplaygame
 20   END

100   DEF PROCplaygame
110     PROCsetupboard : REM and decide who starts.
120     PROCdisplayboard
130     gameover = FALSE
140     REPEAT
150       IF turn$ = "A" THEN  PROCplayerA
                         ELSE  PROCplayerB
160       PROCdisplayboard
170       PROCtestgameover
180     UNTIL gameover
190     PROCannouncewinner
200   ENDPROC
```

In order to show how versatile this structure is, we describe four situations in which it could be used:

(a) The program will act as player A, using PROCplayerA to choose its move. Someone seated at the keyboard acts as the program's opponent and PROCplayerB will organise the input of this player's move.

(b) Two human players seated at the keyboard can use the computer as a board and scorekeeper. PROCplayerA is used to input one player's move and PROCplayerB is used to input the other's.

(c) Two rival programmers want to compare their game programming skills. One programmer can write PROCplayerA to choose a move and the other can write PROCplayerB to choose a move his way. The computer can then be made to play through one or more games by itself in order to decide whose procedure is better.

(d) The serious student of a game such as chess may want to store records of interesting games (on cassette or disk files) and have the program play through these games under his control so that he can analyse them. If, as is quite likely, the chess analyst wanted the program to go back to an earlier stage in the game and replay a sequence of moves or if he wanted to experiment with alternatives to the recorded moves, some slight adjustment to our outline program structure might be necessary.

We now convert our outline program into a complete rogram for a very simple game. The game we use is called Last One Wins' and the rules are:

The 'board' is a pile of counters.
Two players take turns at removing at least one and not more than three counters from the pile.
The player who removes the last counter is the winner.

he computer will play against an opponent. The opponent is o be allowed to decide how many counters there will be at he start of the game and who makes the first move. The ollowing program plays this game very stupidly (by making ompletely random moves) but the program will serve to llustrate a number of points. This game and the program eveloped in this section will be extensively referred to in hapter 8.

```
 10   PROCplaygame
 20   END

100   DEF PROCplaygame
          .
          .
          .
200   ENDPROC

300   DEF PROCsetupboard
310     INPUT "How many counters", counters
320     INPUT "OK. Do you want to start", reply$
330     IF INSTR("Yy",LEFT$(reply$,1))
        THEN turn$ = "B" ELSE turn$ = "A"
340   ENDPROC

400   DEF PROCdisplayboard
410     PRINT
420     PRINT "There are "; counters; " counters left."
430   ENDPROC

500   DEF PROCtestgameover
510     gameover = (counters = 0)
520   ENDPROC
```

```
 600   DEF PROCannouncewinner
 610     IF turn$ = "A" THEN PRINT "You win."
                        ELSE PRINT "I win."
 620   ENDPROC

 700   DEF PROCplayerA
 710     PRINT "My turn."
 720     PROCcheckmovesavailable
 730     IF movesavailable=1 THEN move=1
         ELSE move = RND(movesavailable)
 740     PRINT "I take "; move; " counters."
 750     counters = counters - move
 760     turn$ = "B"
 770   ENDPROC

 800   DEF PROCcheckmovesavailable
 810      IF counters<3 THEN movesavailable = counters
                        ELSE movesavailable = 3
 820   ENDPROC

 900   DEF PROCplayerB
 910     PROCinputmove
 920     counters = counters-move
 930     turn$ = "A"
 940   ENDPROC

1000   DEF PROCinputmove
1010     PROCcheckmovesavailable
1020     INPUT "Your turn. How many do you take", move
1030     IF move>0 AND move<=movesavailable THEN ENDPROC
1040     REPEAT
1050       PRINT "At least one and not more than three."
1060       INPUT "Try again:" move
1070     UNTIL move >0  AND  move <= movesavailable
1080   ENDPROC
```

As the program stands, some of the procedures contain only one or two instructions and you may wonder why we bother to use so many procedures. The advantage of breaking the program up into procedures in this way is that if we want to change or improve any particular aspect of the program's behaviour, we can concentrate our attention on the procedure that controls that aspect. For example, as it stands the program plays rather stupidly, but all the stupidity is confined to one procedure, PROCplayerA. If we wanted the program to play a better game we would concentrate on reprogramming this procedure. (There is in fact a very simple rule that can be used for choosing a good move in this game - think about it.) As another example of the sort of improvement that could be made, we might want to use graphics facilities to produce a pictorial representation of the pile of counters, the display being changed after each move. The changes to enable the program to do this could be concentrated in PROCdisplayboard.

Exercises

1 Change the above program so that it displays a pictorial representation of the pile of counters on the screen. The display should be updated after each move.

2 Change the program so that, after a game, it asks the program's opponent if he would like another game and terminates only if he says NO.

3 Write a program that plays Noughts and Crosses by making completely random moves. Use the structure introduced in the last section as a framework on which to build your program.

Experiment with different board representations. Three possibilities are:

(a) A 3x3 two-dimensional array.

(b) A one-dimensional array of 9 locations.

(c) (Rather difficult) - A single number that is handled by the program as a bit-pattern. The nine least significant bits indicate the position of the X's and the next nine indicate the position of the O's. Thus:

board = ...000001100001010000

might represent the position

		X
	X	O
O		

You are free to decide which bits represent which squares. Individual bits can be isolated from a number by using DIV and logical operations. This opens up the possibility of very efficient testing for winning positions. We can test for the presence of the winning pattern

		X
	X	
X		

by comparing the 'board' with the bit-pattern

.....000000000001010100 (ie. &54 in hex)

as follows:

```
IF (board AND &54)=&54 THEN .....
```

Placing an X in the top left-hand corner square involves

```
board = board OR &100
```

The bit-patterns corresponding to each possible move and each possible winning pattern could be stored in a lookup table or could be calculated as powers of 2.

Binary and hexadecimal notation, and the application of logical operations to bit-patterns are described in Appendix 2. If you get the third version working, you will learn a great deal about binary and hexadecimal representation of numbers.

Chapter 2 Logical processing of colour and interactive graphics

In this chapter we examine in detail the uses of the logical processing facilities available in the GCOL statement. In particular we look at how they can be used to create user defined mappings of the screen memory and to provide interactive graphics facilities.

The GCOL statement controls the way in which new values are loaded into the screen memory. Either a new value (or colour) specified for a particular pixel is loaded directly into the appropriate position in the screen memory:

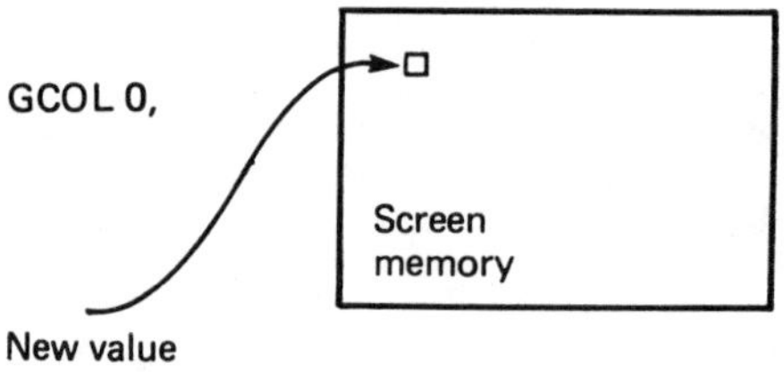

or else a logical operation is performed between the new value and the current value in the screen memory.

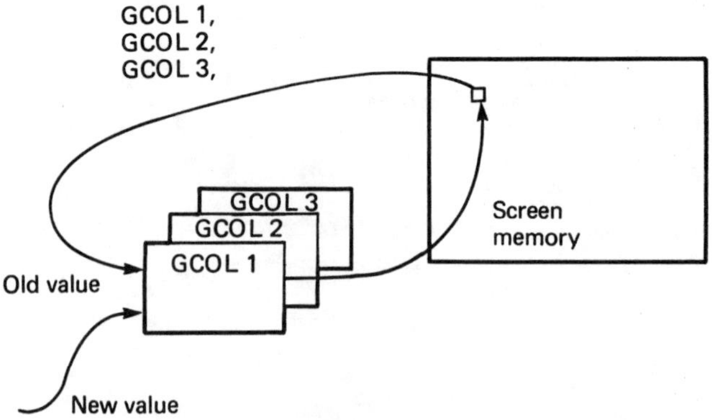

The type of logical operation is specified by the first

parameter in the GCOL statement. The GCOL statement provides powerful logical and colour processing facilities that can be used in a wide variety of graphics applications. Some of these are developed in the remainder of this chapter and others are utilised in the chapter on animation. Without such logical facilities many advanced graphics applications would be impossible. The GCOL facilities are:

GCOL 0, colour	any subsequent plotting will be in the specified colour
GCOL 1, colour	the colour that results from subsequent plotting is produced by performing an OR operation between the specified colour and the existing screen colour at a pixel
GCOL 2, colour	as 1 but the logical operation is AND
GCOL 3, colour	as 1 but the logical operation is EOR (exclusive OR)
GCOL 4, colour	as 1 but the logical operation is NOT (i.e. the colour at any pixel visited is inverted)

The application of logical operations such as OR, AND, EOR and NOT is explained in Appendix 2. For details on the handling of foreground and background colour, consult our companion volume or the User Guide. GCOL 1 and 2 have applications in the dividing of an image into planes such as foreground, background and midground and GCOL 3 and 4 have applications in interactive graphics described later.

2.1 Image planes (GCOL 1 and GCOL 2)

We shall start by considering multi-plane images. A multi-plane image is an abstraction for the convenience of the programmer. He can build up images independently in planes that are (virtually) separate. This is useful in animation (later) and in being able to deal with a composite image, where different planes have a different priority, e.g. foreground, midground and background (below). We look first at the easier problem of constructing separate planes and switching between them, and then at the more general problem of building up a composite image from planes of different priority.

Virtual image planes : separate images
In a four-colour mode, two bits per pixel are used in the computer screen memory. However it is up to the programmer how he uses them. We could set up a scheme where we have two 'independent' planes or a scheme where we have a foreground and a midground plane of the same image. Consider the former scheme. We can set up the two bits at a pixel in this way:

```
0 = 00 = image1 and image2 background
1 = 01 = image1 foreground
2 = 10 = image2 foreground
3 = 11 = image1 and image2 foreground
```

The fourth code (3=11) is necessary to signify that for a particular pixel <u>both</u> image1 and image2 planes are 'on'. Starting with the easier consideration of switching between planes (assuming that both images are already built up) we would proceed as follows:

<u>DISPLAY</u> <u>image1:</u>

```
VDU 19, 0, backgroundcolimage1, 0,0,0
VDU 19, 1, foregroundcolimage1, 0,0,0
VDU 19, 2, backgroundcolimage1, 0,0,0
VDU 19, 3, foregroundcolimage1, 0,0,0
```

Image2 is thus set to the background colour selected for image1 and becomes invisible.

<u>DISPLAY</u> <u>image2:</u>

```
VDU 19, 0, backgroundcolimage2, 0,0,0
VDU 19, 1, backgroundcolimage2, 0,0,0
VDU 19, 2, foregroundcolimage2, 0,0,0
VDU 19, 3, foregroundcolimage2, 0,0,0
```

Now image1 is set to the background colour selected for image2 and becomes invisible.

To plot in the image1 plane, say, we have to proceed as follows for each pixel:

```
0 = 00 becomes 01
1 = 01 remains 01 (point already there)
2 = 10 becomes 11 (image2 point already there)
3 = 11 remains 11 (image2 and image1 point
                               already there)
```

The third column is produced by ORing (inclusive) 01 with the second column and we simply precede any plotting statements with the appropriate GCOL statement:

<u>PLOT image1</u>: precede PLOT statements with GCOL 1, 1

Similarly to plot in the image2 plane:

```
0 = 00 becomes 10
1 = 01 becomes 11
2 = 10 remains 10
3 = 11 remains 11
```

and the appropriate GCOL is:

<u>PLOT image2</u>: precede PLOTs with GCOL 1, 2

The following program builds up a simple image in each image plane then repeatedly switches between them.

```
 10   MODE 5
 20   PROCplotimage1
 30   PROCplotimage2
 40   FOR screen = 1 TO 10
 50     PROCdisplayimage1
 60     PROCdelay
 70     PROCdisplayimage2
 80     PROCdelay
 90   NEXT screen
100   END

110   DEFPROCplotimage1
120     GCOL 1, 1
130     PROCdrawacircle(500, 500, 125)
140   ENDPROC

150   DEFPROCplotimage2
160     GCOL 1, 2
170     PROCdrawatriangle(327, 400, 346)
180   ENDPROC

190   DEFPROCdisplayimage1
200     VDU 19, 0, 2, 0,0,0
210     VDU 19, 1, 1, 0,0,0
220     VDU 19, 2, 2, 0,0,0
230     VDU 19, 3, 1, 0,0,0
240   ENDPROC
```

```
250   DEFPROCdisplayimage2
260     VDU 19, 0, 4, 0,0,0
270     VDU 19, 1, 4, 0,0,0
280     VDU 19, 2, 0, 0,0,0
290     VDU 19, 3, 0, 0,0,0
300   ENDPROC

310   DEFPROCdrawacircle(xc, yc, r)
320     MOVE xc + r, yc
330     FOR theta = 10 TO 360 STEP 10
340       x = r*COS(RAD(theta))
350       y = r*SIN(RAD(theta))
360       x = xc + x : y = yc + y
370       MOVE xc, yc : PLOT 85, x, y
380     NEXT theta
390   ENDPROC

390   DEFPROCdrawatriangle(xs, ys, s)
400     MOVE xs, ys : DRAW xs+s, ys
410     PLOT 85, xs+s/2, ys+s*0.866
420   ENDPROC

430   DEF PROCdelay
440     TIME = 0
450     REPEAT : UNTIL TIME>100
460   ENDPROC
```

In the above program note that we are using completely different colours in each image. Switching between image planes that use the same colour is important in animation (Chapter 4).

Incidentally information common to both planes (such as text, say), need only be plotted once using GCOL 0, 3.

Composite image with priority (3 planes)

Again with a choice of four colours the above scheme can easily be adapted to set up a three-plane composite image (foreground, midground and background). Using GCOL the foreground and midground planes can be independently accessed and anything drawn in the midground plane that is shadowed by anything drawn in the foreground plane is automatically obscured in the composite image. Also we can delete from the foreground, delete from the midground, add to the foreground or add to the midground and the foreground/midground priority is automatically taken into account. Common operations that we might want to perform are:

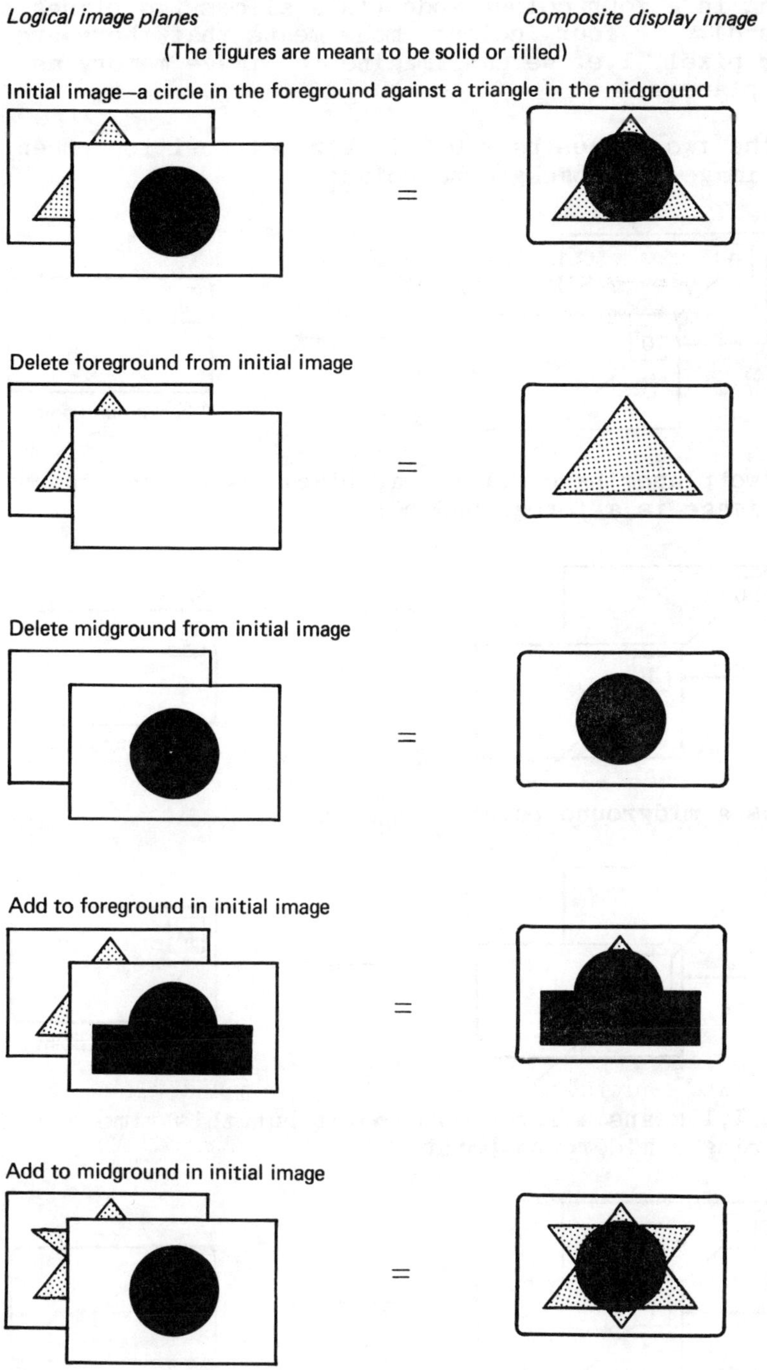
Logical image planes
Composite display image
(The figures are meant to be solid or filled)
Initial image—a circle in the foreground against a triangle in the midground
=
Delete foreground from initial image
=
Delete midground from initial image
=
Add to foreground in initial image
=
Add to midground in initial image
=

How this is accomplished is now explained. Suppose we are operating in a four colour mode (this allows two planes plus background). A four colour mode means that there are two bits per pixel, i.e. we can imagine the image memory as two one-bit planes.

If the two planes have 0,0 in a pixel position, then the display image is a background point:

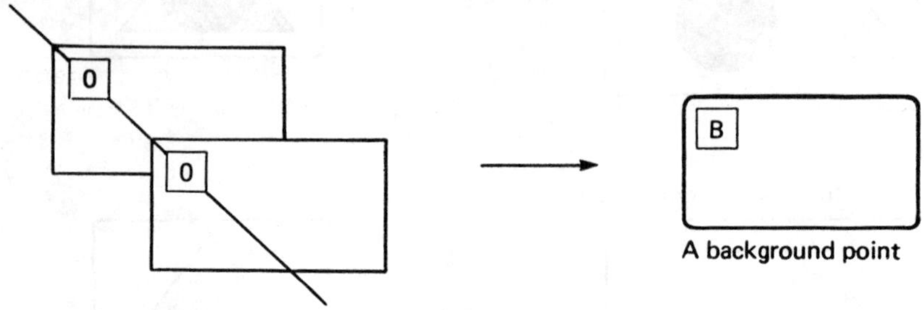

If the two planes have 0,1 in a pixel position then the display image is a foreground point:

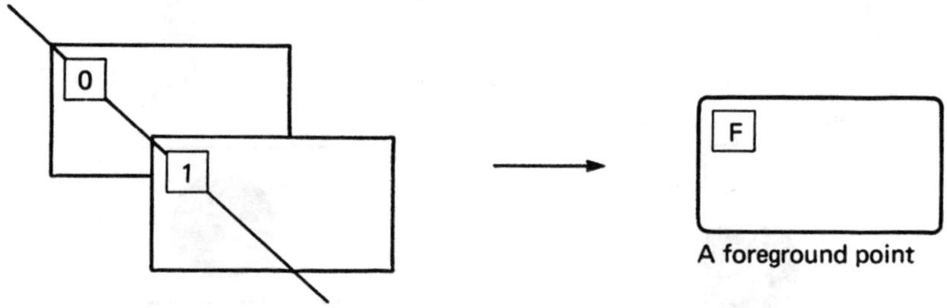

1,0 means a midground point:

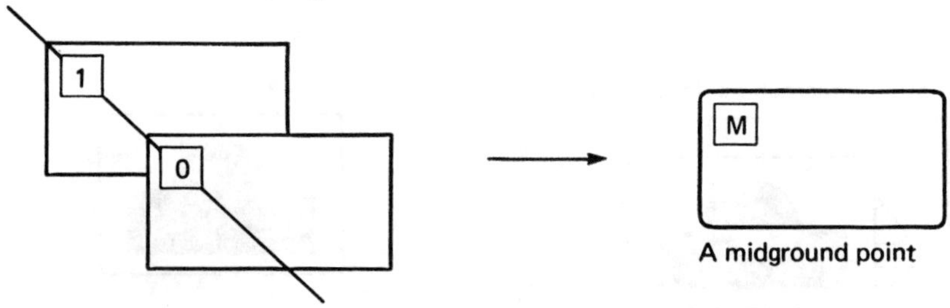

Finally 1,1 means a foreground point but this time one that is obscuring a midground point:

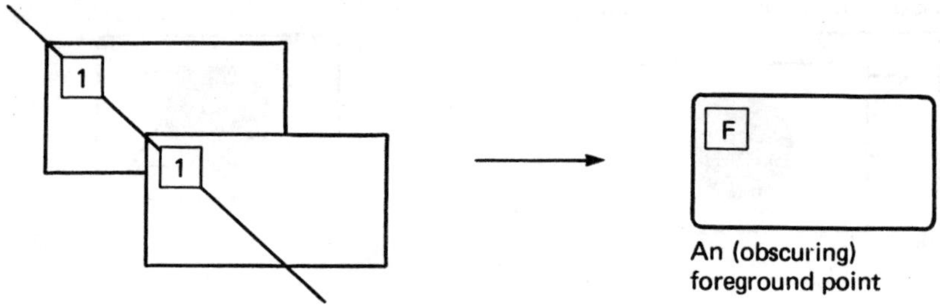

Thus we have:

```
0 = 00 = background point (. in illustrations)
1 = 01 = foreground point (F in illustrations)
2 = 10 = midground  point (M in illustrations)
3 = 11 = foreground point (F in illustrations)
         (obscuring a midground)
```

Note that we use two logical colour codes to represent the foreground. This is because we can have 2 types of foreground points - a foreground point obscuring a background point only, and a foreground point obscuring a midground point. We can now give a few examples of 'plane' plotting and you can generalise from these examples.

To PLOT in the foreground

We precede any plot statements with GCOL 1,1 (inclusive OR):

```
GCOL 1,1
PLOT statements to plot figures in foreground plane
```

Now because

```
     00          OR          01          =          01
 background              foreground             foreground
```

background points are obscured by foreground points:

```
.....................
....FFFFFFFFFFFF.....
....F................
....F................
....FFFFFFFFFF.......
....F................
....F................
....F................
.....................
```

To PLOT in the midground

We precede any PLOT statements with GCOL 1,2 (inclusive OR):

```
GCOL 1,2
PLOT statements to plot a figure in the midground plane
```

Now because

```
      00          OR         10          =          10
  background              midground              midground
```

and

```
        01        OR        10       =        11
  foreground          midground          foreground
```

background points are obscured by midground points as you would expect, but points that are are already foreground remain in the foreground colour (but with code 11 indicating that they are obscuring a midground point). Thus to build up information in these two planes we use GCOL 1 (inclusive OR).

```
......................
....FFFFFFFFFFFF.....
....FM.........MM.....
....F.M.......M.M.....
....FFFFFFFFFF.M.....
....F...M...M...M.....
....F....M.M....M.....
....F.....M.....M.....
......................
```

You can perhaps see from this that after a composite set of planes has been built up any subsequent additions to the foreground or midground will be incorporated into the composite image according to their respective priority.

To DELETE from foreground and midground

Now to delete images or parts of images from planes we use GCOL 2 (AND). To delete a foreground object, we redraw the object after using GCOL 2,2, where the second parameter happens to be the midground colour but is used here as a 'foreground delete code'. To delete a midground object, we use GCOL 2,1. For example to delete from the foreground:

```
GCOL 2, 2
PLOT statements to delete figure from foreground plane
```

and the PLOT statements will be exactly the same as the ones that were used to draw the object being deleted. Now we have

```
      00       AND      10     =     00
  background                      background
```

i.e. background points remain as background

```
      01       AND      10     =     00
  foreground                      background
```

'ordinary' foreground points revert to background

```
      10        AND     10      =      10
  midground                          midground
```

'ordinary' midground points are left unaltered

```
      11        AND     10      =      10
```

'obscured' midground points are now revealed

```
......................
....M...........M.....
....MM.........MM.....
....M.M.......M.M.....
....M..M.....M..M.....
....M...M...M...M.....
....M....M.M....M.....
....M.....M.....M.....
......................
```

Thus GCOL 2 (AND) can be used to delete and reveal. These operations are now demonstrated. The procedures are left undefined (see earlier sections) but should include colour fill. The following program draws a red circle in the foreground plane and a yellow triangle in the midground plane and any geometrical overlap is automatically taken care of. Note line 20; remember that we use 2 codes for the foreground and these of course should be the same colour.

```
10   MODE 5
20   VDU 19, 3, 1, 0,0,0
25   GCOL 1, 1
30   PROCdrawacircle(500, 500, 125)
40   GCOL 1, 2
50   PROCdrawatriangle(327, 400, 346)
60   END
```

To delete the red circle and reveal any previously hidden parts of the yellow triangle we can add:

```
60   keypress = GET
70   GCOL 2, 2
80   PROCdrawacircle(500, 500, 125)
```

which 'undraws' the circle.

A convenient alternative to the above uses of GCOL 1 and GCOL 2 is often useful. Provided that an object being plotted in a plane does not overlap any object that is already present in that plane, then GCOL 3 can be used for both the drawing and deleting process. For example to draw an object in image plane 1:

```
GCOL 3, 1
PLOTs etc to draw the object
```

To delete the object we simply repeat exactly the same GCOL and PLOT statements.

Composite image with priority (5 planes)
On the Model B, in MODE 2, we have 4 bit colour codes (16 colours) and this gives us many more possibilities. The next program is designed to illustrate one such possibility.

In this program, we have set up four planes plus background:

foreground (white)
midground (yellow)
rearground (red)
distant (blue)
background (black)

The different colour codes for a pixel together with their significance are:

code	binary	actual colour	interpretation
1	0001	white	fore
3	0011	white	fore obscuring mid
5	0101	white	fore obscuring rear
7	0111	white	fore obscuring rear, mid
9	1001	white	fore obscuring distant
11	1011	white	fore obscuring distant, mid
13	1101	white	fore obscuring distant, rear
15	1111	white	fore obscuring distant, rear, mid
2	0010	yellow	mid
6	0110	yellow	mid obscuring rear
10	1010	yellow	mid obscuring distant
14	1110	yellow	mid obscuring distant, rear
4	0100	red	rear
12	1100	red	rear obscuring distant
8	1000	blue	distant
0	0000	black	background

Each bit in a colour code represents one of the four planes.

The GCOL 1 colour code for drawing contains a one in the bit position for the plane involved and zeros in the other bit positions. The GCOL 2 colour code for erasing contains a zero bit for the plane in which erasing is taking place and ones for the planes that are to be unaffected. The GCOL statements needed for drawing or erasing in each plane without affecting the other planes are:

	draw	erase
foreground	GCOL 1,1	GCOL 2,14
midground	GCOL 1,2	GCOL 2,13
rearground	GCOL 1,4	GCOL 2,11
distant	GCOL 1,8	GCOL 2, 7

The program repeatedly draws or erases a colour-filled circle, in a plane specified by the user and with centre and radius specified by the user. A plane is specified using one of the keys F(oreground), M(idground), R(earground), D(istant) or Q(uit). You should experiment with the program and observe how the above priority system works when drawing and erasing overlapping circles in different planes.

```
10    MODE 2
20    VDU 28, 0,1, 19,0
30    VDU 24, 0;0; 1279;963;
40    sin5=SIN(RAD(5)) : cos5=COS(RAD(5))
50    VDU 19,  1,7, 0,0,0 : VDU 19,  3,7, 0,0,0
60    VDU 19,  5,7, 0,0,0
70    VDU 19,  9,7, 0,0,0 : VDU 19, 11,7, 0,0,0
80    VDU 19, 13,7, 0,0,0 : VDU 19, 15,7, 0,0,0
90    VDU 19,  2,3, 0,0,0 : VDU 19,  6,3, 0,0,0
100   VDU 19, 10,3, 0,0,0 : VDU 19, 14,3, 0,0,0
110   VDU 19,  4,1, 0,0,0 : VDU 19, 12,1, 0,0,0
120   VDU 19,  8,4, 0,0,0
130   REPEAT : PROCcommand : UNTIL plane$="Q"
140   MODE 7 : END

150   DEF PROCcommand
160     plane$ = FNcommand("Which plane","FMRDQ")
170     IF plane$="Q" THEN ENDPROC
180     PROCcirclespec
190     IF plane$="F" THEN PROCdraworerase(1,14)
200     IF plane$="M" THEN PROCdraworerase(2,13)
210     IF plane$="R" THEN PROCdraworerase(4,11)
220     IF plane$="D" THEN PROCdraworerase(8,7)
230   ENDPROC

240   DEF FNcommand(type$,coms$)
250   LOCAL c$
260     PRINT type$;"(";coms$;")?";
270     REPEAT : c$=GET$ : UNTIL INSTR(coms$,c$)>0
280     CLS
290   =c$
```

```
300   DEF PROCcirclespec
310    INPUT "Centre(x,y)",cx,cy
320    INPUT "Radius",r
330    CLS
340   ENDPROC

350   DEF PROCdraworerase(drawcode,erasecode)
360   LOCAL op$
370     op$ = FNcommand("Draw or Erase","DE")
380     IF op$="D" THEN GCOL 1,drawcode
                   ELSE GCOL 2,erasecode
390     PROCcircle
400   ENDPROC

410   DEF PROCcircle
420   LOCAL oldx,oldy
430     MOVE cx+r,cy
440     oldx=r : oldy=0
450     FOR t=5 TO 360 STEP 5
460       x =  oldx*cos5 + oldy*sin5
470       y = -oldx*sin5 + oldy*cos5
480       MOVE cx,cy
490       PLOT 81,x,y
500       oldx=x : oldy=y
510     NEXT t
520   ENDPROC
```

Another possibility would be to have three priority levels plus background with:

```
3 foreground colours    (spaceships?)
1 midground colour      (planets?)
1 rearground colour     (stars?)
1 background  colour    (sky?)
```

This is discussed in Exercise 5 below.

Exercises

1 Undraw a rectangle by working from the centre as if it were a stage curtain being pulled to each wing. Underneath detail should be revealed in another colour: legendry that might be used in a caption sequence or anything else you fancy.

2 Plot two pictures using values from DATA statements and then repeatedly read a key. Depending on which key was pressed, display the first picture or display the second picture or display both pictures at once (without redrawing them).

3 Certain patterns are used for testing for various types

of colour blindness. These consist of a pattern of dots containing a large letter or number made up of dots in one colour, the rest of the dots being in another colour. Write a program that generates VDU 19 statements to switch through a sequence of colour combinations.

4 Write a program that uses data to draw four graphs (on the same axes) representing four year's sales and then uses VDU 19 commands to display one, two, three or four of the graphs in response to keys pressed by a user.

5 Modify the four-plane demonstration program so that there are three levels of priority, foreground, midground and rearground, with a choice of three foreground colours. You could use the following settings for the colour codes:

code	binary	actual colour	interpretation
1	0001	red	fore
2	0010	green	fore
3	0011	yellow	fore
5	0101	red	fore obscuring mid
6	0110	green	fore obscuring mid
7	0111	yellow	fore obscuring mid
9	1001	red	fore obscuring rear
10	1010	green	fore obscuring rear
11	1011	yellow	fore obscuring rear
13	1101	red	fore obscuring mid, rear
14	1110	green	fore obscuring mid, rear
15	1111	yellow	fore obscuring mid, rear
4	0100	blue	mid
12	1100	blue	mid obscuring rear
8	1000	magenta	rear
0	0000	black	background

You will find that to plot a foreground circle, you may first have to erase any existing foreground colour in the circle.

2.2 Basic interaction techniques (GCOL 3 and GCOL 4)

In this section two interaction techniques are implemented. Both of these use the keyboard, but clearly the principles are the same for either a keyboard or a more convenient device. Both interaction techniques can be used in picture construction and this forms a part of most CAD (Computer Aided Design) systems. Such techniques enable designers to work in a two-dimensional or picture domain. This means for example that an electrical engineer can work with circuit diagrams and an architect with elevations or other projections of buildings, rather than just numbers. Now CAD techniques are an extensive topic by themselves and we shall only be concerned here with picture or line-drawing generation. It is not out of place to examine just briefly how such techniques 'fit in' to CAD programs. A CAD program that accepts a picture as input has to deduce certain information from it. An electrical engineer may draw a circuit diagram as input. A simple but somewhat unrealistic example serves to illustrate the point; say he inputs a series parallel resistor configuration:

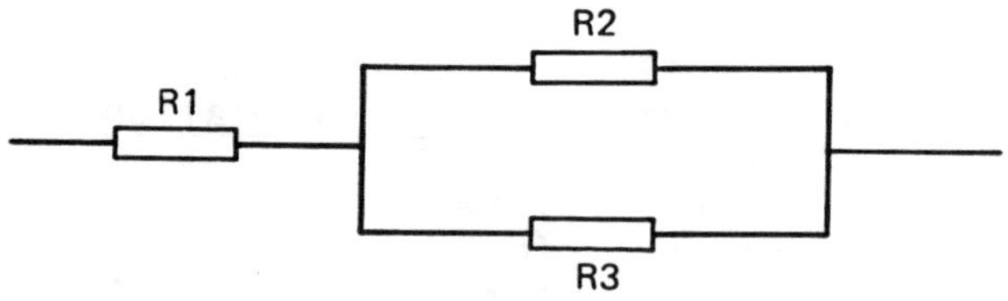

From this the CAD program will have to deduce that a resistor is connected in series to two resistors in parallel and that the total resistance is :

RT = R1 + R2*R3/(R2 + R3)

It can then evaluate numerical calculations and output required information graphically or otherwise back to the user. The CAD program will also be able to cope with alterations to the diagram - additions, deletions etc.

The circuit diagram could be built up using a technique known as 'picking and dragging'. A user is presented with a menu of objects and can pick a particular object and drag it to anywhere on the screen:

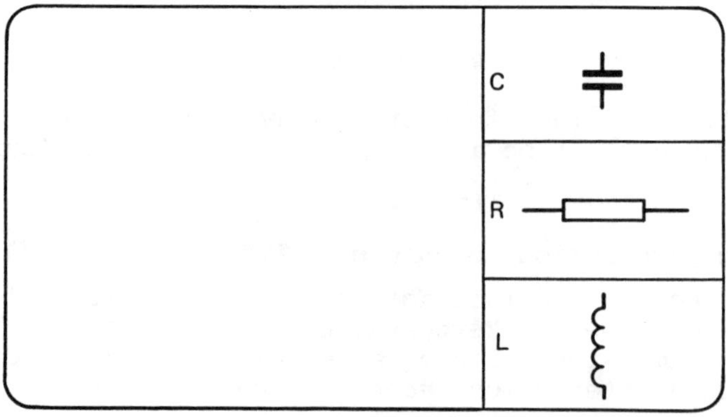

Other operations that might be available on objects are magnification and rotation. Again in the case of an electrical circuit diagram, in parallel with the picture-drawing modules there will be procedures that keep track of the spatial relationship between components. The CAD program can then build up a formula reflecting some required attribute or behaviour of the circuit. This might be transfer characteristic, frequency response, etc. The computer program's view of the problem is numerical or formula based while the engineer's view remains pictorial. This is a tremendous advantage in most design problems.

In the same way an architect may sketch in the elevations of a house and ask for costing, insulation or sunlight calculations.

In the next two sections we look at the front end of such CAD programs firstly by looking at how we can sketch line drawings on the screen, and secondly how we can pick and drag predefined sub-pictures across the screen.

Rubberband line drawing

Using this technique we can build up a sketch or line drawing on the screen, using line segments whose length and direction are controlled from the keyboard. The program starts off by drawing an arbitrary line from (0,0) to (500,500). By using keys R, L, U, and D (Right, Left, Up and Down) as direction indicators we can move the end point of the line anywhere we want. Key F can be used to 'Fix' the end point of the line.

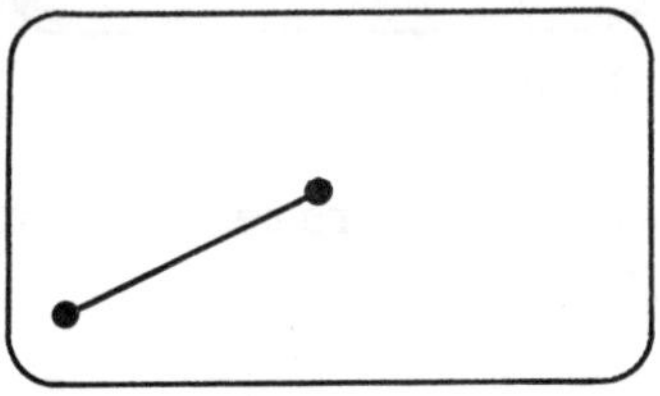

Start of program
Arbitrary line drawn from
(0,0) to (500,500)

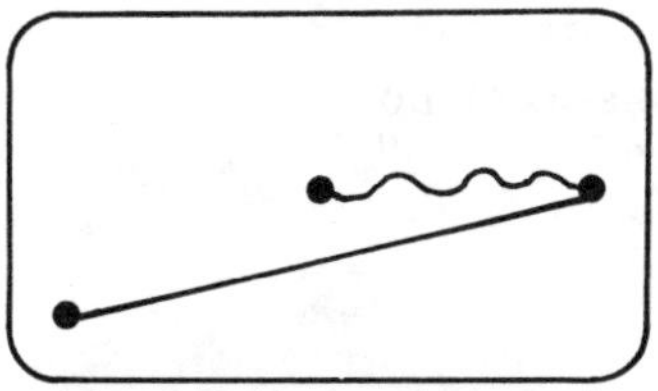

Line endpoint can be moved
anywhere from (500,500)

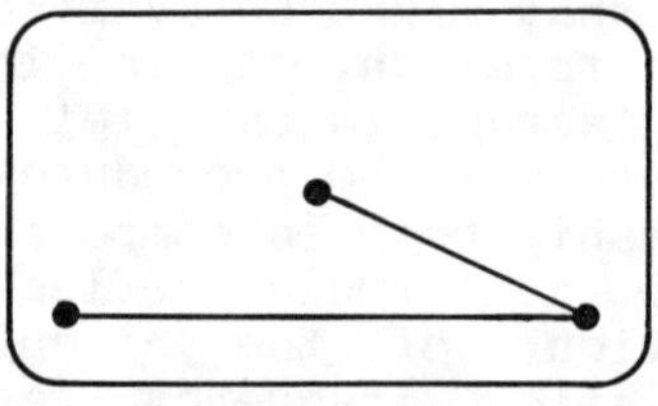

Key F depressed 2nd line arbitrarily drawn to (500,500) and 1st line permanently drawn

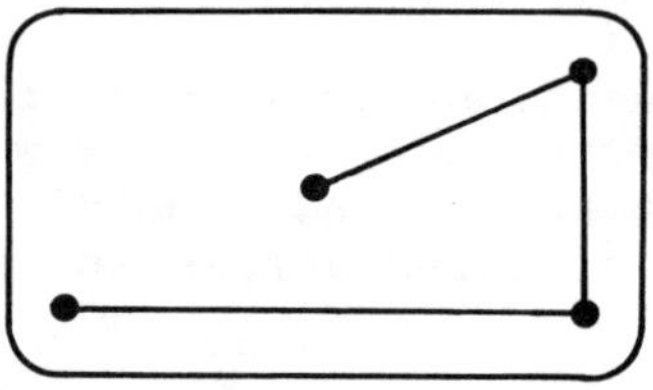

This line can be moved anywhere and key F depressed again

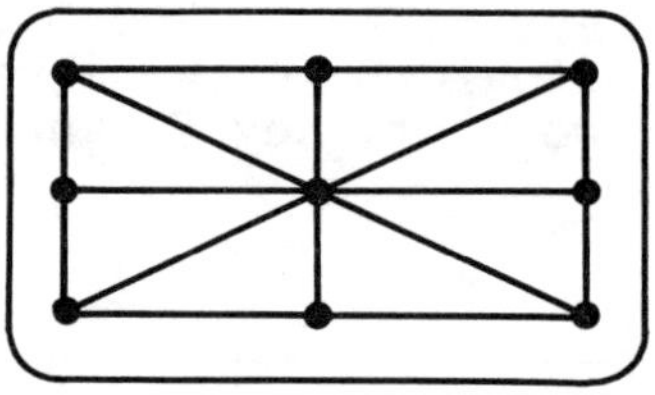

Thus any shape can be built up

Here is a program that illustrates a simple approach to 'rubberbanding'.

```
 10   MODE 4 : xstep = 4 : ystep = 4
 20   xs = 0 : ys = 0
 30   x = 640 : y = 512
 40   GCOL 3, 1
 50   PROCdrawordelete
 60   REPEAT
 70     command$ = GET$
 80     PROCprocesscommand
 90   UNTIL command$ = "Q"
100   MODE 7 : END
```

```
110   DEF PROCprocesscommand
120     IF INSTR("FLRUD",command$)=0 THEN ENDPROC
130     PROCdrawordelete
140     IF command$ = "F" THEN PROCfix
150     IF command$ = "L" THEN x = x - xstep
160     IF command$ = "R" THEN x = x + xstep
170     IF command$ = "U" THEN y = y + ystep
180     IF command$ = "D" THEN y = y - ystep
190     PROCdrawordelete
200   ENDPROC

210   DEF PROCdrawordelete
220     MOVE xs, ys : DRAW x, y
230   ENDPROC

240   DEF PROCfix
250     REM Permanent draw
260     GCOL 0,1 : PROCdrawordelete
270     GCOL 3,1
280     xs = x : ys = y
290     x = 640 : y = 512
300   ENDPROC
```

'xs' and 'ys' always represent the start position of the line currently being drawn and 'x' and 'y' represent the position of the end of the line being moved. The program consists of a REPEAT loop that processes commands UNTIL the key Q (Quit) is typed.

PROCprocesscommand first checks for a valid key. It then calls PROCdrawordelete to delete the line in its current position. If "F" has been pressed, then the line currently being operated on is fixed and the coordinates are set for a new line. One of the coordinates x, y is updated if one of the movement keys (L, R, U, D) has been pressed. The coordinate increments, 'xstep' and 'ystep', are set to the dimensions of a pixel in the mode being used. PROCprocesscommand terminates by drawing a line to the position now specified by the x-y coordinates.

The critical statement in the program is GCOL 3, 1 (exclusive OR). This means that lines can be moved over existing lines without permanently wiping part of them out, as would be the case without this facility.

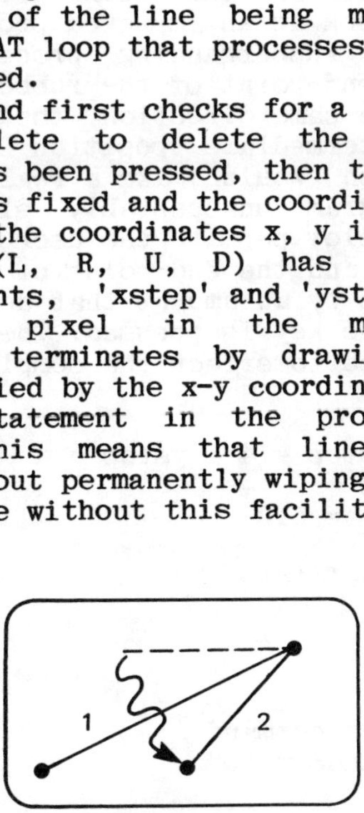

Normally to delete an object we would re-plot the object in the background colour but this would wipe out intersecting parts of existing lines. Using the above method, an existing line disappears only momentarily while the current moving line passes over it. Thus line segment 2 (above) can be swept over existing line segment 1 without rubbing it out. This can be explained by reference to the following table.

1st. DRAW			2nd. DRAW		
old	plotting	new	old	plotting	new
0	1	1	1	1	0
1	1	0	0	1	1

You can see from the bottom row of the table that plotting a 1 on top of a 1 in the first DRAW results in a zero that is restored to a 1 by the 2nd DRAW. The top row of the table gives the effect of a normal draw and erase function. The second DRAW thus erases or undraws, at the same time restoring any holes in existing lines made by the 1st DRAW. We leave it as an exercise to work out why the behaviour is unaltered if GCOL 3 is replaced by GCOL 4.

If you try using this simple program, you will find that it suffers from a number of disadvantages. In order to make it more useful as a line-drawing program, we need to make a number of improvements and extensions.

First, we will look at an improved program structure that will speed up the rubberbanding process. In the above program, when the end-point of the rubberband line is moved several times in the same direction, the line is deleted and redrawn for each intermediate position of the end-point. Using this approach would make a realistic CAD (Computer Aided Design) program unacceptably slow. The improved program structure below permits the user to hold down one of the movement keys and the end-point of the rubberband line is moved in one step by an amount that depends on the length of time for which the key is pressed. The line is deleted and redrawn only once to effect the complete move.

```
 10   MODE 4 : xstep = 4 : ystep = 4
 20   xs = 0 : ys = 0
 30   x = 640 : y = 512
 40   GCOL 3, 1
 50   PROCdrawordelete
 60   *FX 11,10
 70   *FX 12,1
 80   command$=GET$
 90   REPEAT
100     PROCprocesscommand
110   UNTIL command$ = "Q"
120   *FX 12,0
130   MODE 7 : END
```

```
140   DEF PROCprocesscommand
150     PROCcountcoms
160     IF INSTR("FLRUD",command$) = 0 THEN
          command$=GET$ : ENDPROC
170     PROCdrawordelete
180     IF command$ = "F" THEN PROCfix
190     IF command$ = "L" THEN x = x - xstep*coms
200     IF command$ = "R" THEN x = x + xstep*coms
210     IF command$ = "U" THEN y = y + ystep*coms
220     IF command$ = "D" THEN y = y - ystep*coms
230     PROCdrawordelete
240     IF nextcom$="" THEN command$=GET$
                       ELSE command$=nextcom$
250   ENDPROC

260   DEF PROCcountcoms
270     coms=0
280     REPEAT : coms=coms+1 : nextcom$=INKEY$(11)
290     UNTIL nextcom$<>command$
300   ENDPROC

310   DEF PROCdrawordelete
320     MOVE xs, ys : DRAW x, y
330   ENDPROC

340   DEF PROCfix
350     REM Permanent draw
360     GCOL 0,1 : PROCdrawordelete
370     GCOL 3,1
380     xs = x : ys = y
390     x = 640 : y = 512
400   ENDPROC
```

The *FX commands at lines 60 and 70 are used to increase the sensitivity of the keys. *FX 11 sets the delay before repeated copies of a character are sent to the computer by a continually depressed key. *FX 12 sets the delay between subsequent repeats of a character. (Each of these 'operating system commands' must appear on a separate numbered line.)

```
*FX 11,10
```

means that if a key is pressed for less than 10 hundredths of a second, then only one character is sent by that key.

```
*FX 12,1
```

now means that if a key is pressed for more than 10 hundredths of a second, then repeated copies of the character are sent by the key every 1 hundredth of a second.

The program enters PROCprocesscommand having read the next command character. PROCcountcoms is then used to count any repeats of the command character in case the command key is being held down. If the command key is a movement key, then this count is used in changing x or y by an appropriate multiple of the basic increment.

PROCprocesscommand terminates (at line 160 or line 240) by ensuring that 'command$' has been set to the next command character, using GET$ if necessary, ready for the next execution of the main loop.

Now, even although we have speeded it up, the program is still slightly impractical - figures are constructed without the 'pen being lifted off the paper'. That is to say after a line is fixed it is assumed that another line is required. This may not be the case and the easiest way to incorporate a line on/off facility is to have another key controlling this option:

```
221       IF command$ = "O" THEN lineoff = NOT lineoff
```

This IF statement sets up a 'push on/push off' key - a mechanism that we shall use again. Whenever we introduce an extra command key, we must extend the string of permitted commands:

```
160         IF INSTR("FLRUDO",command$)=0 THEN
              command$=GET$ : ENDPROC
```

The variable 'lineoff' is originally set to FALSE:

```
35    lineoff=FALSE
```

Pressing the appropriate key will change its value from FALSE to TRUE or vice versa. PROCdrawordelete can then be:

```
310    DEF PROCdrawordelete
315      IF lineoff THEN ENDPROC
320      MOVE xs, ys : DRAW x, y
330    ENDPROC
```

which prevents the drawing action if the line is switched off. Now, for example, to construct two isolated rectangles we would:

1. Draw the first rectangle

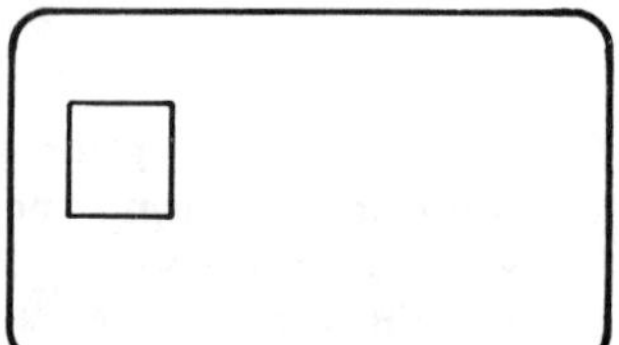

2. Draw a line to the start of the second

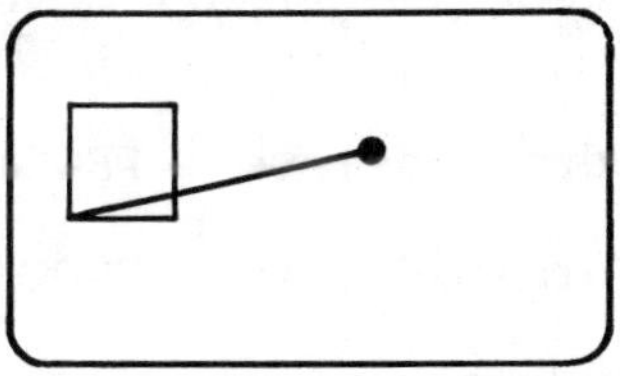

3. Switch off this line (press 0)

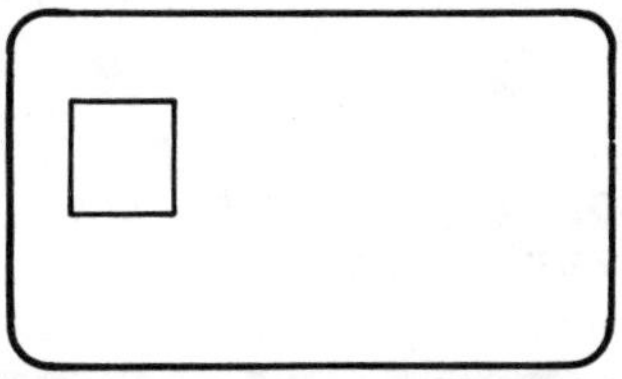

4. Fix the invisible line & press 0

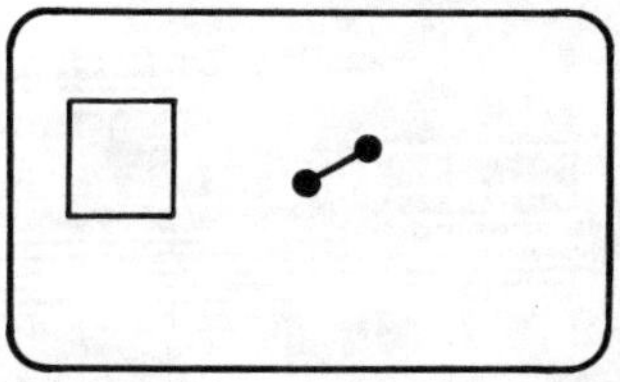

5. Draw the new rectangle

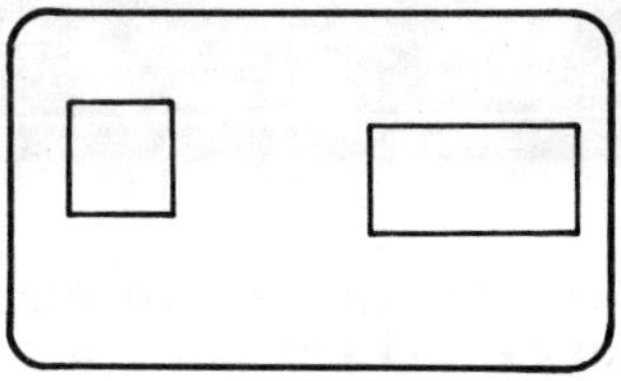

Rubberband drawing aids

There are two useful elaborations that we can make to our rubberband line drawing program. Firstly we can include a horizontal and vertical cursor line to enable us to line up different parts of a drawing. This simply adds another two selections to PROCprocesscommand:

```
 36   hcursor = FALSE : vcursor = FALSE

160       IF INSTR("FLRUDOHV",command$)=0 THEN
            command$=GET$ : ENDPROC

225     IF command$ = "H" THEN hcursor = NOT hcursor
226     IF command$ = "V" THEN vcursor = NOT vcursor
```

This means that the H and V key functions are also push on/push off keys. PROCprocesscommand can now be further elaborated to check if cursors have to be drawn:

```
170      PROCdrawordelete : PROCcheckcursors

230      PROCdrawordelete : PROCcheckcursors

410    DEF PROCcheckcursors
420      IF hcursor THEN MOVE 0,y:DRAW 1279,y
430      IF vcursor THEN MOVE x,0:DRAW x,1023
440    ENDPROC
```

The next photograph shows the cursor being used in the course of a construction.

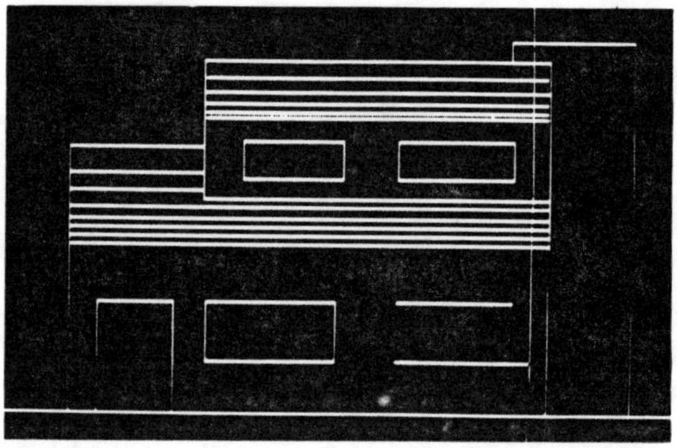

Another useful aid is a length measuring device that indicates the current length of a line. Consider for example measuring the current x projection of the line:

```
 37    printmeasure = FALSE

160        IF INSTR("FLRUDOHVM",command$)=0 THEN
             command$=GET$ : ENDPROC

227      IF command$ = "M" THEN
           printmeasure = NOT printmeasure

235      PROCmeasure

450    DEF PROCmeasure
460      IF printmeasure THEN
           PRINT TAB(3,3); ABS(xs-x)
         ELSE PRINT TAB(3,3); SPC(4)
470    ENDPROC
```

If the measure option is switched on then PROCmeasure is obeyed and prints the current x projection of the line. In the next illustration the hangers on the suspension bridge were accurately positioned using this facility.

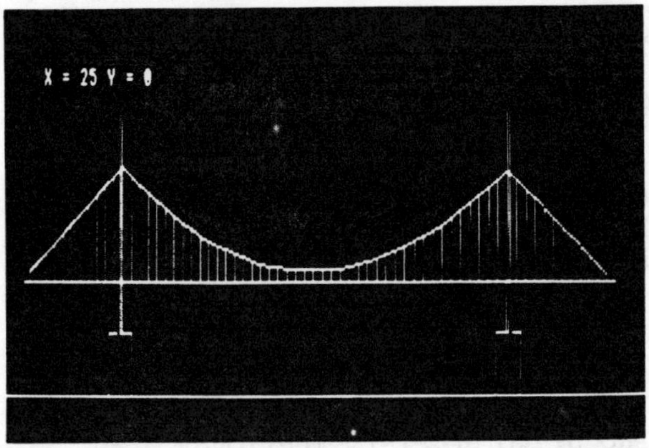

Picking and dragging an object

We have already mentioned the use of this particular technique above so we'll jump straight in to doing it. In the next program we have set up a menu of objects in the right hand side of the screen. An object is selected by typing 1, 2 or 3. In practice, if we were using this technique frequently, an object would be selected from the menu by pointing a light pen at the appropriate position on the screen. When an object is selected it is dragged into position and fixed as before. Instead of dragging a line we are now dragging a complete object.

```
 10   MODE 0 : xstep = 2 : ystep = 4
 20   PROCdrawmenu
 30   GCOL 3,1
 40   PROCpick
 50   REPEAT
 60     x=100 : y=100
 70     PROCdrawordelete(selection$)
 80     *FX 11,10
 90     *FX 12,1
100     command$=GET$
110     fixed = FALSE
120     REPEAT
130       PROCprocesscommand
140     UNTIL fixed
150     *FX 12,0
160     PROCpick
170   UNTIL selection$ = "Q"
180   MODE 7 : END
```

```
190   DEF PROCdrawmenu
200     MOVE 900,0 : DRAW 900,1000
210     PROCdrawresistor(1000,600)
220     PROCdrawcapacitor(1000,400)
230     PROCdrawdiode(1000,200)
240     PRINT TAB(60,12);"1"; TAB(60,18);"2";
                              TAB(60,24);"3"
250   ENDPROC

260   DEF PROCpick
270     PRINT TAB(0,0);"Pick, (1/2/3/Q)";
280     REPEAT : selection$=GET$
290     UNTIL INSTR("123Q",selection$)>0
300     PRINT TAB(0,0);"               ";
310   ENDPROC

320   DEF PROCprocesscommand
330     PROCcountcoms
340     IF INSTR("FLRUD",command$)=0 THEN
          command$=GET$ : ENDPROC
350     PROCdrawordelete(selection$)
360     IF command$="F" THEN
          PROCfix:fixed=TRUE:ENDPROC
370     IF command$="L" THEN x = x-xstep*coms
380     IF command$="R" THEN x = x+xstep*coms
390     IF command$="U" THEN y = y+ystep*coms
400     IF command$="D" THEN y = y-ystep*coms
410     PROCdrawordelete(selection$)
420     IF nextcom$="" THEN command$=GET$
                       ELSE command$=nextcom$
430   ENDPROC

440   DEF PROCcountcoms
450     coms=0
460     REPEAT : coms=coms+1 : nextcom$=INKEY$(11)
470     UNTIL command$<>nextcom$
480   ENDPROC

490   DEF PROCfix
500     GCOL 0,1:PROCdrawordelete(selection$)
510     GCOL 3,1
520   ENDPROC

530   DEF PROCdrawordelete(s$)
540     IF s$="1" THEN PROCdrawresistor(x,y)
550     IF s$="2" THEN PROCdrawcapacitor(x,y)
560     IF s$="3" THEN PROCdrawdiode(x,y)
570   ENDPROC
```

```
580    DEF PROCdrawresistor(x,y)
590      MOVE x,y : PLOT 1,30,0
600      PLOT 1,0,10 : PLOT 1,60,0
610      PLOT 1,0,-20 : PLOT 1,-60,0
620      PLOT 1,0,10 : PLOT 0,60,0
630      PLOT 1,30,0
640    ENDPROC

650    DEF PROCdrawcapacitor(x,y)
660      MOVE x,y : PLOT 1,30,0
670      PLOT 0,0,-30 : PLOT 1,0,60
680      PLOT 0,20,0 : PLOT 1,0,-60
690      PLOT 0,0,30 : PLOT 1,30,0
700    ENDPROC

710    DEF PROCdrawdiode(x,y)
720      MOVE x,y : PLOT 1,30,0
730      PLOT 0,0,-25 : PLOT 1,0,50
740      PLOT 1,25,-25 : PLOT 1,-25,-25
750      PLOT 0,25,25 : PLOT 1,30,0
760    ENDPROC
```

The program to drag an object is identical to the rubberband program with

```
PROCdrawordelete
```

replaced by:

```
PROCdrawordelete(selection$)
```

This procedure selects one out of the three drawing procedures and the selected object is drawn at a position under control of the directional keys. The next illustration shows the screen during execution of the above program.

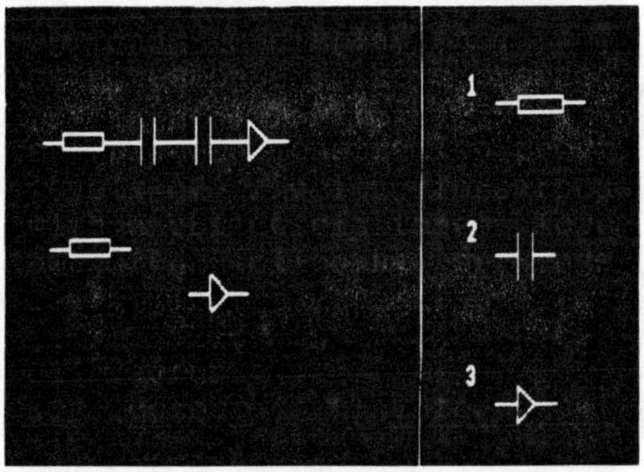

Scaling and rotating a dragged object
Other common facilities in picking and dragging programs are magnification and rotation. For example in the above dragging program, another key option could be "M" for 'Magnify' and T (turn) for rotation. The structural alterations now required in the program are significant. In particular we have to change the way in which we store shape information. Currently this information is embedded in the drawing procedures as parameters of the PLOT 1 statement. The most convenient scheme is to store the current displacement coordinate values for an object in an array. These displacements will of course change as a function of the angle of rotation. Initially we could set up an array for a square, for example, as:

squarex(1)	100	squarey(1)	0
(2)	0	(2)	100
(3)	-100	(3)	0

To draw the square in any (dragged) position (x,y) we need:

```
570   DEF PROCdrawsquare(x, y)
580     MOVE x, y
590     FOR i = 1 TO 3
600       PLOT 1, squarex(i), squarey(i)
610     NEXT i
620     DRAW x, y
630   ENDPROC
```

This is the same scheme as we have in the component drawing procedures (above) except that we are now storing the displacements in an array. Now to rotate an object we would press T (turn) and make the object rotate by a predetermined angular increment of , say, 10 degrees by altering the relative displacements. To do this we simply use a standard two-dimensional rotation transform (see Chapter 3):

```
800   DEF PROCrotate
810   LOCAL x,y
820     sintheta = SIN(RAD(10))
830     costheta = COS(RAD(10))
840     FOR i = 1 TO 3
850       x = x(i) : y = y(i)
860       x(i) = x*costheta + y*sintheta
870       y(i) = -x*sintheta+ y*costheta
880     NEXT i
890   ENDPROC
```

Each time the key is depressed new displacements are

calculated from the previous. Note that the figure is stationary while it is being rotated; it cannot be rotated and dragged at the same time.

Saving a line drawing
An image that has been created by rubberbanding can be saved as a list of coordinates and subsequently regenerated by a simple program reading the coordinates from a file and using DRAW. The coordinates can be saved initially in two parallel arrays and when the drawing is complete, the array contents dumped into a file. The coordinate saving should clearly be part of the 'fixing' process:

```
340   DEF PROCfix
350     REM Permanent draw
360     GCOL 0,1 : PROCdrawordelete
370     GCOL 3,1
375     line = line + 1
376     xcoord(line) = x
377     ycoord(line) = y
380     xs = x : ys = y
390     x = 640 : y = 512
400   ENDPROC
```

Similarly an image that has been created by picking and dragging an object can be saved, most economically, using three parallel arrays. The program would store, for each object, a pair of coordinates followed by a code indicating the class of object drawn at that position. The program would terminate by outputting the contents of the three arrays to a file. The regenerating program would contain the object-generating procedures again called from a shape selection procedure, the appropriate procedure for each shape being selected according to the stored code.

Exercises

1 Improve the rubberband program so that the start coordinate is input from the keyboard.

2 Introduce colour so that the fixed lines are displayed in one colour, but the moving line appears in a contrasting colour.

3 Consult the User Guide and change the rubberband program so that the cursor arrow keys are used for controlling the movement of the endpoints of the line.

4 Write a rubberband program where the permanent lines are to be constrained to the horizontal or vertical direction. For example an imperfectly drawn horizontal

line:

is to be corrected to a perfect horizontal line:

5 Write a picking and dragging program that picks either a hexagon or an equilateral triangle and drags it to a required position, fixes it there and colours it in a colour that is selected by another key. The hexagon and triangle should each have the same length of side so that they can be fitted together.

6 Write a picking and dragging program that will allow such diagrams as the following to be constructed:

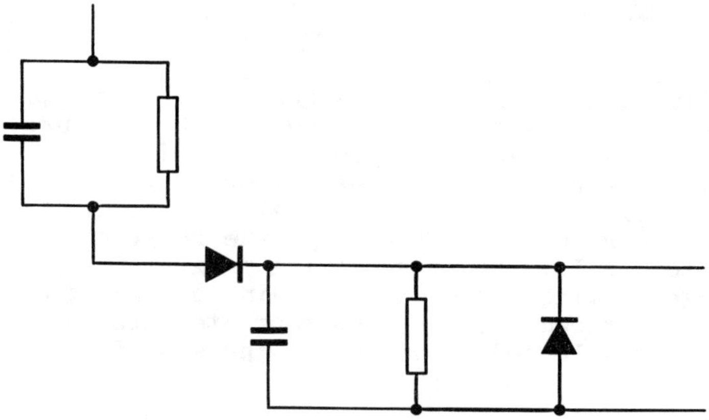

Note that this will have to contain both object dragging and rotation (0 or 90 degrees only) as well as rubberband line drawing.

7 Incorporate the picture-filing suggestions in your programs.

2.3 Colour-fill - general algorithms

The triangular fill facility (PLOT 80 to 87) is generally inconvenient in interactive graphics. In particular figures containing interior holes or concavities are difficult to fill using this method. Also if we are drawing a region outline using a light pen or graphics tablet it is inconvenient to store the coordinates of pixels on the outline. We require a general algorithm that will fill any region already delineated on the screen

Algorithms that fill the interior of any closed figure are sometimes called 'flood-fill' algorithms and they work by assuming that the region to be filled is delineated by a boundary of pixels in a non-background colour and that the interior of the region is '4-connected'. This means that all pixels within the region can be reached one from the other by a sequence of any of the movements up, down, left and right.

There are two approaches that we can make to this problem: one is recursive and is described in Chapter 7; the other is non-recursive and is now described. The algorithm below is extremely slow, but it provides a good introduction to the ideas involved. This algorithm uses a FIFO (first in, first out) buffer or queue. A program that fills the area enclosed by two concentric circles is now given.

```
 10   INPUT "RADII",r1,r2
 20   MODE 1
 30   GCOL 0,1
 40   PROCcircle(r1,640,512)
 50   PROCcircle(r2,640,512)
 60   PROCfillfrom(640+(r1+r2)/2,512)
 70   END

 90   DEF PROCcircle(r,xc,yc)
100   LOCAL t
110     MOVE xc+r,yc
120     FOR t=10 TO 360 STEP 10
130       DRAW xc+r*COS(RAD(t)),yc+r*SIN(RAD(t))
140     NEXT t
150   ENDPROC

200   DEF PROCfillfrom(startx,starty)
210   DIM queuex(500), queuey(500)
220     first=1 : last=0
230     PROCfill(startx,starty)
240     REPEAT
250       PROCunqueue
260       PROCfill(x,y+4)
270       PROCfill(x,y-4)
280       PROCfill(x+4,y)
290       PROCfill(x-4,y)
300     UNTIL first=(last+1) MOD 500
310   ENDPROC
```

```
330  DEF PROCfill(x,y)
340    IF POINT(x,y)>0 THEN ENDPROC
350    PLOT 69,x,y
360    PROCqueue(x,y)
370  ENDPROC

390  DEF PROCqueue(x,y)
400    last=(last+1)MOD500
410    queuex(last)=x
420    queuey(last)=y
430  ENDPROC

450  DEF PROCunqueue
460    x=queuex(first)
470    y=queuey(first)
480    first=(first+1)MOD500
490  ENDPROC
```

PROCfillfrom is initiated from a start point and that start point is coloured and added to a queue (by calling PROCfill). PROCfillfrom then repeatedly takes the first point from the queue and examines each of the neighbouring N, S, E and W points (by calling PROCfill for each of these points in turn). Each time PROCfill is called, it colours the point it is given (if it is not already coloured) and adds that point to the end of the queue. Adding a point to the queue in this way ensures that it will subsequently be removed from the queue and its neighbours examined.

The reason the queue is made a FIFO is to prevent it becoming too large. If for example we made the queue an ordinary stack (LIFO or last in first out), as you may see suggested in computer graphics textbooks, it would gradually fill up and would run out of memory.

For the queue, we use two arrays, one for x-coordinates and one for y-coordinates. Two variables indicate the positions of the 'first' and 'last' items in the queue.

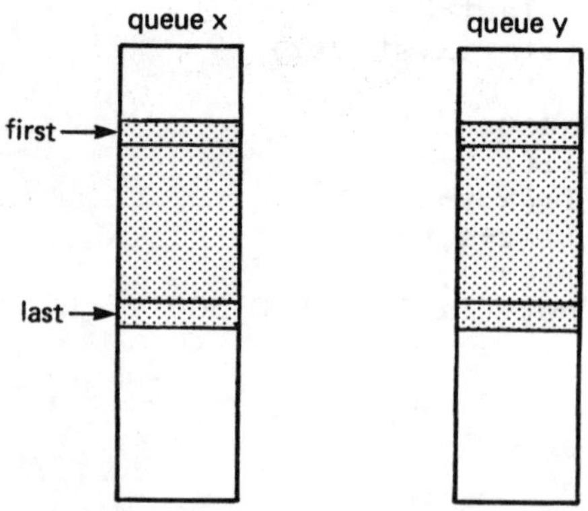

The arrays are treated as circular so that when the end of the queue reaches the end of the arrays, the queue is 'wrapped around' and continued into the space that is now free at the start of the arrays.

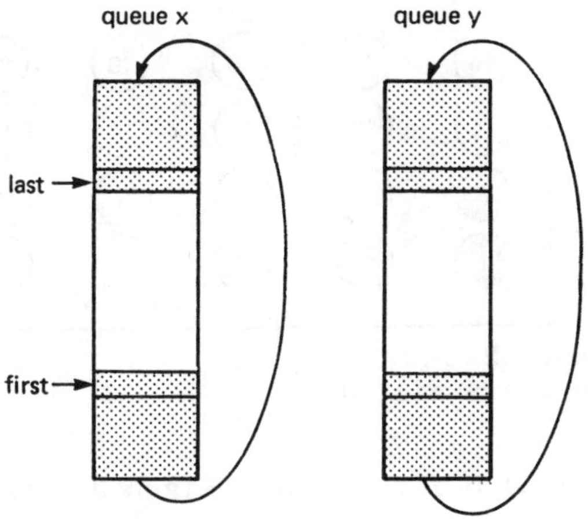

PROCfillfrom repeatedly takes the next point from the queue until the queue is empty. The photograph shows the algorithm in the course of filling. Note that the 'wavefronts' are diagonal. This is a consequence of using a FIFO queue in this particular context.

An illustrative sequence of how the algorithm works in detail is now given for a simple rectangular region. The start point is the bottom left hand corner.

pixel 1 is filled and added to the queue

1st cycle of REPEAT loop in PROCfillfrom
pixel 1 is removed from queue and neighbouring points examined

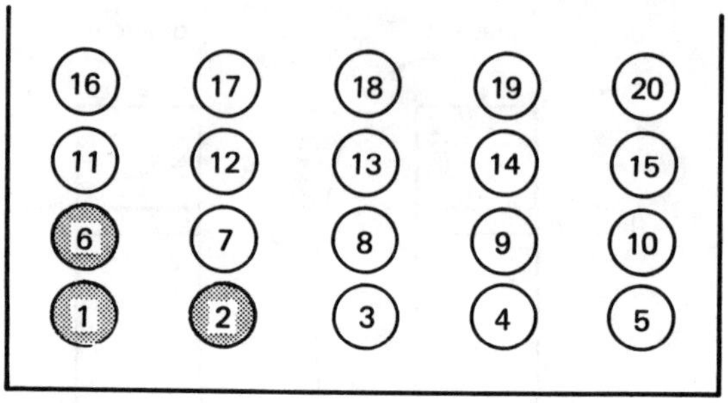

queue is now 6, 2
pixels 6 and 2 are filled

2nd cycle, pixel 6 removed and neighbours examined.

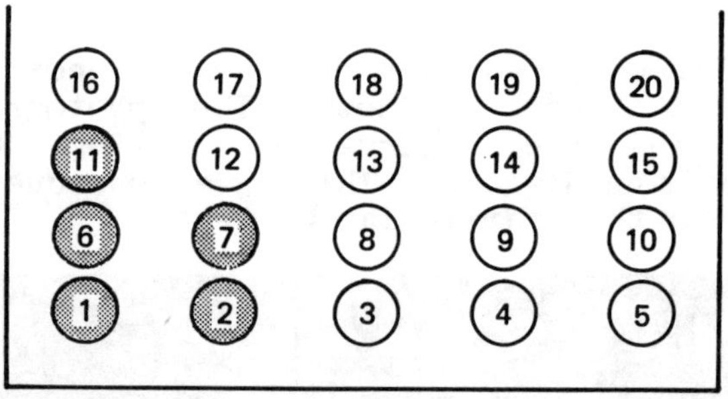

queue is now 2, 11, 7
pixels 11 and 7 are also filled.

3rd cycle, pixel 2 removed and neighbours examined.

queue is now 11, 7, 3
pixel 3 is filled

4th cycle, pixel 11 removed and neighbours examined.

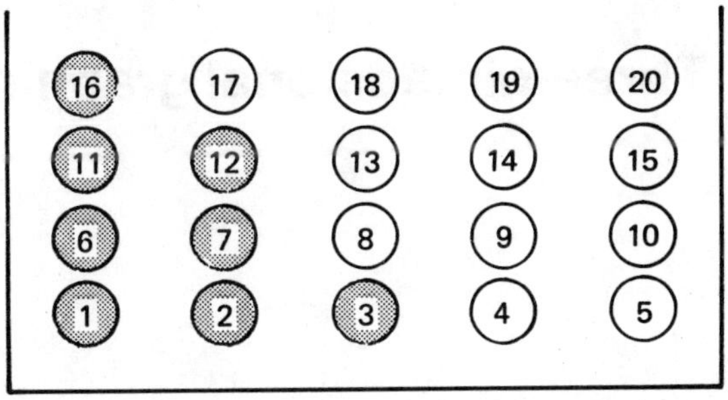

queue is now 7, 3, 16, 12
pixels 16 and 12 are filled

This sequence continues until the queue is empty.

Later versions of the Operating System provide a PLOT command for horizontal filling of a row of pixels up to a boundary. It is convenient to postpone discussion of this facility until Chapter 7 (recursion).

Exercises

1 Draw a checker board or games board pattern using colour-fill.

2 As an aid to understanding the queue fill algorithm, build up on paper a sequence showing a shape being filled from a central point.

3 Write a rubberbanding program that includes a paint option for colouring the region containing the current point.

Chapter 3 Three-dimensional graphics

This chapter looks at handling three-dimensional solids in computer graphics systems. Four important aspects are dealt with. First of all we look at the mathematical techniques for transforming (enlarging, rotating etc.) such models and we shall pave the way for this by looking at analogous operations on two-dimensional models. Secondly we consider how to display such solid bodies on a two-dimensional display or screen system. Thirdly we shall look at how models can be generated mathematically, that is how we can specify the three-dimensional shape of, for example, a cylinder to the computer. Finally we shall dip gently into a classic problem in computer graphics - hidden line removal.

This chapter contains a good deal of fairly straightforward mathematics involving matrix manipulation (mainly multiplication). A lot of the mathematical detail is in Appendices 4 and 5. The transformation procedures, particularly those for creating a screen image from a three-dimensional object, can easily be used as a tool without understanding how they were derived. The procedures used in this chapter will give you most of the tools you require to delve into three-dimensional computer graphics. If, however, you wish to develop your own software, or alter the given procedures, then obviously an understanding of the mathematics is desirable.

Currently there are two main methods for representing three-dimensional solids on computer graphics display devices. The first is the wire frame model. Here the model is defined as a list of vertices together with connectivity information. A two-dimensional representation of this model as seen from a particular viewpoint can then be drawn by using line graphics to join the vertices together. Hidden line removal may also be employed in such models. A more elaborate and more realistic display involves surface modelling. This is much closer to visual reality and here an attempt is made to create an image on the screen rather than a vertex model. Hidden surfaces are removed in the representation and visible surfaces are shaded, taking into account such factors as assumed position of the light source, surface textural characteristics that define reflectivity, etc. Colour graphics is used in such modelling and the end result can be uncannily real.

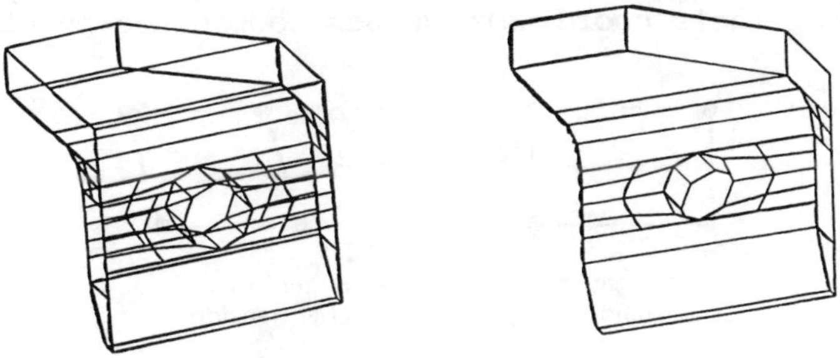

Courtesy Boeing Corporation

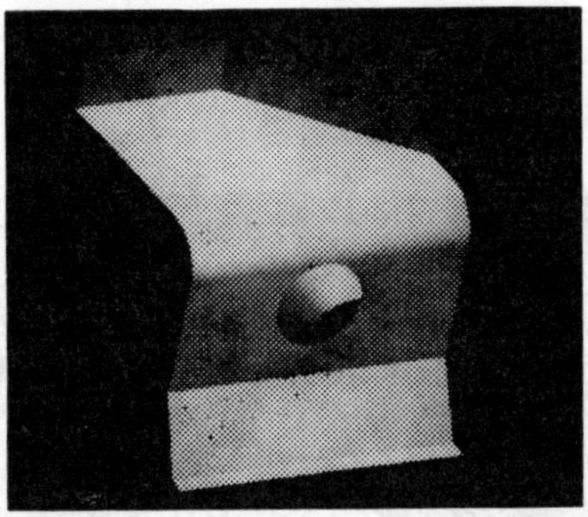

Now with the BBC micro we are limited by practical considerations to wire frame models. In MODE 0 even although the spatial resolution (640x256) is reasonable, each pixel at this resolution is 1 bit in the screen memory. This can only be used to define a surface using lines for its boundaries or by filling it in one uniform colour. To do realistic surface modelling we would need to have say 8 bits/pixel. In MODE 1 four colours are available and this is still insufficient for surface modelling. Colours can be mixed using a technique called 'dithering' or 'super-pixeling' but this results in a further decrease in resolution. However, we can still explore a variety of fascinating techniques used in three-dimensional graphics with wire frame models.

3.1 Two-dimensional transformations and matrix notation

The easiest two-dimensional transformation to implement and one that you have probably used already is translation or movement in one direction. Translation is one of a set of linear transformations that we can apply to a set of coordinates that specify the vertices or corners of a piecewise linear figure.

In the more general case a set of points S is operated on by a transformation T to produce the set S'. This means that a mathematical operation is carried out on all the points in S, changing their coordinate values to produce points in S'.

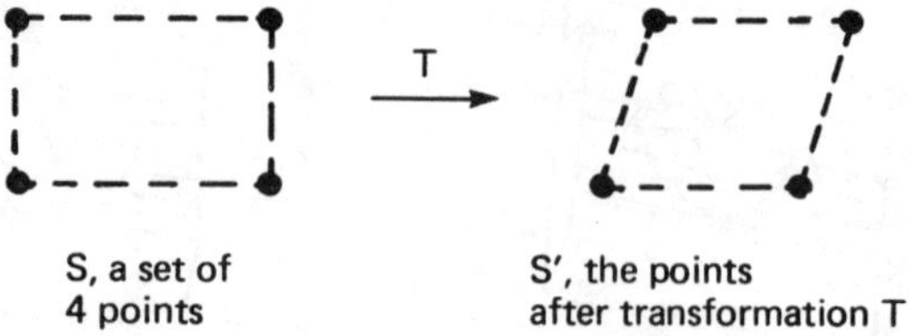

Depending on the operation used this may change the shape of a figure that is defined by drawing straight lines between the points. Consider a set of coordinate points representing a piecewise linear bird. To draw the six seagulls shown below from a single set of (x,y) coordinates in DATA statements we could use the next program.

```
 10   MODE 0
 20   VDU 29, 640; 512;
 30   FOR i = 0 TO 100 STEP 20
 40     PROCdrawseagull(i)
 50   NEXT i
 60   k=GET : MODE 7 : END

 70   DEF PROCdrawseagull(i)
 80     RESTORE
 90     READ noofpoints
100     READ x, y : MOVE x+i, y
110     FOR j = 2 TO noofpoints
120        READ x, y : DRAW x+i, y
130     NEXT j
140   ENDPROC
```

```
150    DATA 17, -110,70
160    DATA -120,90, -110,100, -90,100, -30,70
170    DATA 100,240, 300,160, 130,180, 40,0
180    DATA 140,-60, 60,-130, 0,-40, -140,-130
190    DATA -220,-390, -200,-70, -70,30, -110,70
```

The program effects five simple transformations of the coordinate set in the DATA statements. To change the translation such that, for example, a diagonally displaced set was displaced, we could change lines 100 and 120:

```
100     READ x, y : MOVE x+i, y+i

120         READ x, y : DRAW x+i, y+i
```

This is, however, an approach that would lead us into a different programming notation for each transformation that we used - a rather unsatisfactory state of affairs.

What we will now proceed to develop is a mathematical technique that allows us to specify any transformation as a set of four parameters. We can then have a single procedure that operates on the data set, using these parameters and producing the desired transformation. (We will then find that this system has certain deficiencies that can be overcome by using six parameters.)

To start with we will ignore translation and consider the other two common transformations, rotation and scaling. To rotate a point (x,y) through a clockwise angle, theta, about the origin, the transformation is:

$$xt = x\cos\theta + y\sin\theta$$
$$yt = -x\sin\theta + y\cos\theta$$

and scaling is given by:

$$xt = xS1$$
$$yt = yS2$$

The xt and yt are the transformed values of x and y. S1 is the scaling factor in the x direction and S2 the scaling factor in the y direction. For example, to magnify a figure uniformly we would use S1 = S2 = 3, say. Now we can make the two sets of equations look like each other by re-expressing the scaling equations as:

$$xt = xS1 + y \times 0$$
$$yt = x \times 0 + yS2$$

This enables us to write the operations using matrix notation. (Details on matrix notation and matrix manipulation are to be found in Appendix 4.) Firstly rotation clockwise:

$$(xt, yt) = (x, y)\begin{bmatrix} \cos\theta & -\sin\theta \\ \sin\theta & \cos\theta \end{bmatrix}$$

and scaling:

$$(xt, yt) = (x, y)\begin{bmatrix} S1 & 0 \\ 0 & S2 \end{bmatrix}$$

and this is just a different way of writing the operations expressed as equations above. The notation used for expressing such transformations in matrix form is not standard but is, for better or worse, the de-facto standard in computer graphics. We can now represent various linear transformations as 2x2 matrices:

1) Identity (no effect) $\begin{bmatrix} 1 & 0 \\ 0 & 1 \end{bmatrix}$

2) Rotation (clockwise) $\begin{bmatrix} \cos\theta & -\sin\theta \\ \sin\theta & \cos\theta \end{bmatrix}$

3) Rotation (counter-clockwise) $\begin{bmatrix} \cos\theta & \sin\theta \\ -\sin\theta & \cos\theta \end{bmatrix}$

4) Scaling $\begin{bmatrix} S1 & 0 \\ 0 & S2 \end{bmatrix}$

5) Reflection (about the x-axis) $\begin{bmatrix} 1 & 0 \\ 0 & -1 \end{bmatrix}$

6) Reflection (about the y-axis) $\begin{bmatrix} -1 & 0 \\ 0 & 1 \end{bmatrix}$

7) Y Shear $\begin{bmatrix} 1 & S \\ 0 & 1 \end{bmatrix}$

8) X Shear $\begin{bmatrix} 1 & 0 \\ S & 1 \end{bmatrix}$

Note that we cannot define translation using this system, a point we shall return to in a moment.

Here is a program that will accept the four parameters defining a transformation, using the terminology:

$$\begin{bmatrix} a & c \\ b & d \end{bmatrix}$$

for the transformation matrix.

```
 10   MODE 0
 20   VDU 29, 640; 512;
 30   PROCdrawaxes
 40   PRINT ''"a  c"'''"b  d"; TAB(6,3); "?"
 50   INPUT TAB(9,2)a, TAB(14,2)c, TAB(9,4)b, TAB(14,4)d
 60   READ noofpoints
 70   READ x, y : PROCtransform(x,y)
 80   MOVE xt, yt
 90   FOR i = 2 TO noofpoints
100     READ x, y
110     PROCtransform(x, y)
120     DRAW xt, yt
130   NEXT i
140   k=GET : MODE 7 : END
150   DATA 5, 0,0, 180,0, 180,300, 0,300, 0,0

200   DEF PROCdrawaxes
210     MOVE -640,0 : DRAW 640,0
220     MOVE 0,-512 : DRAW 0,512
230   ENDPROC

300   DEF PROCtransform(x, y)
310       xt = a*x + b*y
320       yt = c*x + d*y
330   ENDPROC
```

Note that we have just one procedure and two lines of calculation to perform any of the above transformations. The illustrations show, for both a rectangle and the more complex seagull, the effect of the transformations.

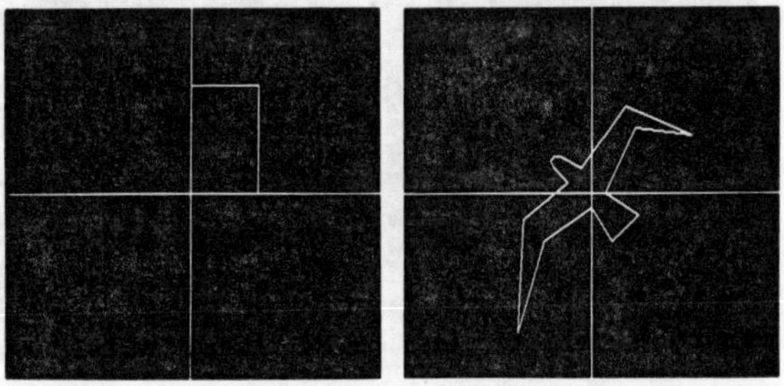

Identity $\begin{bmatrix} 1 & 0 \\ 0 & 1 \end{bmatrix}$

Rotation 30 degrees anticlockwise $\begin{bmatrix} 0.866 & 0.500 \\ -0.500 & 0.866 \end{bmatrix}$

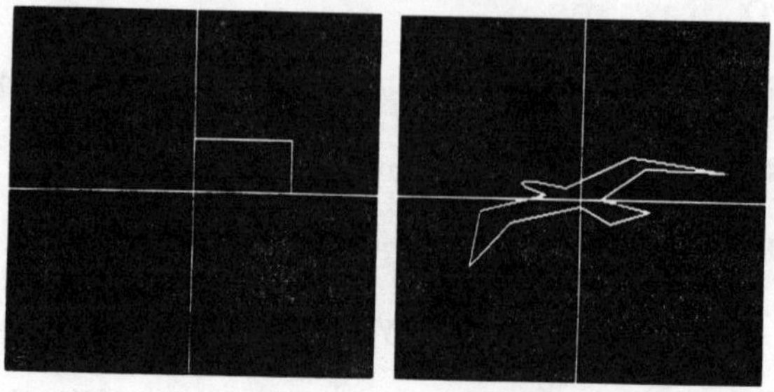

Scaling $\begin{bmatrix} 2 & 0 \\ 0 & 0.5 \end{bmatrix}$

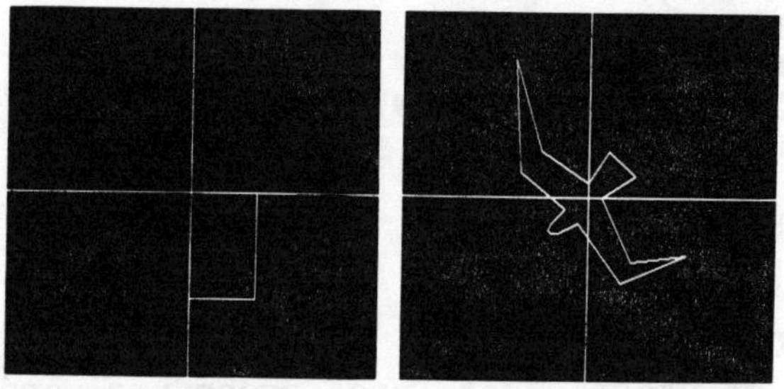

Reflection $\begin{bmatrix} -1 & 0 \\ 0 & -1 \end{bmatrix}$

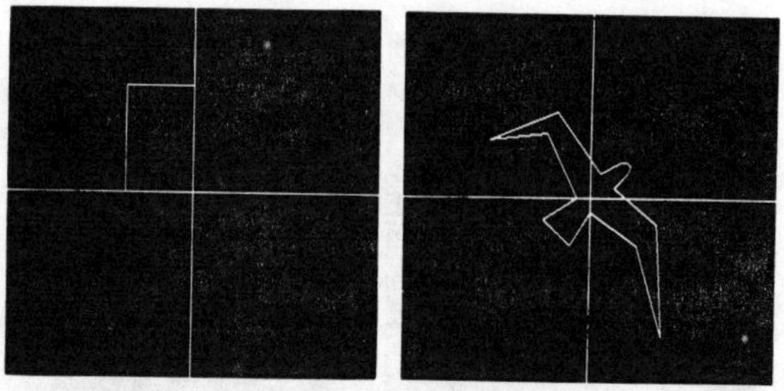

Reflection $\begin{bmatrix} -0 & 0 \\ 0 & 1 \end{bmatrix}$

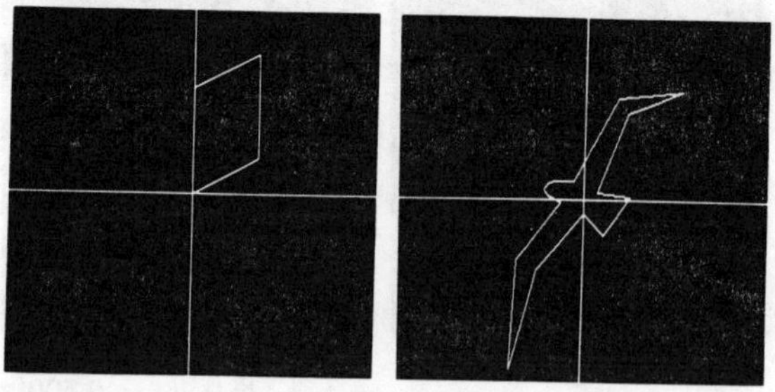

Y shear $\begin{bmatrix} 1 & 1 \\ 0 & 1 \end{bmatrix}$

Now bear in mind that this is only a demonstration program and that normally we would not calculate cosines and sines before supplying these as program input. Rather cos(theta) and sin(theta) would be calculated in the course of execution of a program.

Homogeneous coordinates

The above system for effecting two-dimensional transformations has a number of drawbacks. Firstly it excludes an important transformation (translation). Secondly all the transformations are centred at the origin, (0,0). This is fine in the above examples where the seagull was placed over the origin and one vertex of the rectangle was centred at the origin. Consider a rectangle not centred at the origin and subject to a 30 degree rotation.

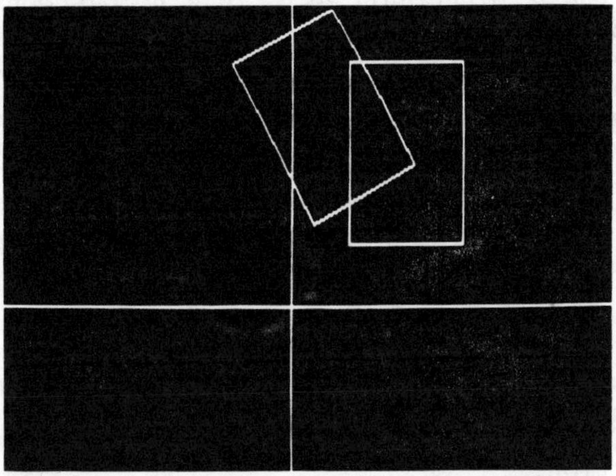

or to a scaling:

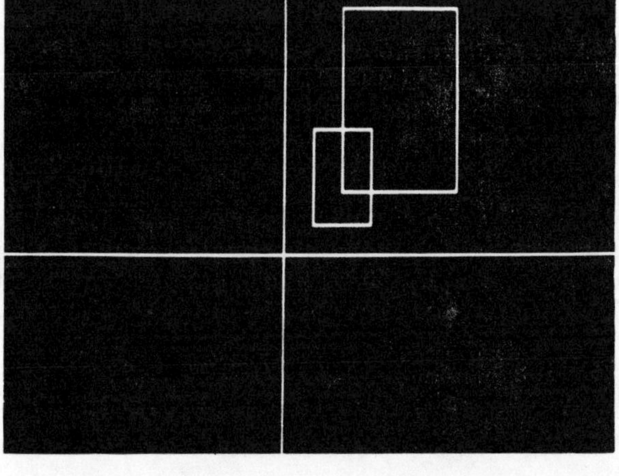

Because the rotation is centred on the origin the rectangle

both rotates and translates. When we are rotating a geometrical figure it is far more likely that we require rotation about an arbitrary point, for example, any one of the vertices of the rectangle, or the intersection of its diagonals. Such a transformation is not available in the above system. Similarly reflections are through the x-axis or the y-axis. Reflections through other lines are not available.

Perhaps most absurd of all is scaling. This also involves a translation. The second illustration shows the rectangle offset from the origin and subject to a shrinking. Again it is highly unlikely that we should ever require scaling complicated by a translation proportional to the magnitude of the scaling. Rather we may require 'pure' scaling about a centre point or vertex.

A homogenous coordinate system is a notation that overcomes these difficulties. In a homogeneous coordinate system a point (x,y) becomes (x/r, y/r, r). It is convenient to make r = 1, avoiding division, giving the representation of a point as (x, y, 1). Because a point is now a three element row matrix, transformation matrices are now 3x3. This system has the immediate advantage that we can now represent the translation transformation with a 3x3 matrix. We can now write down seven common transformation matrices:

1) Translation $$\begin{bmatrix} 1 & 0 & 0 \\ 0 & 1 & 0 \\ Tx & Ty & 1 \end{bmatrix}$$

where Tx is the translation in the x direction and Ty is the translation in the y direction. To check that this works let us translate the point (1, 1, 1)) through a distance of 2 in the x direction:

$$(1, 1, 1) \begin{bmatrix} 1 & 0 & 0 \\ 0 & 1 & 0 \\ 2 & 0 & 1 \end{bmatrix} = ((1 \times 1 + 1 \times 0 + 1 \times 2), (1 \times 0 + 1 \times 1 + 1 \times 0), (1 \times 0 + 1 \times 0 + 1 \times 1))$$

In other words

$$(x, y, 1) \begin{bmatrix} 1 & 0 & 0 \\ 0 & 1 & 0 \\ Tx & Ty & 1 \end{bmatrix} = (x + Tx, y + Ty, 1)$$

Some of the other transformations in our new system are:

2) Rotation (clockwise) $$\begin{bmatrix} \cos\theta & -\sin\theta & 0 \\ \sin\theta & \cos\theta & 0 \\ 0 & 0 & 1 \end{bmatrix}$$

3) Rotation (anti-clockwise) $\begin{bmatrix} \cos\theta & \sin\theta & 0 \\ -\sin\theta & \cos\theta & 0 \\ 0 & 0 & 1 \end{bmatrix}$

These rotations are still centred on the origin.

4) Scaling $\begin{bmatrix} Sx & 0 & 0 \\ 0 & Sy & 0 \\ 0 & 0 & 1 \end{bmatrix}$

5) Reflection (x-axis) $\begin{bmatrix} 1 & 0 & 0 \\ 0 & -1 & 0 \\ 0 & 0 & 1 \end{bmatrix}$

6) X Shear $\begin{bmatrix} 1 & 0 & 0 \\ S & 1 & 0 \\ 0 & 0 & 1 \end{bmatrix}$

To test that these are exactly the same as we had before we can alter the demonstration program to input 6 parameters and perform the matrix multiplication:

```
 40   PRINT ''"a  d"''"b  e"''"c  f";TAB(6,4); "?"
 50   INPUT TAB(9,2)a, TAB(14,2)d,
            TAB(9,4)b, TAB(14,4)e,
            TAB(9,6)c, TAB(14,6)f

300   DEF PROCtransform(x, y)
310       xt = a*x + b*y + c
320       yt = d*x + e*y + f
330   ENDPROC
```

where the input parameters represent six of the coefficients of a 3x3 transformation matrix:

$$\begin{bmatrix} a & d & 0 \\ b & e & 0 \\ c & f & 1 \end{bmatrix}$$

So what have we achieved? Very little as yet! Certainly we have represented translation in a matrix system, but we now need 9 matrix coefficients instead of 4 to achieve the same result. (Actually we have only used 6 of the 9 above, but you will see shortly that nine are convenient when combinations of transformations are considered.) However, the fact that we have included translation in our system now gives us a major advantage - we need no longer restrict ourselves to transformations at the origin. Thus homogeneous coordinates provide a rather roundabout way of adding constants to the transformed x and y values. The advantage of this notation is that transformations can still be represented as matrices which will be useful when considering combinations of transformations.

Generalized two-dimensional transformations
Consider the problem of rotation about any point. Say, for example, we wish to rotate a rectangle, in any position, 30 degrees counter-clockwise about its bottom LH vertex. We can easily do this now:

1) Original rectangle at P(Tx,Ty)

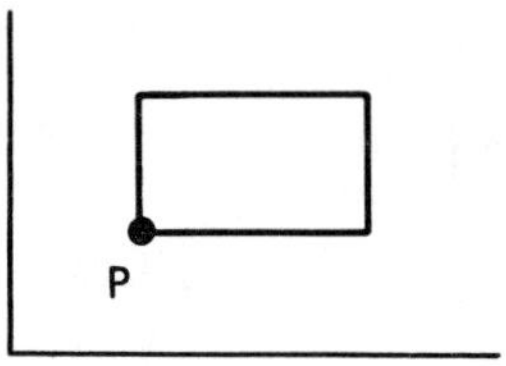

2) Translate to the origin

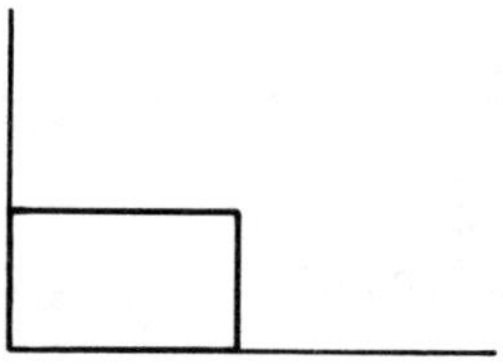

3) Rotate about the origin

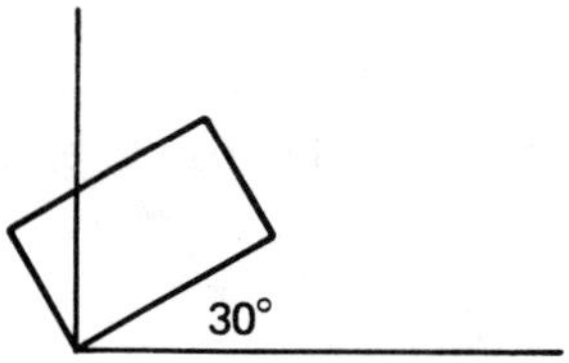

4) Translate to P(Tx, Ty)

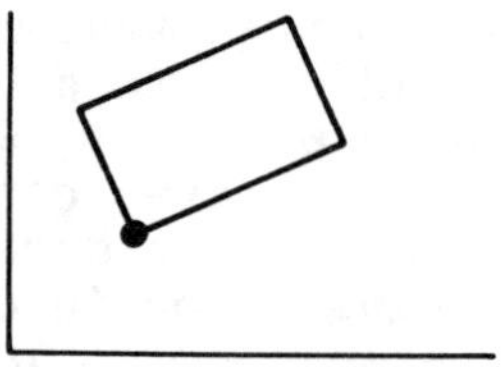

The three operations would be:

$$T1 = \text{translate} = \begin{bmatrix} 1 & 0 & 0 \\ 0 & 1 & 0 \\ -Tx & -Ty & 1 \end{bmatrix}$$

$$R = \text{rotate} = \begin{bmatrix} \cos 30 & \sin 30 & 0 \\ -\sin 30 & \cos 30 & 0 \\ 0 & 0 & 1 \end{bmatrix}$$

$$T2 = \text{translate} = \begin{bmatrix} 1 & 0 & 0 \\ 0 & 1 & 0 \\ Tx & Ty & 1 \end{bmatrix}$$

Now instead of multiplying each point (x,y,1) by three matrices we can multiply the matrices together to obtain a 'net transformation matrix' (Details on matrix multiplication plus a procedure to perform the multiplication are contained in Appendix 4).

net transformation matrix = T1*R*T2

and then multiply each point (x,y,1) by this matrix. A net transformation matrix is always of the form:

$$\begin{bmatrix} a & d & 0 \\ b & e & 0 \\ c & f & 1 \end{bmatrix}$$

and in this case

$$T1{*}R{*}T2 = \begin{bmatrix} \cos 30 & \sin 30 & 0 \\ -\sin 30 & \cos 30 & 0 \\ Tx(1 - \cos 30) + Ty \sin 30 & Ty(1 - \cos 30) - Tx \sin 30 & 1 \end{bmatrix}$$

The same approach can be used for scaling. Say we wanted to shrink the rectangle about its centre point:

1) Original rectangle at P(Tx,Ty)

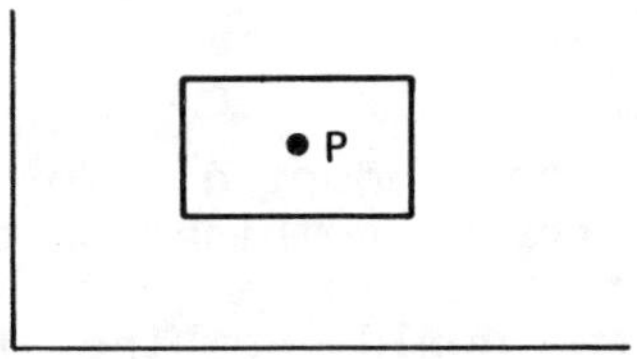

2) Translate to origin

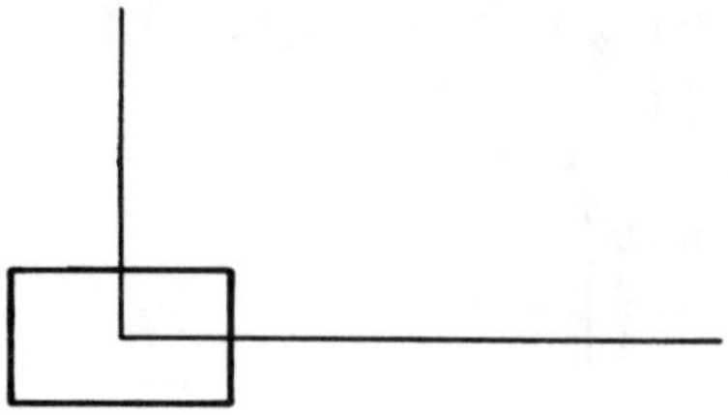

3) Shrink

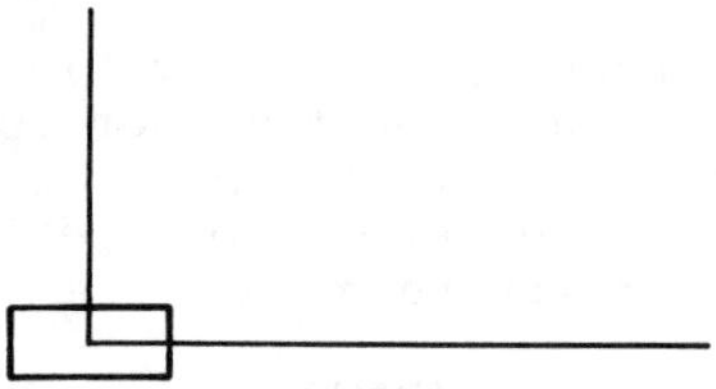

4) Translate to P(Tx,Ty)

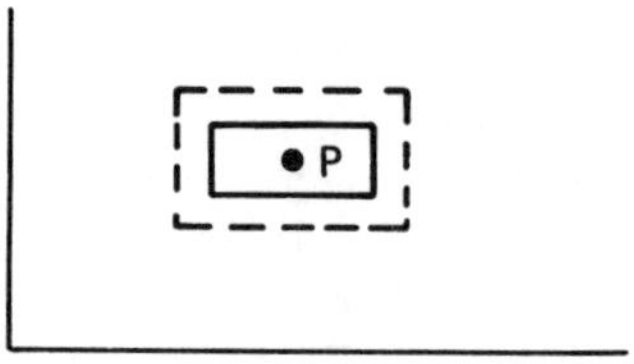

The rectangle has shrunk within itself - the desired transformation. This should be compared with the 2x2 system shrinking illustration (earlier) where the effect of applying a shrink transformation was also to translate the rectangle 'outside itself'.
The net transform matrix for scaling is:

$$\begin{bmatrix} S1 & 0 & 0 \\ 0 & S2 & 0 \\ Tx(1-S1) & Ty(1-S2) & 1 \end{bmatrix}$$

A similar approach can be adopted for the other transformations. Any arbitrary combination of translation scaling and rotation will result in a net transformation matrix. For example we could combine the following transformations into a net transformation matrix:

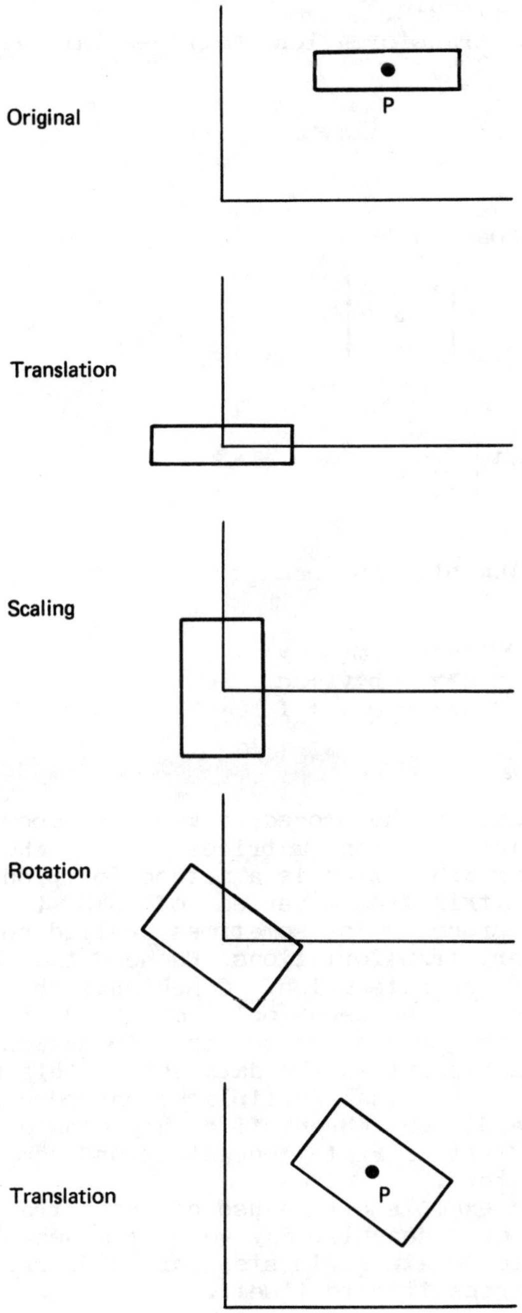
Original
P
Translation
Scaling
Rotation
Translation
P

Now in general transformations are not commutative - the order in which the individual matrices are multiplied to form a net transformation matrix is important. T1*R*T2 is not the same as T1*T2*R.

Because net transformation matrices are <u>always</u> of the form:

$$\begin{bmatrix} a & d & 0 \\ b & e & 0 \\ c & f & 1 \end{bmatrix}$$

The multiplication

$$(xt, yt, 1) = (x, y, 1) \begin{bmatrix} a & d & 0 \\ b & e & 0 \\ c & f & 1 \end{bmatrix}$$

reduces to

$$(xt, yt) = (x, y, 1) \begin{bmatrix} a & d \\ b & e \\ c & f \end{bmatrix}$$

and this is implemented as:

```
300   DEF PROCtransform(x, y)
310       xt = a*x + b*y + c
320       yt = d*x + e*y + f
330   ENDPROC
```

which is identical to the procedure we used above to test the basic transformation matrices. Thus what we have achieved with our 3x3 system is a method for producing a net transformation matrix from a series of 3x3 transformation matrices. The process is sometimes called concatenating (joining together) transformations. We need the 3x3 system to perform the concatenation. Concatenation is clearly advantageous because we need only multiply the matrices together once to obtain the net transformation matrix and then multiply each point in the data set by this matrix. As we have seen this final multiplication reduces to just 4 products and 4 additions. Such efficiency considerations are critically important in real time animation computers such as flight simulators.

Finally as an example of the use of these transformations we return to our seagull. Say we have a seagull drawn at (0,0) and wish to rotate it in steps of 10 degrees, and at the same time shrink it into itself.

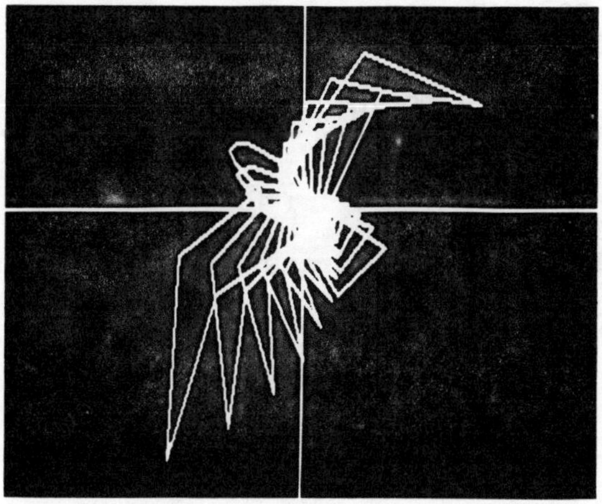

The net transformation matrix for a 10 degree rotation is given by:

$$S*R = \begin{bmatrix} S & 0 & 0 \\ 0 & S & 0 \\ 0 & 0 & 1 \end{bmatrix} \begin{bmatrix} \cos 10 & \sin 10 & 0 \\ -\sin 10 & \cos 10 & 0 \\ 0 & 0 & 1 \end{bmatrix}$$

$$= \begin{bmatrix} S\cos 10 & S\sin 10 & 0 \\ -S\sin 10 & S\cos 10 & 0 \\ 0 & 0 & 1 \end{bmatrix}$$

giving the implementation:

```
a = s*COS(RAD(10)) : d = s*SIN(RAD(10))
b=-d : e=a : c=0 : f=0
```

Remember that our seagull data set is already centred on the origin. If it were not centred at the origin we would apply the net transformation matrix T1*S*R*T2, to scale and rotate the figure.

The program makes repeated application of the rotation and scaling transformation, for different angles and scaling factors. Note that within the main program loop we reduce the scaling and increment 'theta'. The reduction in scale gives the spiral effect and and makes the image easier to interpret.

Now this program contains the three main elements of mathematically generated pictures: a process (FOR loop) to control the repetition of a drawing process; a drawing procedure that can either generate a data set mathematically, or operate with a supplied data set; and a net transformation matrix operating on the data set.

```
 10   MODE 0
 20   VDU 29, 640; 512;
 30   PROCdrawaxes
 40   s = 1 : theta = 0
 50   FOR bird = 1 TO 10
 60     RESTORE 200
 70     a = s*COS(RAD(theta)) : d = s*SIN(RAD(theta))
 80     b=-d : e=a : c=0 : f=0
 90     READ noofpoints
100     READ x, y : PROCtransform(x, y)
110     MOVE xt, yt
120     FOR p = 2 TO noofpoints
130       READ x, y
140       PROCtransform(x, y)
150       DRAW xt, yt
160     NEXT p
170     s = s*0.85:  theta = theta + 10
180   NEXT bird
190   k=GET : MODE 7 : END

200   DEF PROCdrawaxes
210     MOVE -640,0 : DRAW 640,0
220     MOVE 0,-512 : DRAW 0,512
230   ENDPROC

300   DEF PROCtransform(x, y)
310       xt = a*x + b*y + c
320       yt = d*x + e*y + f
330   ENDPROC

340 DATA ...
```

Exercises

1 Write a utility program for constructing net transformation matrices. The individual transformations to be concatenated could be specified as matrices, or by a sequence of commands specifying translation, scaling, rotation and so on.

2 Write a series of programs that generate designs involving the seagull. The illustrations show some suggestions. The first illustration involves scaling only. The second uses scaling, rotation and (non-linear) translation. The third and fourth illustrations just involve translation and a single scale adjustment. They were produced by drawing instances of the seagull at equal angular increments around the circumference of a circle. Changing the radius of the circle, the scale of the seagull and the size of the angular increment will produce literally hundreds of different designs.

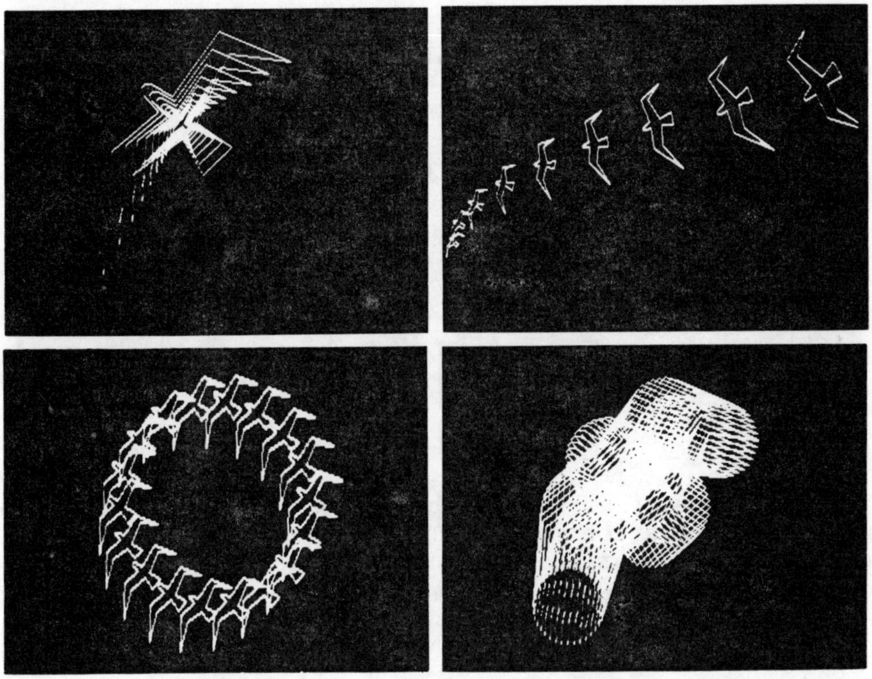

3 Repeat these programs but this time use a motif of your own design. This is most conveniently planned out using graph paper.

3.2 Three-dimensional graphics - general transformations

In this section we extend the techniques used in the two-dimensional transformations for translation, scaling, rotation etc. to deal with three-dimensional objects. Bear in mind that we are dealing with three-dimensional coordinates (x,y,z) that transform under scaling, rotation or whatever to other three-dimensional coordinates (xt,yt,zt) and that we are not yet ready to display a two-dimensional image of a three-dimensional object on the screen. We will thus restrict this section to a short discussion on extending two-dimensional transformations to three-dimensional transformations without developing any programs. The three-dimensional transformation techniques are required before we can deal with the transformation into two dimensions for viewing.

The three-dimensional transformations using homogeneous coordinates (to enable the calculation of net transformation matrices) are all of the form:

$$(xt, yt, zt, 1) = (x, y, z, 1) \begin{bmatrix} a & e & i & 0 \\ b & f & j & 0 \\ c & g & k & 0 \\ d & h & l & 1 \end{bmatrix}$$

where the basic transformation matrices are:

1) Scaling $\begin{bmatrix} Sx & 0 & 0 & 0 \\ 0 & Sy & 0 & 0 \\ 0 & 0 & Sz & 0 \\ 0 & 0 & 0 & 1 \end{bmatrix}$

Overall magnification or shrinking is achieved by:

Magnification $\begin{bmatrix} S & 0 & 0 & 0 \\ 0 & S & 0 & 0 \\ 0 & 0 & S & 0 \\ 0 & 0 & 0 & 1 \end{bmatrix}$

Rotation is easily arrived at by again extending the two-dimensional rotation matrix. To rotate counter-clockwise in two-dimensions about the origin, we used:

$$\begin{bmatrix} \cos\theta & \sin\theta & 0 \\ -\sin\theta & \cos\theta & 0 \\ 0 & 0 & 1 \end{bmatrix}$$

and in the three-dimensional case if we consider the z-axis coming out of the paper, we have:

2) Rotation about the z-axis $\begin{bmatrix} \cos\theta & \sin\theta & 0 & 0 \\ -\sin\theta & \cos\theta & 0 & 0 \\ 0 & 0 & 1 & 0 \\ 0 & 0 & 0 & 1 \end{bmatrix}$

which produces rotation counter-clockwise about the z-axis. That this is a rotation about the z-axis can be seen, informally, from the fact that the matrix multiplication only affects the x and y coefficients. This observation can then be used to write down the other 2 rotation transformations:

3) Rotation about the x-axis $\begin{bmatrix} 1 & 0 & 0 & 0 \\ 0 & \cos\theta & \sin\theta & 0 \\ 0 & -\sin\theta & \cos\theta & 0 \\ 0 & 0 & 0 & 1 \end{bmatrix}$

4) Rotation about the y-axis $\begin{bmatrix} \cos\theta & 0 & -\sin\theta & 0 \\ 0 & 1 & 0 & 0 \\ \sin\theta & 0 & \cos\theta & 0 \\ 0 & 0 & 0 & 1 \end{bmatrix}$

5) Translation

$$\begin{bmatrix} 1 & 0 & 0 & 0 \\ 0 & 1 & 0 & 0 \\ 0 & 0 & 1 & 0 \\ Tx & Ty & Tz & 1 \end{bmatrix}$$

Again we can derive net transformation matrices and, for example, if we wanted to rotate a body about a line parallel to the z-axis which passes through the point (Tx, Ty, 0) we would use:

$$T1*R*T2 = \begin{bmatrix} 1 & 0 & 0 & 0 \\ 0 & 1 & 0 & 0 \\ 0 & 0 & 1 & 0 \\ -Tx & -Ty & 0 & 1 \end{bmatrix} \begin{bmatrix} \cos\theta & \sin\theta & 0 & 0 \\ -\sin\theta & \cos\theta & 0 & 0 \\ 0 & 0 & 1 & 0 \\ 0 & 0 & 0 & 1 \end{bmatrix} \begin{bmatrix} 1 & 0 & 0 & 0 \\ 0 & 1 & 0 & 0 \\ 0 & 0 & 1 & 0 \\ Tx & Ty & 0 & 1 \end{bmatrix}$$

$$= \begin{bmatrix} \cos\theta & \sin\theta & 0 & 0 \\ -\sin\theta & \cos\theta & 0 & 0 \\ 0 & 0 & 1 & 0 \\ -Tx\cos\theta + Ty\sin\theta & -Tx\sin\theta - Ty\cos\theta & 0 & 1 \end{bmatrix} \begin{bmatrix} 1 & 0 & 0 & 0 \\ 0 & 1 & 0 & 0 \\ 0 & 0 & 1 & 0 \\ Tx & Ty & 0 & 1 \end{bmatrix}$$

$$= \begin{bmatrix} \cos\theta & \sin\theta & 0 & 0 \\ -\sin\theta & \cos\theta & 0 & 0 \\ 0 & 0 & 1 & 0 \\ -Tx\cos\theta + Ty\sin\theta + Tx & -Tx\sin\theta - Ty\cos\theta + Ty & 0 & 1 \end{bmatrix}$$

This would be implemented as:

```
xt = x*costheta-y*sintheta-Tx*costheta+Ty*sintheta+Tx
yt = x*sintheta+y*costheta-Tx*sintheta-Ty*costheta+Ty
zt = z
```

where of course the third equation is redundant because the rotation is about the z-axis and the z coordinate is unchanged for all points.

This transformation is effected for the case shown in the following illustration. Since we are not yet ready to actually plot these objects on a display screen the output from the program is shown as a coordinate list.

The transformation is:

theta = 45, Tx = Ty = 3

i.e. rotate 45 degrees counter-clockwise about the vertical line (3,3)

Input coordinates

vertex	x	y	z
1	3	3	3
2	4	3	3
3	4	4	3
4	3	4	3
5	3	3	4
6	4	3	4
7	4	4	4
8	3	4	4

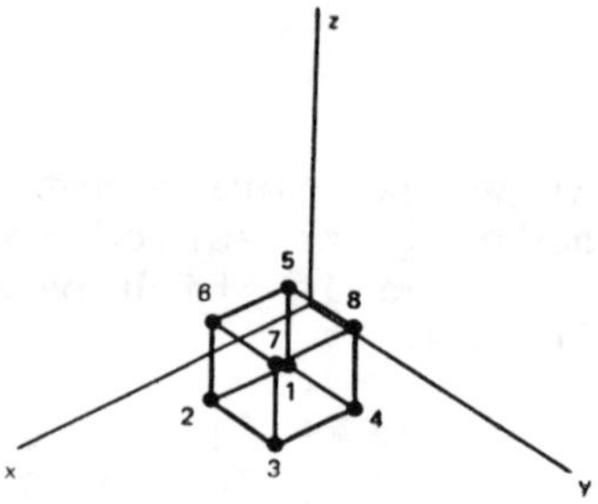

Output coordinates

vertex	x	y	z
1	3.000	3.000	3.000
2	3.707	3.707	3.000
3	3.000	4.414	3.000
4	2.293	3.707	3.000
5	3.000	3.000	4.000
6	3.707	3.707	4.000
7	3.000	4.414	4.000
8	2.293	3.707	4.000

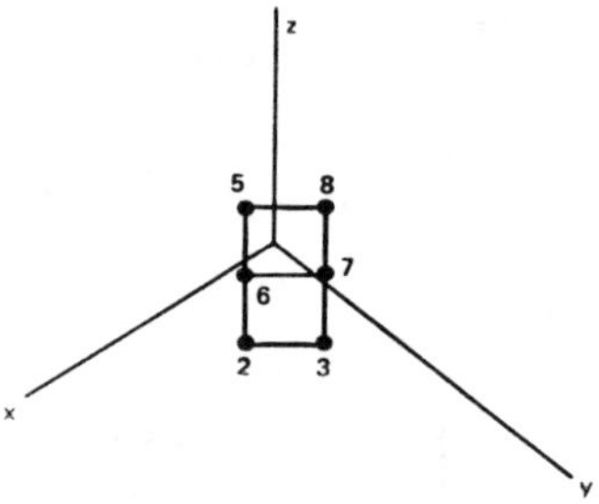

3.3 Three-dimensional graphics - viewing and perspective transformations

Three-dimensional graphics would be a simple extension of two-dimensional graphics - all our 3x3 transformations would become 4x4 transformations and that would be the end of the matter - if we had access to a three-dimensional display device. Of course the display device is two-dimensional and the external complication in three-dimensional graphics comes from the need to map the three-dimensional coordinates of the object to be displayed into the two-dimensional coordinates of the display system. It is convenient to express this as a combination of two transformations - the viewing transformation and the perspective transformation. This is needed in addition to any other of the transformations described above such as scaling, rotation and translation of the three-dimensional object.

We shall specify the coordinates of a three-dimensional object in a so called world coordinate system:

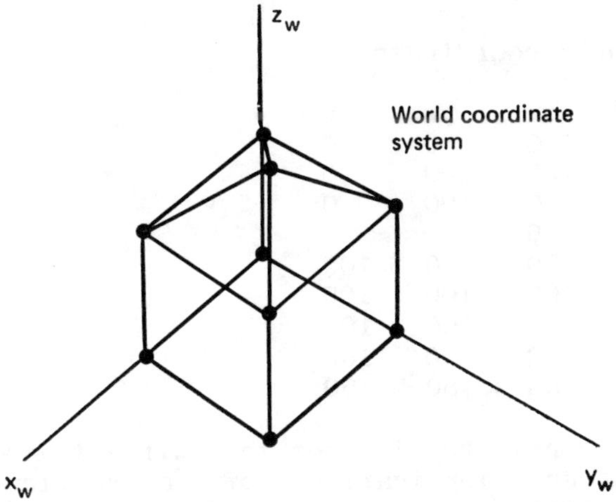

A house with a pyramidal roof could be specified in this system as a list of 9 (x,y,z) points in the world coordinate system.

Our intuition and visual experience with such abstractions as the wire frame model shown above enables us to realise the shape of the solid body that the model represents. Just as we would see different views of the real object as we moved our viewpoint around the sides and over the top, so we can construct two-dimensional representations of these different views from the original wire frame model.

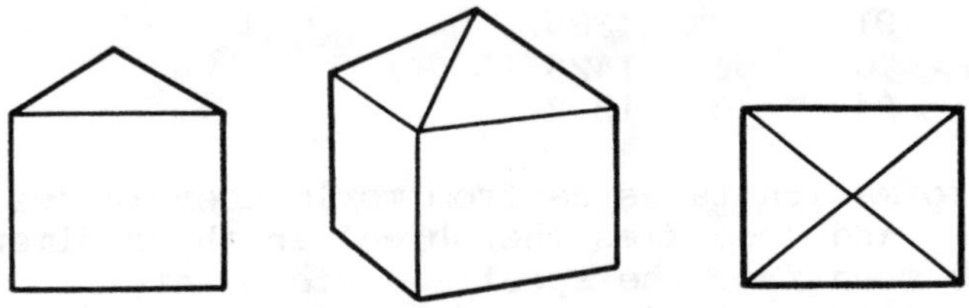

The views can be constructed from the original object by specifying a viewpoint in relation to the object. The so-called 'viewpoint transformation' converts the coordinates expressed in the world coordinate system into 'eye' coordinates expressed in a coordinate system centred at the viewpoint.

Having applied the viewpoint transformation we are still left with a list of three-dimensional coordinates. The transformation that produces a list of two-dimensional or screen coordinates from the viewpoint list is called the perspective transformation.

The process can be illustrated:

World coordinates

vertex	xw	yw	zw
1	100	0	0
2	100	100	0
3	0	100	0
4	0	0	0
5	100	0	100
6	100	100	100
7	0	100	100
8	0	0	100
9	50	50	150

This is a coordinate list for the wire frame house shown above. After application of a particular viewpoint transformation:

Eye coordinates

vertex	xe	ye	ze
1	-42	-69	1442
2	48	-102	1415
3	91	-32	1473
4	0	0	1500
5	-42	-5	1365
6	48	-38	1338
7	91	32	1396
8	0	64	1423
9	24	46	1342

This transformation takes us from world coordinates to eye coordinates and specifies the object in three dimensions as it would be seen from the specified viewpoint.

After application of a perspective transformation we have:

Screen coordinates

vertex	xs	ys
1	-88	-144
2	103	-216
3	185	-66
4	0	0
5	-93	-11
6	108	-84
7	195	69
8	0	135
9	54	102

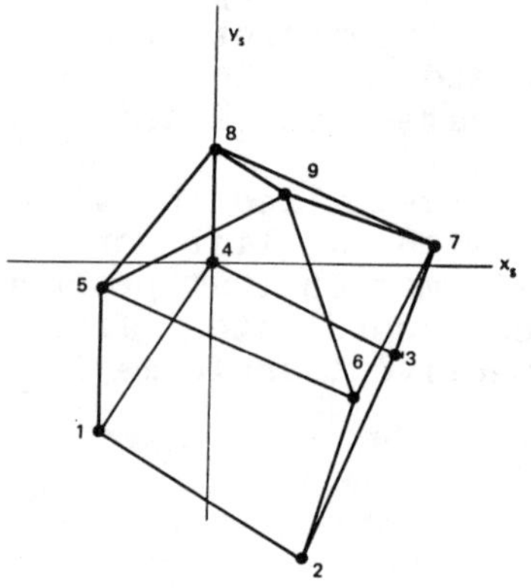

Now it is important to bear in mind that both the the viewpoint transformation and the perspective transformation are particular transformations, arbitrarily chosen for this example. There is an infinity of viewpoint transformations because there is an infinity of viewpoints. There is a large set of perspective transformations depending on the particular criteria that we wish to adopt to transform or map a three-dimensional point into a two-dimensional point.

The viewing transformation

The viewing transformation, V, transforms points in the world coordinate system into the eye coordinate system. The required operation is:

$$(xe, ye, ze, 1) = (xw, yw, zw, 1)V$$

where

$$V = \begin{bmatrix} -\sin\theta & -\cos\theta\cos\phi & -\cos\theta\sin\phi & 0 \\ \cos\theta & -\sin\theta\cos\phi & -\sin\theta\sin\phi & 0 \\ 0 & \sin\phi & -\cos\phi & 0 \\ 0 & 0 & \rho & 1 \end{bmatrix}$$

where rho, theta and phi together specify the viewpoint. The mathematics although not difficult requires a firm appreciation of movements (rotations etc.) in three-dimensional space. The mathematics that lead to this result, together with diagrams illustrating the significance of rho, theta and phi, is given in Appendix 5. If you wish, you can simply accept this result and use the following BASIC implementation:

```
1000   DEF PROCinitviewtransform(rho, theta, phi)
1010    LOCAL sintheta,costheta,sinphi,cosphi
1020    sintheta=SIN(RAD(theta)):costheta=COS(RAD(theta))
1030    sinphi  =SIN(RAD(phi))  : cosphi =COS(RAD(phi))
1040    va = -sintheta : vb = costheta
1050    ve = -costheta*cosphi : vf = -sintheta*cosphi
1060    vg = sinphi
1070    vi = -costheta*sinphi : vj = -sintheta*sinphi
1080    vk = -cosphi : vl = rho
1090   ENDPROC

1100   DEF PROCviewtransform(x, y, z)
1110     xe  = va*x + vb*y
1120     ye  = ve*x + vf*y + vg*z
1130     ze  = vi*x + vj*y + vk*z + vl
1140   ENDPROC
```

PROCinitviewtransform would be called once for a given viewpoint and PROCviewtransform would then be called once for each vertex in the object being viewed.

Now as we have already mentioned this transformation will give us a list of three-dimensional coordinates in the eye coordinate system. What we now need is a perspective transformation that will produce screen coordinates. This is considerably easier to derive than the viewing transformation.

Perspective transformation

The perspective transformation from the eye coordinate system to the screen coordinate system can be illustrated:

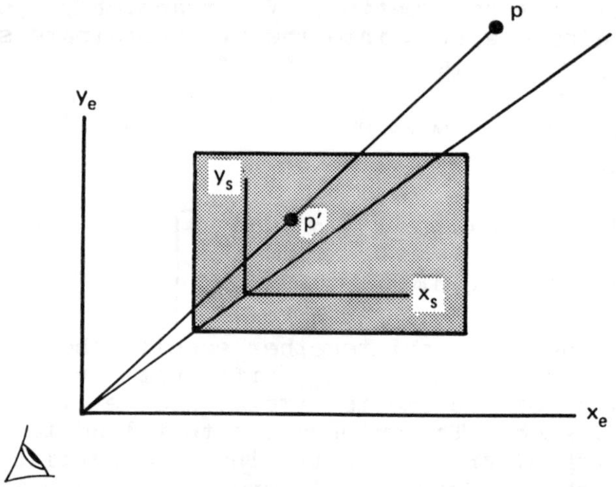

Point p is a point in the eye system, p' is its mapping into the screen coordinate system and d is the distance of the eye from a screen. If we look at the illustration normal to the ye,ze plane we have:

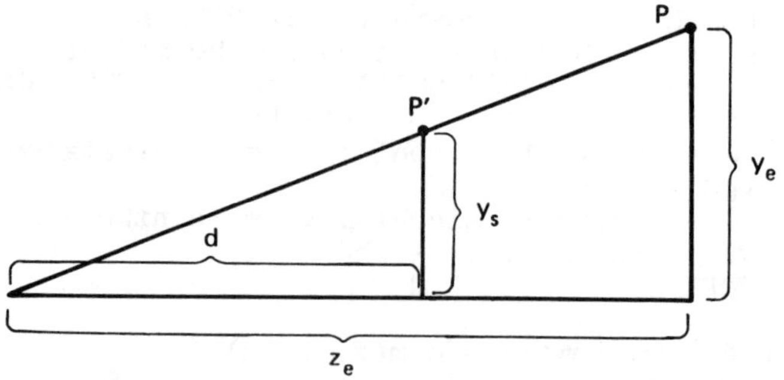

and it is easily seen that:

ys = d*ye/ze

Similarly

xs = d*xe/ze

We can imagine the process as follows. The screen is a plane parallel to the (xe,ye) plane. For every vertex in the object - a collection of points in the eye coordinate system - we can use a line to join the vertex to the origin (the eye). Where each line intersects the screen plane gives us the mapping from the vertex into the screen plane.

There is a family of perspective transformations available but this particular one is the easiest to compute and use, so we will restrict ourselves to it. It is categorised by having a single vanishing point and the xs and ys axes are parallel to the xe and ye axes.

The perspective transformation is implemented by:

```
1150   DEF PROCperspecttransform(xe, ye, ze, d)
1160     xs = d*xe/ze
1170     ys = d*ye/ze
1180   ENDPROC
```

The procedures for carrying out the viewing and perspective transformations will be needed by all the remaining programs in this chapter.

An example using viewing and perspective transformations

Here we turn to that hoary old chestnut - the wire frame cube. This is not so much lack of imagination, as the fact that a wire frame cube is such an intuitively obvious shape. The way in which the parameters input to the program affect the outcome of the program is then easier to understand.

The variables controlling the view are 'd' - the viewing distance, 'rho', 'theta' and 'phi' the spherical coordinates specifying a viewpoint (see Appendix 5). 'theta' is controlled by a FOR loop and the other three parameters are typed in. This means that we 'fly round' the cube at a constant elevation.

```
 10   DIM sx(8), sy(8)
 20   INPUT "rho",rho, "phi",phi, "screen dist, d",d
 30   MODE 0
 40   VDU 29, 640; 512;
 50   FOR theta = 0 TO 90 STEP 10
 60     PROCinitviewtransform(rho, theta, phi)
 70     RESTORE
 80     FOR vertex = 1 TO 8
 90       READ xw, yw, zw
100       PROCviewtransform(xw, yw, zw)
110       PROCperspecttransform(xe, ye, ze, d)
120       sx(vertex) = xs : sy(vertex) = ys
130     NEXT vertex
140     CLG
150     PROCdrawcube
160   NEXT theta
170   k=GET : MODE 7 : END
```

```
180   DATA 100,0,0,  100,100,0,  0,100,0,  0,0,0
190   DATA 100,0,100,  100,100,100,  0,100,100,  0,0,100

200   DEF PROCdrawcube
210     MOVE sx(1), sy(1)
220     FOR vertex = 2 TO 4
230       DRAW sx(vertex), sy(vertex)
240     NEXT vertex
250     DRAW sx(1), sy(1)
260     DRAW sx(5), sy(5)
270     FOR vertex = 6 TO 8
280       DRAW sx(vertex), sy(vertex)
290     NEXT vertex
300     DRAW sx(5), sy(5)
310     FOR vertex = 2 TO 4
320       MOVE sx(vertex+4), sy(vertex+4)
330       DRAW sx(vertex), sy(vertex)
340     NEXT vertex
350   ENDPROC
```

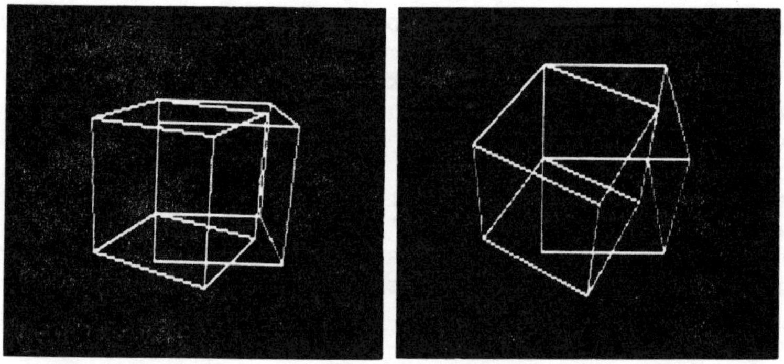

The illustration shows the cube from two different viewpoints. For each, the cube is displayed for two consecutive values of 'theta'. Now admittedly it's not a flight through a wire frame model of Chicago (a recent ambitious example of computer graphics), but you can begin to see the principles involved. The extra complexity in a flight through Chicago program would reside in the techniques necessary to cope with the vast number of vertices necessary to specify the model.

Now there are no checks in this program and certain input values will produce nonsense. Suggested values to start with are:

```
phi = 50 degrees
rho = 400 units
  d = 900 units
```

Now make rho = 300 and see how the views increase in size because the viewpoint has moved closer to the world coordinate system origin. (Incidentally note what happens if you move the viewpoint inside the figure.) Changing the value of 'phi' will alter the elevation of the view. For example try 'phi = 0'. You should be able to understand why we do not get a rotating square from this viewpoint. Now, keeping 'rho' constant, decrease the value of 'd'. This not only makes the object smaller but increases the perspective effect.

Exercises

1 Using the two-dimensional seagull of Section 3.1, assume that each vertex of the bird has a zero z-coordinate. We can then treat it as if it were a cardboard cut-out hanging in three-dimensional space. Write a program that will generate displays of the bird as seen from different viewing positions.

2 Organise a 'fly round' a house shape. Include a few windows and doors in the three-dimensional specification of the house.

3 Organise a 'fly round' any other three-dimensional shape with which you are familiar.

4 Select a particular viewpoint and modify the wire frame cube program so that it draws only three 'visible' faces. Ornament each face of this display with an appropriately scaled two-dimensional seagull. The seagull must of course be in the same plane as the face it is ornamenting.

3.4 Constructional techniques

Now that we have developed a viewing and perspective transform that allows us to display, on a two-dimensional screen, a mapping of a three-dimensional object, we can turn our attention to simple techniques for constructing wire frame and other models. Of course not all models that we may wish to construct can be defined mathematically, or at least it may be exceedingly difficult to so specify them. Such models, car body shapes for example, may be built up as data files from perhaps diverse sources that may include some mathematical modelling together with interaction from a device such as a light pen or a graphics tablet.

In this section we will consider generating surfaces specified mathematically as functions of two variables (f(x,y)). We will also look at generating simple convex bodies made up of plane faces.

Display of f(x,y)
Functions of two variables can be generated and displayed by plotting variations along lines of constant x, constant y, or both. The illustration shows the function

$$f(x,y) = \cos(x) + \cos(y)$$

plotted along lines of constant x:

The program is:

```
 10   INPUT rho, theta, phi, d
 20   PROCinitviewtransform(rho, theta, phi)
 30   MODE 0 : VDU 29, 640; 512;
 40   FOR xw = 360 TO -360 STEP -20
 50     PROCscreen(xw, -360, FNf(xw,-360)) : MOVE xs,ys
 60     FOR yw = -340 TO 360 STEP 20
 70       PROCscreen(xw, yw, FNf(xw,yw)) : DRAW xs,ys
 80     NEXT yw
 90   NEXT xw
100   k=GET : MODE 7 : END

110   DEF FNf(x,y) = 100*(COS(RAD(x)) + COS(RAD(y)))

120   DEF PROCscreen(x,y,z)
130   LOCAL xe,ye,ze
140     PROCviewtransform(x, y, z)
150     PROCperspecttransform(xe, ye, ze, d)
160   ENDPROC
```

To plot in the other direction the control variables in the FOR loops can be reversed. Note that when displaying functions of two variables the viewpoint position can be critical if the features of the function are to be visually recognisable. The illustrations shown were produced with

```
rho   =  1500
theta =  30
phi   =  45
    d =  2000
```

The high values of 'rho' and 'd' are necessary because we have arbitrarily scaled the function by 100 (otherwise a value in the range -2 to 2 would have been produced). The function itself is composed of humps and valleys symmetrically disposed about the origin. You can see that the tips of the peaks and valleys are confused by 'crossovers'. These can be removed by a fairly easy hidden line removal algorithm for plots of f(x,y) (see the last section in this chapter). The result of applying a hidden line algorithm is shown in the second photograph. If such a hidden line removal algorithm is to be applied then the function lines must be plotted in the order of decreasing x. (i.e. the one nearest to the viewpoint is plotted first.)

Finally the interpretation of f(x,y) may be assisted by drawing the world coordinate axes on the plot. This is easily accomplished by:

```
 35 PROCdrawaxes

170   DEF PROCdrawaxes
180     PROCscreen(-360,0,0) : MOVE xs,ys
190     PROCscreen( 360,0,0) : DRAW xs,ys
200     PROCscreen(0,-360,0) : MOVE xs,ys
210     PROCscreen(0, 360,0) : DRAW xs,ys
220     PROCscreen(0,0,-360) : MOVE xs,ys
230     PROCscreen(0,0, 360) : DRAW xs,ys
240   ENDPROC
```

Generating wire frame models

A number of commonly used convex bodies can be generated by sweeping a plane or a line through 360 degrees. The simplest figure in this class is a cylinder. In the next program 74 vertices on the top and bottom circumferential edges of a cylinder are generated by sweeping the line (i.e the line end-points)

```
-100, 0, 100
-100, 0, 0
```

through 360 degrees at 10 degree increments.

```
10   noofpoints=2 : noofvertices=37*noofpoints
20   DIM object(3,noofvertices),cylinder(2,noofvertices)
30   MODE 0 : VDU 29, 640; 512;
40   INPUT "rho",rho, "theta",viewtheta,
           "phi",phi, "screen dist,d",d
50   PROCinitialise
60   PROCinitviewtransform(rho, viewtheta, phi)
70   PROCworldtoscreen : PROCplotcylinder
80   k=GET : MODE 7 : END

200  DEF PROCinitialise
210  LOCAL sintheta,costheta, theta, p,v
220    v = 0
230    FOR theta = 0 TO 360 STEP 10
240      RESTORE
250      sintheta = SIN(RAD(theta))
260      costheta = COS(RAD(theta))
270      FOR p = 1 TO noofpoints
280        v = v+1
290        READ x, y, z
300        object(1, v) = x*costheta + y*sintheta
310        object(2, v) = -x*sintheta + y*costheta
320        object(3, v) = z
330      NEXT p
340    NEXT theta
350  ENDPROC
360  DATA -100,0,0,  -100,0,100

400  DEF PROCworldtoscreen
410  LOCAL v
420    FOR v = 1 TO noofvertices
430      PROCviewtransform(object(1,v),object(2,v),object(3,
440      PROCperspecttransform(xe,ye,ze,d)
450      cylinder(1,v) = xs
460      cylinder(2,v) = ys
470    NEXT v
480  ENDPROC

500  DEF PROCplotcylinder
510  LOCAL v
520    MOVE cylinder(1, 1), cylinder(2, 1)
530    FOR v = 3 TO noofvertices STEP 2
540      DRAW cylinder(1,v), cylinder(2,v)
550    NEXT v
560    MOVE cylinder(1,2), cylinder(2,2)
570    FOR v = 4 TO noofvertices STEP 2
580      DRAW cylinder(1,v), cylinder(2,v)
590    NEXT v
600    FOR v = 1 TO noofvertices STEP 2
610      MOVE cylinder(1,v), cylinder(2,v)
620      DRAW cylinder(1,v+1), cylinder(2,v+1)
630    NEXT v
640  ENDPROC
```

The transformation required to rotate the line about the zw-axis is

$$\begin{bmatrix} \cos\theta & -\sin\theta & 0 & 0 \\ \sin\theta & \cos\theta & 0 & 0 \\ 0 & 0 & 1 & 0 \\ 0 & 0 & 0 & 1 \end{bmatrix}$$

and this is applied 37 times in the program for values of 'theta' of 0, 10, 20,...,360. Thus 74 vertices are generated and stored in the array 'object'. This array is then processed by PROCworldtoscreen that produces the screen coordinates. PROCworldtoscreen repeatedly uses the two procedures PROCviewtransform and PROCperspecttransform. The screen coordinates are stored in array 'cylinder' and this array is plotted by PROCplotcylinder. The cylinder vertices are loaded into array 'cylinder' as follows:

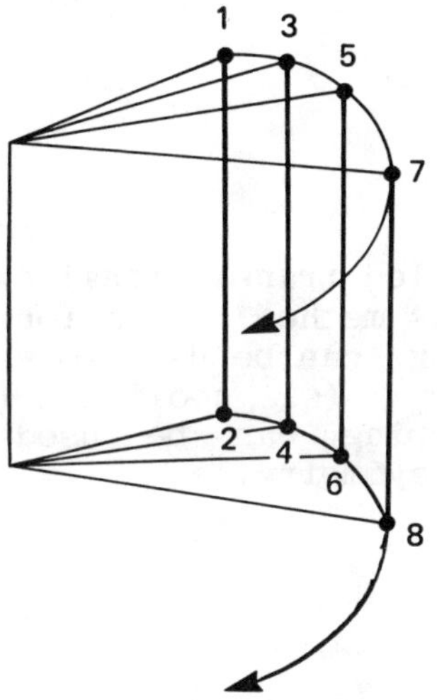

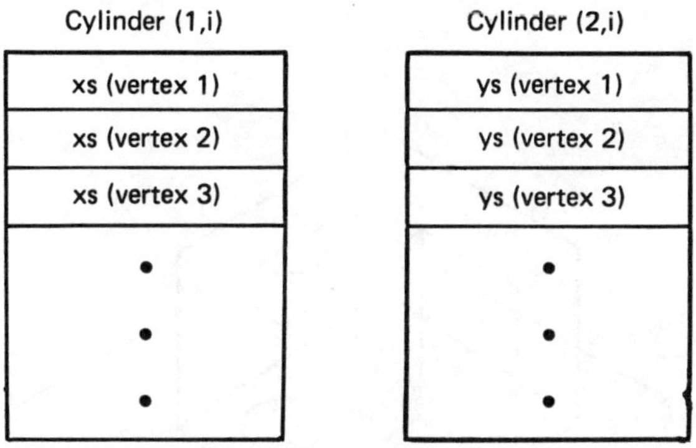

This structure is reflected in the structure of the procedure that plots the cylinder.

It is easy to see that the same effect could be achieved by sweeping a circle (a regular polygon) along the long axis of the cylinder.

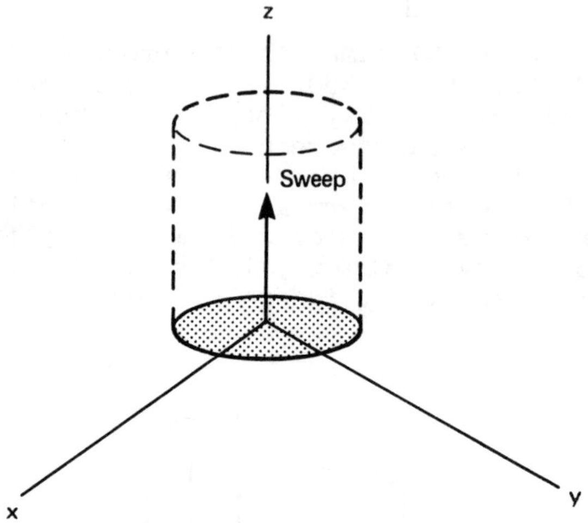

This method is called translational sweeping to distinguish it from the previous method - rotational sweeping. Just as rotational sweeping can be used to generate any solid with rotational symmetry (a cooling tower for example) translational sweeping can be used to generate any solid with translational symmetry.

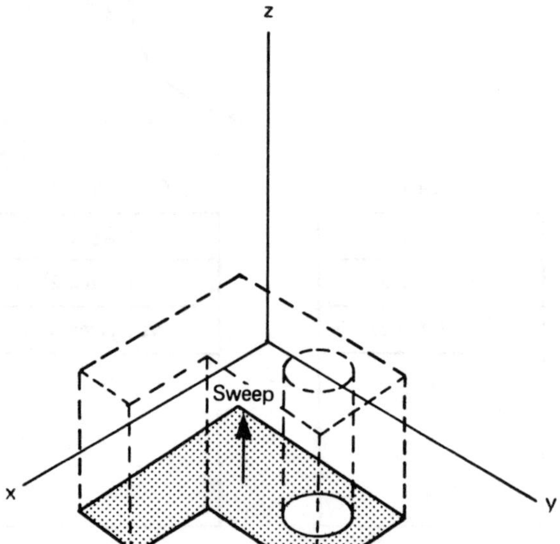

When you execute the last program note the speed of plotting from the calculated screen coordinate array, compared with the speed of calculation of these coordinates. You can generate models and store the vertex arrays in files or DATA statements, but this will, of course, give an instance of the model from one viewpoint only.

This structure can be used to generate related figures. Changing one vertex in the DATA statement will cause the program to generate cones instead of cylinders. Using a function definition rather than DATA statements can enable spheres (rotating a semicircle) and cooling towers (rotating a segment of a hyperbola) for example, to be generated.

Exercises

1 Edit the above program so that it generates the other common 'mathematical solids' such as a cone, a truncated cone and a sphere.

2 Write a program to generate a wire frame model of a body with rotational symmetry. The program should allow the user to generate a profile using the rubberband techniques described in Chapter 2. (An example of this process is shown in the first illustration.) By recording each vertex in the rubber band profile the program should then generate a rotationally symmetric wire frame model. This is simply a matter of generating circles of appropriate radius at each vertex. The 'vertical' wire frame lines are constructed by joining points on the circumferences of these circles at equal angular increments.

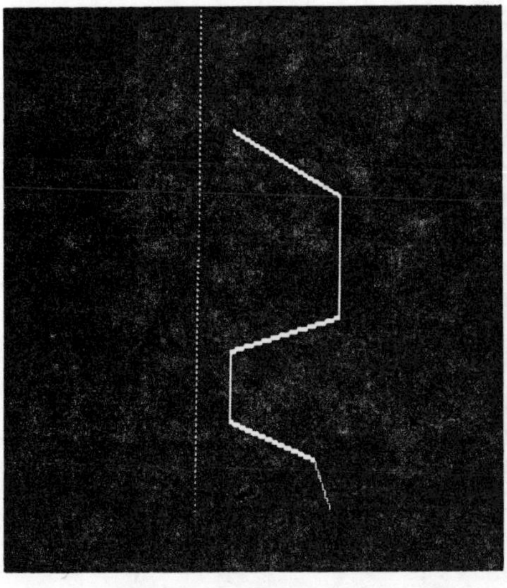

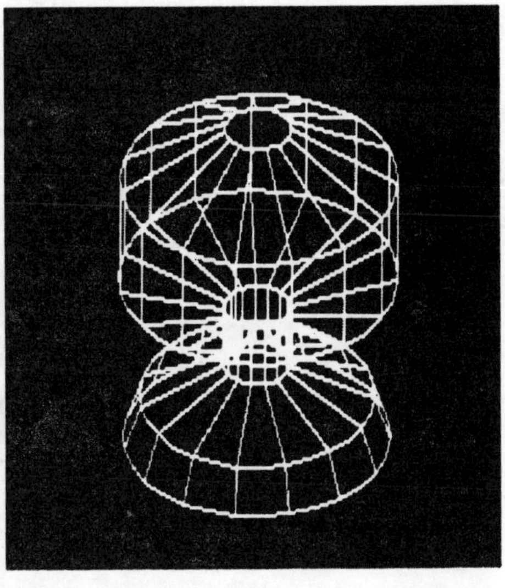

Three dimensional transformations - composite bodies
Composite models can be built up using instances of already generated structures. Say, for example, that we wanted to generate a model consisting of four cylinders as shown, perhaps to represent the four wheels of a motor car.

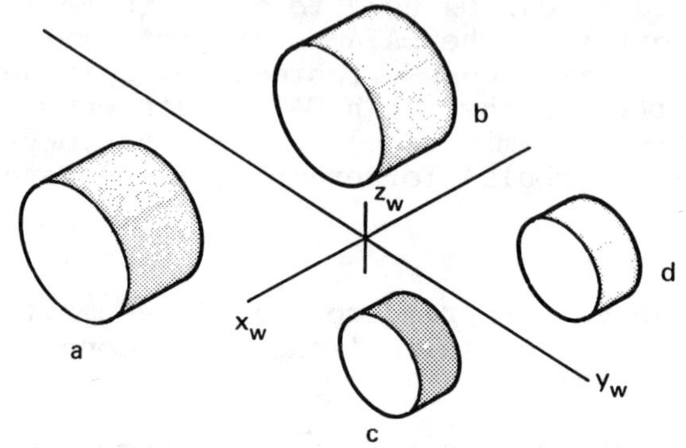

We could start by generating the cylinder in the correct orientation (long axis parallel to the (xw, yw) plane, but let us consider instancing the cylinders in their correct orientation and position from data generated by the previous program - an upright cylinder.

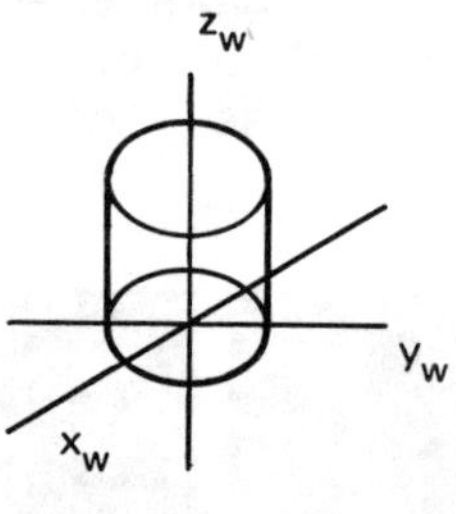

To instance the four cylinders in their required positions and orientations we could use various combinations of the following transformations:

T1

T1 move the cylinder down so that its long axis is centred at the origin

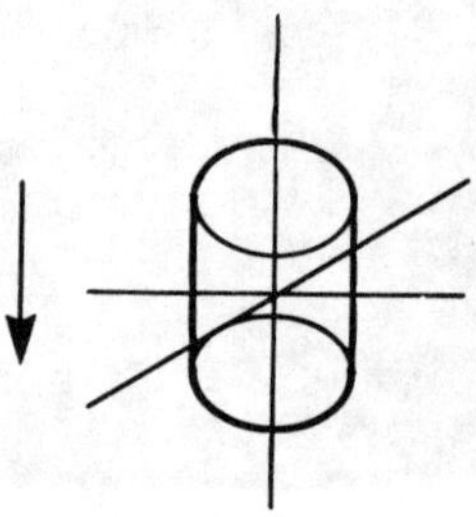

R1 rotate 90 degrees about the yw-axis - the cylinder in this position can now be used in each of the subsequent transformations

R1

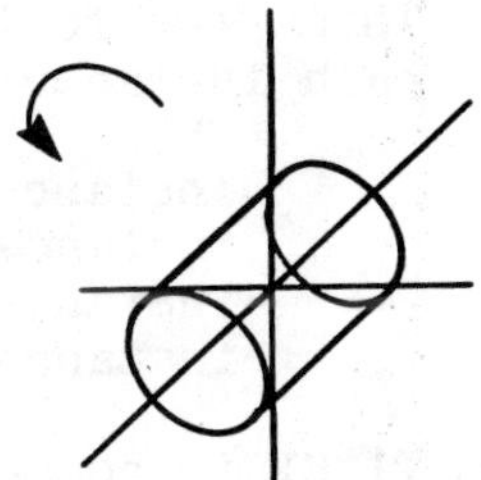

T2 translate 100, -100, 0 and DRAW an instance of the cylinder

T2

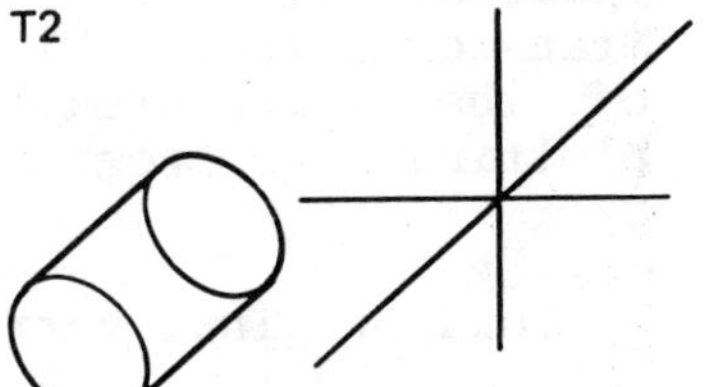

T3 translate (-100, -100, 0) and DRAW an instance of the cylinder

T3

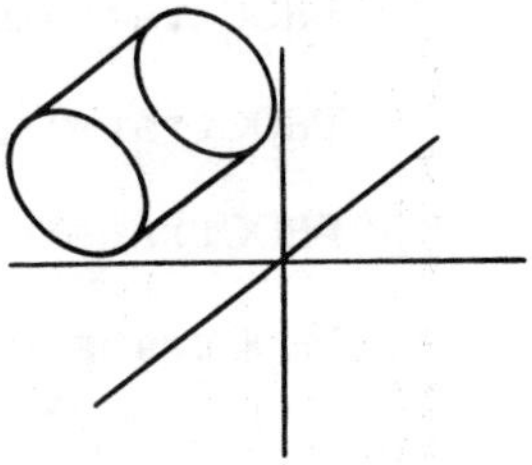

S1*T4 shrink by half and translate (75, 150, 0); DRAW an instance of the cylinder

S1*T4

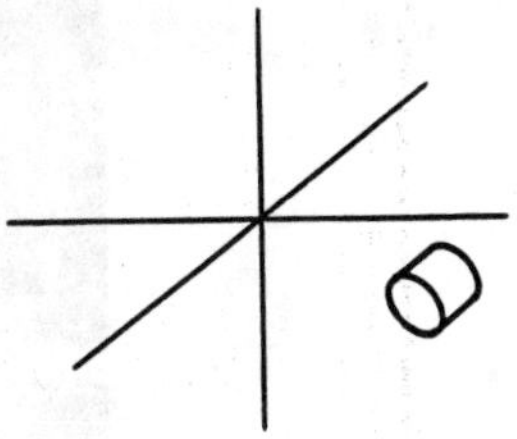

S1*T5 shrink by half and translate (-75, 150, 0); DRAW an instance of the cylinder

S1*T5

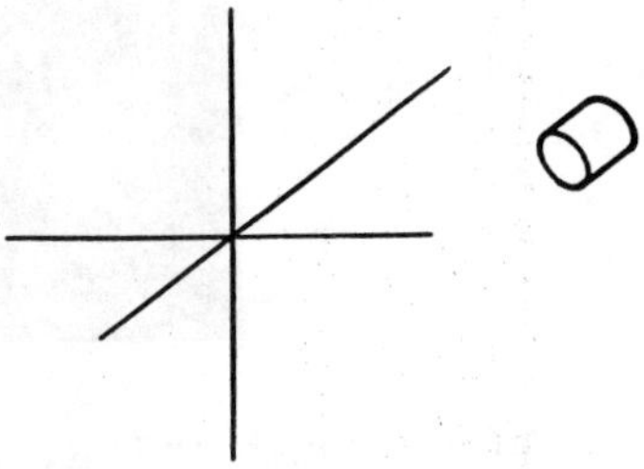

Thus the following transformation matrices are required for each instance:

```
instance A    T1*R1*T2
instance B    T1*R1*T3
instance C    T1*R1*S1*T4
instance D    T1*R1*S1*T5
```

T1*R1 is common to all transformations. We can organise the program by having two arrays, one in which to store the original cylinder in world coordinates, after the common transformation T1*R1. The other array would store the result of the transformations T2, T3, S1*T4 and S1*T5 prior to plotting. The program structure would be:

```
read original vertex file into the vertex array 'object'

PROCtransformT1R1

PROCtransformT2 : PROCworldtoscreen : PROCplotcylinder

PROCtransformT3 : PROCworldtoscreen : PROCplotcylinder

PROCtransformS1T4 : PROCworldtoscreen : PROCplotcylinder

PROCtransformS1T5 : PROCworldtoscreen : PROCplotcylinder
```

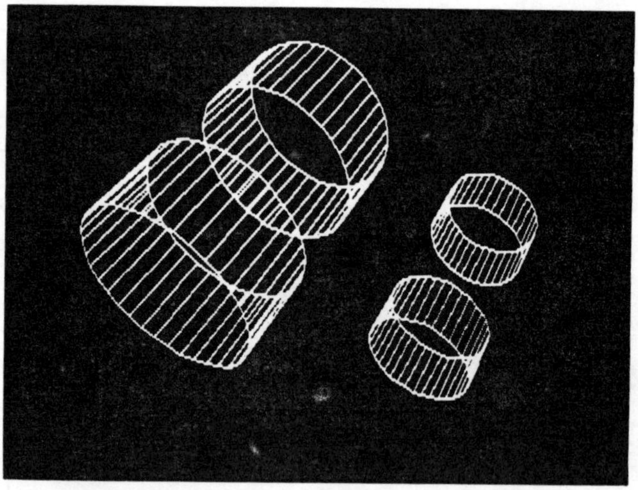

PROCtransformT1R1 operates on and outputs to the array 'object' originally initialised with the vertex data produced by the previous program. All the other procedures output to the array 'target' and can be the same procedure supplied with different parameters according to the transformation being carried out. The array 'target' is the input to PROCworldtoscreen and this produces the array 'cylinder' containing the screen coordinates for PROCplotcylinder. Thus we are using three arrays - 'object', which stores the original cylinder and the cylinder after the common transform T1*R1, 'target', which stores each cylinder after it is subject to the remaining transforms and 'cylinder', which stores the final screen coordinates for each generated cylinder. The transformations are:

$$T1*R1 = \begin{bmatrix} 1 & 0 & 0 & 0 \\ 0 & 1 & 0 & 0 \\ 0 & 0 & 1 & 0 \\ 0 & 0 & -50 & 1 \end{bmatrix} \begin{bmatrix} \cos 90 & 0 & -\sin 90 & 0 \\ 0 & 1 & 0 & 0 \\ \sin 90 & 0 & \cos 90 & 0 \\ 0 & 0 & 0 & 1 \end{bmatrix}$$

$$= \begin{bmatrix} 0 & 0 & -1 & 0 \\ 0 & 1 & 0 & 0 \\ 1 & 0 & 0 & 0 \\ -50 & 0 & 0 & 1 \end{bmatrix}$$

$$T2 = \begin{bmatrix} 1 & 0 & 0 & 0 \\ 0 & 1 & 0 & 0 \\ 0 & 0 & 1 & 0 \\ 100 & -100 & 0 & 1 \end{bmatrix}$$

$$T3 = \begin{bmatrix} 1 & 0 & 0 & 0 \\ 0 & 1 & 0 & 0 \\ 0 & 0 & 1 & 0 \\ -100 & -100 & 0 & 1 \end{bmatrix}$$

$$S1*T4 = \begin{bmatrix} 0.5 & 0 & 0 & 0 \\ 0 & 0.5 & 0 & 0 \\ 0 & 0 & 0.5 & 0 \\ 0 & 0 & 0 & 1 \end{bmatrix} \begin{bmatrix} 1 & 0 & 0 & 0 \\ 0 & 1 & 0 & 0 \\ 0 & 0 & 1 & 0 \\ 75 & 150 & 0 & 1 \end{bmatrix}$$

$$= \begin{bmatrix} 0.5 & 0 & 0 & 0 \\ 0 & 0.5 & 0 & 0 \\ 0 & 0 & 0.5 & 0 \\ 75 & 150 & 0 & 1 \end{bmatrix}$$

$$S1*T5 = \begin{bmatrix} 0.5 & 0 & 0 & 0 \\ 0 & 0.5 & 0 & 0 \\ 0 & 0 & 0.5 & 0 \\ 0 & 0 & 0 & 1 \end{bmatrix} \begin{bmatrix} 1 & 0 & 0 & 0 \\ 0 & 1 & 0 & 0 \\ 0 & 0 & 1 & 0 \\ -75 & 150 & 0 & 1 \end{bmatrix}$$

$$= \begin{bmatrix} 0.5 & 0 & 0 & 0 \\ 0 & 0.5 & 0 & 0 \\ 0 & 0 & 0.5 & 0 \\ -75 & 150 & 0 & 1 \end{bmatrix}$$

Examination of the transformations shows that only 12 parameters need be specified:

$$\begin{bmatrix} a & e & i \\ b & f & j \\ c & g & k \\ d & h & l \end{bmatrix}$$

and this is implemented as the procedure PROCtransform in the program below. PROCinitialise can initialise array 'object' either by generating the cylinder as described previously, or by reading previously generated vertices.

```
 10  noofpoints=2 : noofvertices=noofpoints*37
 20  DIM object(3,noofvertices),
         target(3,noofvertices),
         cylinder(2,noofvertices)
 30  MODE 0 : VDU 29, 640; 512;
 40  INPUT "rho",rho, "theta",viewtheta,
          "phi",phi, "screen dist,d",d
 50  PROCinitviewtransform(rho,viewtheta,phi)
 60  PROCinitialise : PROCtransformT1R1
 80  PROCtransform(1,0,0,100,0,1,0,-100,0,0,1,0)
 90  PROCworldtoscreen : PROCplotcylinder
100  PROCtransform(1,0,0,-100,0,1,0,-100,0,0,1,0)
110  PROCworldtoscreen : PROCplotcylinder
120  PROCtransform(0.5,0,0,75,0,0.5,0,150,0,0,0.5,0)
130  PROCworldtoscreen : PROCplotcylinder
140  PROCtransform(0.5,0,0,-75,0,0.5,0,150,0,0,0.5,0)
150  PROCworldtoscreen : PROCplotcylinder
160  k=GET : MODE 7 : END

400  DEF PROCworldtoscreen
410  LOCAL v
420    FOR v = 1 TO noofvertices
425 REM ***** note change in next line *****
430      PROCviewtransform(target(1,v),
                  target(2,v),target(3,v))
440      PROCperspecttransform(xe,ye,ze,d)
450      cylinder(1,v) = xs
460      cylinder(2,v) = ys
470    NEXT v
480  ENDPROC

700  DEF PROCtransformT1R1
710  LOCAL v, x,z
720    FOR v = 1 TO noofvertices
730      x = object(1,v) : z = object(3,v)
740      object(1,v) = z - 50
750      object(3,v) = -x
760    NEXT v
770  ENDPROC
```

```
800   DEF PROCtransform(a,b,c,d,e,f,g,h,i,j,k,l)
810   LOCAL v, x,y,z
820     FOR v = 1 TO noofvertices
830       x = object(1,v) : y = object(2,v)
840       z = object(3,v)
850       target(1,v) = a*x + b*y + c*z + d
860       target(2,v) = e*x + f*y + g*z + h
870       target(3,v) = i*x + j*y + k*z + l
880     NEXT v
890   ENDPROC
```

Off-line animation - moving modelled objects
You can see from the time taken to execute the above example that real-time animation of such mathematically generated objects is impossible on the BBC micro. Some graphics processors are designed to perform real time animation of three-dimensional scenes - notably flight simulators - but most animation of this kind is generated off-line. A frame is built up and stored and quickly transformed into a screen image. As far as the BBC micro is concerned even storing frames in the form of final position vertex arrays in disc files will still not facilitate animation in BASIC. The MOVE and DRAW utilities still take too long to construct a picture. Off-line animation could however be performed in BASIC by single shotting with a cine camera and the techniques used are worthy of study.

Let us return to the four wheel model. Say that we want to generate a sequence of 10 frames with the wheel set moving from left to right. Of course it is not just a matter of taking a two-dimensional image and moving it to the right (two-dimensional animation) because if we are animating with respect to a stationary observer, each frame will be different because of the changing position of the object with respect to the stationary viewpoint.

To make the wheels move forward in a straight line (along say the yw-axis) we have to apply an increasing yw translation to each wheel object in turn, and keep the viewpoint stationary. This could be accomplished in the above program by inserting another common transformation prior to the individual wheel transformations and drawing sequences. The required transformation is:

$$Ta = \begin{bmatrix} 1 & 0 & 0 & 0 \\ 0 & 1 & 0 & 0 \\ 0 & 0 & 1 & 0 \\ 0 & d & 0 & 1 \end{bmatrix}$$

where d is the inter-frame displacement along the yw-axis. The procedure can output into array 'object' so that the displacements accumulate:

```
900    DEF PROCdisplace
910    LOCAL v
920      FOR v = 1 TO 74
930        object(2,v) = object(2,v) + displacement
940      NEXT v
950    ENDPROC
```

The whole program would then be looped, providing one frame for each execution of the loop.

```
         :
 55    INPUT "displacement", displacement
         :
 75    FOR frame=1 TO 10
 76      CLG
         :
150      PROCworldtoscreen : PROCplotcylinder
155      PROCdisplace : k = GET
156    NEXT frame
```

The illustration shows just two frames (superimposed) that are produced by the first two executions of the frame loop in the program.

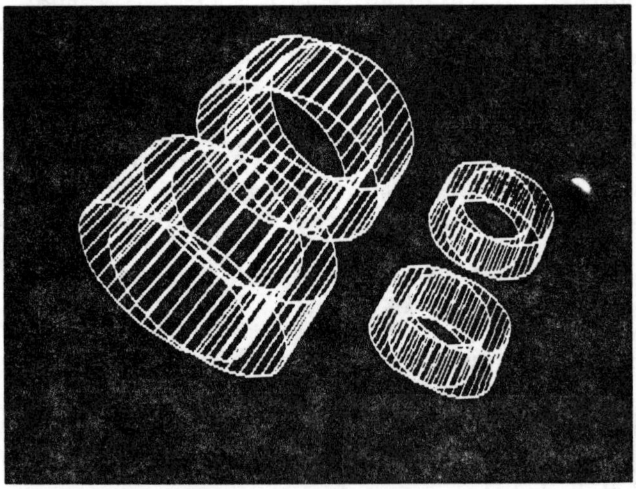

Local coordinate systems
The method used above to instance the four wheels is somewhat less than satisfactory. What we are doing is taking one cylinder , subjecting it to increasing yw displacements and then translating it into four wheel positions.

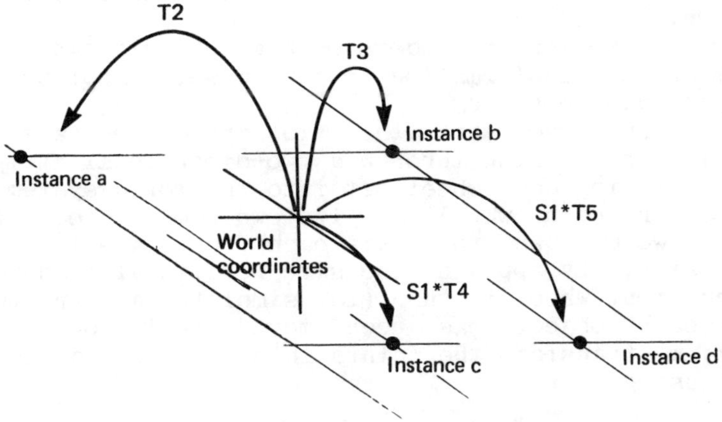

What if the car was turning? Then not only would the front wheels have to be rotated about the zw-axis, but each wheel's (x,y) displacement would be different. In general it makes more sense to divide the problem into four sub-problems with a separate <u>local</u> coordinate system for each wheel.

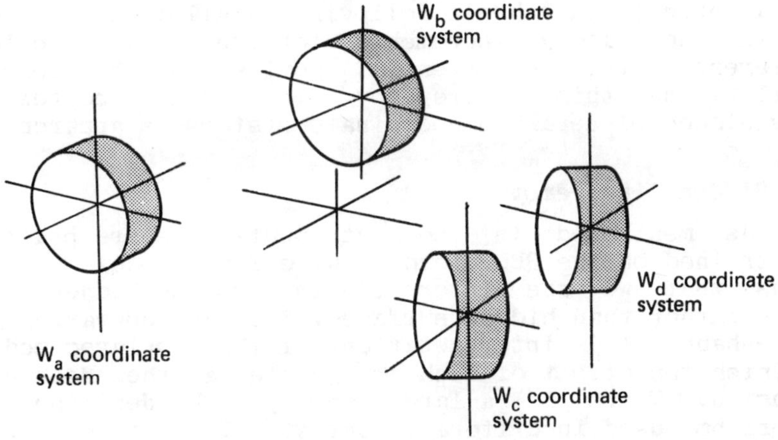

We can then start by having an instance of a cylinder in each of the four coordinate systems. The set of points in Wa, representing a wheel, would be exactly the same as the set of points in Wb. Similarly the set in Wc would be identical to those in Wd. To start off with a frame in which all the wheels were pointing straight ahead, we would transform the wheel points into the world coordinate system (from their own local system) by transforming each sub-coordinate system into the world coordinate system. Remember that to transform a coordinate system we apply the inverse translation transformation. Previously we had a cylinder at the centre of the world system and instanced it four times as shown.

Now we have four cylinders each with their own coordinate system and a transformation to give a set of points in the world coordinate system.

You can see that the two approaches are exactly equivalent by working through a two-dimensional example. Now prior to taking each wheel set into the world system we can operate on each wheel in its own coordinate system. For example, we may want to rotate each front wheel about its own z-axis, by applying the same rotational transformation to each front wheel in turn (to simulate a car turning). After each object has been moved in its own coordinate system, we transform the points into the world coordinate system using:

$$(xwi, ywi, zwi, 1) \begin{bmatrix} -Tx & 0 & 0 & 0 \\ 0 & -Ty & 0 & 0 \\ 0 & 0 & -Tz & 0 \\ 0 & 0 & 0 & 1 \end{bmatrix}$$

where i = a, b, c or d.

The inter-frame x and y increments for the front wheels are identical, the wheels following parallel circumferential tracks. The x and y increments for the rear wheels are different, the differential drive in the rear axle facilitating this discrepancy. In such a context the convenience of separate coordinate systems is apparent.

3.5 Hidden line removal

Now as mentioned in the introduction we are practically constrained on the BBC micro to wire frame models and this means that we are interested in removing hidden lines or edges rather than hidden surfaces. Such an operation tends to enhance the interpretation of the displayed model and diminish the effect of such ambiguities as the Necker cube illusion. There is a large variety of hidden line removal algorithms used in different contexts. There is no standard approach or algorithm, the algorithm used depends on the application or context. One thing is certain, hidden line removal will add an execution time penalty to your program.

Algorithms can either operate in object space where the calculations are carried out in the world coordinate system or in display space where the calculations are carried out in the display coordinate system. Hybrid algorithms use information from both the object and the image space domain. One of the most direct approaches to the problem of hidden surface removal is the depth buffer or z-buffer algorithm. In this algorithm we keep a record of the intensity of a pixel together with its depth or value of its 'ze' coordinate (depth information comes from object space and the algorithm, although primarily a display space algorithm, needs some information from the object domain). The need for a two-dimensional buffer to store the 'depth' of each pixel gives the algorithm its name and of course is the major disadvantage of the technique - it requires considerable extra storage. The algorithm operates on the polygons that delineate the boundary of a surface that has been mapped into the screen coordinate system. It can be stated as:

(1) Initially set depth(x,y) to a large value and intensity(x,y) to the background.

(2) For every polygon in the scene find all the pixels that lie within the polygon

For each pixel:

(a) Calculate its z value

(b) If the z value < depth(x,y) (eye coordinates) then depth(x,y) becomes the z value and intensity(x,y) becomes the intensity of the pixel, otherwise leave depth(x,y) and intensity(x,y) unaltered.

Now the point of this digression is firstly to point out that it is completely general and will work for any group of objects or scene. Secondly it operates on individual pixels. On the BBC micro if we are restricting ourselves to BASIC then we have no easy access in a wire frame model to the 'bright' pixels joining two vertices - we only have access to the end points. Efficient general purpose hidden line removal algorithms need to be integrated with the scan conversion process - the process that converts for example the statement 'DRAW x,y' into a line of the required bright pixels. We will now look at two special cases of hidden line removal. Firstly consider the plotting of a function of two variables.

Hidden line removal - f(x,y)

This is a display space or image space algorithm and depends on the fact that the function is plotted along lines of constant x starting with the profile nearest to the observer. The algorithm needs two arrays at the horizontal resolution of the display (640 in MODE 0). In these arrays, say 'max(ys)' and 'min(ys)', we keep the current highest and lowest values of ys - the screen y value. When plotting a new function or profile along a line of constant x it is deemed to be visible when above the profile stored in 'max' and below the profile stored in 'min'.

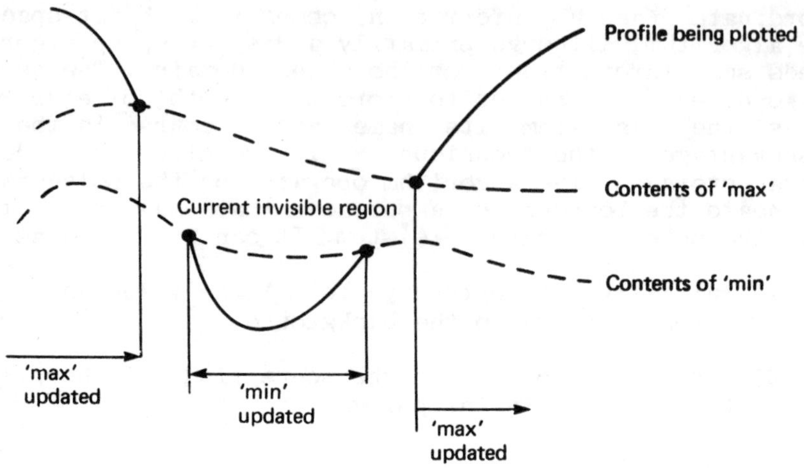

The algorithm is:

(1) Initialise 'max' to the minimum y screen coordinate and 'min' to the maximum y screen coordinate.

(2) For all x profiles or contours

```
For all x profiles or contours
   For each y along the profile
      Calculate xs and ys
      IF ys>max(xs)      THEN DRAW xs,ys : max(xs)=ys
      ELSE IF ys<min(xs) THEN DRAW xs,ys : min(xs)=ys
      ELSE MOVE xs,ys
```

This simple algorithm however has two drawbacks. The arrays 'max' and 'min' must each have 640 elements. However, if we increment y by 20 degrees in the object space (as we did in the original program) the algorithm will produce only 37 xs values for each profile where the size of the intervals between values depends on the viewpoint. When the arrays are updated with new information gaps will be left. Another effect of these gaps is that when plotting does start it may not necessarily coincide with the previous x profile.

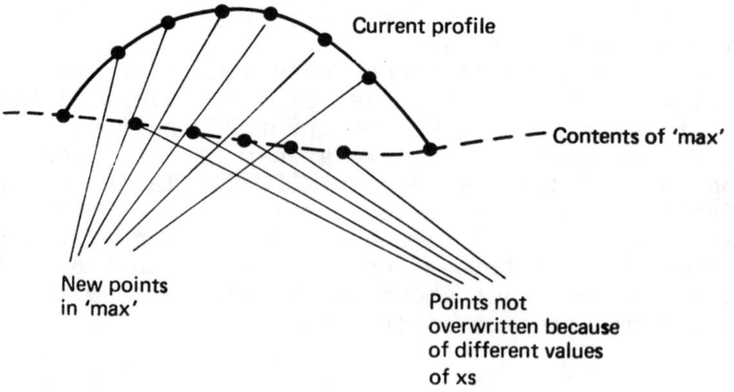

There are two possible solutions to this problem. We could reduce the increments in y to a point where all the elements in 'max' and 'min' are guaranteed to be accessed. For the function and viewpoint used earlier this would have to be about 1/2 degree. The plotting time would then be inordinately long, because of excessive use of the trigonometric functions. Another approach is to 'interpolate' between successive screen points generated by the program, i.e. to examine each pixel on a line between two successive screen points. It is the latter method that is implemented in the next program. The output from the program was displayed earlier alongside the same function plotted without hidden line removal. Note that, with the long variable names and readable layout used here, there is no room to run the program in MODE 0. As presented, the program runs in MODE 4. The photograph was taken by running a compacted version of the program in MODE 0. Techniques for compacting programs are given at the end of Chapter 10.

```
 10   INPUT rho, theta, phi, d
 20   PROCinitviewtransform(rho, theta, phi)
 30   MODE 4 : VDU 29, 640; 512;
 32   PROCinithiddenlineremoval
 40   FOR xw = 360 TO -360 STEP -20
 50     PROCscreen(xw, -360, FNf(xw,-360)) : MOVE xs,ys
 55     prevxcell = (640+xs) DIV xstep : prevys = ys
 60     FOR yw = -340 TO 360 STEP 20
 70       PROCscreen(xw,yw,FNf(xw,yw)) : PROCcheckplot
 80     NEXT yw
 90   NEXT xw
100   k=GET : MODE 7 : END

110   DEF FNf(x,y) = 100*(COS(RAD(x)) + COS(RAD(y)))

120   DEF PROCscreen(x,y,z)
130   LOCAL xe,ye,ze
140     PROCviewtransform(x, y, z)
150     PROCperspecttransform(xe, ye, ze, d)
160   ENDPROC

300   DEF PROCinithiddenlineremoval
310   LOCAL c
320     xstep = 4 : cells = 1279 DIV xstep
330     DIM min(cells), max(cells)
340     FOR c = 0 TO cells
350       min(c) = 512 : max(c) = -512
360     NEXT c
370   ENDPROC
```

```
400   DEF PROCcheckplot
410   LOCAL xcell, yinc,nextys, c
420     xcell = (xs+640) DIV xstep
430     IF xcell=prevxcell THEN PROCpoint(xcell,ys)
440     yinc = (ys-prevys)/(xcell-prevxcell)
450     nextys = prevys
460     FOR c = prevxcell TO xcell
470       nextys = nextys + yinc
480       PROCpoint(c, nextys)
490     NEXT c
500     prevxcell = xcell : prevys = ys
510   ENDPROC

520   DEF PROCpoint(c,y)
530     LOCAL x : x = c*xstep - 640
540     IF c<0 OR c>cells THEN MOVE x,y : ENDPROC
550     IF y<max(c) AND y>min(c) THEN MOVE x,y : ENDPROC
560     IF y<min(c) THEN min(c) = y
570     IF y>max(c) THEN max(c) = y
580     DRAW x,y
590   ENDPROC
```

All in all you can see that great care must be taken when setting up hidden line removal if inordinately long processing is to be avoided.

Hidden line removal - back surface elimination

This is another special case method that works for single convex polyhedrons. It is not really an algorithm but a straightforward application of vector mathematics. It can be used as the basis of a more general algorithm that will deal with scenes containing many convex polyhedral objects. It is an object space procedure and although we are removing edges, paradoxically it is the surfaces defined by the edges that we consider.

Given a viewpoint we determine whether or not a face is visible from that viewpoint. Consider the next illustration showing a cube decomposed into 6 surfaces. Pointing out of each surface we have a line that is normal or perpendicular to the surface. This line or vector determines the orientation of the plane. It is called a surface normal vector. From the viewpoint we can construct 'line of sight' lines or vectors to any point on each surface. If we construct a line of sight vector to meet the surface vector, then the angle between these two vectors gives us a visibility test. The surface is visible from the viewpoint if, and only if, the angle between these two vectors is less than 90 degrees.

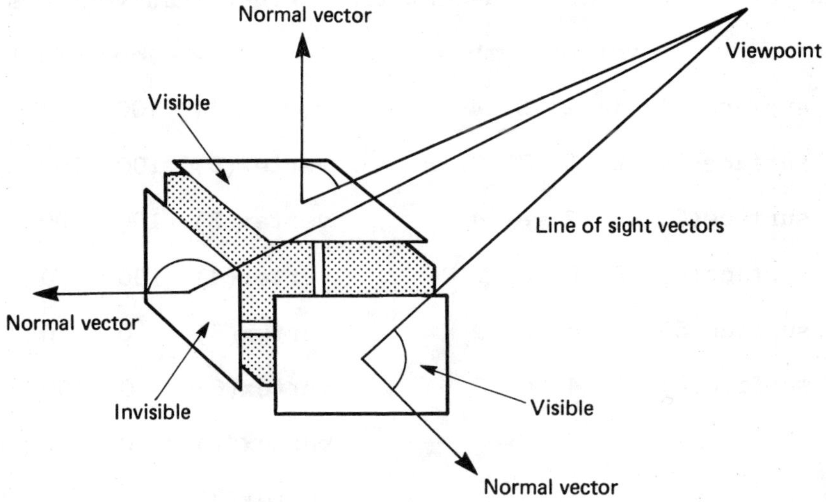

In the next program we have implemented back surface elimination for the wire frame cube. PROChidden_line_remove tests each of the 6 surfaces for visibility. If a surface is visible its edges are plotted. The main program is:

```
 10   DIM vertex(3,8), surface(6,4)
 20   DIM vector1(3), vector2(3)
 30   DIM visible(6)
 40   INPUT "rho",rho, "theta",theta, "phi",phi,
            "screen dist,d",d
 50   costheta=COS(RAD(theta)) : sintheta=SIN(RAD(theta))
 60   cosphi=COS(RAD(phi)) : sinphi=SIN(RAD(phi))
 70   xview = rho*sinphi*costheta
 80   yview = rho*sinphi*sintheta
 90   zview = rho*cosphi
100   PROCinitviewtransform(rho,theta,phi)
110   MODE 0 : VDU 29, 640; 512;
120   PROCinitialise
130   PROChidden_line_remove
140   FOR surfaceno = 1 TO 6
150     IF visible(surfaceno) THEN
          PROCtransform_and_plot(surfaceno)
160   NEXT surfaceno
170   k=GET : MODE 7 : END
```

We need to set up a data structure to associate a surface with its edges and this is implemented by using two arrays 'surface' and 'vertex'. The array 'vertex' contains a list of the coordinates of the 8 vertices in the cube, and 'surface' contains for each surface a list of vertex numbers that define the surface. This data structure means that we can deal with surfaces as entities rather than vertices.

	vertex number			
surface(1)	1	2	3	4
surface(2)	2	6	7	3
surface(3)	3	7	8	4
surface(4)	6	5	8	7
surface(5)	1	5	6	2
surface(6)	1	4	8	5

	coordinates		
vertex(1)	100	0	0
vertex(2)	100	100	0
vertex(3)	100	100	100
vertex(4)	100	0	100
vertex(5)	0	0	0
vertex(6)	0	100	0
vertex(7)	0	100	100
vertex(8)	0	0	100

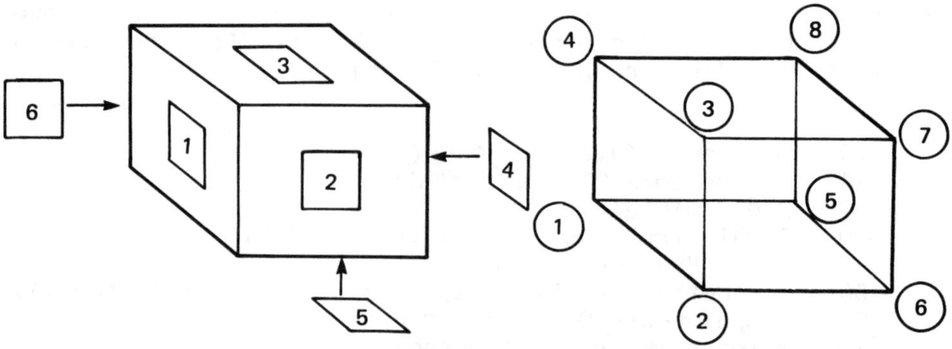

A surface must contain (for the vector mathematics) vertices listed in counter-clockwise order as seen from outside the object. Thus the surface number 2 is specified in the second row of array 'surface' which will contain the vertex numbers 2, 6, 7 and 3. Thus to access surface number 2 for calculation or plotting we would indirectly access the array 'vertex' as follows:

```
vertex(surface(2,1))
vertex(surface(2,2))
vertex(surface(2,3))
vertex(surface(2,4))
```

PROCinitialise sets up this DATA structure. Note that this is another disadvantage of the method - either the construction of surfaces in the object needs to be explicitly stated as here, or the method that constructs the solid must do so in such way that consecutive vertices relating to one surface are listed in counter-clockwise order (looking in from outside the object).

```
180    DEF PROCinitialise
190    LOCAL v, vertexno,surfaceno
200      FOR v = 1 TO 8
210        READ vertex(1,v), vertex(2,v), vertex(3,v)
220      NEXT v
230      FOR surfaceno = 1 TO 6
240        FOR vertexno = 1 TO 4
250          READ surface(surfaceno, vertexno)
260        NEXT vertexno
270      NEXT surfaceno
280    ENDPROC

290    DATA 100,0,0,  100,100,0,  100,100,100,  100,0,100
300    DATA 0,0,0,  0,100,0,  0,100,100,  0,0,100
310    DATA 1,2,3,4,  2,6,7,3,  3,7,8,4
320    DATA 6,5,8,7,  1,5,6,2,  1,4,8,5
```

PROChidden_line_remove lists the method broken down into further procedure calls.

```
330    DEF PROChidden_line_remove
340      FOR surfaceno = 1 TO 6
350        PROCcalc_surface_vectors(surfaceno)
360        PROCcalc_normal_vector
370        PROCcalc_line_of_sight_vector(surfaceno)
380        PROCvisibility_test(surfaceno)
390      NEXT surfaceno
400    ENDPROC
```

The first thing that we do is to calculate the components of a pair of vectors lying <u>in</u> the surface. These are two vectors emanating from the first vertex. We do this for each surface and calculate the components of vector1 and vector2, storing them in arrays 'vector1' and 'vector2'.

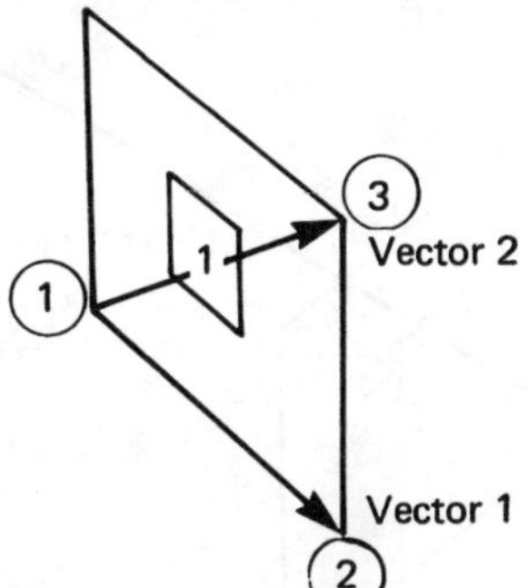

```
410    DEF PROCcalc_surface_vectors(surfaceno)
420      FOR i = 1 TO 3
430        vector1(i) = vertex(i, surface(surfaceno,2))
                               - vertex(i,surface(surfaceno,1))
440        vector2(i) = vertex(i, surface(surfaceno,3))
                               - vertex(i,surface(surfaceno, 1))
450      NEXT i
460    ENDPROC
```

The 'cross product' of vector1 and vector2 gives a normal vector or a vector perpendicular to the surface and joining the surface at the first vertex. This has components 'normalx', 'normaly' and 'normalz'.

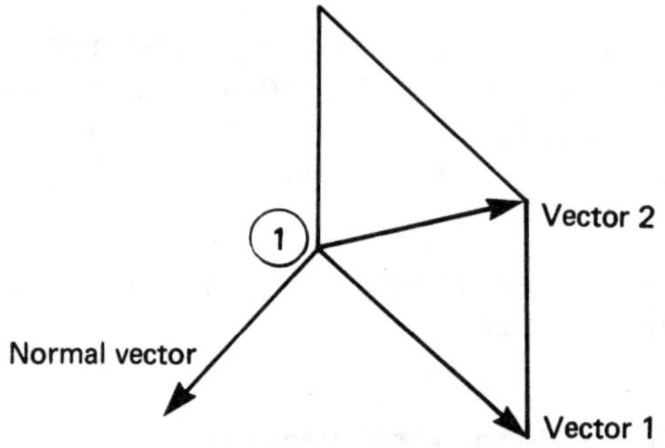


```
470    DEF PROCcalc_normal_vector
480      normalx = vector1(2)*vector2(3) -
                            vector2(2)*vector1(3)
490      normaly = vector1(3)*vector2(1) -
                            vector2(3)*vector1(1)
500      normalz = vector1(1)*vector2(2) -
                            vector2(1)*vector1(2)
510    ENDPROC
```

We can then calculate the components of the vector that joins the viewpoint to the vertex containing the normal vector and apply the visibility test.

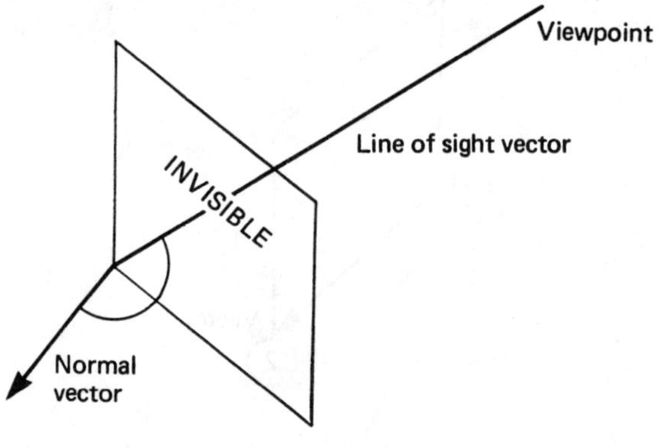

```
520   DEF PROCcalc_line_of_sight_vector(surfaceno)
530     lineofsightx = xview -
                      vertex(1,surface(surfaceno,1))
540     lineofsighty = yview -
                      vertex(2,surface(surfaceno,1))
550     lineofsightz = zview -
                      vertex(3,surface(surfaceno,1))
560   ENDPROC

570   DEF PROCvisibility_test(surfaceno)
580     visible(surfaceno) = normalx*lineofsightx
                           + normaly*lineofsighty
                           + normalz*lineofsightz > 0
590   ENDPROC
```

The visibility test calculates the 'dot product' of the line of sight and normal vectors. If the magnitude of the dot product is less than zero the the angle between the two vectors is greater than 90 degrees. Finally we need a standard transformation and plotting procedure for a surface:

```
600   DEF PROCtransform_and_plot(surfaceno)
610   LOCAL vertexno, startx,starty
620     PROCscreenvertex(surfaceno,1)
630     MOVE xs,ys : startx=xs : starty=ys
640     FOR vertexno = 2 TO 4
650     PROCscreenvertex(surfaceno,vertexno)
660       DRAW xs,ys
670     NEXT vertexno
680     DRAW startx,starty
690   ENDPROC

700   DEF PROCscreenvertex(s,v)
710     PROCviewtransform(vertex(1, surface(s,v)),
                          vertex(2, surface(s,v)),
                          vertex(3, surface(s,v)))
720     PROCperspecttransform(xe,ye,ze,d)
730   ENDPROC
```

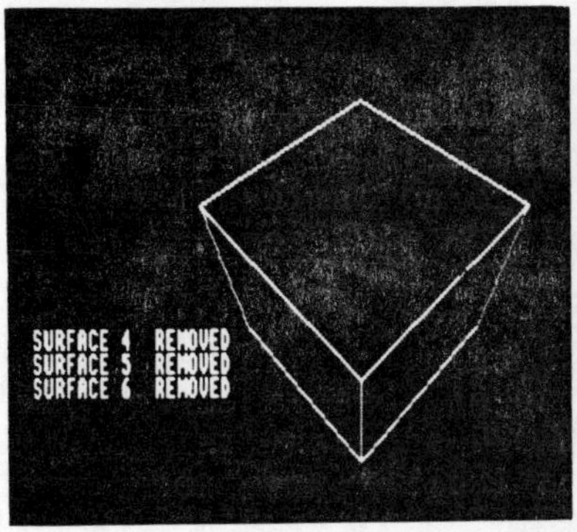

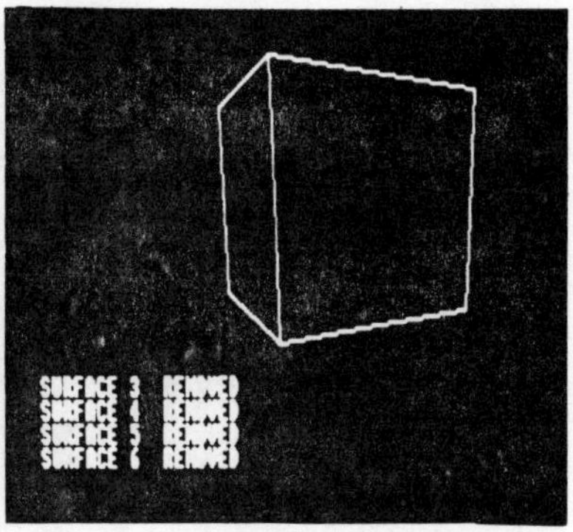

The illustration shows views of the cube together with a list of the surfaces removed for two different viewpoints.

Exercises

1 Apply hidden line removal to plots of a variety of three-dimensional functions f(x,y).

2 Apply the hidden surface removal algorithm to a variety of three-dimensional shapes - a house, a tetrahedron, and so on. You will need to extend the dimensions of the arrays used if there are more than eight vertices or if there are surfaces with more than four vertices. If the number of vertices in a surface varies within the same object, a separate array will be needed to record the number of vertices in each surface.

3 Organise a 'fly round' each object used in the last exercise, with hidden line removal.

Chapter 4 Animation techniques

The commonest animation technique that you are likely to use on your BBC micro will be character animation, where objects are moved about the screen by printing and reprinting characters. In any of the graphics modes, a character shape can be displayed by a PRINT statement in considerably less time than it would take to draw the same shape using graphics commands. This is because of the fast techniques used to fill the area of the screen memory that is to be occupied by the character. In MODE 7, character printing is even faster than in the graphics modes.

We shall see later in the chapter how to define our own character shapes but for the time being, the objects being moved will be strings of standard characters. Such simple animation of words and numbers is a powerful tool in computer-assisted learning systems as we shall demonstrate shortly.

Although the use of DRAW and PLOT facilities for animation is limited by lack of speed, towards the end of the chapter we shall look into techniques for the animation of simple line drawings such as stick figures.

4.1 Word animation and computer assisted learning

Displaying character information on a screen in a way that is interesting and informative finds applications in many branches of interactive computing. Currently one of the more exotic of these is to replace the conventional electromechanical instrumentation in large complex passenger aircraft with a single animated computer display.

Here as a case study of word animation we look at animating the control flow in a program of reasonable complexity. Explaining to someone how a complicated program works has always been a problem, and in this section, we look at ways of animating a character display to bring a programming technique to life. The technique we shall animate is a simple sort method. Sorting techniques are discussed in Chapter 6, but here we use one of the simplest approaches to sorting a list into order - a simple exchange sort. The program that we wish to animate is presented first. It reads ten items into an array from DATA statements and sorts the items into order. We could think of the data as representing, say, a simple stocklist. Each item is a string consisting of a character (a 'department code') followed by a 3-digit integer (a 'stock number'). The items are sorted in the array so that the numbers are in ascending numerical order.

```
100   noofitems=10
110   DIM item$(noofitems)
120   PROCsetuptable
130   PROCexchsort
140   FOR i=1 TO noofitems:PRINT item$(i):NEXT
150   END

200   DEF PROCsetuptable
210   LOCAL i
220     FOR i=1 TO noofitems
230       READ item$(i)
240     NEXT i
250     DATA G 291, D 251, H 123, C 243
260     DATA C 523, L 145, H 391, L 265
270     DATA H 367, H 443
280   ENDPROC

300   DEF PROCexchsort
310     LOCAL i, posnsmallest
320     FOR i = 1 TO noofitems-1
330       PROCfindsmallestentryfrom(i)
340       PROCswop(i, posnsmallest)
350     NEXT i
360   ENDPROC

400   DEF PROCfindsmallestentryfrom(i)
410   LOCAL next
420     posnsmallest = i
430     FOR next = i+1 TO noofitems
440       IF   RIGHT$(item$(next),3)
             < RIGHT$(item$(posnsmallest),3)
          THEN posnsmallest=next
450     NEXT next
460   ENDPROC

500   DEF PROCswop(k,l)
510   LOCAL temp$
520     temp$=item$(k):item$(k)=item$(l):item$(l)=temp$
530   ENDPROC
```

What we shall do now is modify the program so that while the contents of the array are being sorted, the contents of the array are also displayed on the screen, and values being moved around in store are also moved around on the screen.

The initial layout of the display that we shall use is illustrated in the first photograph.

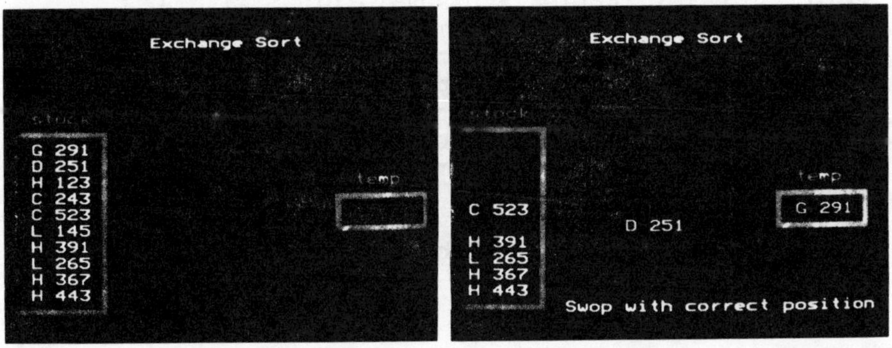

The program will run in MODE 7 using Teletext codes to obtain colour effects and Teletext graphics characters to draw the boxes. (For a summary of these codes, see Appendix 3. For further information on Teletext consult the User Guide.) Note that a Teletext colour or graphics effect is obtained by 'printing' a special character code just before the characters that are to be affected. These special codes appear on the screen as spaces. Their effect lasts only for the line on which they appear. We assume that these codes have been given names at the start of our animation program:

```
10    red$=CHR$(129) : green$=CHR$(130)
20    yellow$=CHR$(131):white$=CHR$(135)
30    blue$=CHR$(132):cyan$=CHR$(134)
40    gb$=CHR$(148) : flash$=CHR$(136)
```

where 'gb$' stands for 'graphics blue code'. The other codes will be used for changing the colours of words on the screen, so as to draw attention to them during animation. For example a common technique to animate a scan through a list is to display the list and change the colour of each item to a highlight colour and back again. The highlight colour then appears to move down the list.

The array 'item$' and the variable 'temp$' together with their contents are initially displayed by PROCsetupdisplay.

```
600   DEF PROCsetupdisplay
610   LOCAL y
620     CLS
630     VDU 23;8202;0;0;0;
640     midx = 16 : leftx=3
650     basey=(24-noofitems) DIV 2
660     tempx=30 : tempy = basey + noofitems DIV 2
```

```
670      PRINT TAB(leftx,basey-1);blue$;"items"
680      PRINT TAB(tempx,tempy-2);blue$;"temp"
690      PRINT TAB(tempx-2,tempy-1);gb$;"h,,,,,,,4";
700      PROCbars(tempx,tempy)
710      PRINT TAB(tempx-2,tempy+1);gb$;"*,,,,,,,%"
720      PRINT TAB(leftx-2,basey);gb$;"h,,,,,,,4";
730      FOR y=1 TO noofitems
740        PROCdisplayrec(y,white$)
750      NEXT y
760      PRINT TAB(leftx-2,basey+noofitems+1) ;
                                   gb$;"*,,,,,,,%"
770    ENDPROC

800    DEF PROCbars(x,y)
810      PRINT TAB(x-2,y);gb$;"j";TAB(x+6,y);gb$;"5"
820    ENDPROC

840    DEF PROCdisplayrec(r,c$)
850      PRINT TAB(leftx-2,basey+r) ;
                      gb$; "j"; c$; item$(r); gb$; "5"
860    ENDPROC
```

In order to animate our sort method, we must move a string in our display whenever it is moved in store. To do this, we shall use a procedure PROCmove called in PROCswop.

```
500    DEF PROCswop(k,l)
510    LOCAL temp$
512    LOCAL sk$,sl$
514      sk$=yellow$+item$(k) : sl$=yellow$+item$(l)
520      temp$=item$(k):item$(k)=item$(l):item$(l)=temp$
522      PROCmove(sk$,leftx,basey+k,tempx,tempy)
524      PROCmove(sl$,leftx,basey+l,leftx,basey+k)
526      PROCmove(sk$,tempx,tempy,leftx,basey+l)
530    ENDPROC
```

PROCmove requires 5 parameters. The first parameter is the string that is to be moved on the screen. We have arranged for the moving string to be highlighted in yellow by including a yellow control code in the string when the procedure is called, the next two are the coordinates of the start position of the string (where it is already displayed) and the final two parameters are the coordinates of the final position of the string.

The most convenient way to arrange for the movement of strings in this type of animation is to establish a highway in the centre of the screen and break all movements down into three stages: horizontal, vertical and horizontal again. The second photograph shows a string in the process of moving up the central highway. In detail, we must:

(1) Move the string horizontally on to the central (vertical) highway.

(2) Move the string up or down the highway to its final vertical position.

(3) Move the string horizontally into its final position.

This approach eliminates the problem of calculating 'trajectories' for the movement between two points and also eliminates the possibility of a moving string wiping out other information that is already on the screen.

Here is the definition of PROCmove together with subsidiary procedures for horizontal and vertical movement. PROCbars is used for restoring the bars at the sides of the array or variable when they have been wiped out by a string moving horizontally into or out of one of the boxes.

```
 900   DEF PROCmove(s$,x1,y1,x2,y2)
 910   LOCAL x,y,xdir,ydir
 920     xdir = SGN(midx-x1)
 930     FOR x=x1 TO midx-xdir STEP xdir
 940       PROCstepx(s$,x,y1,xdir)
 950     NEXT x
 960     PROCbars(x1,y1)
 970     IF y1<>y2 THEN  ydir=SGN(y2-y1) :
              FOR y=y1 TO y2-ydir STEP ydir :
                 PROCstepy(s$,midx,y,ydir) :
              NEXT y
 980     xdir = SGN(x2-midx)
 990     FOR x = midx TO x2-xdir STEP xdir
1000       PROCstepx(s$,x,y2,xdir)
1010     NEXT x
1020     PROCbars(x2,y2)
1030   ENDPROC

1040   DEF PROCstepx(s$,x,y,xdir)
1050     PRINT TAB(x+xdir-1,y);" ";s$;" ";
1060     PROCdelay(1)
1070   ENDPROC

1080   DEF PROCstepy(s$,x,y,ydir)
1090     PRINT TAB(x,y);"        ";TAB(x,y+ydir);s$;
1100     PROCdelay(1)
1110   ENDPROC

1120   DEF PROCdelay(d)
1130   LOCAL t
1140     t=TIME+d
1150     REPEAT:UNTIL TIME>t
1160   ENDPROC
```

The vertical and horizontal movement procedures each require a parameter indicating the direction of the movement. For example in the case of PROCstepx, the parameter 'xdir' will have the value 1 for movement from left to right and -1 for movement from right to left.

We can further improve the instructive value of the display by adding text explaining what is happening during the sort and by highlighting information in the array in different colours to signify its status as the sort proceeds. For example, once a value has been moved to its correct position, we can highlight it in red. Here are PROCexchsort and PROCfindsmallestentryfrom rewritten to use these facilities.

```
300   DEF PROCexchsort
310     LOCAL i, posnsmallest
315     PROCheading("Exchange Sort")
320     FOR i = 1 TO noofitems-1
325       go=GET:PROCexplain("Find next smallest")
330       PROCfindsmallestentryfrom(i)
335       go=GET:PROCexplain("Swop with correct position")
340       PROCswop(i, posnsmallest)
345       PROCcolourrec(posnsmallest,white$)
346       PROCcolourrec(i,red$)
350     NEXT i
355     go=GET:PROCexplain("Sort completed")
356     PROCcolourrec(noofitems,red$):go=GET
360   ENDPROC

400   DEF PROCfindsmallestentryfrom(i)
410   LOCAL next
420     posnsmallest = i
425     PROCcolourrec(posnsmallest,yellow$)
430     FOR next = i+1 TO noofitems
435     PROCcolourrec(next,green$):PROCdelay(10)
436     PROCcolourrec(next,white$)
440       IF   RIGHT$(item$(next),3)
              < RIGHT$(item$(posnsmallest),3)
          THEN PROCcolourrec(posnsmallest,white$) :
               posnsmallest=next :
               PROCcolourrec(next,yellow$)
450     NEXT next
460   ENDPROC
```

PROCheading and PROCexplain position a given string in an appropriate place on the screen and PROCcolour simply prints the required colour code before a string at the position specified.

```
1200    DEF PROCheading(s$)
1210      PRINT TAB(13,1);white$;s$
1220    ENDPROC

1230    DEF PROCexplain(s$)
1240    LOCAL spaces
1250      PRINT TAB(leftx+8,basey+noofitems+1);white$;s$;
1260      spaces = 30-leftx-LEN(s$)
1270      PRINT STRING$(spaces," ");
1280    ENDPROC

1290    DEF PROCcolourrec(r,c$)
1300      PRINT TAB(leftx,basey+r);c$
1310    ENDPROC
```

Any sort algorithm can be animated using this technique and the following procedure animates a bubble sort. Again this sort method is explained fully in Chapter 6.

```
1400    DEF PROCbubble
1410    LOCAL i,last
1420      PROCheading("Simple bubble sort")
1430      FOR last = noofitems TO 2 STEP -1
1440        go=GET
1450        PROCcolourrec(1,yellow$)
1460        PROCexplain("Bubble scan")
1470        FOR i = 2 TO last
1480          PROCcolourrec(i,yellow$)
1490          IF RIGHT$(item$(i),3) < RIGHT$(item$(i-1),3)
              THEN PROCswop(i,i-1)
              ELSE PROCdelay(10)
1500          PROCcolourrec(i-1,white$)
1510        NEXT i
1520        PROCcolourrec(last,red$)
1530        PROCexplain("Last "+STR$(noofitems-last+1)+
                                            " now in position")
1540      NEXT last
1550      go=GET
1560      PROCcolourrec(1,red$)
1570      PROCexplain("Sort completed")
1580      go=GET
1590    ENDPROC
```

Exercises

1 Design an animated sequence to illustrate the behaviour of the BASIC statement

The sequence should stress the fact that the contents of 'y' are not changed, but are copied into 'x'.

2 Animate the sequence of BASIC statements for exchanging the contents of two variables:

```
temp = x
   x = y
   y = temp
```

3 When you have read Chapter 6, animate some of the techniques described there; for example, sifting sort, binary search, hash table access and so on.

4.2 User-defined characters

In modes 0, 1, 2, 4 and 5, the screen is divided up into a number of 'pixels'. For example, in modes 1 and 4, there are 320x256 pixels.

In modes 3 and 6, the screen is divided into horizontal strips of pixels which are separated by strips of background colour. Each strip is 8 pixels deep.

In any of modes 0 to 6, printing a character has the effect of filling an 8x8 group of pixels with a pattern of foreground and background colour. For example, the pattern for "A" is:

Also associated with each character is an ASCII code number in the range 0 to 255. This code is used inside the computer to refer to the character. The ASCII code for "A" is 65. When the character whose code number is 65 is to be displayed on the screen by a PRINT statement, the above pattern of foreground and background colour is inserted into the screen memory where information is stored about what is currently displayed on the screen.

The user is normally free to define the character shapes that are associated with ASCII code numbers 224 to 255, and this is particularly useful when creating shapes for use in animation. In fact, on later versions of the operating system (OS 1.2 onwards), it is possible for the user to define shapes for a much greater range of ASCII codes. We shall explain how to do this shortly.

Once a new character shape has been defined, it can be displayed on the screen at the same speed as the predefined characters that we have used so far in this chapter.

The use of user-defined character shapes has two advantages over the use of PLOT instructions to draw shapes. Firstly, as we have already seen, a character shape is displayed on the screen at a much greater speed than can be achieved by using PLOT facilities. Secondly, the sequence of PLOT statements needed to draw a complex shape such as a spaceship would be rather lengthy.

Single character shapes

Let us demonstrate the process of defining new character shapes by defining some Greek letters. These could be useful to a scientist or a mathematician wishing to display mathematical equations. The shape required for alpha is

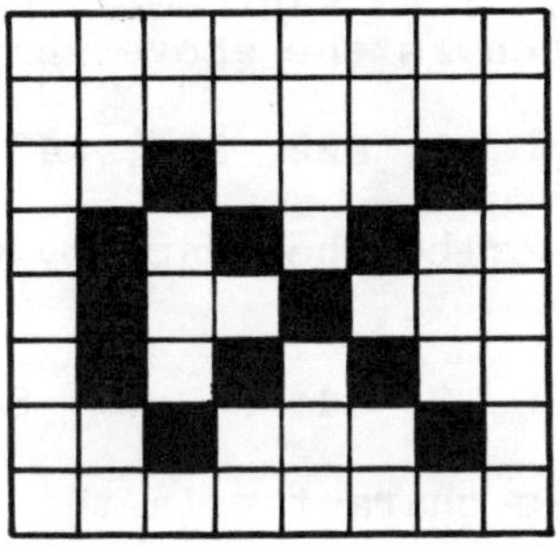

Note that in MODES 2 and 5, a pixel (and therefore a character) is elongated horizontally. Each row in the 8x8 pattern can be viewed as a byte (eight bits - see Appendix 2), and each byte can be written as an integer in the range 0 to 255. Thus the above pattern can be described as a list of 8 bytes or a list of 8 integers:

bytes	integers
00000000	0
00000000	0
00100010	34
01010100	84
01001000	72
01010100	84
00100010	34
00000000	0

A byte can also be written in the form of two hexadecimal

digits. Four bits correspond to one hexadecimal digit as described in Appendix 2. Because of this correspondence, it is usually easier to write a pattern of 8 bits in hex than to convert it into an integer:

bytes	hex
00000000	0
00000000	0
00100010	&22
01010100	&54
01001000	&48
01010100	&54
00100010	&22
00000000	0

In order to define our new character shape, we must choose the ASCII code that we are going to use for the character and we must then calculate the sequence of 8 integers (in decimal or hex) that describes its shape. The ASCII code is associated with the required shape by using the VDU 23 command. For example, if we want ASCII character number 224 to appear on the screen as the above shape, we can use

```
10   VDU 23, 224, 0, 0, &22, &54, &48, &54, &22, 0
```

We could equally describe the shape by writing the bytes in decimal:

```
10   VDU 23, 224, 0, 0, 34, 84, 72, 84, 34, 0
```

We can display this character in the centre of the screen in MODE 4 by:

```
20   MODE 4
30   PRINT TAB(20,10); CHR$(224)
```

or by:

```
20    alpha$ = CHR$(224)
30    PRINT TAB(20, 10); alpha$
```

or we can incorporate it in strings:

```
20    alpha$ = CHR$(224)
30    particle$ = alpha$ + "-particle"
40    ray$ = alpha$ + "-ray"
50    PRINT ray$; "s consist of a stream of";
                  particle$; "s."
```

Here are some further VDU 23 statements for defining the next three letters in the Greek alphabet.

```
20    VDU 23, 225, 0, 0, &1E, &12, &3C, &24, &7C, &40
30    VDU 23, 226, 0, 0, &42, &24, &18, &24, &24, &18
40    VDU 23, 227, &C, &10, &10, &8, &3C, &44, &38, 0
```

Composite character shapes
We can build up bigger objects by defining a number of different character shapes that can be printed together to make up the overall shape of the object. For example, let us define a vintage car for use in MODE 1 or 4. We use a row of three characters for the basic car shape:

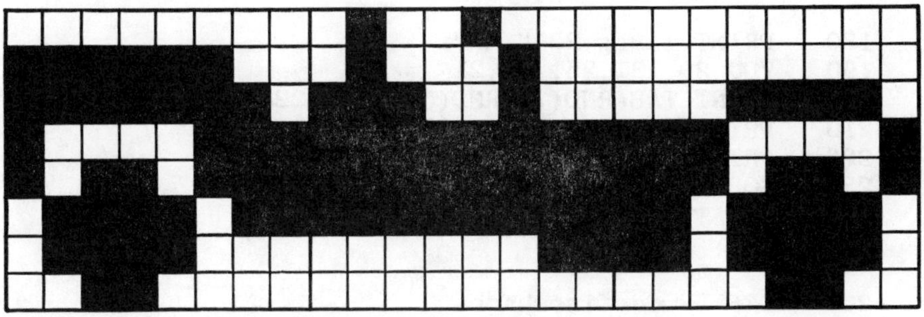

The three characters required are defined by the bit patterns:

```
00000000   01001000   00000000
11111100   01000100   00000000
11111110   11100100   00011110
10000111   11111111   11100001
10110111   11111111   11101101
01111011   11111111   11011110
01111000   00000011   11011110
00110000   00000000   00001100
```

Here is a program that uses these characters together with some other groups of user-defined characters.

```
 10   MODE 1 : VDU 23;8202;0;0;0;
 20   VDU 19,2,2,0,0,0
 30   PROCdefineshapes
 40   PROCbackground
 50   COLOUR 2 : PRINT TAB(1,3)tree$
 60   y=3
 70   COLOUR 1 : PRINT TAB(2,y)car$

 80   FOR x=2 TO 31
 90     SOUND 0,-10,6,1 : SOUND 0,-11,7,1
100     TIME=0 : REPEAT:UNTIL TIME>10
110   COLOUR1 : PRINT TAB(x,y)" ";car$
120   NEXT x

130   x=32
140   FOR y=4 TO 22
150     PRINT TAB(x,y-1)"   "
160     PRINT TAB(x,y)car$
170   NEXT y

180   PRINT TAB(x,22)"   "
190   VDU 28, 31,25, 39,21
200   PRINT TAB(RND(7),RND(5));CHR$224;
210   PRINT TAB(RND(7),RND(5));CHR$225;
220   PRINT TAB(RND(7),RND(5));CHR$226;
230   SOUND 0,-10,6,20
240   K=GET : MODE 7
250   END

260   DEF PROCdefineshapes
270     VDU 23, 224, 0,&FC,&FE,&87,&B7,&7B,&78,&30
280     VDU 23, 225, &48,&44,&E4,&FF,&FF,&FF,3,0
290     VDU 23, 226, 0,0,&1E,&E1,&ED,&DE,&DE,&C
300     car$=CHR$224 + CHR$225 + CHR$226
310     VDU 23, 227, 0,&77,&42,&72,&12,&12,&72,0
320     VDU 23, 228, 0,&77,&55,&57,&54,&54,&74,0
330     st$=CHR$227 + CHR$228
340     VDU 23, 240, 0,0,0,0,0,0,&38,&FE
350     VDU 23, 241, &3,&F,&3F,&FF,&FF,&FF,&F,1
360     VDU 23, 242, &FF,&FF,&FF,&FF,&FF,&FF,&FF,&FF
370     VDU 23, 243, &C0,&F0,&FC,&FF,&FF,&FF,&F0,&80
380     VDU 23, 244, &3C,&3C,&3C,&3C,&3C,&3C,&7E,&7E
390     tree$=CHR$244 + CHR$8 + CHR$8 + CHR$11 +
              CHR$241 + CHR$242 + CHR$243 +
              CHR$8 + CHR$8 + CHR$11 + CHR$240
400   ENDPROC

410   DEF PROCbackground
420     PROCrocks
430     PRINT TAB(29,3)st$
440   ENDPROC
```

```
450   DEF PROCrocks
460     GCOL 0,3
470     MOVE 0,888
480     DRAW 999,888
490     DRAW 999,200
500     DRAW 1020,300
510     PLOT 85,1060,200
520     DRAW 1100,310
530     PLOT 85,1120,200
540     DRAW 1160,270
550     PLOT 85,1180,200
560     DRAW 1220,350
570     PLOT 85,1220,200
580   ENDPROC
```

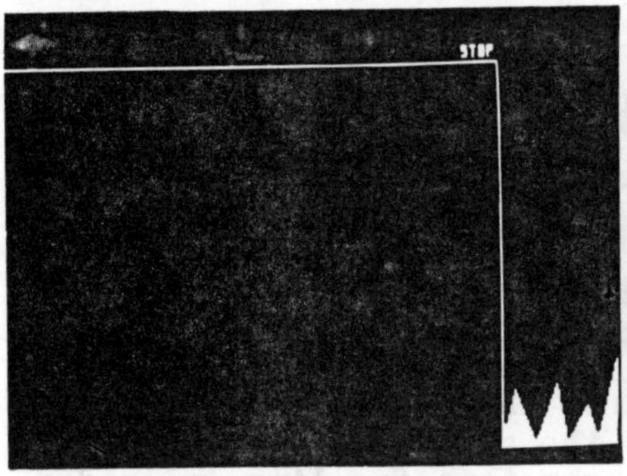

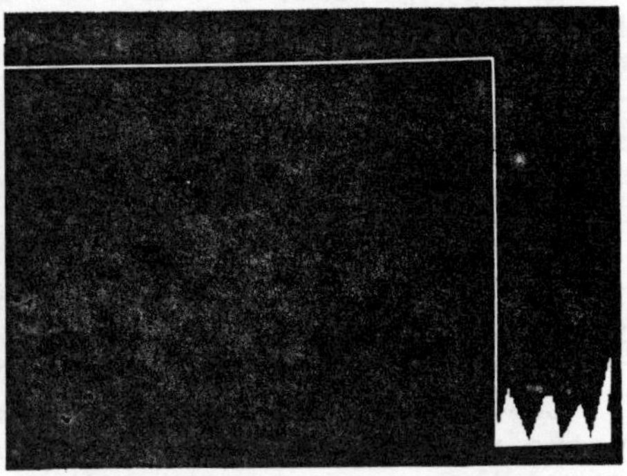

We have moved the car horizontally and vertically in exactly the same way as we moved words in Section 4.1. There are a number of other interesting features in this program:

(1) The string 'tree$' has been made up of a combination of user-defined characters, backspace characters (CHR$ 8) and 'up' characters (CHR$ 11).

(2) The 'stop' sign consists of two user-defined characters - we can obtain small letters in modes whose normal characters are too large.

(3) The crash is simulated by printing the three separate characters constituting the car at random positions in a text window drawn round the rocks. The text window is created by the VDU 28 statement at line 190.

Designing characters on paper is a tedious process and it is sometimes useful to have a computer program that assists us in the design process. A listing of such a program appeared in our earlier book (The BBC micro book: BASIC, Sound and

Graphics) and this program (with others) is also available on cassette. The use of multi-frame character images was extensively covered in the earlier book and we will not go into it here. However, we shall be using user defined characters in various contexts in the rest of this chapter.

'Exploding' the space for user-defined characters
Under normal circumstances, the user can define up to 32 of his own character shapes for ASCII codes 224 to 255 (&E0 to &FF). The bit patterns defining the shapes of these characters are stored by the operating system at store locations &C00 to &CFF. Actually, codes 128 to 255 all initially refer to this space, four codes corresponding to each character shape. For example, once character 224 has been defined, characters 128, 160 and 192 (&80, &A0 and &C0) all produce the same shape as character 224. When constructing large numbers of frames for large multi-character images, more than 32 new character shapes may need to be defined. The space used by the operating system for storing character shapes can be extended or 'exploded' by using the command

```
*FX 20, 1
```

After this command has been obeyed, all the character codes from 32 up to 255 can be redefined. However, the operating system stores the bit pattern defining most of these shapes at the bottom of the storage area that is normally occupied by the user's BASIC program and the above command must be issued before any program that uses this facility is loaded. The system must then be told to load the program above the space needed for character definitions by changing the value of the system variable PAGE which contains the address of the storage location at which the user's BASIC program is stored. PAGE must be increased by an amount which depends on the character codes that are going to be redefined.

character codes to be defined	increase in PAGE
128-159 (&80-&9F)	no change needed
160-191 (&A0-&BF)	PAGE = PAGE + &100
192-223 (&C0-&DF)	PAGE = PAGE + &200
224-255 (&E0-&FF)	PAGE = PAGE + &300
32-63 (&20-&3F)	PAGE = PAGE + &400
64-95 (&40-&5F)	PAGE = PAGE + &500
96-127 (&60-&9F)	PAGE = PAGE + &600

Exercises

1 Add some more sound effects to the car program, for example a squeal of brakes.

2 Add an extra tree in the middle of the car's route towards the cliff edge. When the car has passed in front of the tree, the tree trunk will need to be redrawn.

3 Arrange for the 'stop' sign to fall down the cliff with the car and break up on the rocks.

4.3 Arcade game animation

The really elaborate commercial arcade games are programmed in assembly code and take anything from two to six man months to write. Features of the computer that are not easily accessible to BASIC programmers are employed. Another important factor is speed. An assembly code program executes more quickly than its equivalent written in BASIC. This is because it is generally more efficient and also when a BASIC program is being executed the interpreter is executed at the same time. Such speed is important in animated games in general but particularly so in games where many animated events are (apparently) taking place simultaneously at different points on the screen.

As long as we are not too ambitious we can write interesting games in BASIC, but we must take care that the techniques we use in our programs are as efficient as possible. In this section, we shall look at two aspects of such games - keeping track of the status of a number of moving objects and keeping track of where moving objects are allowed to go (for example, in a Pacman type maze).

Even if we were going to do serious arcade game programming in assembly language, we would need techniques similar to those that we are going to describe, and these techniques are best introduced in BASIC.

Keeping track of moving objects

Arcade game animation of any complexity usually involves two representations of the objects being moved. First of all there is the screen display, which is represented inside the computer by the contents of the screen memory. A code stored in the screen memory indicates the colour of the corresponding pixel on the screen. Such a representation is not convenient for keeping track of the position and status of an object such as a spaceship, which would occupy more than one pixel on the display. We usually have to store separately additional information about an object: for example, coordinates, direction of motion, orientation, etc. It is this information that is repeatedly examined by the program when deciding what action to take next and the number of objects that can be handled in a BASIC arcade game depends on the speed at which this information can be examined and updated. The choice of representation is often critical, making the difference between a slow-moving and uninteresting game, and a fast-moving successful one. We shall illustrate this point with a simple space invader game.

Moving groups of objects - a fleet of space invaders

There are two approaches to the problem of keeping track of a number of objects. Where objects are scattered about the screen, there is no alternative but to store a list of their coordinates, this list being updated each time the objects are moved. The number of separate objects that can be handled quickly enough in this way in a BASIC program is fairly small.

In the case of a group of objects such as a fleet of 'space invaders' which are moving in unison in a tight formation, it is often more convenient to handle the group as if it were a single object. We can use a single string to represent each row of invaders (or indeed a single string to represent the whole fleet). Here is a simple introductory program that moves a small fleet of 'spaceships' backwards and forwards across the screen, each pass bringing them a step closer to the bottom of the screen.

```
 10   MODE 5
 20   VDU 23,1,0;0;0;0;
 30   VDU 23,224,&18,&18,&18,&3C,&7E,&C3,&7E,&3C
 40   VDU 23,225,0,&24,&7E,&5A,&7E,&7E,&FF,&C3
 50   VDU 23,226,&A5,&FF,&FF,&18,&DB,&99,&FF,0
 60   DIM fleet$(3)
 70   fleet$(0)="  "+CHR$(224)+" "+CHR$(224)+"   "
 80   fleet$(1)=" "+CHR$(225)+" "+CHR$(225)+" "+
                    CHR$(225)+" "+CHR$(225)+" "
 90   fleet$(2)=fleet$(1)
100   fleet$(3)="  "+CHR$(226)+" "+CHR$(226)+" "+
                     CHR$(226)+"  "
110   fleetx%=0:fleety%=0:fleetdir%=1
120   PROCprintfleet
130   REPEAT
140     PROCmovefleet
150   UNTIL fleety%=27
160   END

300   DEF PROCprintfleet
310   LOCAL r%
320     FOR r%=0 TO 3
330       COLOUR r% MOD 2 + 1
340       PRINT TAB(fleetx%,fleety%+r%);fleet$(r%)
350     NEXT r%
360   ENDPROC
```

```
400   DEF PROCmovefleet
410     fleetx%=fleetx%+fleetdir%
420     IF fleetx%>10 OR fleetx%<0 THEN
           fleetdir%=-fleetdir% :
           fleetx%=fleetx%+fleetdir% :
           PRINT TAB(fleetx%,fleety%);"       " :
           fleety%=fleety%+1
430     PROCprintfleet
440   ENDPROC
```

Grouping the spaceships into strings in this way makes the animation considerably more convenient (and faster) than it would be if the coordinates for each ship were stored separately and each ship moved in turn.

An interesting alternative to the use of the COLOUR statement at line 330 would be to include colour control codes in the strings representing the fleet. For example, printing the string:

```
CHR$(17) + CHR$(1)
```

is exactly equivalent to obeying the statement:

```
COLOUR 1
```

(see Appendix 3). Strings like the above could be added to the start of each row of the fleet.

Removing ships from the fleet

There are various types of arcade games that could be developed from the previous program. For example, we shall shortly introduce a 'gunsight' controlled by a user at the keyboard whose aim is to destroy the invading fleet. If one of the invaders is destroyed, then clearly it must be replaced by a space in the string in which it is stored. A further elaboration appears in games of the 'Galaxian' family where spaceships are repeatedly selected from the main fleet to launch an individual attack on the user and his gun. This involves searching through the fleet to find such an attacker, deleting it from the fleet and then keeping a separate record of its subsequent movements.

Changing individual characters in a BASIC string is a fairly cumbersome process. For example, to remove the second invader from the third row of the fleet, we could use

```
fleet$(3) = LEFT$(fleet$(3),4) +" "+ RIGHT$(fleet$(3),4)
```

As well as being cumbersome, this process is slow - the whole string is copied as a result of obeying the above statement. All that really needs to be done is to overwrite one character in the string and we now introduce an alternative method of storing a string that makes changing an individual character in the string easier and quicker.

Indirection operators - $ and ?

The BBC computer store consists of a sequence of numbered storage locations or 'words' where each word contains one byte (see Appendix 2). A string simply consists of a sequence of bytes (character codes) stored in consecutive words of computer store. When we store a string in a BASIC string variable, we do not have access to the individual bytes, except by using the MID$ function. We cannot easily change one of the characters in the string without copying the whole string.

An alternative method for storing a string of fixed size is to allocate a block of storage locations in which we can store the character codes of our string. We use an ordinary BASIC variable in which to record the number or 'address' of the storage location at the start of the block. The block of store is allocated by a variant of the DIM statement. For example,

```
DIM s% 5
```

allocates a block of store containing 6 locations and stores the address of the start of the block in the variable 's%'. For instance, the computer might allocate a block of store starting at location 4504

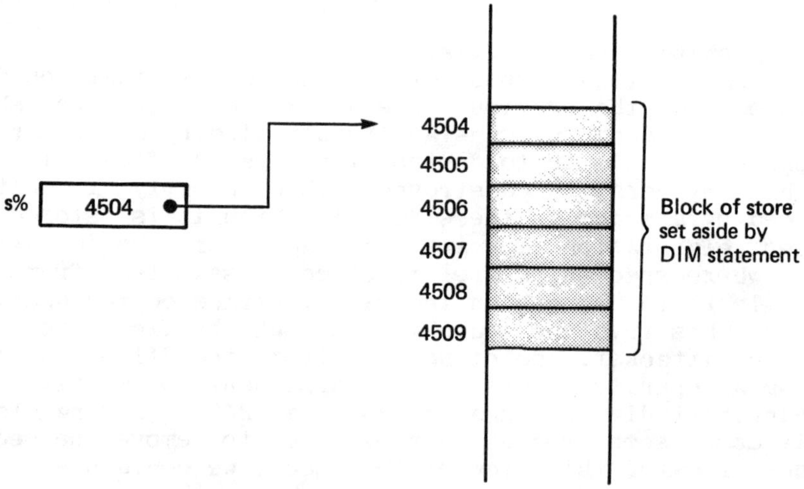

We can now store a string of up to 5 characters in this block by using, for example:

```
$ s% = "ASTMS"
```

The $ operator is called a 'string indirection' operator and it means that the string is to start in the computer word whose address is held in 's%'. The end of the string is marked by an additional character code 13.

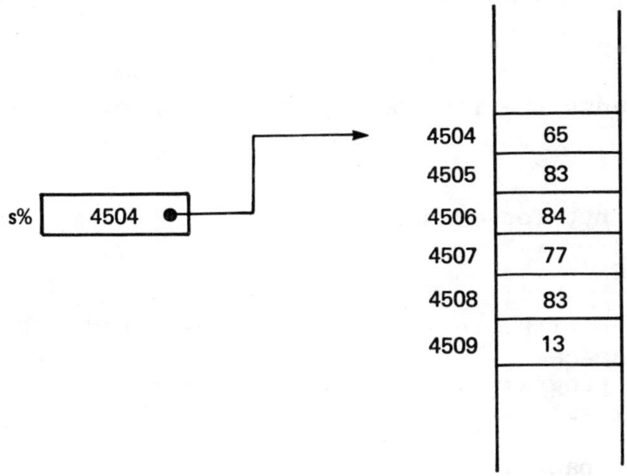

We can print the string by:

```
PRINT $ s%
```

Storing the string in this way allows us to change individual characters in the string without copying the rest of the string. To do this we can use the indirection operator '?'. The '?' can be used either as a unary operator or as a binary operator. For example,

```
PRINT ? s%
```

would print 65. The '?' causes the computer to refer to the storage location whose address is the value of 's%'. This corresponds to the use of PEEK operations in other BASIC dialects. The same effect could be obtained by

```
PRINT ? 4504
```

but it is better not to rely on the computer allocating the same storage locations every time the program is run. We can change the first character by

```
? s% = ASC("B")
```

which corresponds to the POKE operation in other BASIC dialects. In order to access the third character in the string, we could use

```
PRINT ? (s% + 2)
```

In this case the computer refers to the storage locations whose address is the value of the expression following the '?'. However, the '?' can be used as a binary operator and the above is equivalent to

```
PRINT s% ? 2
```

Now we can access the ith code in our string by

```
PRINT s% ? i
```

and change it by, for example

```
s% ? i = 32
```

which sets the ith. character to ASCII code 32 which represents a space.

The next program illustrates various ways of using the above facilities.

Shooting down space invaders

This program is the kernel of a space invaders or Galaxian type program for you to experiment with. The program moves the same fleet of invaders down the screen and the user at the keyboard controls a 'gunsight' (a letter A) that moves left and right at the bottom of the screen. Pressing the space-bar causes a 'laser' to fire at the invading fleet.

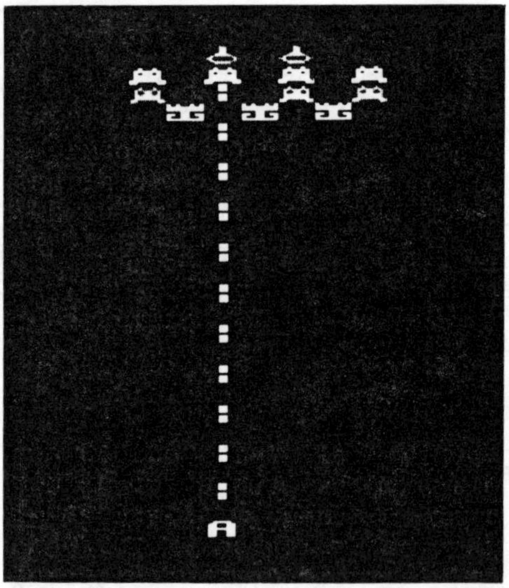

As it stands, it is quite easy to shoot down the invaders, but there are many ways in which the program could be improved. Some of these are suggested as exercises below. There are a number of important points illustrated in this program and these are explained below.

```
 10   MODE 5
 20   VDU 23,1,0;0;0;0;
 30   VDU 23,224,&18,&18,&18,&3C,&7E,&C3,&7E,&3C
 40   VDU 23,225,0,&24,&7E,&5A,&7E,&7E,&FF,&C3
 50   VDU 23,226,&A5,&FF,&FF,&18,&DB,&99,&FF,0
 60   DIM fleet$(3)
 70   fleet$(0)="   "+CHR$(224)+" "+CHR$(224)+"   "
 80   fleet$(1)=" "+CHR$(225)+" "+CHR$(225)+" "+
                     CHR$(225)+" "+CHR$(225)+" "
 90   fleet$(2)=fleet$(1)
100   fleet$(3)="  "+CHR$(226)+" "+CHR$(226)+" "+
                      CHR$(226)+"  "
110   DIM f%(3)
120   DIM s% 49
130   $s% = "*********"
140   FOR r%=0 TO 3
150     f%(r%) = s%+(r%+1)*10
160   NEXT
170   PROCinitialise
180   REPEAT
190     PROCgun
200     PROCmovefleet
210   UNTIL fleety%=27 OR invaders=0
220   *FX 12,0
230   MODE 7 : END

300   DEF PROCinitialise
310     *FX 11,5
320     *FX 12,5
330     FOR r%=0 TO 3
340       $f%(r%) = fleet$(r%)
350     NEXT
360     fleetx%=0 : fleety%=0 : fleetdir%=1
370     fdelay%=10 : ftime%=fdelay% : TIME = 0
380     invaders = 13
390     PROCprintfleet
400     gx%=10 : gy%=31 : gun$="A"
410     PRINT TAB(gx%,gy%); gun$;
420     invaders% = 13
430     b$=CHR$(11) + CHR$(11) + "" + CHR$(8)
440     e$=CHR$(11) + CHR$(11) + " " + CHR$(8)
450   ENDPROC

500   DEF PROCprintfleet
510   LOCAL r%
520     FOR r%=0 TO 3
530       COLOUR r% MOD 2 + 1
540       PRINT TAB(fleetx%,fleety%+r%);$f%(r%)
550     NEXT r%
560   ENDPROC
```

```
600   DEF PROCmovefleet
610   IF TIME<ftime% THEN ENDPROC
620     ftime% = TIME + fdelay%
630     fleetx%=fleetx%+fleetdir%
640     IF fleetx%>10 OR fleetx%<0 THEN
           fleetdir%=-fleetdir% :
           fleetx%=fleetx%+fleetdir% :
           PRINT TAB(fleetx%,fleety%);"              " :
           fleety%=fleety%+1
650     PROCprintfleet
660   ENDPROC

700   DEF PROCgun
710     LOCAL k$,nx%
720     k$=INKEY$(0)
730     IF k$=" " THEN PROCfire : ENDPROC
        ELSEIF k$="Z" THEN nx%=gx%-1
        ELSEIF k$="X" THEN nx%=gx%+1    ELSE ENDPROC
740     IF nx%<0 THEN nx%=0 ELSE IF nx%>18 THEN nx%=18
750     PRINT TAB(gx%,gy%); " "; TAB(nx%,gy%); gun$;
760     gx%=nx%
770     *FX 15,1
780   ENDPROC

800   DEF PROCfire
810   LOCAL r%
820     PROCtesthit
830     PROCtrack(r%,b$)
840     PROCtrack(r%,e$)
850     PRINT TAB(gx%,r%);" ";
860     *FX 15,1
870   ENDPROC

900   DEF PROCtesthit
910   LOCAL p%, y%
920     IF gx%<=fleetx% THEN r%=0:ENDPROC
930     IF gx%>fleetx%+7 THEN r%=0:ENDPROC
940     p%=f%(3)+gx%-fleetx%+10 : y%=fleety%+4
950     REPEAT : p%=p%-10 : y%=y%-1
960     UNTIL ?p%>32
970     IF ?p%=42 THEN r%=0:ENDPROC
980     ?p%=32 : invaders=invaders-1 : r%=y%
990   ENDPROC

1000  DEF PROCtrack(r%,s$)
1010  LOCAL y%
1020    PRINT TAB(gx%,gy%);
1030    FOR y%= 29 TO r% STEP -2
1040      PRINT s$;
1050    NEXT y%
1060  ENDPROC
```

As before, the array 'fleet$' contains the strings representing the complete fleet, but in this program these strings are copied into a separate block of store for use during animation. The statement:

```
120   DIM s% 49
```

allocates a block of 50 locations and this block is divided up into 5 sub-blocks. The first string (accessed as '$ s%') contains 9 stars and the reason for this is explained shortly. The next four groups of 10 locations each contain one row of the fleet (9 characters plus character code 13). The four addresses of these sub-blocks are stored in the locations of the array f%. Before the attack, the fleet is copied (by PROCinitialise) into the four sub-blocks. (lines 330 to 350). We can picture the representation of the fleet as:

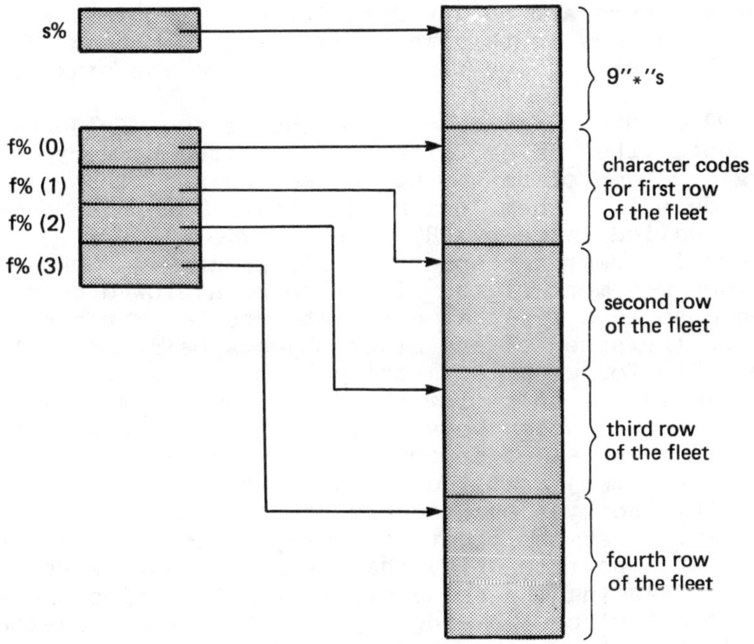

The movement of the fleet is organised in exactly the same way as before. the only difference now is that row 'r%' of the fleet is printed by

```
540         PRINT TAB(fleetx%,fleety%+r%);$f%(r%)
```

which tells the computer to print the string contained in the block of store whose address is contained in f%(r%). One advantage of storing the fleet in this way is that we can scan rapidly through a sequence of the locations that contain the fleet by using the '?' operator. The way in which we have taken advantage of this in the program is in the check to see whether an invader has been hit when the 'gun' is fired (PROCtesthit).

If the x-coordinate of the gun is within the appropriate range, we must examine the fleet locations in the line of fire and find the invader (if any) that is closest to the gun. PROCtesthit thus calculates an address 10 beyond the location to be checked in the fourth row of the fleet (at line 940). By repeatedly subtracting 10 from the address we examine all the locations of the fleet that are in the line of fire. The REPEAT loop terminates (line 960) if a location is found with a character code greater than 32. Thus it stops when an invader is found, or when it reaches one of the "*"s (code 42) which were put there for that very purpose. We can be sure that the loop will terminate at a "*" even if there are no invaders in the line of fire. Using a block of markers in this way eliminates the need for an additional test to see if we have reached the start of the fleet.

Once PROCtesthit has calculated the range (r%) of the laser shot, the laser effect is created by very rapidly printing a column of dashes up the screen and then equally rapidly deleting them (with spaces). This is done by PROCtrack called twice by PROCfire.

Another interesting aspect of this program is the way in which the movement of the fleet has been slowed down. This has been done in a way that does not create unwanted side effects on the speed of any other objects being moved by the program. If, for example, a delay loop was inserted at line 205 this would not only slow the fleet down, but would make the response to the keys controlling the gunsight very sluggish. A much better approach is to keep a record of the next time (ftime%) that the invaders are to be moved and if this time has not yet ben reached, then PROCmovefleet exits immediately. When the fleet is moved, 'ftime%' is increased by 'fdelay%', the time delay that is required between fleet movements. Changing the value of 'fdelay%' changes the speed of the fleet without having any effect on the behaviour of other objects being moved by the program. Of course we cannot increase the speed of the fleet indefinitely. We are limited by the speed at which the BASIC interpreter can cycle through the main loop in the program.

Finally note the way that the command

```
*FX 15, 1
```

is used after a key has been processed. This command flushes any waiting characters that are queued up in the input buffer and simply avoids a build-up of unprocessed input characters. The other two *FX commands used are

```
*FX 11, 5
*FX 12, 5
```

which changes the 'auto-repeat' timings of the keys and makes them more responsive.

```
*FX 12, 0
```

changes the 'auto-repeat' behaviour back to normal. (See the User Guide for details if you are not familiar with this facility.)

Exercises

1 As the space invaders program stands, it is quite easy to shoot down the invaders by holding down the fire button. Arrange for a forced delay, or 'reload time' after each firing. The fire button should have no effect during this period.

2 Structure the program so that it repeats the game after each player has finished. Record the time taken or calculate a score for each player and keep a league table similar to that used in the 'multiplication competition' (Chapter 1).

3 Experiment with different techniques for creating the effect of a 'laser shot'. For example, drawing and deleting a dotted line would be quicker than printing and deleting a large number of characters. Now try the effect of obeying the two statements

```
VDU 19, 0,7, 0,0,0
VDU 19, 0,0, 0,0,0
```

The instantaneous change of actual background colour from black to white and back again creates a 'gunflash' effect.

4 Arrange for an 'explosion' when an invader is hit. The explosion could be represented by two or three user-defined characters displayed in quick succession.

5 Arrange for the invaders to send out an occasional 'missile' which drifts down the screen towards the player's gun, forcing him to take avoiding action.

6 Add sound effects to your program.

4.4 Controlling movement within a maze

Many arcade games involve movement that is restricted to part of the screen. The commonest example of this type of game is the extremely popular 'Pacman'. Here movement takes place within a maze. A program controlling such animation needs to keep a record of which regions of the screen are prohibited and this record must be kept in such a way that the program can recognise very quickly that a particular character position is out of bounds. We could very easily represent a maze on the screen (in MODE 1 or 4 say) marking the walls of the maze with one character and the paths with another. The program could then store a record of the shape of the maze in a two-dimensional array with one location for each character position on the area of the screen being used. (We shall omit the bottom line of the screen from our maze as this makes it easier to avoid accidental scrolling.) The array declaration is:

```
DIM maze%(39, 30)
```

Each location in this array could contain a value (TRUE or FALSE say) indicating whether or not the corresponding character position was part of a path or part of the maze walls. However, although simple, this representation is rather wasteful of memory space. It occupies 1240 BASIC variables, each of which occupies 4 memory locations - nearly 5K of memory altogether.

A much more appropriate representation for this sort of information is a bit map where the status of each character position on the screen is recorded as a single bit. Each BASIC variable occupies four 8-bit words, 32 bits in all, and so we can pack the information about one column of character positions into a single BASIC variable. We can represent the complete maze by a one-dimensional array:

```
DIM bitmap%(39)
```

where each location in this array will contain information about one column of character positions. This representation of the maze occupies only 160 bytes of memory - a considerable saving. Of course, such a saving would lose some of its value if it slowed down the process of recognizing the status of a character position on the screen. However, by careful use of logical operations (see below) we can avoid too much loss of speed.

Manual construction of a maze

We can construct a maze by hand and code it up as a pattern of ones and zeroes where we use ones to represent the maze wall, and zeros to represent the paths. For example

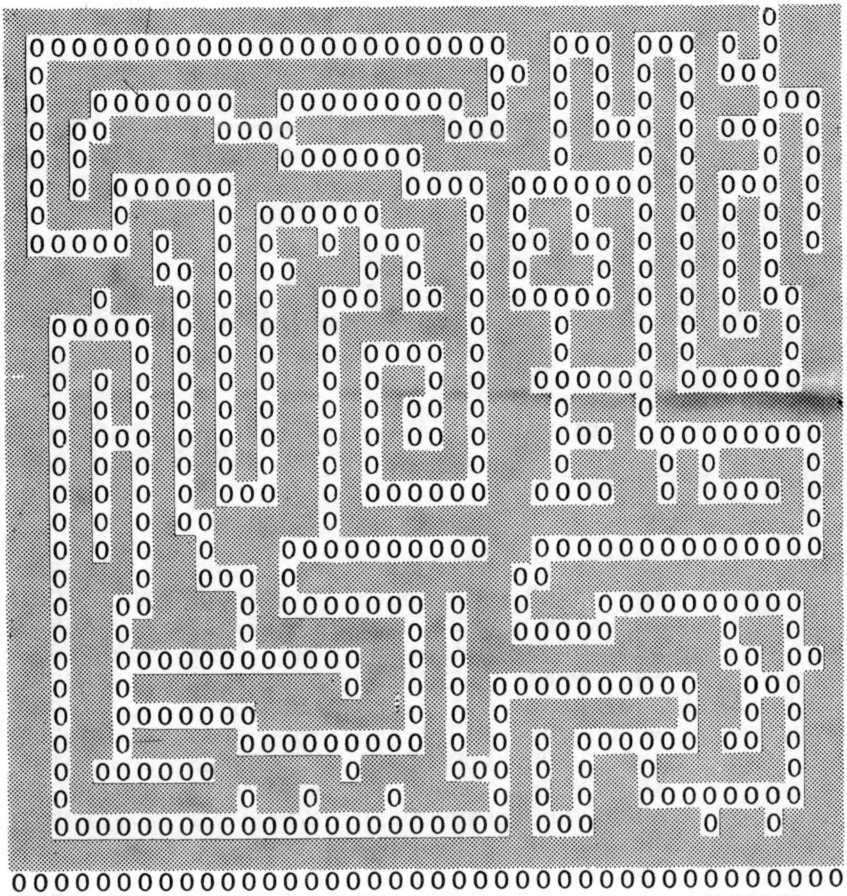

Remember that one column of the binary representation of the maze is to be stored in a single word of our 'bitmap' array. We have included a row of zeros corresponding to the bottom row of the screen which is not used. The easiest way of inputting the above maze to a program is to code each column reading from bottom to top in hex (Appendix 2). A pattern of 32 bits can be represented as a group of 8 hexadecimal digits. Thus 39 8-digit hexadecimal numbers, one for each column of the maze, can be supplied to a program in DATA statements. Here is a short program to draw a maze from such data.

```
10    MODE 1
20    VDU 23,224,&FF,&FF,&FF,&FF,&FF,&FF,&FF,&FF
30    VDU 23;8202;0;0;0;
40    DIM bitmap%(39),mask%(30)
50    PROCsetmasks
60    PROCdrawmaze
70    K=GET : END
```

```
  80   DEF PROCsetmasks
  90     mask%(0)=1
 100     FOR m=1 TO 30
 110       mask%(m)=mask%(m-1)*2
 120     NEXT m
 130   ENDPROC

 140   DEF PROCdrawmaze
 150     LOCAL x,y,path$,wall$
 160     path$=" " : wall$=CHR$(224)
 170     FOR x=0 TO 39:READ bitmap%(x):NEXT
 180     COLOUR 1
 190     FOR y = 0 TO 30
 200       FOR x=0 TO 39
 210         IF bitmap%(x) AND mask%(y) THEN PRINT wall$;
                                        ELSE PRINT path$;
 220     NEXT:NEXT
 230   ENDPROC

1000   DATA &7FFFFFFF, &7F707E07, &601743F7, &4ED55800,
            &685557AB, &6B155029, &4FD45FFF, &68D74001,
            &6AD47FFD, &62D70001, &7AD7DFAF, &7A9558A1,
            &42B55A3D, &5EB40381, &42A5DABF, &7E8FF83B,
            &40FFFFE1, &57F4002D, &5015FFA5, &5FF50BB5
1010   DATA &58152895, &4BD5EED5, &5BD40855, &5257FB55,
            &5B500255, &4B57FF55, &5B47FD45, &5B7C006D,
            &490DFFED, &5D6C0025, &5563FFB5, &557801B5,
            &557FFCB5, &554007B5, &501F7635, &57F012E5,
            &5FFFF68D, &400006FD, &7FFFFE01, &7FFFFFFF
```

This program uses a logical AND operation at line 210 to test whether position x,y in the maze is marked with a 1 representing the maze wall.

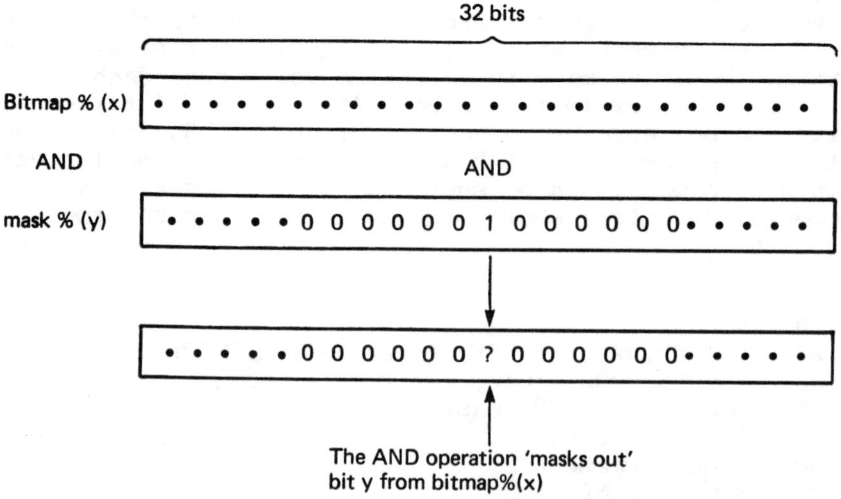

To do this we need to test whether bitmap%(x) has a 1 in bit position y. This is done by 'masking' bitmap%(x) with a bit-pattern or 'mask' that contains only a single 1 in position y and zeros everywhere else. The result of the AND operation between bitmap%(x) and mask%(y) is non-zero only if there is a 1 in position y of bitmap%(x).

The array containing the masks needed in the above operation is initialised by PROCsetmasks which makes use of the fact that multiplying an integer by 2 corresponds to shifting the corresponding bit-pattern along one place.

A maze design program

Before we look at the problem of moving objects around within the maze, here is a program that will make it easier to design a maze. It starts with a screen full of colour (the maze wall colour). You can move around the screen with keys L(eft), R(ight), U(p) and D(own). Switch to path drawing mode with P, switch to wall drawing mode with W and switch to move mode (where you can move around without changing the maze) with M. To set a bit to 1 in the bit map, the maze design program uses an OR operation with the appropriate mask and to set a bit to 0 in the bit map, an AND NOT operation is performed. These both appear at line 490. See Appendix 2 for further details on logical operators.

```
 10   MODE 1
 20   VDU 23,224,&FF,&FF,&FF,&FF,&FF,&FF,&FF,&FF
 30   VDU 19,2,11,0,0,0
 40   VDU 23;8202;0;0;0;
 50   DIM bitmap%(39),mask%(30)
 60   PROCsetmasks
 70   PROCconstructmaze
 80   MODE 7:PRINT "10000 DATA &";~bitmap%(0);
 90   FOR i=1 TO 19:PRINT ",&";~bitmap%(i);:NEXT
100   PRINT'"10010 DATA &";~bitmap%(20);
110   FOR i=21 TO 39:PRINT ",&";~bitmap%(i);:NEXT
120   PRINT:END
130
140   DEF PROCsetmasks
150     mask%(0)=1
160     FOR m=1 TO 30
170       mask%(m)=mask%(m-1)*2
180     NEXT m
190   ENDPROC

210   DEF PROCconstructmaze
220     COLOUR 129
230     VDU 28,0,30,39,0 : CLS : VDU 28,0,31,39,0
240     COLOUR 128
250     FOR y = 0 TO 39 : bitmap%(y)=&FFFFFFFF : NEXT
260     x=0:y=0:wall=FALSE:moving=TRUE
```

```
270      star$ = "*" + CHR$(8)
280      wall$ = CHR$(224) + CHR$(8)
290      path$ = " " + CHR$(8)
300      COLOUR 2:PRINT TAB(x,y);star$;:COLOUR 1
310      REPEAT
320        command$=GET$
330        PROCprocess(command$)
340      UNTIL command$="F"
350    ENDPROC

370    DEF PROCprocess(c$)
380      IF INSTR("LRUDWPM",c$)=0 THEN ENDPROC
390      IF bitmap%(x) AND mask%(y) THEN PRINT wall$;
400      IF c$="L" THEN IF x>0 THEN x=x-1
410      IF c$="R" THEN IF x<39 THEN x=x+1
420      IF c$="U" THEN IF y>0 THEN y=y-1
430      IF c$="D" THEN IF y<30 THEN y=y+1
440      IF c$="W" THEN wall=TRUE:moving=FALSE
450      IF c$="P" THEN wall=FALSE:moving=FALSE
460      IF c$="M" THEN moving=TRUE
470      COLOUR 2:PRINT TAB(x,y); star$;:COLOUR 1
480      IF moving THEN ENDPROC
490      IF wall THEN
            bitmap%(x)=bitmap%(x) OR mask%(y)
         ELSE bitmap%(x)=bitmap%(x) AND NOT mask%(y)
500    ENDPROC
```

A maze-running mouse

We now present a program that draws the same maze as before and controls a mouse as he runs about exploring the maze.

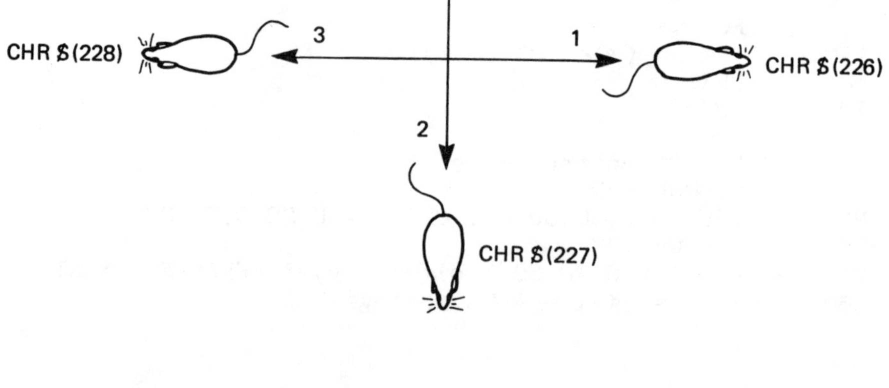

In applications like this, it is often necessary to design more than one user-defined character for the object being animated so as to be able to display the object in different orientations. In this case we have defined four versions of the mouse pointing in the four different directions in which he can move. These directions are numbered 0, 1, 2, and 3.

The mouse starts in the middle and its position and orientation are represented by its x-y coordinates ('mx%', 'my%') and a direction code (mdir%) which is set to 0, 1, 2 or 3.

The program makes the mouse explore the maze by repeatedly calling PROCmove and it is the definition of this procedure that determines the mouse's general behaviour. In the first version of the program (lines 470 to 510), at each step the mouse takes, this procedure counts in 'n%' the number of directions in which the mouse can move (excluding the direction from which it has just come). The possible directions are listed in the array 'possdir%'. The value of n% determines the action taken. If n% = 0, then it has reached a dead end and must turn back the way it came. If n% = 1 then it moves in that one direction, otherwise it makes a random choice from the directions available. Note the use of arrays 'xinc%' and 'yinc%' which are used to quickly convert direction codes (0, 1, 2 or 3) into x and y increments for a direction.

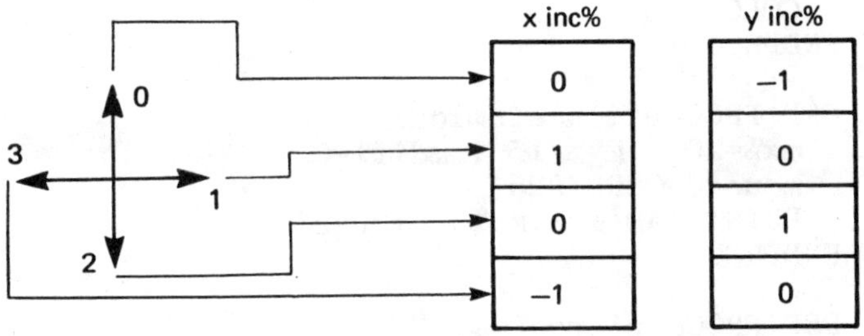

An attempt has been made to make the behaviour of the mouse more realistic by inserting time delays at appropriate points. For example it pauses when it has a choice of routes. The position and duration of such delays is worth experimenting with.

```
10   MODE 1
20   VDU 23,224,&FF,&FF,&FF,&FF,&FF,&FF,&FF,&FF
30   VDU 23,225,&10,&38,&38,&7C,&38,&10,&10,&10
40   VDU 23,226,0,8,&1E,&FF,&1E,8,0,0
50   VDU 23,227,&10,&10,&10,&38,&7C,&38,&38,&10
60   VDU 23,228,0,&10,&78,&FF,&78,&10,0,0
70   VDU 23;8202;0;0;0;
80   DIM bitmap%(39),mask%(30)
90   DIM xinc%(3), yinc%(3), possdir%(3)
```

```
100 xinc%(0)=0 : xinc%(1)=1 : xinc%(2)=0 : xinc%(3)=-1
110 yinc%(0)=-1 : yinc%(1)=0 : yinc%(2)=1 : yinc%(3)=0
120 PROCsetmasks
130 PROCdrawmaze
140 PROCputmouseinmiddle
150 PROCexplore
160 K=GET
170 END

180 DEF PROCsetmasks
190   mask%(0)=1
200   FOR m=1 TO 30
210     mask%(m)=mask%(m-1)*2
220   NEXT m
230 ENDPROC

240 DEF PROCdrawmaze
250   LOCAL x,y,path$,wall$
260   path$=" " : wall$=CHR$(224)
270   FOR x=0 TO 39:READ bitmap%(x):NEXT
280   COLOUR 1
290   FOR y = 0 TO 30
300     FOR x=0 TO 39
310       IF bitmap%(x) AND mask%(y) THEN PRINT wall$;
                                     ELSE PRINT path$;
320   NEXT:NEXT
330   COLOUR 3
340 ENDPROC

350 DEF PROCputmouseinmiddle
360   mx%=20 : my%=15 : mdir%=0
370   mouse$=CHR$(225)
380   PRINT TAB(mx%,my%); mouse$
390 ENDPROC

400 DEF PROCexplore
410   REPEAT
420     PROCmove
430   UNTIL my%=0
440 ENDPROC

450 DEF PROCmove
460 LOCAL fromdir%,newdir%,n%,d%
470   fromdir% = (mdir%+2) MOD 4
480   n% = 0
490   FOR d%=0 TO 3
500     IF d%<>fromdir% THEN
           IF    (bitmap%(mx%+xinc%(d%))
              AND   mask%(my%+yinc%(d%))) = 0
           THEN n%=n%+1 : possdir%(n%)=d%
510   NEXT d%
```

```
520      IF n%=0 THEN newdir%=fromdir%
         ELSEIF n%=1 THEN newdir%=possdir%(1)
         ELSE PROCdelay(20):newdir%=possdir%(RND(n%))
530      PROCturn(newdir%)
540      PROCstep
550    ENDPROC

560    DEF PROCturn(d%)
570      IF d%=mdir% THEN ENDPROC
580      mdir%=d% : mouse$=CHR$(225+d%)
590      PRINT TAB(mx%,my%);mouse$;
600      PROCdelay(10)
610    ENDPROC

620    DEF PROCstep
630    LOCAL nx%,ny%
640      nx%=mx%+xinc%(mdir%)
650      ny%=my%+yinc%(mdir%)
660      PRINT TAB(mx%,my%);" ";TAB(nx%,ny%);mouse$;
670      mx%=nx% : my%=ny%
680    ENDPROC

690    DEF PROCdelay(d)
700    LOCAL t
710      t=TIME+d
720      REPEAT : UNTIL TIME>t
730    ENDPROC

1000   DATA  ...  as before
```

The next photograph shows part of the maze in which the area explored by the mouse has been marked with 'droppings'.

A straightforward modification to the program was used to obtain this display.

```
74    VDU 23,229,0,0,0,&18,&18,0,0,0
76    dropping$ = CHR$(229)
          :
660     PRINT TAB(mx%,my%); dropping$;
              TAB(nx%,ny%); mouse$;
```

We have simply replaced the space used to delete the mouse when it is being moved by a character consisting of a white spot.

Marking dead ends

The only use made of the bit map so far is to mark the position of the walls of the maze. However, we could easily make the program extend the prohibited region, while the program was running, by adding ones to the bit map on paths that have been found to be dead ends. We recognise a dead end at line 520 (n% = 0) and can set a variable 'deadend%' to TRUE. When there is a choice of paths (n% > 1) we can set 'deadend%' to FALSE. We then modify PROCstep so that if 'deadend%' is TRUE, then the square being moved from is marked in the bit map as prohibited. Because 'deadend%' remains TRUE until a choice of paths is encountered, all squares down the dead end will be marked on the way out. We can also modify the program so that the 'droppings' are left only in the dead ends.

```
75    VDU 19,2,2,0,0,0
          :
520     IF n%=0 THEN deadend% = TRUE:newdir%=fromdir%
        ELSEIF n%=1 THEN newdir%=possdir%(1)
        ELSE deadend%=FALSE : PROCdelay(20):
             newdir%=possdir%(RND(n%))
          :
630   LOCAL nx%,ny%,dropcol%
635   IF deadend% THEN
         bitmap%(mx%) = bitmap%(mx%) OR mask%(my%) :
         dropcol%=2
      ELSE dropcol%=0
          :
660     COLOUR dropcol% : PRINT TAB(mx%,my%);dropping$;
661     COLOUR 3 :        PRINT TAB(nx%,ny%);mouse$;
```

The spot is now printed in COLOUR 2 to mark dead ends, or in COLOUR 0 elsewhere. Printing a character in COLOUR 0 (the background colour) has the same effect as printing a space.

Exercises

1 Experiment with time delays in the mouse program to make him appear hesitant in different places.

2 Make the mouse look down each direction that is recognised as a possibility when he is considering which way to go.

3 Add sound effects to the mouse program, for example a 'frustrated squeak' when it hits a dead end and an 'excited squeak' if it reaches the exit. (Perhaps the exit could be made more interesting by adding a a user-defined character to represent a piece of cheese.)

4 The mouse frequently returns to his 'den' in the centre after exploring part of the maze. Make him curl up and sleep in the corner of the den whenever this happens. (You will need to define one or two characters to represent a sleeping mouse.)

5 Change the mouse program so that the mouse is controlled from the keyboard with keys telling it to turn left, right, up or down. Record the time taken by a user at the keyboard to find the way out of the maze. (Note that we have defined PROCdelay in such a way that it does not alter the variable TIME.)

4.5 Animating line drawings

Up to now we have looked at animation using characters and this is the most commonly used mechanism in microcomputer animation. It has spawned a vast industry of computer games, and such character animation techniques must be the most commonly viewed computer image. In many applications, however, the use of character animation is inconvenient and we may wish to compose 'frames' of an animated sequence by drawing lines. This may be because we wish to animate a sequence that is mathematically defined (the cross section of a piston engine driving a crankshaft, for example), or because we want to animate using frames that have been drawn by hand on a graphics tablet. In either case the source material will be a list of coordinates and the most convenient tool to deal with a list of coordinates is the PLOT statement.

When film cartoons are made by hand, animated effects are created by drawing and photographing a large number of frames which are then displayed by a projector at a speed that gives the impression of continuous movement.

Computer animation packages now exist that help the cartoon artist to create animated films. Such a package typically includes programs that help the artist to design scenes from the film, using commands for interactively drawing lines and colouring regions. An animation package also includes programs for carrying out tasks such as 'in-betweening', a tedious and time-consuming job carried out by the 'in-betweeners' or junior artists of the cartoon film industry. Here, the main frames of a film are created on the screen by an artist and the hundreds of in-between frames that bridge the gaps between the main frames are generated by the animation package, each frame being photographed as it is created.

If you have the facilities for making films and wish to use your BBC micro for creating cartoons, then the full power of the graphics facilities can be used in drawing each frame of the film. The time taken to change the image on the screen is not critical as each frame of the film will be photographed only when the changes on the screen are complete. It can take many hours of program runs to create a few seconds of film in this way.

In this section we will look at techniques for animating line drawings. Although the graphics facilities on the BBC micro are extremely powerful and versatile, they are generally too slow for the animation of large objects drawn with line drawing and colour fill facilities. However, line drawings such as simple stick figures can be fairly successfully animated in real time.

Frames for animating a stick man

In order to animate a line drawing we need to draw a sequence of separate frames representing the object in different stages of movement. There are many ways in which these frames could be presented to the computer, but, in our illustrative example of line drawing animation, we shall present each frame in the form of a DATA statement containing a list of coordinates that describe a stick man. We shall animate the man so that he appears to walk across the screen. The frames that we shall use are displayed simultaneously in the first photograph.

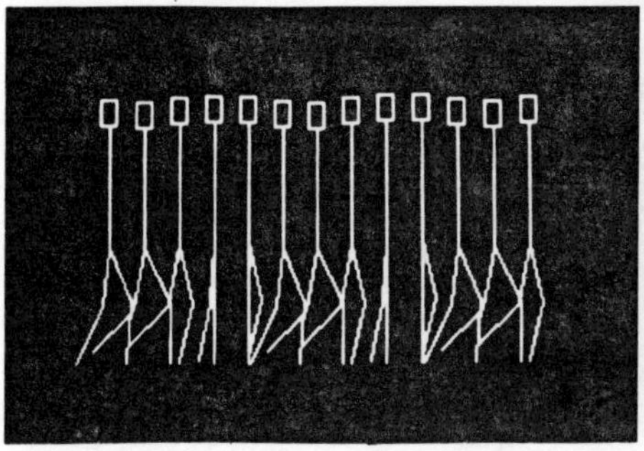

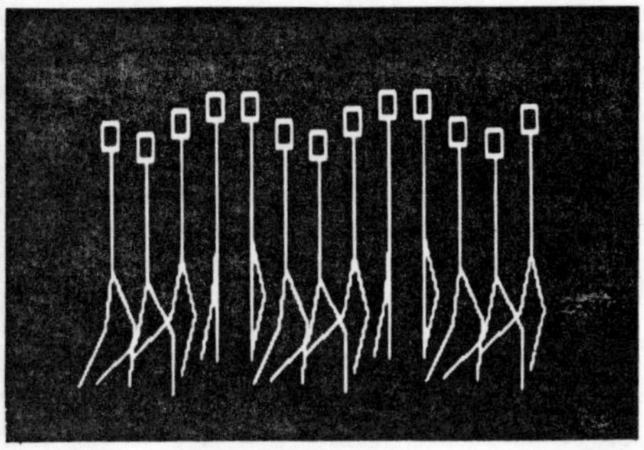

There are in fact only five different frames, which are displayed repeatedly. In the interests of brevity, we have omitted the arms. We will create the required walking effect by displaying and then deleting successive representations of the man, each one being displayed a little further across the screen than the previous one. Note that the vertical height of the head varies depending on the way in which the legs are bent. This effect is exaggerated in the second photograph and such exaggeration could be used to put more of a 'spring' in his step.

Representing frames for stick figures

The DATA statement for a frame will contain 9 values. The first is a y-increment to give the rise and fall of the body from frame to frame. The back is always in the same orientation and so it need not be specified for each frame. The next 8 values in a frame DATA statement represent four x-y pairs. These are

(1) the coordinates of the first knee relative to the top of the leg,

(2) the coordinates of the first foot relative to the first knee,

(3) the coordinates of the second knee relative to the top

of the leg, and

(4) the coordinates of the second foot relative to the second knee.

We use the following nomenclature:

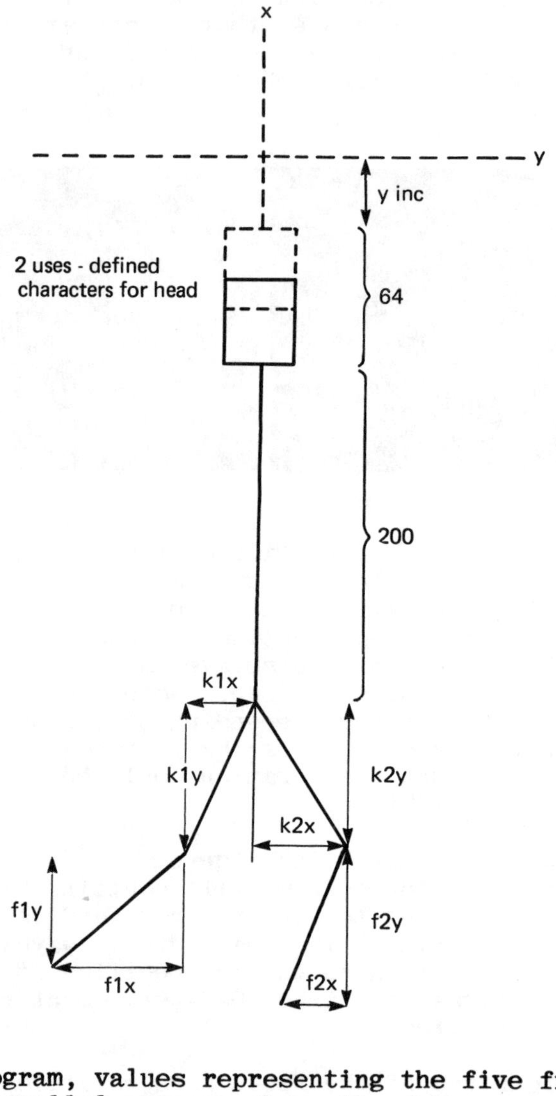

In the program, values representing the five frames will be stored in parallel arrays, where the frames are numbered 0 to 4. The 'yinc' values for a frame is not stored but is used to calculate a y-coordinate for starting to draw the frame and a y-coordinate for the top of the legs. It is these two values that are stored along with the other coordinates from the DATA statement for a frame. The head is drawn by printing two user-defined characters. We use the VDU 5 statement to arrange that characters are printed at the current graphics position.

Designing frames for stick figures

When calculating coordinates for stick figures, it is necessary to bear in mind that distances between joints should not vary from frame to frame. The possible knee coordinates relative to the top of the leg were constructed by marking the top of the leg on a piece of graph paper and using that point as the centre of a circle whose radius was the distance from the top of the leg to the knee.

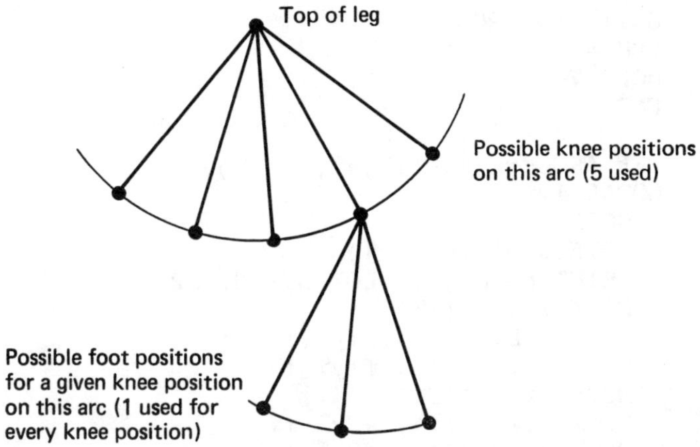

Associated with each knee position is a set of possible foot positions. These can also be obtained by drawing a circle of appropriate radius centred on the required knee position.

Animation by repeated deleting and drawing

Here is a first attempt at a program that makes the stick man walk across the screen. It works by repeatedly deleting and redrawing the man. Deletion is achieved by 'drawing' in the background colour. The flickering effect which is the main drawback of this program will be rectified shortly.

```
10   DIM k1x%(4), k1y%(4), f1x%(4), f1y%(4),
         k2x%(4), k2y%(4), f2x%(4), f2y%(4),
         hy%(4),  ly%(4)
20   y% = 600
30   FOR f=0 TO 4
40     READ yinc%, k1x%(f), k1y%(f), f1x%(f), f1y%(f),
                   k2x%(f), k2y%(f), f2x%(f), f2y%(f)
50     hy%(f)=y%+yinc% : ly%(f)=hy%(f)-264
60   NEXT f
```

```
70   VDU 23,224,0,0,0,0,&FF,&81,&81,&81
80   VDU 23,225,&81,&81,&81,&81,&81,&81,&81,&FF
90   head$=CHR$(224)+CHR$(8)+CHR$(10)+CHR$(225)
100  MODE 1 : VDU 5
110  x%=16 : xinc%=16
120  frame%=0
130  PROCdrawman(0,x%,0,3)

140  REPEAT
150    nx%=x%+xinc%
160    PROCdrawman(frame%,x%,0,0)
170    frame%=(frame%+1) MOD 5
180    PROCdrawman(frame%,nx%,0,3)
190    x%=nx%
200  UNTIL x%>1200
210  VDU 4
220  MODE 7
230  END

300  DEF PROCdrawman(f%,x%,l%,c%)
310  LOCAL ly%
320    GCOL l%,c%
330    MOVE x%-16,hy%(f%)
340    PRINT head$; : PLOT 0,-16,-32
350    DRAW x%,ly%(f%)
360    PLOT 1,k1x%(f%),k1y%(f%) :
       PLOT 1,f1x%(f%),f1y%(f%)
370    MOVE x%,ly%(f%)
380    PLOT 1,k2x%(f%),k2y%(f%) :
       PLOT 1,f2x%(f%),f2y%(f%)
390  ENDPROC

1000 DATA -10,40,-92,-8,-98,-10,-99,-50,-90
1010 DATA -14,50,-86,0,-100,-20,-98,-70,-68
1020 DATA -6,25,-97,-25,-97,-20,-98,-70,-68
1030 DATA 0,0,-100,0,-100,-8,-100,-20,-95
1040 DATA 0,25,-97,-25,-97,0,-100,0,-100
```

The man is drawn (or deleted) by PROCdrawman which accesses one of the sets of values stored in the 'frame arrays'. The first parameter of the procedure selects the frame to be drawn. The second parameter specifies the x-coordinate (the y-coordinate is stored as part of the frame). The remaining two parameters specify the logical plotting operation and colour code to be used in drawing the man. In this program, the colour is either 3 (for draw) or 0 (for delete). The logical plotting operation is always 0, but this parameter is needed in the next version of the program.

Image plane switching

The flickering effect exhibited by the above program was due to the fact that we could see the man being erased and redrawn. In order to eliminate this flickering effect, we need to arrange for the erasing and redrawing process to take place invisibly. To do this, we need to work with two separate 'image planes' and display one plane on the screen while the erasing and redrawing process is being carried out in the other plane.

In MODE 1, the colour of each pixel is coded as a two-bit number. We saw in Chapter 2 that, instead of treating the screen as a single image plane in which each pixel is one of four colours, we can treat it as two separate image planes in which each pixel is one of two colours. In each MODE 1 pixel, one of the two bits is taken to represent the colour of a pixel in one plane and the other bit is taken to represent the colour of the corresponding pixel in the other plane. The alternative significance of each two-bit colour code is given by the following table:

Single image plane		Two separate image planes	
colour code	bit pattern	plane 1	plane 2
0	00	0	0
1	01	1	0
2	10	0	1
3	11	1	1

To switch between planes 1 and 2, we use VDU 19 statements to associate different combinations of actual colours with our four colour codes. For example, if we want 0 to be the background colour code and 1 to be the foreground colour code in each of planes 1 and 2, then we can selectively display one of the two planes by selecting one of the two actual colour combinations given in the following table:

Colour code	Actual colour settings	
	plane 1 displayed plane 2 hidden	plane 2 displayed plane 1 hidden
0	background	background
1	foreground	background
2	background	foreground
3	foreground	foreground

If we are using the same background and foreground colours in plane 1 as in plane 2, colour code 0 is always set to the background colour and colour code 3 is always set to the foreground. If the background colour is black and the foreground colour is white, then the colour codes 0 and 3 are correctly initialised in MODE 1. To switch plane 1 on and plane 2 off, we need only use:

```
VDU 19, 1,7, 0,0,0
VDU 19, 2,0, 0,0,0
```

and to switch plane 1 off and plane 2 on, we use

```
VDU 19, 1,0, 0,0,0
VDU 19, 2,7, 0,0,0
```

A new shape can be plotted in plane 1 by preceding the plotting instructions by

```
GCOL 1,1
```

A shape can be erased from plane 1 by replotting it after

```
GCOL 2,2
```

(see Chapter 2). Similarly, a shape can plotted in plane 2 by preceding the plotting instructions by

```
GCOL 1,2
```

and erased by redrawing the shape after

```
GCOL 2,1
```

The following is an outline of how we use the above technique to conceal the deleting and redrawing process while an object is being moved about the screen:

```
Set x,y to the initial position of the object
Switch plane 1 on, plane 2 off
Draw first frame in plane 1

REPEAT
   Calculate newx,newy
   Draw next frame at newx,newy in off plane
   Switch planes
   Erase frame at position x,y in plane that is now off
   x=newx : y=newy
UNTIL final position reached
```

The next program fills in the details needed to make our man walk across the screen. Note that the speed at which the man walks can be varied by changing the x-increment (xinc%) between frames. (For very fast or slow motion, it may be necessary to change the stride length in the 5 basic frames used.) An alternative way of slowing him down is, of course, to insert a delay loop.

```
        .
        .
        .
110    x%=16 : xinc%=16
120    frame%=0
130    PROCswitchon(1)
140    PROCdrawman(0,x%,1,on%)
150    REPEAT
160      nx%=x%+xinc% : nf% = (frame%+1) MOD 5
170      PROCdrawman(nf%,nx%,1,off%)
                  : REM hidden draw in new position
180      PROCswitchon(off%)
190      PROCdrawman(frame%,x%,2,on%)
                  : REM hidden delete in off frame!
200      x% = nx% : frame% = nf%
210    UNTIL x%>1200
220    VDU 4
230    k=GET : MODE 7
240    END

300    DEF PROCdrawman(f%,x%,l%,c%)
          .
          .
        as before
          .
          .
390    ENDPROC

400    DEF PROCswitchon(screen%)
410      on% = screen% : off% = 3-on%
420      VDU 19, on%, 7, 0,0,0
430      VDU 19, off%,0, 0,0,0
440    ENDPROC
          .
          .
          .
```

Exercises

1 Extend The DATA statements used to represent the frames for our stick man so that arm positions can be specified. Extend PROCdrawman accordingly.

2 Add feet to the stick man.

3 Multiply The y-increment values by a 'bounce factor' and experiment with the effects obtained.

4 Give the man a dog on a lead.

5 Design a set of frames for a stick-horse and make it walk, trot or gallop across the screen.

4.6 Palette changing

The 'palette' of actual colours associated with the colour codes for a mode can be changed instantaneously with the VDU 19 statement and we have already used this statement in several programs in this chapter as well as in Chapter 2. In 'The BBC Micro Book' we demonstrated how palette changing could be used to animate, spinning disks, for example. We finish the present chapter with a further demonstration of the use of this technique to create the illusion of movement. We shall use the same stick man as we used in the last section, but this time we shall create an army of stick men marching across the screen. To produce this effect, we need to have available a colour for each different frame as well as a background colour. In this case, we need at least six colours and we must therefore run the program in MODE 2. (This causes a slight change in the shape of the man because of the different resolution.)

The program starts by setting colours 0 to 5 to black, selecting colour 5 as the background colour (GCOL 0, 133) and clearing the screen. The program then cycles frames 0 to 4 as before, drawing them at success positions on the screen, but this time frame 0 is drawn in colour 0, frame 1 in colour 1 and so on. At this stage the men are invisible. The animation effect is now created by cycling through the colours 0 to 4, at each step using VDU 19 statements to switch the previous colour to black and the next colour to white. This creates the impression that a succession of men is continually marching across the screen.

```
      :
      :
 70   VDU 23,224,0,0,0,0,&F,9,9,9
 80   VDU 23,225,9,9,9,9,9,9,9,&F
 90   head$=CHR$(224)+CHR$(8)+CHR$(10)+CHR$(225)
100   MODE 2 : VDU 5
110   x%=16 : xinc%=48
120   FOR c=0 TO 5:VDU 19,c,0,0,0,0:NEXT
130   GCOL 0,133 : CLG

140   frame%=0
150   REPEAT
160     PROCdrawman(frame%,x%,0,frame%)
170     frame%=(frame%+1) MOD 5
180     x%=x%+xinc%
190   UNTIL x%>1220
```

```
200   frame%=0
210   REPEAT
220     nf%=(frame%+1) MOD 5
230     VDU 19,frame%,0,0,0,0
240     VDU 19,nf%,7,0,0,0
250     PROCdelay(10)
260     frame%=nf%
270   UNTIL INKEY$(0)=" "
280   VDU 4 : K=GET : MODE 7 : END

300   DEF PROCdrawman(f%,x%,l%,c%)
        :
     as before
        :
390   ENDPROC

400   DEF PROCdelay(d)
410   LOCAL t
420     t=TIME+d
430     REPEAT : UNTIL TIME>t
440   ENDPROC

        :
   DATA as before
        :
```

Exercises

1 Create the effect of a bouncing ball by drawing a number of balls in different vertical positions (non-overlapping) and in different colours, and then using palette changing.

2 Create the effect of a rotating sphere by first drawing a circle and then drawing lines of longitude in different colours. Then use palette changing to reveal each line of longitude in turn.

Chapter 5 Advanced uses of sound

In this chapter we look at two of the more advanced uses of the SOUND statement. We first of all consider how to synchronise the playing of two and three part melodies. This is a sequential processing problem and similar problems often occur in computer science, for example, in operating systems.

We then look at the intriguing business of getting the computer to generate or compose music. There are two aspects to this. First of all we can get the computer to imitate music of a particular style by supplying it with a sufficient number of examples of tunes in the style that we require to mimic. Secondly we can get the computer to compose its own original music, by using a constrained random number generator. Both of these methods will provide pleasing results if sufficient thought is put into the programming techniques.

5.1 Playing a two-voice melody

Although careful use of the ENVELOPE statement can produce moderately pleasing effects with a single voice (single SOUND statement), it is always obvious that the sound is generated by a fairly basic synthesiser. A lot of the resulting musical inadequacies can be overcome by using 2 or 3 voices or sound channels simultaneously. Before we can do this there are queuing and synchronisation problems that have to be overcome.

Synchronisation of two voices

Consider playing melodies simultaneously from parallel arrays or separate data streams containing, for each melody line, a pitch and duration value. We could fetch elements alternately from each melody array and send them alternately to two sound channels. A queuing problem arises whenever notes of different durations appear at corresponding points in each melody line - the usual situation in musical arrangements. To start with we'll consider the problem with 2 voices or channels. The following example should make things clear. A sequence of 4 minims is to be initiated in one channel at the same time as a series of quavers in the other channel:

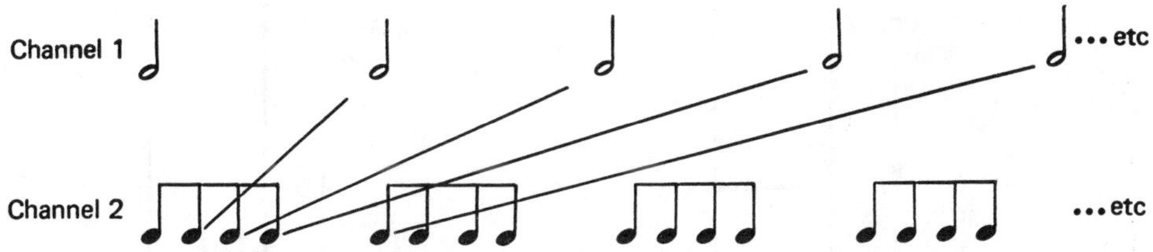

We could attempt to play the melodies by fetching a note from the channel 1 data stream or array and sending it to the channel 1 queue. We then fetch a note from the channel 2 data stream and send it to the channel 2 queue etc. (By 'send' we mean execute a SOUND statement.) This approach would be perfectly satisfactory if there were a limitless queue associated with each channel. However a channel queue can only hold a maximum of 5 requests.

By sending notes alternately to each channel, we have created the correspondence shown by the sloping lines. The program will be held up when it attempts to send the seventh minim to the channel 1 queue. The first minim will still be sounding and the next five have filled the queue. There are also five notes on the channel 2 queue but these are shorter and will be dealt with more frequently than the channel 1 notes. When the first minim on channel 1 has been played, four notes on channel 2 will have finished, leaving only two notes in the queue. The second minim on channel 1 now starts to play, making room for the seventh minim in the queue. This enables one further quaver to be added to the channel 2 queue before the program is again held up on attempting to add the eighth minim to the channel 1 queue. Thus while the second minim is being played on channel 1, only three quavers are available to be played on channel 2.

To solve this problem, we must arrange in this particular case to execute SOUND statements for channel 2 more frequently than for channel 1. Once the SOUND statement for the first note on channel 1 has been obeyed, no further channel 1 SOUND statements need be obeyed until SOUND statements have been obeyed for the first four notes on channel 2. In general, we must keep the total duration of notes for which channel 1 SOUND statements have been executed approximately equal to the total duration of notes for which channel 2 SOUND statements have been executed.

One way to solve the problem is to merge the voices into one DATA stream that contains channel numbers as well as pitch and duration values. This, however, makes the problem of transposition from the musical score to the DATA statement horrendous. The complexity of the synchronisation task has to be handled in the manual transposition process rather than in the program.

One simple way to achieve synchronisation between two or more voices is to keep a 'clock' running for each voice of the melody as shown.

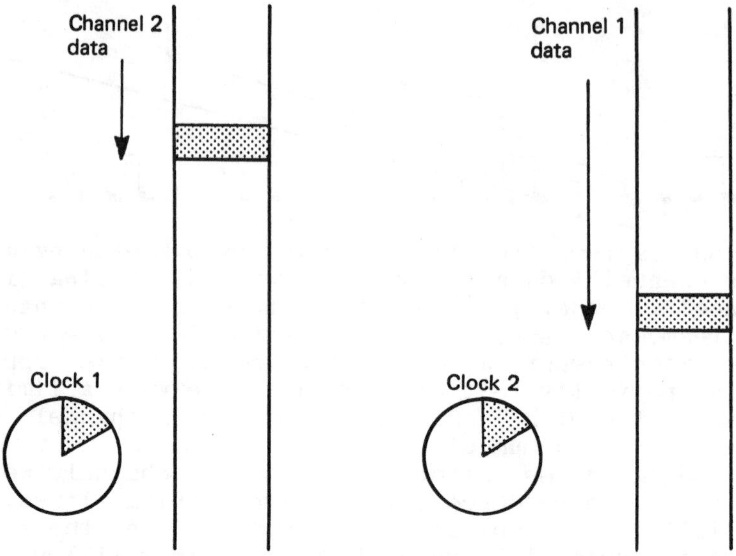

In general the current note for each channel will be in a different position in the data streams. The clocks will tend to show equal elapsed times. Each time a SOUND statement is obeyed, the duration of the note is added to the clock associated with that channel. At each step we must obey a SOUND statement for the channel whose clock shows the least elapsed time. We require to repeat the following operation:

```
IF clock1 > clock2 THEN SOUND statement for channel 2

                   ELSE SOUND statement for channel 1
```

The program then selects one out of two alternative courses of action and this ensures that the channels free run and are not subject to interference from each other. Effectively we have removed the artificial connection in the parallel data streams between notes in different channels that have different duration values.

An alternative method of playing notes of a two-voice melody from separate data streams is to use the function ADVAL to test the channel queue status. For example, the expression 'ADVAL(-6)' has a value indicating the number of empty places on the channel 1 queue (-7 for channel 2 and -8 for channel 3). Thus, we could use:

```
IF ADVAL(-6)>0 AND voice 1 not yet finished THEN
                        SOUND statement for channel 1
IF ADVAL(-7)>0 AND voice 2 not yet finished THEN
                        SOUND statement for channel 2
```

This ensures that no SOUND statement is obeyed if a channel queue is full. The end effect is exactly the same as that of the clock algorithm. Using ADVAL, a separate test is needed to check whether a voice has finished, whereas with the clock method this possibility can be dealt with by setting the clock to a large value when the last SOUND statement for that voice is obeyed. The clock algorithm also makes it easy to incorporate a common musical requirement - emphasis of the first note in every bar. Here the state of a clock could be used to recognise the first note of a bar.

Transposing
Another tedious task to be overcome before we start getting the machine to play arrangements is transposing from a musical score to a set of pitch numbers and associated notation. Transposing directly from the black dots to pitch numbers and durations in 1/20ths of a second can be tedious and error prone. You can write a graphics 'picking and dragging' program to input the music onto a screen stave, and this is a commonly adopted approach, but we have not space for that. Instead we shall adopt a character convention, and list the music in DATA statements using the following tables.

code	musical convention	duration (for metronome 150)	
t	1/32	1	DEMISEMIQUAVER
s	1/16	2	SEMIQUAVER
ds	dotted 1/16	3	
e	1/8	4	QUAVER
de	dotted 1/8	6	
q	1/4	8	CROTCHET
dq	dotted 1/4	12	
h	1/2	16	MINIM
dh	dotted 1/2	24	DOTTED MINIM
w	whole	32	SEMIBREVE

Remember that there are notes that cannot be accurately represented at this tempo. For example a dotted 1/32 is 1.5 (only 1 or 2 can be used as a duration parameter in a SOUND statement). Similarly a 1/16 triplet is 4/3 per note, an 1/8 triplet 8/3 per note and a 1/4 triplet 16/3 per note.

Pitch values are represented using the convention:

pitch values		pitch number
C	(C below middle C)	5
C'	(middle C)	53
C''	(C above middle C)	101
C'''		149
C''''		197
C'#	(middle C sharp)	57
C'b	(middle C flat)	49
R	rest	255

We do not cater for a key signature, but insert sharps and flats explicitly.

The character codes in the DATA statements will be converted into pitch and duration codes by the program. In all our programs for playing two or three part music, we shall use two two-dimensional arrays to hold up to three voices for an arrangement. These can be pictured as:

	pitch values for voice 1
pitch	pitch values for voice 2
	pitch values for voice 3

	duration values for voice 1
duration	duration values for voice 2
	duration values for voice 3

The first program uses only the first two rows of these arrays. There are also three one-dimensional arrays used to record the number of notes in each voice, a count of the notes SOUNDed for each voice and the 'clock' recording the total duration of the notes SOUNDed for each voice.

A two-voice Bach minuet

The next program is a complete program that can be used to play two voices of a melody where the two voices are supplied separately in DATA statements using the above notation. The data in this case is a two-voice Bach minuet.

```
10    ENVELOPE 1,1,0,0,0,0,0,0,126,-4,0,-63,126,100
20    ENVELOPE 2,1,0,0,0,0,0,0,126,-4,0,-63,126,100
30    ENVELOPE 3,1,0,0,0,0,0,0,126,-4,0,-63,126,100
40    DIM pitch(3,100), duration(3,100), noofnotes(3),
        nextnote(3), clock(3)
50    tempo=1
60    PROCinitialise(1)
70    PROCinitialise(2)
80    PROCplaytwovoices
90    END

200   DEF PROCinitialise(voice)
210   LOCAL note,pitch$,duration$,dur$,dur,
          notename$,position,prime$,octave
220     READ noofnotes(voice)
230     FOR note = 1 TO noofnotes(voice)
240       READ pitch$, duration$
250       dur$=RIGHT$(duration$,1)
255       dur =INSTR("tseqhw",dur$)
260       duration(voice,note)=2^(dur-1)*tempo
270       IF INSTR(duration$,"d") THEN
             duration(voice,note) =
                                 duration(voice,note)*3/2
280       notename$=LEFT$(pitch$,1)
290       position=INSTR("C-D-EF-G-A-BR",notename$)
300       IF position=13 THEN pitch(voice,note)=255
          ELSE pitch(voice,note)=1+4*position
310       IF RIGHT$(pitch$,1) = "#" THEN
             pitch(voice,note) = pitch(voice,note) + 4
320       IF RIGHT$(pitch$,1) = "b" THEN
             pitch(voice,note) = pitch(voice,note) - 4
330  X see below   prime$ = "'" : octave = 0
340       FOR j=2 TO LEN(pitch$)
350         IF MID$(pitch$,j,1) = prime$
                                THEN octave = octave +1
360       NEXT j
370       pitch(voice,note) = pitch(voice,note)+octave*48
380     NEXT note
390   ENDPROC

400   DEF PROCplaytwovoices
410     nextnote(1)=0 : nextnote(2)=0
420     clock(1)=0 : clock(2)=0
430     finished=0
440     SOUND &101,0,0,8 : SOUND &102,0,0,8
450     REPEAT
460       IF clock(1) > clock(2) THEN PROCsound(2)
                                  ELSE PROCsound(1)
470     UNTIL finished=2
480    ENDPROC
```

Repl. 330 IF INSTR(Pitch$,"<") THEN octave = -1: GOTO 370
ELSE Prime$="'": octave =0

```
 600   DEF PROCsound(voice)
 610   LOCAL n,envelope
 620     nextnote(voice)=nextnote(voice)+1
 630     n=nextnote(voice)
 640     clock(voice)=clock(voice)+duration(voice,n)
 650     IF pitch(voice,n)=255 THEN envelope=0
                                  ELSE envelope=voice
 660     SOUND voice,envelope,pitch(voice,n),
                                      duration(voice,n)
 670     IF n=noofnotes(voice) THEN
            finished=finished+1:clock(voice)=2000000
 680   ENDPROC

 700   DEF PROCround(leader,follower,delay)
 710   LOCAL l,f
 720     pitch(follower,1)=255:duration(follower,1)=delay
 730     f = 1
 740     FOR l=1 TO noofnotes(leader)
 750       f = f + 1
 760       pitch(follower,f)=pitch(leader,l)
 770       duration(follower,f)=duration(leader,l)
 780     NEXT l
 790     noofnotes(follower)=f
 800   ENDPROC
1000   DATA 74, D'',q,G',e,A',e,B',e,C'',e,D'',q,G',e,
            R,e,G',e,R,e,E'',q
1010   DATA C'',e,D'',e,E'',e,F''#,e,G'',q,G',e,R,e,
            G',e,R,e,C'',q,D'',e
1020   DATA C'',e,B',e,A',e,B',q,C'',e,B',e,A',e,G',e,
            F'#,q,G',e,A',e,B',e
1030   DATA G',e,B',q,A',h,D'',q,G',e,A',e,B',e,C'',e,
            D'',q,G',e,R,e,G',e
1040   DATA R,e,E'',q,C'',e,D'',e,E'',e,F''#,e,G'',q,
            G',e,R,e,G',e,R,e
1050   DATA C'',q,D'',e,C'',e,B',e,A',e,B',q,C'',e,
            B',e,A',e,G',e,A',q
1060   DATA B',e,A',e,G',e,F'#,e,G',h,G,q
1070   DATA 37, B,h,A,q,B,dh,C',dh,B,dh,A,dh,G,dh,D',e,
            R,e,B,q,G,q,D',e,R,e
1080   DATA D',e,C',e,B,e,A,e,B,h,A,q,G,q,B,q,G,q,C',dh,
            B,e,R,e,C',e,B,e,A,e,G,e
1090   DATA A,h,F',q,G',h,B',q,C'',q,D'',q,D',q,G',dh
```

There is one further point to note in the above program. We have started PROCplaytwovoices with statements that play two synchronised rests, one on each of the two channels that are being used. By the time that these rests have finished being 'played', the program will have started to obey SOUND statements for the two voices and further use of synchronisation parameters is rendered unnecessary by the 100% timing accuracy of the sound generator. Provided that our two voices start in step, they will remain in step.

5.2 Simple canons or rounds

You can arrange the voices yourself if you have sufficient musical knowledge, but there are many compositions that will produce pleasing results on your micro. One particular intriguing musical form that is easy to transpose into a number of voices (because the second and third voices are derivable from the theme) is the canon.

The simplest and most familiar form of canon is the round. 'Frere Jacques' is a common example. A theme (called the initiating voice or leader) enters. The second voice (identical to the theme in the case of a round) enters after a time interval. The round is of course written in such a way that it harmonises with itself. Thus the theme performs two functions, firstly as a melody in its own right and secondly as a harmony or counterpoint to itself.

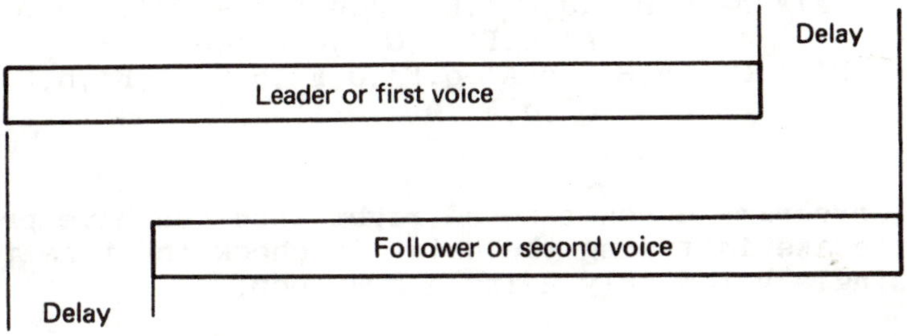

Now the follower is identical to the leader in the case of a round. In canons in general, it is mathematically derivable from it. Thus to play two or more voices only one theme need be transposed into a program.

A two-voice round - Frere Jacques

We can easily modify the above program to play a round. The next program plays 'Frere Jacques' as a two voice round with a two-bar delay. The procedure PROCround produces the two rows of our arrays necessary to play a round on two channels. In this procedure we effectively displace the follower by the delay, where the delay is specified to the procedure in multiples of the smallest possible note (𝅘𝅥𝅯).

```
10   ENVELOPE 1,1,0,0,0,0,0,0,63,10,0,-63,63,110
20   ENVELOPE 2,1,0,0,0,0,0,0,126,-4,0,-63,126,100
30   ENVELOPE 3,1,0,0,0,0,0,0,126,-4,0,-63,126,100
40   DIM pitch(3,100), duration(3,100),
         noofnotes(3), nextnote(3), clock(3)
50   tempo=1
60   PROCinitialise(1)
70   PROCround(1,2,64)
80   PROCplaytwovoices
90   END
```

```
        .
        .
        .
   700  DEF PROCround(leader,follower,delay)
   710  LOCAL 1,f
   720    pitch(follower,1)=255:duration(follower,1)=delay
   730    f = 1
   740    FOR 1=1 TO noofnotes(leader)
   750      f = f + 1
   760      pitch(follower,f)=pitch(leader,1)
   770      duration(follower,f)=duration(leader,1)
   780    NEXT 1
   790    noofnotes(follower)=f
   800  ENDPROC

  1000  DATA 32, F',q,G',q,A',q,F',q,F',q,G',q,A',q,
                     F',q,A',q,B'b,q,C'',h
  1010  DATA A',q,B'b,q,C'',h,C'',e,D'',e,C'',e,B'b,e,
                     A',q,F',q,C'',e,D'',e
  1020  DATA C'',e,B'b,e,A',q,F',q,F',q,C',q,F',h,F',q,
                     C',q,F',h
```

If the program doesn't sound right then you have probably made a mistake in typing the data. To check the tune through play a single voice only using a FOR loop:

```
FOR note = 1 TO noofnotes
  SOUND 1,1, pitch(1,note), duration(1,note)
NEXT note
```

These three lines should replace the call of PROCplaytwovoices.

Contrasting ENVELOPES can be used to effect, and we leave you to experiment with these. Now the theme in the above program is rather banal and boring but it is necessary to verify that your program works before moving on to the serious stuff.

5.3 Synchronizing three (or more!) voices

Before moving on to more complex canons, we first present a procedure to synchronise music consisting of three separate voices. In the next program, we have replaced PROCplaytwovoices with PROCharmonise which can organise the playing of three voices. In fact it will organise the playing of any number of voices from one upwards as specified by its parameter. It could be used to play more than three voices if we had more than three musical sound channels available. Each execution of the REPEAT loop in this procedure picks out a channel that has fallen behind and issues a SOUND statement for that channel.

A three-voice round - Frere Jacques
The next program indicates the changes needed to arrange and play a three-voice round using the same DATA as before.

```
 10   ENVELOPE 1,1,0,0,0,0,0,0,63,10,0,-63,63,110
 20   ENVELOPE 2,1,0,0,0,0,0,0,126,-4,0,-63,126,100
 30   ENVELOPE 3,1,0,0,0,0,0,0,126,-4,0,-63,126,100
 40   DIM pitch(3,100), duration(3,100),
          noofnotes(3), nextnote(3), clock(3)
 50   tempo = 1
 60   PROCinitialise(1)
 70   PROCround(1,2,64)
 80   PROCround(2,3,64)
 90   PROCharmonise(3)
100   END
        :
400   DEF PROCharmonise(noofvoices)
410   LOCAL voice,slowest,sync
420     sync = (noofvoices-1)*&100
430     FOR voice=1 TO noofvoices
440       SOUND sync+voice,0,0,8
450       clock(voice)=0 : nextnote(voice)=0
460     NEXT voice
470     finished=0
480     REPEAT
490       slowest=1
500       FOR voice=1 TO noofvoices
510         IF clock(voice)<clock(slowest)
            THEN slowest=voice
520       NEXT voice
530       PROCsound(slowest)
540     UNTIL finished=noofvoices
550   ENDPROC
        :
```

5.4 Bach's 'Musical Offering'

J. S. Bach's amazing work 'The Musical Offering' contains a number of canons of different forms. The American mathematical philosopher Douglas Hofstader, said of the work 'All in all, the Musical Offering represents one of Bach's supreme accomplishments in counterpoint. It is itself one large intellectual fugue, in which many ideas and forms have been woven together, and in which playful double meanings and subtle allusions are commonplace. And it is a very beautiful creation of the human intellect which we can appreciate forever'.

Crab canons or canons in retrograde motion

One of the rarest forms of canon is the crab canon or canon in retrograde motion. It is a rare form presumably because it is so difficult to write. In a crab canon there is no delay, both themes enter simultaneously. The first voice plays the theme from the start and the second voice plays the same theme backwards from the end.

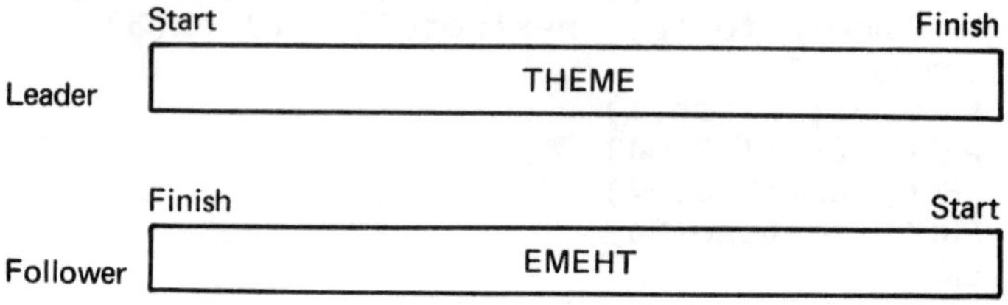

Bach's No. 9 canon from 'The Musical Offering' is a crab canon. It contains a theme with long duration notes followed by a counterpoint. The theme is played against the reverse of the counterpoint, followed by the counterpoint playing against the reverse of the theme. This structure is obvious when you listen to the music.

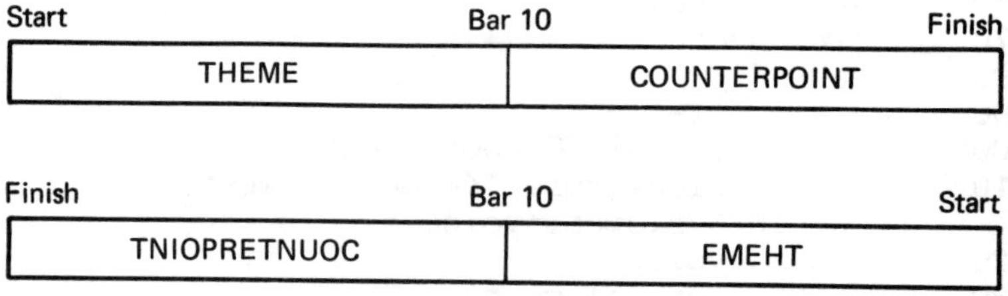

The next program includes a procedure to generate the arrays for a crab canon and includes the DATA for Bach's crab canon.

```
10    ENVELOPE 1,1,0,0,0,0,0,0,63,10,0,-63,63,110
20    ENVELOPE 2,1,0,0,0,0,0,0,126,-4,0,-63,126,100
30    ENVELOPE 3,1,0,0,0,0,0,0,126,-4,0,-63,126,100
40    DIM pitch(3,100), duration(3,100),
          noofnotes(3), nextnote(3), clock(3)
50    tempo=1
60    PROCinitialise(1)
70    PROCcrab(1,2)
80    PROCharmonise(2)
90    END
      :
```

```
700   DEF PROCcrab(voice,othervoice)
710   LOCAL n1,n2
720     n1=noofnotes(voice)
730     FOR n2=1 TO noofnotes(voice)
740       pitch(othervoice,n2)=pitch(voice,n1)
750       duration(othervoice,n2)=duration(voice,n1)
760       n1=n1-1
770     NEXT n2
780     noofnotes(othervoice)=noofnotes(voice)
790   ENDPROC

1000  DATA 90,C',h,E'b,h,G',h,A'b,h,B,h,R,q,G',h,F'#,h,
      F',h,E',h,E'b,h,D',q,D'b,q,C',q,B,q,G,q,C',q,
      F',q,E'b,h,D',h,C',h,E'b,h,G',e,F',e,G',e,C'',e,
      G',e,E'b,e,D',e,E'b,e,F',e,G',e,A',e,B',e,C'',e
1010  DATA E'b,e,F',e,G',e,A'b,e,D',e,E'b,e,F',e,G',e,
      F',e,E'b,e,D',e,E'b,e,F',e,G',e,A'b,e,B'b,e,
      A'b,e,G',e,F',e,G',e,A'b,e,B'b,e,C'',e,D''b,e,
      B'b,e,A'b,e,G',e,A',e,B',e,C'',e,D'',e,E''b,e,C'',e
1020  DATA B'b,e,A'b,e,B',e,C'',e,D'',e,E''b,e,F'',e,
      D'',e,G',e,D'',e,C'',e,D'',e,E''b,e,F'',e,E''b,e,
      D'',e,C'',e,B',e,C'',q,G',q,E'b,q,C',q
```

(a)

5.5 Mirror canons or canons in contrary motion

In this form the follower is derived from the leader by inverting the intervals in the leader. This means that when the leader ascends the follower descends by exactly the same interval. A familiar tune that will work as a mirror canon is 'Good King Wenceslas'. A time delay of half a bar is needed between the leader and the follower.

We now look at canon No. 4 from the 'Musical Offering'. This is a three-part arrangement, a variation of the 'Royal Theme' - the centre piece of the work - providing the upper voice. The higher canonic part enters first followed by its exact inversion half a bar later (delay = 8 notes):

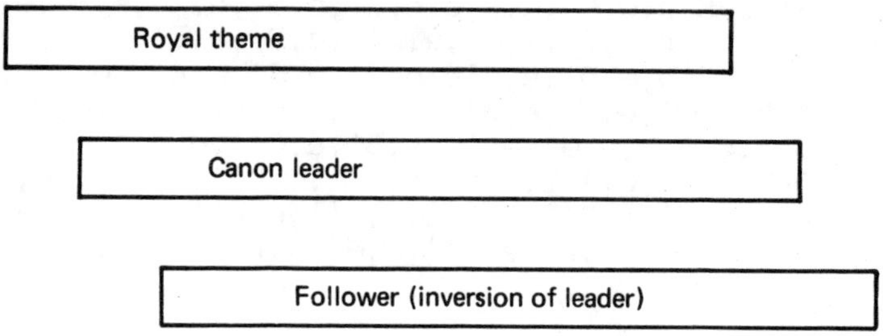

In a mirror canon there is a common note about which the reflection occurs. In this case it is Eb (the third degree of the C minor scale - the key of the work). Thus C in the leader becomes G in the follower and vice versa. If all that is a bit technical bear in mind that it is just a rule for deriving the first note of the follower. Once the first note of the follower is fixed we derive the remainder by inverting the intervals in the leader. The leader in this case starts as the sequence:

```
C  Bb  Ab  G  F ...
 \/  \/  \/\/
 T   T   S  T  ...
```

i.e. a descending sequence of tone, tone, semitone, tone,... The follower thus begins (in the octave below):

```
G  A  B  C  D ...
 \/\/\/\/
 T  T  S  T  ...
```

i.e. an <u>ascending</u> sequence of tone, tone, semitone, tone,... The next program contains the procedure required to generate the arrays for the inverted part from the data for the canon. It uses the data for the 'Royal Theme' together with the canon data.

```
     :
  50  tempo=2
  60  PROCinitialise(1)
  70  PROCinitialise(2)
  80  PROCinvert(2,3,-68,16*tempo)
  90  PROCharmonise(3)
 100  END
     :
 700  DEF PROCinvert(voice,othervoice,shift,delay)
 710  LOCAL n1,next1,n2,lastpitchon1,lastpitchon2
 720    IF delay >0 THEN pitch(othervoice,1)=255 :
                duration(othervoice,1)=delay : n2=1
        ELSE n2=0  :REM n2 counts notes in other voice.
 730    next1=1  :REM next1 is next note in voice.
 740    REPEAT  :REM to copy rests and find first note.
 750     IF pitch(voice,next1)=255 THEN
          n2=n2+1:pitch(othervoice,n2)=255:
          duration(othervoice,n2)=duration(voice,next1):
          next1 = next1+1
 760    UNTIL pitch(voice,next1)<>255
 770    n2=n2+1
 780    pitch(othervoice,n2)=pitch(voice,next1)+shift
 790    lastpitchon1=pitch(voice,next1)
 800    lastpitchon2=pitch(othervoice,n2)
 810    duration(othervoice,n2)=duration(voice,next1)
 820    next1=next1+1
 830    FOR n1=next1 TO noofnotes(voice)
 840      n2=n2+1
 850      nextinterval=-(pitch(voice,n1)-lastpitchon1)
 860      IF pitch(voice,n1)=255 THEN
             pitch(othervoice,n2)=255
          ELSE
             pitch(othervoice,n2) =
                     lastpitchon2+nextinterval :
             lastpitchon1=pitch(voice,n1) :
             lastpitchon2=pitch(othervoice,n2)
 870      duration(othervoice,n2)=duration(voice,n1)
 880    NEXT n1
 890    noofnotes(othervoice)=n2
 900  ENDPROC

1000  DATA 22, C'',q,E''b,q,G'',q,A''b,q,B',q,R,e,G'',e,
        F''#,q,F'',q,E'',q,E''b,dq,D'',e,D''b,e,C'',e,
        B',e,A',s,G',s,C'',e,F'',e,E'',e,E''b,e,D'',q
1010  DATA 46,R,s,C'',s,B'b,s,A'b,s,G',s,F',s,E'b,s,
        D',s,C',s,B,s,C',s,D',s,E'b,e,C',e,R,e,G',e,
        C'',s,D'',s,C'',s,B'b,s,A',s,A,s,G,s,A,s,B,e,
        G',de,G,s,A,s,B,s,C',s,D',s,E'b,s,D',s,C',e,
        D',e,E'b,e,Ab,e,G,s,D',s,C',s,B,s,R,s,F',s,
        E',s,D',s,C',dq
```

(c)

Exercises

1 Arrange for the voice synchronisation procedures to recognise the first note in a bar and emphasise it slightly by playing it with a different envelope. (Define envelope 4 for this purpose).

2 Animate a piece of music by drawing vertical lines at successive x positions, one line for each note as the note is played. The height of a line should be proportional to the pitch of the corresponding note.

3 Animate a piece of music by displaying the notes on a musical stave as they are played.

4 Transpose 'Good King Wenceslas' into our musical notation and play it as a mirror canon as suggested in the text.

5 Modify PROCharmonise to handle sound channels numbered from zero upwards. Write a procedure that generates, from the voice 1 data, a set of pitch and duration values for playing a 'drumbeat' on Channel 0. (There is room in our arrays for these - the zero subscripts were not used.) You can experiment with different rules for generating the drumbeat. For example, you might have a drumbeat only at the start of each bar, or every time the start of a note on voice 1 coincides with the natural 'beat' of the music.

5.6 Automatic composition

Music has been called 'a compromise between chaos and monotony'. The next two programs provide two contrasting examples. The first is an example of 'chaos' and the second represents structured monotony. The first program selects a note or pitch, channel, envelope and duration entirely at random.

```
 10  ENVELOPE 1,1, 0,0,0,0,0,0,
              126,-4,0,-63,126,100
 20  ENVELOPE 2,1, 0,0,0,0,0,0,
              63,10,0,-63,63,110
 30  ENVELOPE 3,1, 0,0,0,0,0,0,
              126,-8,0,-10,126,50

 40  FOR note=1 TO RND(100)
 50    channel = RND(3)
 60    envelope = RND(3)
 70    pitch = RND(256)-1
 80    duration=RND(32)
 90    SOUND channel,envelope,pitch,duration
100  NEXT note
```

The second program produces a monotonous sequence, the nature of which should be clear from a reading of the program.

```
 10  ENVELOPE 1,1, 0,0,0,0,0,0,
              126,-4,0,-63,126,100
 20  ENVELOPE 2,1, 0,0,0,0,0,0,
              63,10,0,-63,63,110
 30  ENVELOPE 3,1, 0,0,0,0,0,0,
              126,-8,0,-10,126,50

 40  FOR note = 1 TO 20
 50    SOUND 1,1,53,8
 60  NEXT note
 70  key=GET
 80  FOR pitch=53 TO 101 STEP 4
 90    SOUND 1,1,pitch,8
100  NEXT pitch
110  key=GET
120  FOR phrase = 1 TO 10
130    SOUND 1,1,53,8
140    SOUND 1,1,69,8
150    SOUND 1,1,81,8
160    SOUND 1,1,101,8
170  NEXT phrase
```

In this section, we explore ways of getting the BBC micro to compose its own music. In order for a computer to compose interesting music, there must be some degree of randomness involved, otherwise the music produced would be monotonous. But the music must also satisfy certain rules that make it recognisable as music to the listener. Incidentally, the rules that make music acceptable vary from culture to culture and from period to period. For example, Oriental music sounds strange to Western ears and the music of Beethoven (18th to 19th century) would probably have shocked Palestrina (16th century). The ear needs educating in the rules that are prevalent at a particular period.

Random music is not necessarily unpleasant, particularly if the texture of the music is controlled. The next program illustrates this point and plays music selecting two random numbers to drive the pitch and duration in a SOUND statement. Superimposed on this basic method we have added three effects:

(1) An echo (Two SOUND statements referencing separate envelopes)

(2) Insertion of a glissando or slide (de rigueur in arcade games) at random instants, and

(3) Insertion of pitch distortion at random instants.

The net effect is not uninteresting. Note that the pitch distortion is inserted by changing the parameters in a single ENVELOPE statement. In this case we could have used two ENVELOPE statements with different parameters and selected, but the setting and resetting of ENVELOPE parameters (PROCpitchset and PROCpitchreset) is the general structure required for dynamically changing ENVELOPE parameters and back again in a playing loop.

```
 10  ENVELOPE 1,1, 0,0,0,0,0,0,
              126,-4,0,0,126,100
 20  ENVELOPE 2,1, 0,0,0,0,0,0,
              63,-4,0,0,63,50
 30  prevnote = 0
 40  FOR I = 1 TO 100
 50    note = RND(255)
 60    IF note MOD 11 = 0 THEN PROCslide(prevnote,note)
 70    IF note MOD 7 = 0 THEN PROCpitchset
 80    SOUND 1,1,note,RND(8)
 90    SOUND 1,2,note,RND(8)
100    prevnote = note
110    PROCpitchreset
120  NEXT
130  END
```

```
140  DEF PROCslide(old,new)
150    IF old>new THEN step = -1 ELSE step = 1
160    SOUND &1001,0,0,0
170    FOR i = old TO new STEP step
180      SOUND &1001,0,0,0
190      SOUND &11,1, i, 2
200      PROCpitchreset
210    NEXT
220  ENDPROC

230  DEF PROCpitchset
240    pi1 = 16:pi2 = -16: pi3 = 16
250    pn1 = 2: pn2 = 4:  pn3 = 2
260    ENVELOPE 1,1, pi1,pi2,pi3,pn1,pn2,pn3,
                     126,-4,0,0,126,100
270  ENDPROC

280  DEF PROCpitchreset
290    ENVELOPE 1,1, 0,0,0,0,0,0,
                     126,-4,0,0,126,100
300  ENDPROC
```

5.7 Generating rhythms

Rhythm is a very important component of music of all cultures. Indeed in some primitive cultures, music consists of rhythm and very little else. In this section, we shall examine ways of making a computer generate a rhythmic structure that is similar to that of a simple folk tune.

In music, rhythm is concerned with the grouping of notes into beats, of beats into bars, bars into phrases and so on. In the Oxford Companion to Music, the entry under 'phrase' states that any simple four-line hymn or folk-tune falls clearly into two halves or 'sentences'. Each sentence falls into two phrases and each phrase normally consists of four bars (although this is sometimes varied). We shall use this simple model for our first attempts at automatic composition.

To a computer scientist or linguist, the above description suggests the use of a 'generative grammar' to describe the structure of a piece of music. Such grammars are used extensively by computer scientists to describe the structure of programming languages. Such structures are, for example, reflected in the construction of a compiler. In this case, we might start with the rule

```
TUNE ::= SENTENCE SENTENCE
```

which we read as 'A tune consists of a sentence followed by another sentence'. ::= is a special symbol meaning 'consists of' or 'can be rewritten as'.

We could then go on to define

```
SENTENCE ::= PHRASE PHRASE
PHRASE   ::= BAR BAR BAR BAR
```

or we might decide that the last bar of a phrase should have a different structure from the other bars:

```
PHRASE ::= BAR1 BAR1 BAR1 BAR2
```

where a BAR2 will have a different definition from a BAR1. Rules like these are usually referred to as 'rewrite rules'. The left-hand side of the rule can be rewritten as the right-hand side.

A more complicated example of a musical grammar might start off with

```
PIECE ::= SONATA | RONDO | FUGUE
```

The sign '|' is read as 'or', thus the above rewrite rule states that a piece is either a sonata or a rondo or a fugue. The definition might continue with

```
SONATA ::= EXPOSITION DEVELOPMENT RECAPITULATION
```

Simple rewrite rules provide a concise notation for describing the structure of language or music, but they have many limitations and the system has to be 'augmented' for more advanced applications.

Returning to our simple folk-tune example, the structure of the rules constituting the grammar can be directly reflected in the structure of a BASIC program that generates a piece of music from the grammar. In the next program, the rule defining a tune has been transcribed directly into into a procedure that generates a tune.

```
DEF PROCtune               Corresponds to rule
  PROCsentence
  PROCsentence          TUNE ::= SENTENCE SENTENCE
ENDPROC
```

PROCsentence is defined similarly. These two procedures could have been combined into one, a tune being defined as four phrases, but it is always advisable to maintain a procedure structure that reflects the structure of the process being modelled. We may decide later that the first sentence in a tune should have a slightly different structure than the second. Defining a tune in terms of sentences and a sentence in terms of phrases will make it easier to incorporate changes like this.

PROCphrase is defined in a similar way. It makes three identical calls of PROCbar and then a fourth call of PROCbar to generate the last bar of the phrase. The type of bar to be generated has been indicated by a parameter.

```
DEF PROCphrase
LOCAL bar                          Corresponds to rule
  FOR bar=1 TO 3
    PROCbar(minnote)         PHRASE ::= BAR1 BAR1 BAR1 BAR2
  NEXT bar
  PROCbar(16)
ENDPROC
```

The parameter indicates the minimum duration permitted for the final note of the bar and we have created the last bar of a phrase (a BAR2) by supplying a different parameter, 16. This indicates that the bar generated by this call should have a final note of duration at least 16 time units, i.e. a minim. Forcing a phrase to end with a longish note gives an impression of rounding off the phrase. The first three bars of a phrase are allowed to terminate with the shortest permitted note available for the tune being composed. This value is called 'minnote' and is input to the program as a parameter. The value input determines the overall 'tempo' of the piece.

The 'grammar' of a bar will depend on the number of beats in a bar (another input parameter). For example, in 2/4 time, we could have

BAR1 ::= CROTCHETGROUP CROTCHETGROUP | MINIMGROUP

This means 'a bar can be a group of notes equivalent to a crotchet followed by another crotchet group, or a bar can consist of a group of notes equivalent to a minim.' We shall not allow note groupings to cut accross the 'beat' structure of the bar. We could define

CROTCHETGROUP ::= 

assuming a semiquaver as the minimum permitted note (duration = 2). For convenience, we insist that notes in a group all have the same duration. We do not permit

CROTCHETGROUP ::= 

A minim group is defined as

MINIMGROUP ::= 

Recall that we require a phrase to terminate with at least a minim. With two beats to the bar, this means

BAR2 ::= 

The complete grammar for 2/4 time is listed next. The whole process of generating a sequence of symbols (in this case notes of a certain duration) using rewrite rules can be viewed as a tree structure. Using choice where choice is available we could generate the tree shown below. This particular tree is just one of a large number that could be generated from the rewrite rules. The tree structure or hierarchy is reflected directly in the procedure hierarchy or structure.

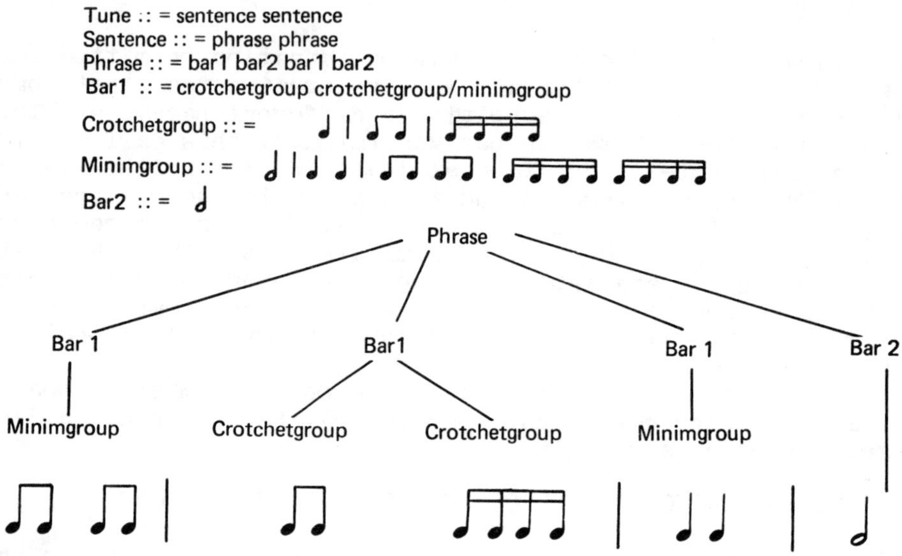

BAR1 and BAR2 would be defined slightly differently if we had three or four (or more) beats to the bar.

The definitions of BAR1 and BAR2 are implemented in a fairly ad hoc fashion in PROCbar in the program.

```
 10  ENVELOPE 1,1, 0,0,0,0,0,0,
              126,-8,0,-63,126,50
 20  ENVELOPE 2,1, 0,0,0,0,0,0,
              100,-8,0,-80,100,50
100  INPUT "Beats per bar",timesig
110  INPUT "Minimum note",minnote
120  PROCtune
130  END

200  DEF PROCtune
210    PROCsentence
220    PROCsentence
230  ENDPROC
```

```
240  DEF PROCsentence
250    PROCphrase
260    PROCphrase
270  ENDPROC

280  DEF PROCphrase
290  LOCAL bar
300    FOR bar=1 TO 3
310      PROCbar(minnote)
320    NEXT bar
330    PROCbar(16)
340  ENDPROC

350  DEF PROCbar(minfinish)
360    envelope = 1
370    beatsleft=timesig
380    REPEAT
390      PROCselectgroup
400      IF beatsleft=0
                        THEN PROCsubdividegroup(minfinish)
                        ELSE PROCsubdividegroup(minnote)
410      FOR note=1 TO nextgroup DIV duration
420        PROCplaynote
430      NEXT note
440    UNTIL beatsleft=0
450  ENDPROC

460  DEF PROCselectgroup
470  LOCAL g,timeleft
480    timeleft=beatsleft*8
490    IF beatsleft=1 OR timeleft=minfinish THEN
          nextgroup=timeleft:beatsleft=0:ENDPROC
500    REPEAT:g=RND(beatsleft)
510    UNTIL beatsleft-g=0 OR timeleft-g*8>=minfinish
520    nextgroup=g*8
530    beatsleft=beatsleft-g
540  ENDPROC

550  DEF PROCsubdividegroup(mindur)
560    IF nextgroup=mindur OR nextgroup MOD mindur<>0
       THEN duration=nextgroup:ENDPROC
570    REPEAT
580      duration=2RND(5)
590    UNTIL nextgroup MOD duration=0ANDduration>=mindur
600  ENDPROC

610  DEF PROCplaynote
620    pitch=53
630    SOUND 1,envelope,pitch,duration:envelope = 2
650  ENDPROC
```

PROCbar repeatedly chooses a group consisting of a random

number of whole notes that is less than or equal to the number of beats left to be played, subject to the constraint imposed by the 'minimum last note' parameter. Each group chosen is then split into an equal number of notes whose duration divides into the group chosen and whose duration is less than or equal to the minimum permitted duration. The notes of the group are then played (all on Middle C).

One further enhancement that assists the listener's perception of rhythm is to use a slightly louder envelope for the first note of a bar than is used for the remaining notes of the bar.

Listen to some of the output from this program and you will find that the 'sentence', phrase, bar and beat structure is usually fairly evident.

5.8 Generating pitch values

We now turn our attention to the pitch of the notes played in the tune so that we can impose a melodic sequence on the rhythmic structure.

Playing random notes from a scale

A particular piece of music (or at least a section of a piece of music) is usually confined to notes taken from a set of notes that are closely related to each other in some way. The set of notes, or 'scale', used contributes in a large way to the 'character' of the music. We can easily alter our 'Rhythm on Middle C' program so that it selects random notes from a particular scale. The next program indicates the modifications needed to do this.

```
 10  ENVELOPE 1,1, 0,0,0,0,0,0,
              126,-4,0,-63,126,100
 20  ENVELOPE 2,1, 0,0,0,0,0,0,
              100,-4,0,-80,100,80
 30  READ scalelength
 40  DIM scalenote(scalelength)
 50  FOR n=1 TO scalelength
 60    READ scalenote(n)
 70  NEXT
 80  DATA 4, 53,69,81,101

 90  keynote=scalenote(1)
100  INPUT "Beats per bar",timesig
110  INPUT "Minimum note",minnote
120  PROCtune
130  END

200  DEF PROCtune
210    PROCsentence(FALSE)
220    PROCsentence(TRUE)
230  ENDPROC
```

```
240  DEF PROCsentence(finalsent)
250    PROCphrase(FALSE)
260    PROCphrase(finalsent)
270  ENDPROC

280  DEF PROCphrase(finalph)
290  LOCAL bar
300    FOR bar=1 TO 3
310      PROCbar(minnote,FALSE)
320    NEXT bar
330    PROCbar(16,finalph)
340  ENDPROC

350  DEF PROCbar(minfinish,finalbar)
360    envelope = 1
370    beatsleft=timesig
380    REPEAT
390      PROCselectgroup
400      IF beatsleft=0
                      THEN PROCsubdividegroup(minfinish)
                      ELSE PROCsubdividegroup(minnote)
410      FOR note=1 TO nextgroup DIV duration
420        PROCplaynote(note=nextgroup DIV duration AND
                           beatsleft=0 AND finalbar)
430      NEXT note
440    UNTIL beatsleft=0
450  ENDPROC
         .
         .
         .
610  DEF PROCplaynote(finalnote)
620    IF finalnote THEN pitch=keynote
       ELSE pitch=scalenote(RND(scalelength))
630    SOUND 1,envelope,pitch,duration
640    envelope=2
650  ENDPROC
```

The DATA statement at line 80 defines the number of notes and the pitch values for the scale used, in this case a major arpeggio.

One further addition has been made to this program. A new parameter is passed to each of PROCsentence, PROCphrase and PROCbar to indicate whether it is the final example of that construction in the tune. This enables the program to recognise the last note of the tune and constrain it to fall on the keynote of the scale.

Try running the program with notes taken from the major arpeggio and you will obtain a moderately pleasing if rather monotonous effect. Then try some of the other scales listed here.

Scale	Interval sequence
major	8 8 4 8 8 8 4
diminished	4 8 4 8 4 8 4 8
blues	12 8 4 4 12 8
Hindu	8 8 4 8 4 8 8
whole tone	8 8 8 8 8 8
dorian minor	8 4 8 8 8 4 8
aeolian minor	8 4 8 8 4 8 8
harmonic minor	8 4 8 8 4 12 4
pentatonic	8 8 12 8 12

In subsequent sections, we shall use notes taken from the following extended major scale:

This is the scale of C major extended downwards by three notes to lower G and up one note to upper D.

First order probability distribution of notes

Once the set of notes (the key) on which a tune will be played has been determined, there are a number of further constraints that can be applied in order to make a tune mimic a particular style. In music of a particular style, certain notes and combinations of notes will be more common than others. It is fairly obvious that Mozart does not sound like Stravinsky and this difference can be quantified to a certain extent using the techniques now described.

One way of making our program select pitch values more systematically is to make it use probability distributions when selecting the pitch of a note to be played. The simplest (and least satisfactory) type of distribution that can be used is the first order probability distribution.

The table below shows the result of a 'first order analysis' of 9 simple well-known tunes taken from a child's recorder tutor (Baa Black Sheep, Bobby Shaftoe, etc.).

g	a	b	c	d	E	F	G	A	B	C	D
3.4	0.7	3.4	15.0	12.6	13.8	8.5	14.3	8.0	11.1	6.3	2.9

If we imagine all these tunes being played in C major, on the 12 notes from lower G to upper D, then the figures in the table give, as percentages, the relative frequency of occurrence of each note over the nine tunes analysed. Thus, 3.4% of the notes in these tunes were bottom G, 15% of the notes were Middle C and so on. (These percentages were part of the output produced by a program which is discussed later.)

We now explain how to generate a note so that the probability of getting a particular note matches its entry in the table. The tunes generated by doing this will not be much better than those obtained by choosing a random note from the scale, but the basic technique used is easily extended to deal with higher order probability distributions discussed next.

We first set up an array containing the above percentages. In order to select a note, we generate a random number in the range 0 to 100 and add up values from the array until the total exceeds the random number generated (see below). The number of percentages added determine the note from the scale that is selected.

(1)	(2)	(3)	(4)	(5)	(6)	(7)	(8)	(9)	(10)	(11)	(12)
3.4	0.7	3.4	15.0	12.6	13.8	8.5	14.3	8.0	11.1	6.3	2.9

rand=RND(1)*100 Say, for example, rand=43.5. Then the first 6 values in freq1 are added before we obtain a total that exceeds 43.5. This means that we play the 6th note in the scale.

pitch=scalenote(6)

This approach is implemented in the next program.

```
 10  ENVELOPE 1,1, 0,0,0,0,0,0,
              126,-4,0,-63,126,100
 20  ENVELOPE 2,1, 0,0,0,0,0,0,
              100,-4,0,-80,100,80
 30  READ scalelength
 40  DIM scalenote(scalelength)
 50  FOR n=1 TO scalelength
 60    READ scalenote(n)
 70  NEXT
 80  DATA 12, 33,41,49,53,61,69,73,81,89,97,101,109
 90  keynote=scalenote(4)
100  PROCsetupfreqtable1
110  INPUT "Beats per bar",timesig
120  INPUT "Minimum note",minnote
130  notesplayed=0
140  PROCtune
150  END
      :
```

```
  610 DEF PROCplaynote(finalnote)
  620   IF finalnote THEN pitch=keynote
                      ELSE PROCselectpitch1
  630   SOUND 1,envelope,pitch,duration
  640   notesplayed=notesplayed+1
  650   envelope=2
  660 ENDPROC

  670 DEF PROCsetupfreqtable1
  680 LOCAL lb1,l,n,fileno
  690   DIM freq1(12)
  700   FOR n=1 TO 12
  710     READ freq1(n)
  720   NEXT n
  730 ENDPROC

  740 DEF PROCselectpitch1
  750 LOCAL rand, n, sum
  760   rand=RND(1)*100
  770   n=0 : sum=0
  780   REPEAT
  790     n=n+1:sum=sum+freq1(n)
  800   UNTIL sum>=rand
  810   pitch=scalenote(n)
  820   lastnoteplayed=n
  830 ENDPROC
10010 DATA 3.4,  0.7, 3.4, 15.0, 12.6, 13.8,
           8.5, 14.3, 8.0, 11.1,  6.3,  2.9
```

Note sequences are much more important in composing melodies, and if we want to constrain the note sequences that are chosen by our program, we must consider higher order probabilities.

Second order probability distributions

The use of second order probability distributions makes the choice of a note depend on the preceding note.

The next table shows the second order distributions resulting from an analysis of our 9 simple tunes.

	g	a	b	c	d	E	F	G	A	B	C	D
g	42.9	0.0	0.0	28.6	14.3	7.1	0.0	7.1	0.0	0.0	0.0	0.0
a	0.0	0.0	66.7	0.0	33.3	0.0	0.0	0.0	0.0	0.0	0.0	0.0
b	21.4	0.0	7.1	50.0	21.4	0.0	0.0	0.0	0.0	0.0	0.0	0.0
c	0.0	0.0	12.7	40.0	14.5	18.2	10.9	3.6	0.0	0.0	0.0	0.0
d	7.7	0.0	7.7	26.9	28.8	13.5	9.6	5.8	0.0	0.0	0.0	0.0
E	0.0	3.5	0.0	17.5	26.3	21.1	14.0	17.5	0.0	0.0	0.0	0.0
F	0.0	2.9	0.0	0.0	20.0	45.7	8.6	22.9	0.0	0.0	0.0	0.0
G	0.0	0.0	0.0	3.5	1.8	15.8	21.1	22.8	31.6	0.0	1.8	1.8
A	0.0	0.0	0.0	0.0	0.0	0.0	3.0	24.2	18.2	48.5	0.0	6.1
B	0.0	0.0	0.0	0.0	0.0	0.0	0.0	13.0	13.0	43.5	23.9	6.5
C	0.0	0.0	0.0	0.0	0.0	3.8	0.0	3.8	3.8	30.8	42.3	15.4
D	0.0	0.0	0.0	0.0	0.0	0.0	0.0	33.3	16.7	8.3	25.0	16.7

One row in this table corresponds to one of our notes and the entries in a row give the percentage of occasions on which each of the other notes followed the note to which the row corresponds. For example, row 1 indicates that lower G is followed by another lower G on 42.9% of occasions, by Middle C on 28.6% of occasions, by D next to Middle C on 14.3% of occasions, by E on 7.1% of occasions and by upper G on 7.1% of occasions.

The modifications to the previous program needed to generate notes according to the second order probability distributions are presented in the next program.

```
      :
  100 PROCsetupfreqtable1
  101 PROCsetupfreqtable2
      :
  610 DEF PROCplaynote(finalnote)
  620   IF finalnote THEN pitch=keynote
        ELSE IF notesplayed=0 THEN PROCselectpitch1
                               ELSE PROCselectpitch2
      :
  840 DEF PROCsetupfreqtable2
  850 LOCAL l,n
  860   DIM freq2(12,12)
  870   FOR l=1 TO 12
  880     FOR n=1 TO 12
  890       READ freq2(l,n)
  900   NEXT:NEXT
  910 ENDPROC

  920 DEF PROCselectpitch2
  930 LOCAL rand, n, sum
  940   rand=RND(1)*100
  950   n=0 : sum=0
  960   REPEAT
  970     n=n+1 : sum=sum+freq2(lastnoteplayed,n)
  980   UNTIL sum>=rand
  990   pitch=scalenote(n)
 1000   lastbut1=lastnoteplayed : lastnoteplayed=n
 1010 ENDPROC

10010 DATA  3.4, 0.7,  3.4, 15.0, 12.6, 13.8,
            8.5, 14.3, 8.0, 11.1, 6.3, 2.9
20010 DATA 42.9, 0.0,  0.0, 28.6, 14.3,  7.1,
            0.0,  7.1, 0.0,  0.0, 0.0, 0.0
20020 DATA  0.0, 0.0, 66.7,  0.0, 33.3,  0.0,
            0.0,  0.0, 0.0,  0.0, 0.0, 0.0
          ... (second order probabilities)
```

The first note of the tune is generated using first order probabilities (there is no previous note on which to base its selection). From then on, a note is generated using the row of the second-order probability table that corresponds to the previous note played. This eliminates the occasional violent leaps in pitch that occurred with the previous version of the program. The second-order probabilities associated with such violent leaps are mostly 0. The use of second order probability thus encourages the program to use commonly acceptable pitch intervals between consecutive notes.

Third order probability distributions
If we want the program to use commonly used sequences of notes, we can move on to third order distributions where the probability of choosing a note will depend on the two previous notes played. The next table gives the results of a third order analysis of our 9 tunes.

Each possible sequence has a probability distribution associated with it and that distribution is used to choose the next note. Many of the rows in a complete version of this table would contain all zeros - if you consult the previous table, you will see that many combinations of two notes never occur.

The next program uses the first order distribution to choose its starting note, the second order distributions to choose the second note and from then on it uses the third order distributions.

```
       :
 100  PROCsetupfreqtable1
 101  PROCsetupfreqtable2
 102  PROCsetupfreqtable3
       :
 610  DEF PROCplaynote(finalnote)
 620    IF finalnote THEN pitch=keynote
        ELSE IF notesplayed=0 THEN PROCselectpitch1
        ELSE IF notesplayed=1 THEN PROCselectpitch2
                                ELSE PROCselectpitch3
       :
1020   DEF PROCsetupfreqtable3
1030   LOCAL lbl,l,n
1040     DIM freq3(12,12,12)
1050     REPEAT
1060       READ lbl,l
1070       FOR n=1 TO 12
1080         READ freq3(lbl,l,n)
1090       NEXT n
1100     UNTIL lbl=0
1110   ENDPROC
```

Previous two note numbers		frequency distributions of following notes											
1	1	0.0	0.0	0.0	33.3	33.3	16.7	0.0	16.7	0.0	0.0	0.0	0.0
1	4	0.0	0.0	33.3	33.3	0.0	33.3	0.0	0.0	0.0	0.0	0.0	0.0
1	5	0.0	0.0	0.0	100.0	0.0	0.0	0.0	0.0	0.0	0.0	0.0	0.0
1	6	0.0	0.0	0.0	100.0	0.0	0.0	0.0	0.0	0.0	0.0	0.0	0.0
1	8	0.0	0.0	0.0	0.0	0.0	0.0	0.0	0.0	100.0	0.0	0.0	0.0
2	3	0.0	0.0	50.0	50.0	0.0	0.0	0.0	0.0	0.0	0.0	0.0	0.0
2	5	0.0	0.0	0.0	100.0	0.0	0.0	0.0	0.0	0.0	0.0	0.0	0.0
3	1	66.7	0.0	0.0	33.3	0.0	0.0	0.0	0.0	0.0	0.0	0.0	0.0
3	3	0.0	0.0	0.0	100.0	0.0	0.0	0.0	0.0	0.0	0.0	0.0	0.0
3	4	0.0	0.0	0.0	50.0	16.7	16.7	16.7	0.0	0.0	0.0	0.0	0.0
3	5	33.3	0.0	33.3	0.0	0.0	0.0	33.3	0.0	0.0	0.0	0.0	0.0
4	3	28.6	0.0	0.0	42.9	28.6	0.0	0.0	0.0	0.0	0.0	0.0	0.0
4	4	0.0	0.0	5.0	50.0	10.0	15.0	15.0	5.0	0.0	0.0	0.0	0.0
4	5	37.5	0.0	0.0	0.0	25.0	25.0	12.5	0.0	0.0	0.0	0.0	0.0
4	6	0.0	20.0	0.0	20.0	0.0	0.0	30.0	30.0	0.0	0.0	0.0	0.0
4	7	0.0	16.7	0.0	0.0	33.3	50.0	0.0	0.0	0.0	0.0	0.0	0.0
4	8	0.0	0.0	0.0	0.0	0.0	0.0	0.0	100.0	0.0	0.0	0.0	0.0
5	1	100.0	0.0	0.0	0.0	0.0	0.0	0.0	0.0	0.0	0.0	0.0	0.0
5	3	25.0	0.0	0.0	50.0	25.0	0.0	0.0	0.0	0.0	0.0	0.0	0.0
5	4	0.0	0.0	36.4	0.0	36.4	18.2	0.0	9.1	0.0	0.0	0.0	0.0
5	5	0.0	0.0	0.0	20.0	53.3	6.7	6.7	13.3	0.0	0.0	0.0	0.0
5	6	0.0	0.0	0.0	28.6	14.3	14.3	28.6	14.3	0.0	0.0	0.0	0.0
5	7	0.0	0.0	0.0	0.0	80.0	20.0	0.0	0.0	0.0	0.0	0.0	0.0
5	8	0.0	0.0	0.0	0.0	0.0	0.0	33.3	66.7	0.0	0.0	0.0	0.0
6	2	0.0	0.0	100.0	0.0	0.0	0.0	0.0	0.0	0.0	0.0	0.0	0.0
6	4	0.0	0.0	0.0	50.0	10.0	20.0	20.0	0.0	0.0	0.0	0.0	0.0
6	5	0.0	0.0	0.0	53.3	20.0	6.7	13.3	6.7	0.0	0.0	0.0	0.0
6	6	0.0	0.0	0.0	0.0	25.0	50.0	8.3	16.7	0.0	0.0	0.0	0.0
6	7	0.0	0.0	0.0	0.0	12.5	0.0	0.0	87.5	0.0	0.0	0.0	0.0
6	8	0.0	0.0	0.0	0.0	0.0	60.0	10.0	20.0	10.0	0.0	0.0	0.0
7	2	0.0	0.0	0.0	0.0	100.0	0.0	0.0	0.0	0.0	0.0	0.0	0.0
7	5	0.0	0.0	42.9	0.0	14.3	42.9	0.0	0.0	0.0	0.0	0.0	0.0
7	6	0.0	0.0	0.0	12.5	56.3	18.7	0.0	12.5	0.0	0.0	0.0	0.0
7	7	0.0	0.0	0.0	0.0	0.0	66.7	33.3	0.0	0.0	0.0	0.0	0.0
7	8	0.0	0.0	0.0	12.5	0.0	0.0	37.5	37.5	12.5	0.0	0.0	0.0
8	4	0.0	0.0	50.0	50.0	0.0	0.0	0.0	0.0	0.0	0.0	0.0	0.0
8	5	0.0	0.0	0.0	0.0	100.0	0.0	0.0	0.0	0.0	0.0	0.0	0.0
8	6	0.0	0.0	0.0	33.3	22.2	11.1	11.1	22.2	0.0	0.0	0.0	0.0
8	7	0.0	0.0	0.0	0.0	0.0	75.0	16.7	8.3	0.0	0.0	0.0	0.0
8	8	0.0	0.0	0.0	7.7	7.7	15.4	15.4	23.1	30.8	0.0	0.0	0.0
8	9	0.0	0.0	0.0	0.0	0.0	0.0	5.6	22.2	22.2	50.0	0.0	0.0
8	11	0.0	0.0	0.0	0.0	0.0	0.0	0.0	0.0	0.0	0.0	100.0	0.0
8	12	0.0	0.0	0.0	0.0	0.0	0.0	0.0	0.0	0.0	0.0	0.0	100.0
9	7	0.0	0.0	0.0	0.0	0.0	100.0	0.0	0.0	0.0	0.0	0.0	0.0
9	8	0.0	0.0	0.0	0.0	0.0	0.0	71.4	14.3	14.3	0.0	0.0	0.0
9	9	0.0	0.0	0.0	0.0	0.0	0.0	0.0	16.7	0.0	83.3	0.0	0.0
9	10	0.0	0.0	0.0	0.0	0.0	0.0	0.0	25.0	6.3	0.0	68.8	0.0
9	12	0.0	0.0	0.0	0.0	0.0	0.0	0.0	0.0	0.0	50.0	0.0	50.0
10	8	0.0	0.0	0.0	0.0	0.0	0.0	0.0	0.0	100.0	0.0	0.0	0.0
10	9	0.0	0.0	0.0	0.0	0.0	0.0	0.0	16.7	33.3	33.3	0.0	16.7
10	10	0.0	0.0	0.0	0.0	0.0	0.0	0.0	10.0	10.0	65.0	0.0	15.0
10	11	0.0	0.0	0.0	0.0	0.0	9.1	0.0	9.1	9.1	0.0	36.4	36.4
10	12	0.0	0.0	0.0	0.0	0.0	0.0	0.0	66.7	0.0	0.0	33.3	0.0
11	6	0.0	0.0	0.0	0.0	0.0	100.0	0.0	0.0	0.0	0.0	0.0	0.0
11	8	0.0	0.0	0.0	0.0	0.0	0.0	0.0	0.0	0.0	0.0	100.0	0.0
11	9	0.0	0.0	0.0	0.0	0.0	0.0	0.0	100.0	0.0	0.0	0.0	0.0
11	10	0.0	0.0	0.0	0.0	0.0	0.0	0.0	0.0	37.5	62.5	0.0	0.0
11	11	0.0	0.0	0.0	0.0	0.0	0.0	0.0	0.0	0.0	45.5	54.5	0.0
11	12	0.0	0.0	0.0	0.0	0.0	0.0	0.0	50.0	50.0	0.0	0.0	0.0
12	8	0.0	0.0	0.0	0.0	0.0	0.0	0.0	0.0	66.7	0.0	0.0	33.3
12	9	0.0	0.0	0.0	0.0	0.0	0.0	0.0	50.0	0.0	0.0	0.0	50.0
12	10	0.0	0.0	0.0	0.0	0.0	0.0	0.0	0.0	0.0	100.0	0.0	0.0
12	11	0.0	0.0	0.0	0.0	0.0	0.0	0.0	0.0	0.0	100.0	0.0	0.0
12	12	0.0	0.0	0.0	0.0	0.0	0.0	0.0	0.0	0.0	0.0	100.0	0.0

```
 1120   DEF PROCselectpitch3
 1130   LOCAL rand,n,sum
 1140     rand=RND(1)*100
 1150     n=0 : sum=0
 1160     REPEAT
 1170       n=n+1
 1175       sum=sum+freq3(lastbut1,lastnoteplayed,n)
 1180     UNTIL sum>=rand
 1190     pitch=scalenote(n)
 1200     lastbut1=lastnoteplayed : lastnoteplayed=n
 1210   ENDPROC
10010   ...
20010   ...
30010   DATA 1, 1, 0.0,  0.0,  0.0, 33.3, 33.3, 16.7,
                   0.0, 16.7,  0.0,  0.0,  0.0,  0.0
30020   DATA 1, 4, 0.0,  0.0, 33.3, 33.3,  0.0, 33.3,
                   0.0,  0.0,  0.0,  0.0,  0.0,  0.0
                   ... (third-order frequencies)
```

The music generated by the program faithfully imitates the banality of the source material.

5.9 A program to generate probability frequency tables

In case you want to analyse your own favourite type of music, we present the following program which was used to generate the distributions of the three frequency tables.

```
 10   DIM freq1(12), freq2(12,12), freq3(12,12,12)
 20   INPUT "Number of tunes",nooftunes
 30   FOR tune=1 TO nooftunes
 40     PROCanalysetune
 50   NEXT tune
 60   PROCstandardisetable1
 70   PROCstandardisetable2
 80   PROCstandardisetable3
 90   PROCoutputtable1
100   PROCoutputtable2
110   PROCoutputtable3
120   END

130   DEF PROCanalysetune
140   LOCAL scale$,lastbut1$,last$,next$,
            lastbut1,last,next
150     READ scale$
160     READ lastbut1$,last$,next$
170     lastbut1=INSTR(scale$,lastbut1$)
180     last=INSTR(scale$,last$)
190     freq1(lastbut1)=freq1(lastbut1)+1
200     freq1(last)=freq1(last)+1
210     freq2(lastbut1,last)=freq2(lastbut1,last)+1
```

```
220      REPEAT
230        next=INSTR(scale$,next$)
240        IF next=0 THEN PRINT "Error in DATA ";tune;
                                " ";scale$;" ";next$
250        freq1(next)=freq1(next)+1
260        freq2(last,next)=freq2(last,next)+1
270        freq3(lastbut1,last,next) =
                         freq3(lastbut1,last,next)+1
280        lastbut1=last:last=next
290        READ next$
300      UNTIL next$="Z"
310    ENDPROC

330    DEF PROCstandardisetable1
340    LOCAL n,total
350      total=0
360      FOR n=1 TO 12
370        total=total+freq1(n)
380      NEXT n
390      FOR n=1 TO 12
400        freq1(n)=freq1(n)*100/total
410      NEXT n
420    ENDPROC

440    DEF PROCstandardisetable2
450    LOCAL l,n
460      FOR l=1 TO 12
470        total=0
480        FOR n=1 TO 12
490          total=total+freq2(l,n)
500        NEXT n
510        IF total>0 THEN
              FOR n=1 TO 12:freq2(l,n)=freq2(l,n)*100/total:
              NEXT n
520      NEXT l
530    ENDPROC

540    DEF PROCstandardisetable3
550    LOCAL lb1,l,n,total
560      FOR lb1=1 TO 12
570        FOR l=1 TO 12
580          total=0
590          FOR n=1 TO 12
600            total=total+freq3(lb1,l,n)
610          NEXT n
620          IF total=0 THEN freq3(lb1,l,0)=0 ELSE
              FOR n=1 TO 12 :
               freq3(lb1,l,n)=freq3(lb1,l,n)*100/total:
              NEXT n : freq3(lb1,l,0)=100
630        NEXT l
640      NEXT lb1
650    ENDPROC
```

```
660   DEF PROCoutputtable1
670   LOCAL n
680     PRINT "10000 DATA ";
690     @%=&20105
700     FOR n=1 TO 12
710       PRINT ;freq1(n); :IF n<12 THEN PRINT ",";
720     NEXT n
730     PRINT
740   ENDPROC

750   DEF PROCoutputtable2
760   LOCAL l,n,lineno
770     lineno=20010
780     FOR l=1 TO 12
790       @%=5
800       PRINT lineno;" DATA ";
810       @%=&20105
820       FOR n=1 TO 12
830         PRINT ;freq2(l,n); :IF n<12 THEN PRINT ",";
840       NEXT n
850       PRINT
860       lineno=lineno+10
870     NEXT l
880   ENDPROC

890   DEF PROCoutputtable3
900   LOCAL lb1,l,n,lineno
910     lineno=30010
920     FOR lb1=1 TO 12
930       FOR l=1 TO 12
940         IF freq3(lb1,l,0)>0 THEN PROCoutline3
950       NEXT l
960     NEXT lb1
970     @%=&90A
980     PRINT ;lineno;
             " DATA 0,0, 0,0,0,0,0,0,0,0,0,0,0,0"
990     REM *** DATA terminator ***
1000  ENDPROC

1010  DEF PROCoutline3
1020    LOCAL n
1030    @%=5
1040    PRINT ;lineno;" DATA ";lb1;",";l;",";
1050    @%=&20105
1060    FOR n=1 TO 12
1070     PRINT;freq3(lb1,l,n);:IF n<12 THEN PRINT ",";
1080    NEXT n
1090    PRINT
1100    lineno=lineno+10
1110  ENDPROC
```

```
1120   DATA gabcdEFGABCD, G,A,B,G,A,A,B,C,C,B,B,G,A,B,
        G,A,A,B,C,D,G,D,D,C,B,A,B,C,D,A,D,D,C,B,A,B,C,
        D,A,G,A,B,G,A,A,B,C,C,B,B,G,A,B,G,A,A,B,C,D,G,Z
1130   DATA defgaBCDEFGA, g,g,g,C,B,D,B,C,D,D,D,g,f,a,
        f,d,g,f,g,C,B,D,B,g,a,C,a,f,g,g,B,D,B,g,B,D,B,
        a,C,a,f,a,C,a,B,D,B,g,B,D,B,a,C,a,f,g,g,Z
1140   DATA defgaBCD, g,B,C,D,C,B,a,g,a,d,d,a,g,B,C,D,
        C,B,a,g,a,d,d,g,B,g,g,C,B,a,g,f,a,d,d,a,g,B,C,
        D,C,B,a,g,a,d,d,g,Z
1150   DATA ***cdEFGABC,  c,c,G,G,A,B,C,A,G,F,F,E,E,d,
        d,c,G,G,G,F,F,F,E,E,E,d,G,G,G,F,G,A,F,E,d,d,c,Z
1160   DATA ***cdEFGABC,  E,F,G,G,A,B,C,E,E,G,G,A,B,C,
        G,C,C,B,B,A,A,G,G,A,G,F,E,d,c,Z
1170   DATA ***gaBCDE,    D,B,D,D,B,D,E,D,C,B,a,B,C,D,
        g,g,g,g,g,a,B,C,D,D,a,a,C,B,a,g,Z
1180   DATA *******GABCD, B,B,B,B,B,B,B,D,G,A,B,C,C,C,
        C,C,B,B,B,B,A,A,B,A,D,B,B,B,B,B,B,B,D,G,A,B,C,
        C,C,C,C,B,B,B,D,C,B,A,G,Z
1190   DATA defgaBCDE,    D,E,D,C,B,g,g,a,B,a,g,f,d,d,
        D,E,D,C,B,g,g,B,e,f,g,B,g,C,a,B,g,g,C,e,a,g,f,
        d,d,B,g,C,a,B,g,g,B,e,f,f,g,Z
1200   DATA fgabcDEF,     f,b,b,b,b,b,a,b,c,c,c,c,c,c,
        D,D,D,D,F,E,D,D,c,c,c,c,F,F,D,D,D,D,D,E,c,c,c,
        c,F,E,D,c,b,c,c,b,a,b,b,b,b,Z
```

The string at the start of the DATA for a tune establishes the range of notes for the tune starting three notes below the keynote. There then follow the names of the notes in the tune in the order in which they appear. The program prints the tables in the form of DATA statements numbered from 10000 upwards that can be absorbed into another program. To do this, type

```
*SPOOL "freqtables"
RUN
*SPOOL
```

and the DATA statements for the tables will be stored on cassette. These can be added to any program by typing

```
*EXEC "freqtables"
```

Note that as is stands the program does not cater for accidentals and would have to be extended for these.

Now the question is: does using probability tables to mimic a musical genre produce anything worth listening to. One of the problems with this method is that you can make music more and more 'Bach-like' or 'Mozart-like' by using higher and higher probability orders, but as the music becomes more and more like the target style it becomes less and less original. In the limit if you take a high enough order probability distribution, you are taking so much information from say Bach tunes that the program will eventually generate an actual Bach tune (give or take a few notes).

So finally we return to letting the computer do its own thing and get it to play some 12 bar blues.

5.10 Micro blues

The next program plays or improvises on a 12 bar blues. It does not use probability tables but selects notes from two jazz blues scales (Bb and Eb, DATA statement 860). It utilises a rhythmic chordal accompaniment and the three voices are synchronised using PROCinitialise, PROCharmonise and PROCsound which were described earlier. Voices 2 and 3 consist of a simple blues chord progression taken from DATA statements 700 and 710. These are loaded up into rows 2 and 3 of the three row pitch and duration arrays. PROCjazz initialises row 1 of this array by randomly selecting starting notes for a phrase from the appropriate scale. The rhythm for a phrase is randomly selected from a set of DATA statements (1301 onwards).

```
  10   ENVELOPE 1,1,0,0,0,0,0,0,63,10,0,-63,63,126
  20   ENVELOPE 2,1,0,0,0,0,0,0,126,-4,0,-100,126,100
  30   ENVELOPE 3,1,0,0,0,0,0,0,126,-4,0,-100,126,100
  40   DIM pitch(3,200), duration(3,200),
          noofnotes(3), nextnote(3), clock(3)
  50   tempo = 1
  60   PROCinitialise(2)
  70   PROCinitialise(3)
  80   PROCjazz
  90   PROCharmonise(3)
 100   END

 200   DEF PROCinitialise(voice)
         .
         .  as before
         .
 390   ENDPROC

 400   DEF PROCharmonise(noofvoices)
         .
         .  as before
         .
 550   ENDPROC

 600   DEF PROCsound(voice,sync)
         .
         .  as before
         .
 680   ENDPROC
```

```
700   DATA 24, A#,h,A#,dq,A#,e,R,w,A#,e,A#,e,R,q,A#,dq,
        A#,e,R,w,C'#,h,C'#,dq,C'#,e,R,w,A#,h,A#,dq,
        A#,e,R,w,D'#,w,C'#,w,A#,h,A#,dq,A#,e,A#,w
710   DATA 24, D',h,D',dq,D',e,R,w,D',e,D',e,R,q,D',dq,
        D',e,R,w,G,h,G,dq,G,e,R,w,D',h,D',dq,D',e,R,w,
        R,w,R,w,D',h,D',dq,D',e,D',w

800   DEF PROCjazz
810     DIM Bb(13), Eb(13)
820     ii = 0
830     FOR note=1 TO 13
840       READ Bb(note)
850     NEXT note
860     DATA 45,57,65,69,73,85,93,105,113,117,121,133,141
870     FOR note = 1 TO 13
880       Eb(note) = Bb(note) + 20
890     NEXT note
900     PROCplaytheblues
910     noofnotes(1)=ii
920   ENDPROC

930   DEF PROCplaytheblues
940     PROCplaybars(4,"Bb")
950     PROCplaybars(2,"Eb")
960     PROCplaybars(6,"Bb")
970   ENDPROC

980   DEF PROCplaybars(n, key$)
990     FOR bar = 1 TO n
1000      FOR phrase = 1 TO 2
1010      PROCselectstartnote
1020      PROCselectupdown
1030      PROCselectphrase
1040      PROCplayphrase(key$)
1050    NEXT phrase
1060  NEXT bar
1070  ENDPROC

1080  DEF PROCselectstartnote
1090    startnote = RND(13)
1100  ENDPROC

1110  DEF PROCselectphrase
1120    sphrase=RND(6)
1130    restoreto = 1300 + sphrase
1140    RESTORE restoreto
1150  ENDPROC
```

```
1160    DEF PROCplayphrase(key$)
1170      READ noofnotes
1180      note = startnote
1190      FOR i = 1 TO noofnotes
1200        READ length
1210        ii = ii + 1: duration(1,ii) = length
1220      IF key$ = "Eb"  THEN pitch(1,ii) = Eb(note)
                          ELSE pitch(1,ii) = Bb(note)
1230        note=note+ updown
1240        IFnote > 13 OR note < 1 THEN note=7
1250      NEXT i
1260    ENDPROC

1270    DEF PROCselectupdown
1280      IF RND(2) = 2 THEN updown= -1 ELSE updown=  1
1290    ENDPROC

1301 DATA 8,2,2,2,2,2,2,2,2
1302 DATA 4,4,4,4,4
1303 DATA 1,16
1304 DATA 1,16
1305 DATA 4,2,6,2,6
1306 DATA 11,1,2,1,2,1,2,1,2,1,2,1
```

Exercises

1 Select your favourite style of music, analyse a sample, generate a set of probability frequency tables and produce a program that composes in that style. You may find that you need to experiment with the rhythm generating program in order to produce rhythms that are appropriate for your kind of music.

2 The 'creative' part of the 'micro blues' program could be significantly improved by adding more constraints. For example:

(a) The intervals used in the phrases are all major or minor seconds (one step in the scale sequence - line 1220). The interval between notes could be varied.

(b) Rests or gaps of silence should be introduced, space is very important in music.

(c) Fast note phrases used consecutively should be followed by a long note.

(d) Repetition of a phrase should be occasionally introduced.

(e) There are further harmonic constraints if you know the blues progression.

Chapter 6 Storing, sorting, searching and indexing

The general term 'data structures' is given to any way of organising information handled by a program. Simple data structures that you will have met already are one-dimensional arrays and two-dimensional arrays. One-dimensional arrays facilitate random access to a list of numbers or strings. Two-dimensional arrays also allow random access and impose an organisation on the data that reflects the reality of a two-dimensional data source. For example a population map is a two-dimensional table of integers where each integer is the population of, say, a square mile zone of a geographical area. It is natural to retain this two-dimensional ordering within the program and it makes for easier and more natural programming.

The material in this chapter is concerned with building more complex data structures using combinations of arrays. The first raison d'etre of data structures is to retain a 'natural' organisation and thus ease the task of the programmer. This is very important as easy and natural programming structures make for correct programs.

The second reason for organising data into structures is that individual 'entries' may vary considerably in size. Allocating the same space for each entry, i.e. space large enough for the largest entry, would be wasteful. Instead we may allow the entries to occupy exactly the storage space that they require, and set up a table that 'points' to the start of each entry.

The third important reason for using data structures is that if our collection of data is very large, the imposition of a data structure may be necessary to enable efficient searching. A related consideration here is the amount of memory space available. It may be that only part of the data set, held on disk say, can be brought into the memory at any time.

The information stored in connection with a particular application is called a data set, data base or data bank. A useful concept is that the data structure mirror-images a natural or artificial organisation of data in the real world. We may for example initialise, first thing in the morning, the main memory data structures of a stock control program and organise a sequential file into a series of departments, articles, classes etc. This data may be changed during the day, as stock levels change, for example, and be dumped back into a sequential file to sleep in its 'unstructured' form overnight. This is not the whole story because the disk files may themselves be subject to an organisational framework. This is certainly the case when the main store data structure is such that it can only hold a very small part of the data set. In this case the files themselves will be organised to reflect the organisational framework of the data, and the data structure in this case resides in the file structure. The general topic of structured files and data structures has come to be known as database organisation. In this chapter we will be concerned with the simpler problem of main memory data structures. These may contain information that is built up by a program while it is running, or they may be initialised from a sequential file where all of the file is taken into the data structure.

The distinguishing features of these cases can be illustrated. Consider first of all a small index for a book. This may have to undergo transformations such as addition of a new entry, sorting, checking for duplicate entries etc. The length of each entry is short and there may only be a few entries. The entire index could be held in a sequential file, and, providing each entry is de-limited, read into an array of strings. The array can then be randomly accessed and otherwise manipulated by the program. The whole of the data base is contained in the main memory data structure.

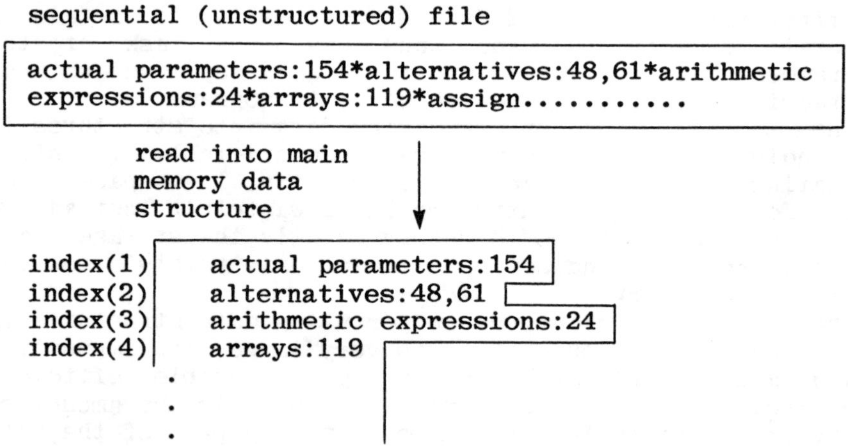

Now if we intend to store and manipulate an English dictionary the situation is completely different. The data base cannot be held in main memory and the required structures will be set up on disk. The disk file(s) will be subject to an imposed framework.

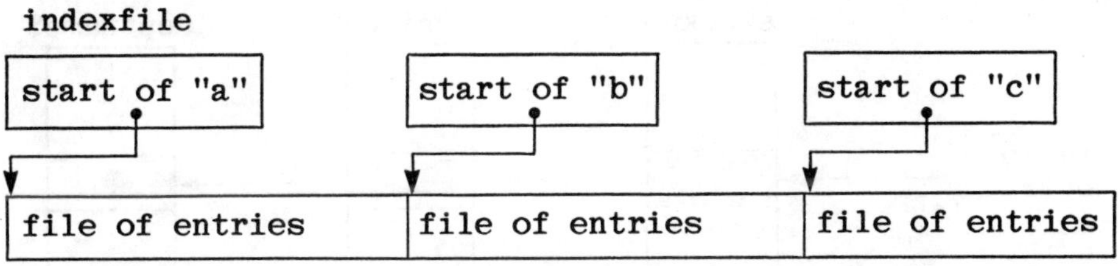

Depending on the manipulation that has to be performed by the program such a simple structure may be inadequate and the hierarchy may have to be 'deepened'

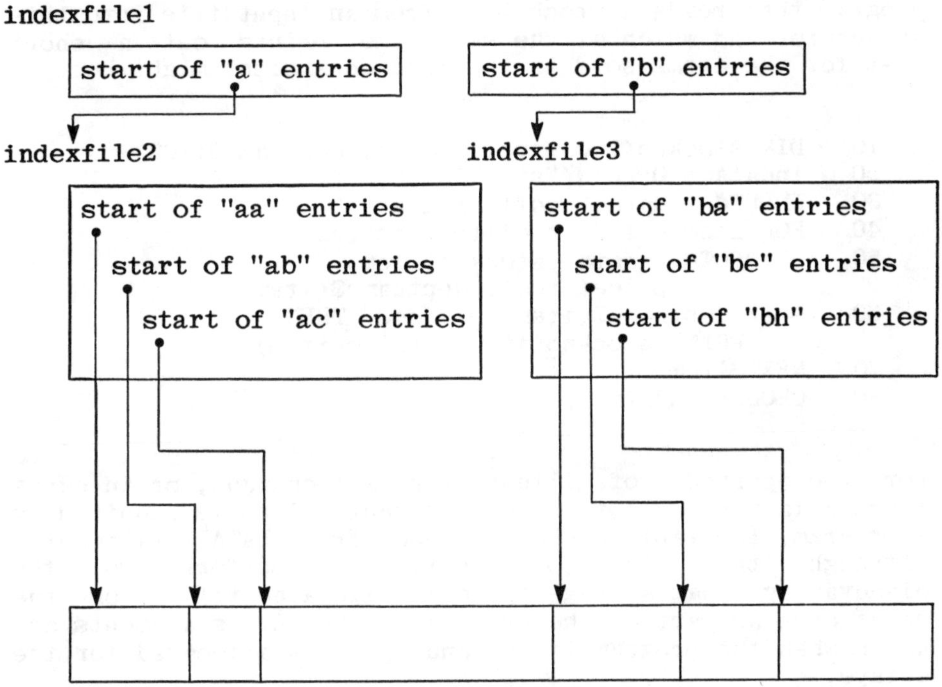

6.1 Tables

Many computer applications involve storing a table of information where each entry in the table consists of several related values. For example we may want to store a stock table, where each entry in the stock table consists of a stock number, a price and a department name. An appropriate data structure could be constructed in Basic from three parallel arrays.

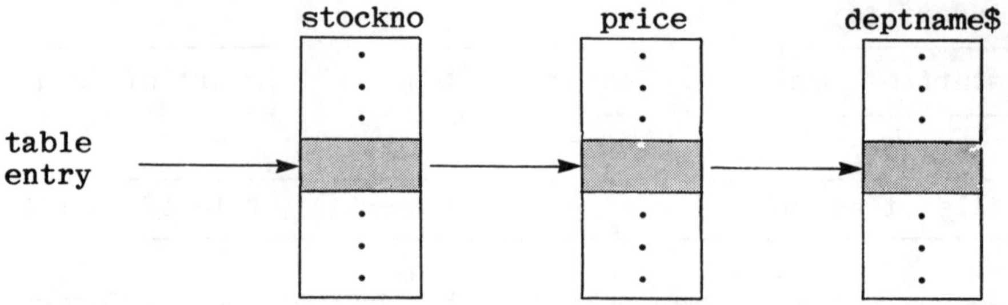

Any three corresponding elements in these arrays will then be referred to as a table entry. Each element of a table entry will be referred to as a field of that entry. A program that reads a stock list from an input file into this structure, and which at the same time prints out a short list for the items sold in the food department might be:

```
10    DIM stockno(100), price(100), deptname$(100)
20    indata = OPENIN("stockdata")
30    INPUT# indata, noofitemsinstock
40    FOR item = 1 TO noofitemsinstock
50      INPUT# indata, stockno(item),
                price(item), deptname$(item)
60      IF deptname$(item) = "food" THEN
          PRINT stockno(item), price(item)
70    NEXT item
80    CLOSE# indata
```

For the purpose of illustrating a technique, or in cases where a fairly small table of constant values is required by a program, the table could be read from DATA statements. Although this is convenient, it suffers from the disadvantage that storage space is allocated twice for the data; once as part of the program in the DATA statements and again when the program is run and space is allocated for the arrays.

In the following examples we will omit the details concerning the initialisation of a data structure from a file or DATA statement if this is simply a sequential transfer of information to arrays.

6.2 Searching a table - linear search

Having seen how to set up or organise a simple table we will now look at some common operations that are performed on tables. Searching a table for a particular entry is a common problem. An example is a Basic interpreter, the program that processes and obeys your Basic programs. An interpreter program builds up a table of variable names. Each entry in the table consists of the variable name together with a memory address that the interpreter allocates to that name the first time it encounters it.

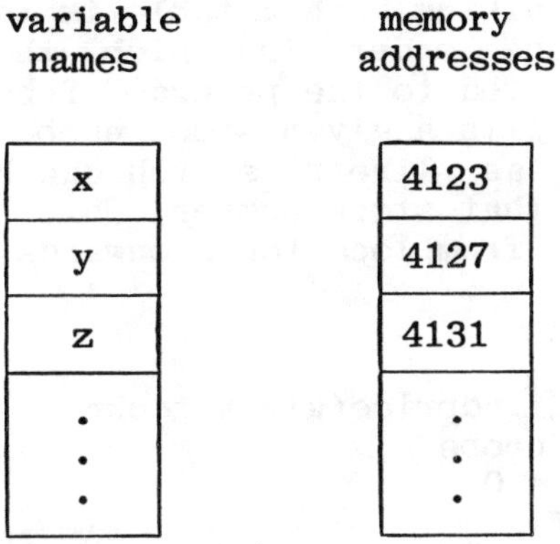

Each time a variable name is encountered the interpreter has to access the table for a memory address. The statement:

```
x = (x + y)/(a*a + b)
```

would involve six accesses to this table. Interpreting a program may involve thousands of table accesses and the method used for the search becomes critically important in such applications. Now when we are searching tables we usually have given one field of an entry and the point of the search is to find the other field(s) associated with this 'key' field. For example in the stocklist we may be using the stock number entry as a key. The problem is then: given a particular stock number, find the associated price.

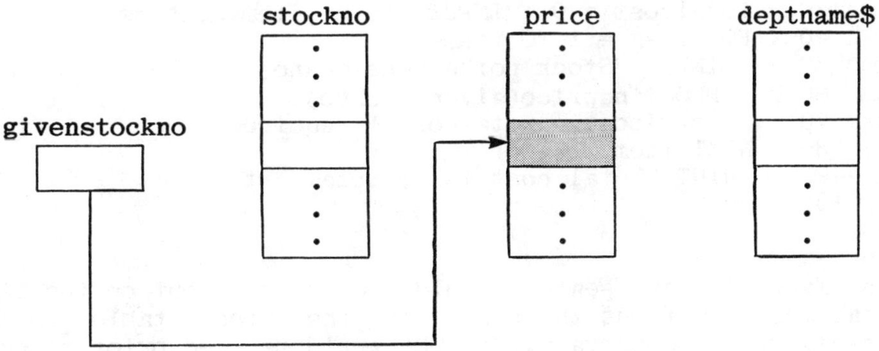

Table searching methods are concerned with organising the table in such a way that finding the field or fields associated with a key is quick and efficient. The simplest approach to organising such a table is to store the entries in the table in the order in which the information was originally presented to the program. Subsequently, when the price of an item with a given stock number is required, the technique known as linear search can be used to find the entry containing that stock number. This involves scanning through the table from location 1 onwards until the required entry is found.

```
400  DEF PROCfindprice(givenstockno)
410    LOCAL probe
420    probe = 0
430    REPEAT
440      probe = probe + 1
450    UNTIL stockno(probe) = givenstockno
460    requiredprice = price(probe)
470  ENDPROC
```

(We have here assumed that the given stock number will be found in the table.) Consider now a complete customer order consisting of a list of stock numbers for the items a customer requires. Let us assume that he requires only one of each type of item. The total number of items required is indicated at the start of the order. The cost of his order can be calculated by:

```
 10  DIM stockno(100), price(100)
 20  PROCsetupstocktable    :REM from file or DATA
 30  totalcost = 0 : INPUT "No of items",items
 40  FOR item = 1 TO items
 50    INPUT "Stock no:"givenstockno
 60    PROCfindprice(givenstockno)
 70    totalcost = totalcost + requiredprice
 80  NEXT item
 90  PRINT "Total cost is "; totalcost
100  END
```

In fact linear search could be carried out on the DATA statements, without the need for the stock table to be transferred to arrays. RESTORE would be used prior to each search. However, this could not be done for the more efficient search methods introduced later.

If there are n records in a table, linear search involves, on average, the examination of n/2 entries before a required record is found. For example if the stocklist is 1000 items long and each order to be processed contains on average 350 items, then processing an order involves examining 175000 entries. In most applications, particularly where n is large, this is unacceptable. In the following sections, we shall be discussing different ways of organising the information in a table, usually with a view to finding an entry containing a given key more quickly than is possible with linear search. To facilitate more efficient methods of searching we first look at sorting.

Exercises

1 Write a program that repeatedly accepts input of a French word and responds with the equivalent English word. Use a fairly small dictionary for the exercise and initialise it from DATA statements. Assume that each word has a unique translation. If a given word is not found in the dictionary, the program should report this. The program should use linear search to look for a dictionary entry.

2 Modify the previous program so that the user can specify whether he requires translation of a word from French to English or English to French.

3 Write a program that will analyse a short piece of English text and report the total number of different words used in the text and the number of times each word was used. The text should be read from a file (write a separate program to set up the file). As it reads the text, the program will have to build up a table of words encountered, together with a count of the number of occurrences of each word so far. Differences between upper and lower case letters can be ignored by converting all lower case letters into upper case.

4 Use the animation procedures developed in Chapter 4 (Section 4.1) to animate a linear search for a particular entry. Each entry should be highlighted in a different colour as it is examined and the required entry should be highlighted in a flashing colour when it has been found.

5 The membership list for a society consists of an integer n followed by a list of n entries where each entry consists of a person's name (surname first) and a membership number (an integer). Write a program that will read and store the membership list in an appropriate table. The program should then input an integer m followed by m membership numbers. For each number presented, the program should find and print out the name of the member with that number.

6.3 Ordered data - sorting

It is often more convenient or even necessary for the entries involved in an application to be stored in some specified order. This ordering is usually determined by one of the entry fields. For example, we can organise a set of entries so that a particular string field appears in alphabetic order. Alternatively we may organise them so that a numeric field appears in increasing or decreasing order. We can then refer to a table as being sorted on a particular field.

As an example, we consider the problem of sorting the stock entries used previously so that the stock numbers are in increasing numerical order. We present three of the simplest sort algorithms that can be used to sort the entries stored in an array into a required order. Let us assume that initially we have n records stored in the stocklist arrays used previously.

Simple exchange sort

A simple exchange sort is perhaps the easiest algorithm to describe. It is also the least efficient. For a simple exchange sort we can describe the algorithm, using the stocklist example:

```
find the entry with the smallest stock no.
swop it with the first entry (stockno(1), price(1) etc.)
find the entry with the second smallest stock no.
 (at this stage we need only look at 2nd entry onwards)
swop it with the second entry
find the entry with the third smallest stock no.
 (at this stage we need only look at 3rd entry onwards)
                    .
                    .
                   etc.
```

in other words:

```
 10   DIM stockno(100), price(100)
 20   PROCsetupstocktable
 30   PROCsortstocktable(noofitemsinstock)
 40   PROCoutputstocktable
 50   END

400   DEF PROCsortstocktable(n)
410   LOCAL i
420     FOR i = 1 TO n-1
430       PROCfindsmallestentryfrom(i)
440       PROCswop(i, posnsmallest)
450     NEXT i
460   ENDPROC
```

```
500   DEF PROCfindsmallestentryfrom(i)
510     LOCAL next
520     posnsmallest = i
530     FOR next = i+1 TO n
540       IF stockno(next) < stockno(posnsmallest) THEN
              posnsmallest = next
550     NEXT next
560   ENDPROC

600   DEF PROCswop(i, j)
610     LOCAL temp
620     temp = stockno(i)
630     stockno(i) = stockno(j)
640     stockno(j) = temp
650     temp = price(i)
660     price(i) = price(j)
670     price(j) = temp
                 .
                 .  etc. for all other fields in the entry
                 .
680   ENDPROC
```

PROCsetsupstocktable will initialise the arrays from a file or DATA statements and PROCoutputstocktable will print the arrays.

Bubble sort
Depending on the state of the data a bubble sort can be considerably more efficient than an exchange sort. Sometimes data is already partially ordered and in such a context a bubble sort is preferred. Consider the following program fragment:

```
FOR i = 2 To n
  IF stockno(i) < stockno(i-1) THEN PROCswop(i, i-1)
NEXT i
```

If this is executed once, the entry with the largest stock number is picked up and carried to the end of the arrays, and in the process some of the other entries are moved closer to their correct position in the ordering. If we execute the same fragment of program again, but this time using:

```
FOR i = 2 TO n-1
```

the entry with the second largest stock no. will be carried to the second last position in the arrays.

Repeated application of this process eventually sorts the entries into order:

```
400   DEF PROCsortstocktable(n)
410   LOCAL i, last
420     FOR last = n TO 2 STEP -1
430       FOR i = 2 TO last
440        IF stockno(i) < stockno(i-1) THEN
              PROCswop(i,i-1)
450       NEXT i
460     NEXT last
470   ENDPROC
```

This first approximation can be considerably improved. Each time lines 430-450 are obeyed, not only is one entry carried to its correct position, but other entries may also be moved closer to their final positions. Thus lines 430-450 may not have to be obeyed n-1 times before the entries are in order. If at some stage, obeying lines 430-450 does not move any entries then they must already be in order and the process can be terminated. This is an occurrence that that is more and more likely to happen as n increases.

Secondly, in the process of obeying lines 430-450, we may find that 'stockno(last)' is already in its correct position. This can be detected while lines 430-450 are being obeyed by keeping a note of the number of the last record moved down. Thus we have:

```
400   DEF PROCsortstocktable(n)
410   LOCAL i, last, lastonemoveddown
420     last = n
430     REPEAT
440       lastonemoveddown = 0
450       FOR i = 2 TO last
460         IF stockno(i) < stockno(i-1) THEN
              PROCswop(i, i-1) : lastonemoveddown = i-1
470       NEXT i
480       last = lastonemoveddown
490     UNTIL last < 2
500   ENDPROC
```

Sifting sort
Finally we modify the central idea used in the bubble sort algorithm and introduce the algorithm known as 'sifting'. When two entries are found to be in the wrong order, instead of simply exchanging them, we move the second one back past all the entries which should come after it, moving all these entries forward one place to make room for it. The first operation to be performed in this algorithm is to look for the first out of sequence number and store it temporarily.

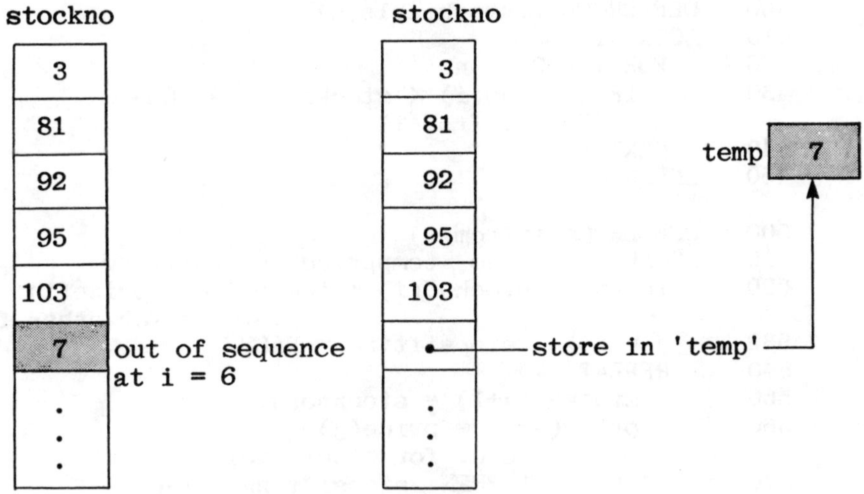

The next step is to 'sift' until we find the correct position in the sequence for the contents of 'temp'.

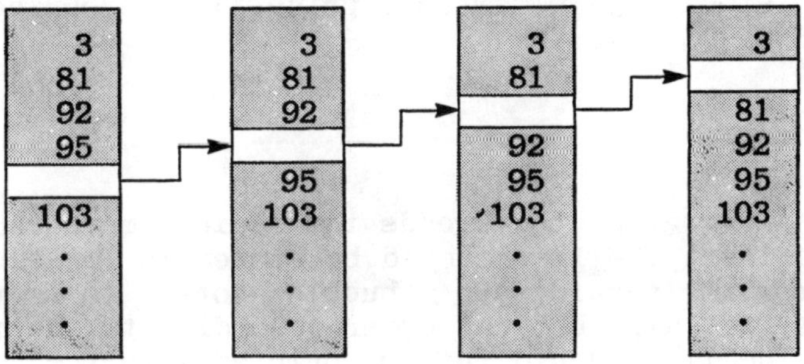

Finally the contents of 'temp' are inserted back into 'stockno'.

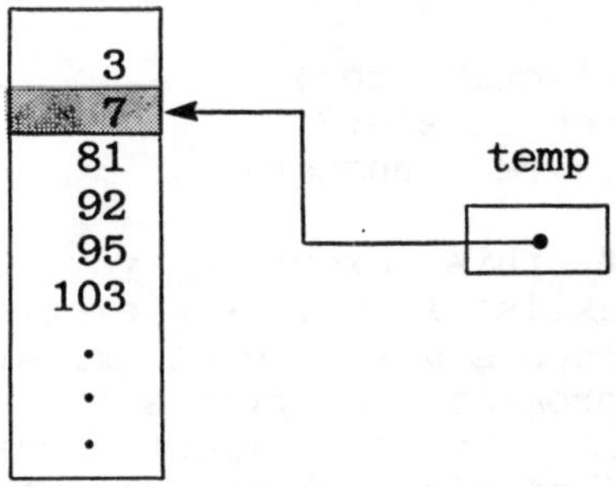

The process is best imagined in the illustrations as the 'white space' made 'empty' by storing the number to be repositioned in 'temp', sifting backwards. The program is:

```
400   DEF PROCsortstocktable(n)
410   LOCAL i
420     FOR i = 2 TO n
430       IF stockno(i) < stockno(i-1) THEN
            PROCsiftfrom(i)
440     NEXT i
450   ENDPROC

500   DEF PROCsiftfrom(i)
510   LOCAL j, tempno, tempprice, stopsifting
520     tempno = stockno(i) : tempprice = price(i)
                                  ... etc for other fields
530     j = i-1 : stopsifting = FALSE
540     REPEAT
550       stockno(j+1) = stockno(j)
560       price(j+1) = price(j)
              ... etc. for other fields
570       IF j = 1 THEN  stopsifting = TRUE
          ELSE IF tempno > stockno(j-1) THEN
                   stopsifting = TRUE
          ELSE j = j-1
580     UNTIL stopsifting
590     stockno(j) = tempno : price(j) = tempprice ...
610   ENDPROC
```

Exercises

1 Write a program that reads the society membership list used earlier. The list should be stored in a table and the program should use 'bubble sort' to sort these records into alphabetical order according to the member's names. The list should then be printed with the names in order.

2 The stock list for a small department store consists of a list of records, where each record contains three items:

```
department code (1 character)
stock number    (an integer)
price           (a real number)
```

For the purposes of this exercise you can either construct a sample stocklist in DATA statements or write a short program that inputs a sample stocklist and saves it in a file. Write a program that prints the stock list in such a way that the department codes are in alphabetical order and, within each department, the stock numbers are in ascending numerical order. Two approaches are possible.

EITHER define a FNinorder(recordno1, recordno2) and use this to compare two records during sorting,

OR sort the stocklist twice, firstly on the stock numbers and then on the departments codes, making sure that two records with the same department code remain in order determined previously by their stock numbers.

6.4 Ordered data - binary chopping

Now that we have examined techniques that sort entries into order we can return to the problem of table searching. If the information in a table is already ordered on a particular field, or can be sorted before further processing takes place, then the technique known as 'logarithmic search' or 'binary search' can be used for finding the entry that contains a given key in that field. Use of this search algorithm requires the examination of approximately $\log_2 n$ entries in order to find the entry containing a given key.

This algorithm starts by examining the entry approximately in the middle of the table. The given key is compared with the appropriate field of this middle entry and if they are the same, the search is terminated successfully. If the given key comes before the value in this field, the first half of the table must be searched, otherwise the last half of the table must be searched. The same process is repeated on the first half or the last half of the table, the area in which the required key is known to lie being repeatedly halved in this way until the key has been found.

In the program that implements this technique, the variable 'probe' has as its final value the number of the entry containing the given stock number. The entries in the table are assumed to be in ascending order of stock number.

```
 10   DIM stockno(100), price(100)
 20   PROCsetupstocktable
 30   PROCsortstocktable(noofitemsinstock)
         :
         :
700   DEF PROCfindprice(givenstockno)
710   LOCAL first,last, stopsearching,found
720     first = 1
730     last = noofitemsinstock
740     stopsearching = FALSE : found = FALSE
750     REPEAT
760       PROCchoptable
770     UNTIL stopsearching
780     IF found THEN requiredprice = price(mid)
        ELSE PRINT "Entry does not exist." :
             requiredprice = 0
790   ENDPROC
```

```
800   DEF PROCchoptable
810     mid = (first + last) DIV 2
820      IF stockno(mid) = givenstockno THEN
          stopsearching = TRUE : found = TRUE : ENDPROC
830      IF stockno(mid) > givenstockno THEN
          last = mid - 1 ELSE first = mid + 1
840      IF first > last THEN stopsearching = TRUE
850   ENDPROC
```

The process can be illustrated for a particular arbitrary sequence:

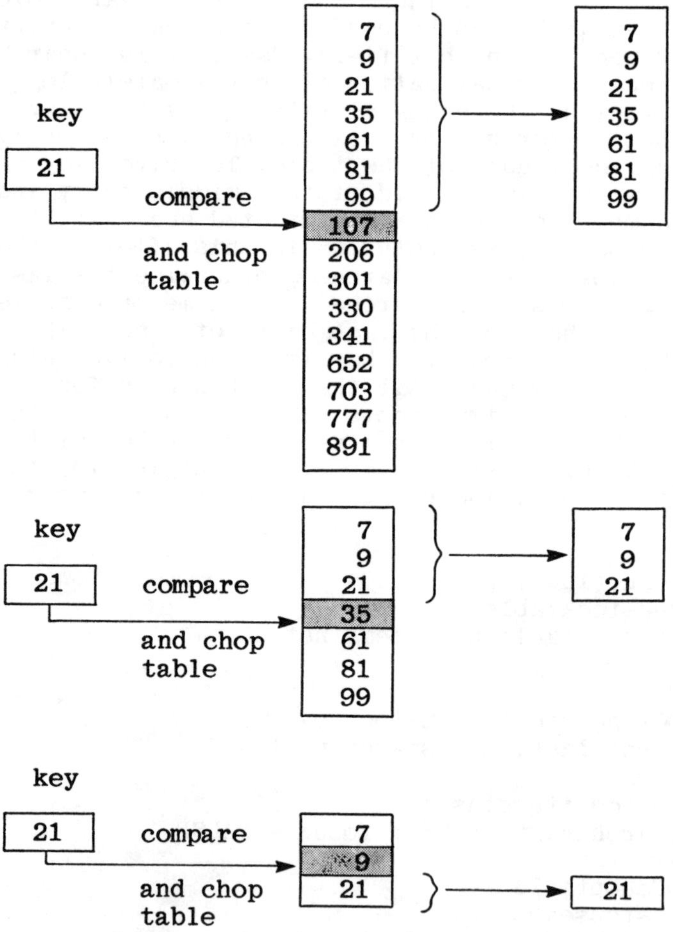

It is interesting to compare the average number of steps required by a linear search in a table of n records with the average number of steps required by a logarithmic search, for different values of n:

number of entries	linear search	logarithmic search
n	average no. of steps is n/2	average no. of steps is $\log_2 n$
4	2	2
16	8	4
128	64	7
1024	512	10
8192	4096	13

It must be remembered that sorting algorithms are themselves fairly time consuming and this must be balanced against the subsequent saving in look-up time. If also, new data is to be continually added to the table, it would be very inconvenient to have to keep moving the information already in the table in order to insert a new entry in its correct position. However, there are applications in which all the entries in the table are present in advance and where the table needs to be sorted for some other reason: for example, so that an ordered listing of the table can be generated for reference by a human user.

Other techniques are available for organising and accessing tables in cases where the table does not need to be ordered or where new entries are continually being added. Such techniques are described later.

Exercises

1 Write a program that sorts the French-English dictionary used earlier so that the French words are stored in alphabetical order.

2 Modify the earlier French-English word translator program so that it uses binary search to find a French word in the ordered table produced by the previous exercise.

3 Use the procedures of Chapter 4, Section 4.1, to animate a sifting sort.

6.5 Direct access

If the keys to be looked up in a table are such that we can define a function that calculates a unique value from each possible key and the values calculated by the function are in a suitably small range, then this function can be used for deciding where in a table to insert an entry associated with a given key and where to find it later.

Consider the problem of storing in a table the name of each animal kept in a zoo together with the name of the keeper assigned to look after each animal. Let us impose the highly artificial restriction that all the animals kept have names beginning with different letters. We require a program which, given the name of the animal, prints the name of the keeper assigned to look after that animal (or an error message indicating that no animal of that description is kept). We can use the initial letter of an animal's name to determine the location in the table in which the animal's entry is to be stored.

We need two parallel arrays and it is convenient in this case to number the locations of these arrays from 0 to 25.

```
10   DIM animal$(25), keeper$(25)
```

Remember that the locations in a BASIC array are numbered from 0 upwards, but location 0 is often ignored. Here we will use slot 0 for the animal whose name begins with "a". A number in the range 0 to 25 can be easily calculated from a given 'firstletter$':

```
entryno = ASC(firstletter$) - ASC("a")
```

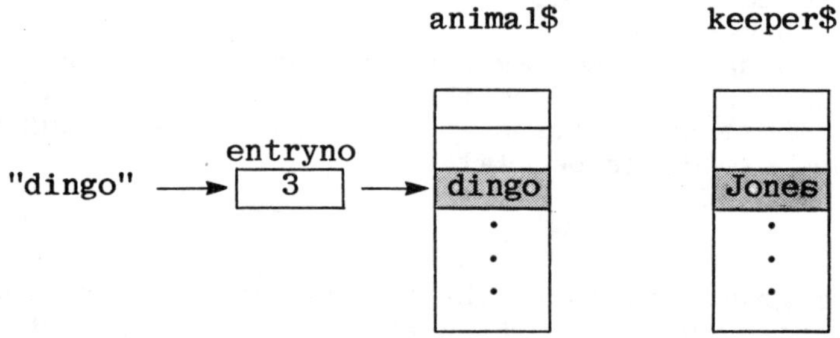

This table can be initialised from DATA statements:

```
200   DEF PROCsetupzootable
210   LOCAL noofanimals, i, entryno
220     READ noofanimals
230     FOR i = 1 TO noofanimals
240       READ nextanimal$, nextkeeper$
250       firstletter$ = LEFT$(nextanimal$,1)
260       entryno = ASC(firstletter$) - ASC("a")
270       animal$(entryno) = nextanimal$
280       keeper$(entryno) = nextkeeper$
290     NEXT i
300   ENDPROC
```

After the DIM statement at line 10 has been obeyed, all array locations contain the empty string. If fewer than 26 animals are kept, then after the table has been initialised some of the animal fields will still have an empty string stored in them. An empty string indicates that there is no animal whose name begins with the corresponding letter.

To respond to an inquiry about a particular animal we need:

```
400   DEF PROCfindkeeper(givenanimal$)
405   LOCAL entryno
410     entryno = ASC(LEFT$(givenanimal$,1)) - ASC("a")
420     IF animal$(entryno) = givenanimal$ THEN
          PRINT "Keeper is "; keeper$(entryno)
        ELSE PRINT "There is no animal of that name."
430   ENDPROC
```

There is now no searching required to find the entry containing information about the animal with a given name, hence the term 'direct access'.

As another example of direct access, consider the stock table used previously. If the stock numbers are such that the last two digits of each number uniquely identify an item we could use these two digits to directly access the stock table. We can initialise the stock table with:

```
 10   DIM  stockno(99), price(99)
        :
        :
200   DEF PROCsetupstocktable
210   LOCAL noofotemsinstock, i, entryno
220     READ noofitemsinstock
230     FOR i = 1 TO noofitemsinstock
240       READ nextstockno, nextprice
250       entryno = nextstockno MOD 100
260       stockno(entryno) = nextstockno
270       price(entryno) = nextprice
280     NEXT i
290   ENDPROC
```

Again there will be empty space in the table if we have fewer than 100 items in stock. Since numeric array locations are initialised to 0, the unused locations still contain 0 after the stock list has been read. Now for a given stock number, the location (if any) containing the associated price is 'price(givenstockno MOD 100)'.

In general, if the function f is to be used for direct access to a table of entries, we can picture f being used as follows:

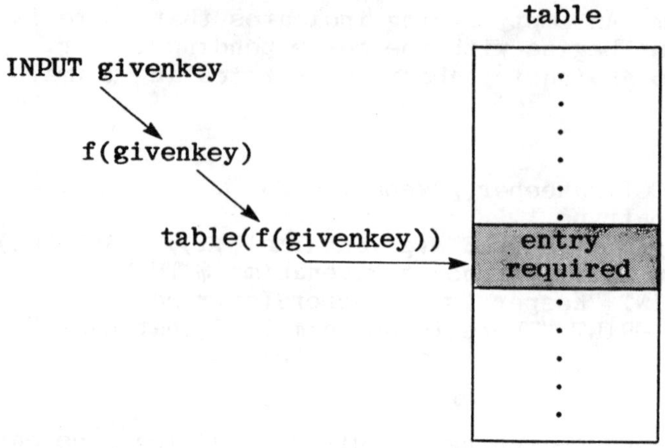

In the first example the function was:

```
f(givenkey$) = ASC(LEFT$(givenkey$,1)) - ASC("a")
```

and in the second example

```
f(givenkey) = givenkey MOD 100
```

The first function has 26 possible values and the second 100, so 26 entries can be stored in the first case and 100 in the second.

6.6 Direct access to a subtable

Even if we cannot define a function that calculates a unique table subscript for each key, we can easily extend the ideas introduced in the previous section to the situation where more than one key gives rise to the same function value. One way of doing this involves allocating a subtable to hold the entries corresponding to one value of the access function. Given a particular key we evaluate f(key) and use this value to tell us in which subtable the entry with that key is stored.

In the zoo-keeper example, we will allow for up to 10 animals whose names begin with each initial letter. We will thus allow for a maximum of 260 animals, some of which have names beginning with the same letter. Associated with each subtable is an integer value indicating the number of entries in that subtable. We can use linear search for storing and accessing entries within one such subtable. The complete table, then, will consist of 26 of these subtables, one for each initial letter.

In general, we can picture the process of accessing the table as:

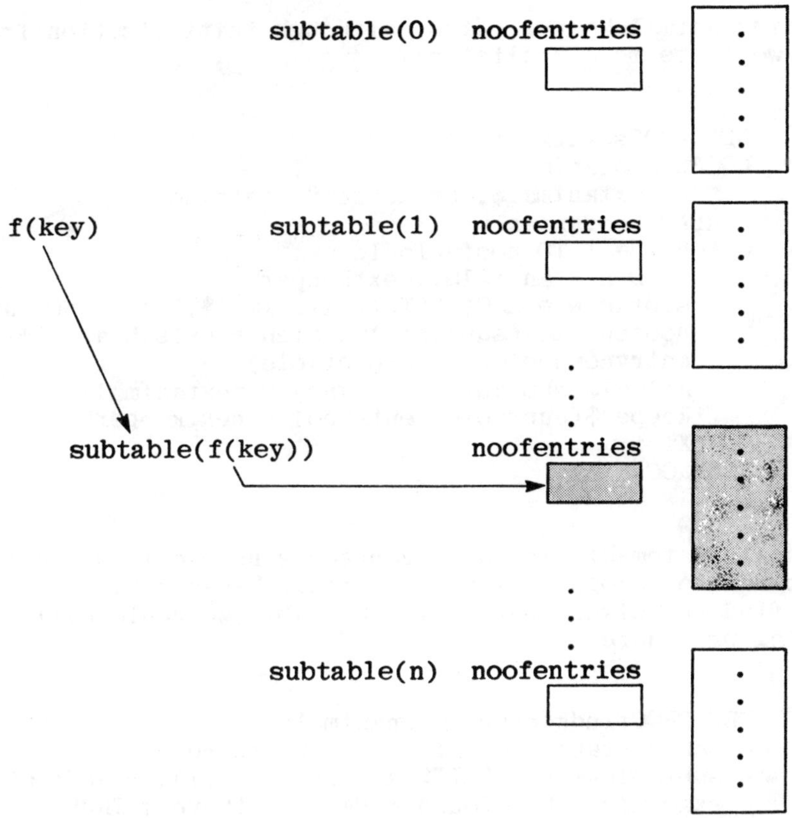

We can set up this data structure for the zoo table using three arrays (or more if there were more fields associated with each animal): a one-dimensional array containing the 'noofentries' values, and two two-dimensional arrays to store the subtables:

```
10   DIM noofentries(25), animal$(25,10), keeper$(25,10)
```

noofentries	animal$			keeper$		
3	aardvark	adder	agama	Bloggs	Jones	Smith
1	baboon			Brown		
2	camel	coyote		Smith	Watt	
.	.	.	.	.	.	.
.	.	.	.	.	.	.

We can initialise the structure from DATA statements

containing animal-keeper pairs (although initialisation from a file would be more realistic).

```
200    DEF PROCsetupzootable
210    LOCAL noofanimals, i,
             nextanimal$,nextkeeper$, entryno
220      READ noofanimals
230      FOR i = 1 TO noofanimals
240        READ nextanimal$, nextkeeper$
250        subtable = ASC(LEFT$(nextanimal$,1)) - ASC("a")
260        noofentries(subtable)=noofentries(subtable)+1
270        entryno=noofentries(subtable)
280        animal$(subtable, entryno) = nextanimal$
290        keeper$(subtable, entryno) = nextkeeper$
300      NEXT i
310    ENDPROC
```

Additional statements would of course be needed if we wanted the program to recognise when a subtable became full.

To find a given entry in the table we could call the following procedure:

```
400    DEF PROCfindkeeper(givenanimal$)
410    LOCAL subtable, examined, found,there
420      subtable = ASC(LEFT$(givenanimal$,1)) - ASC("a")
430      examined = 0 : found = FALSE : there = TRUE
440      REPEAT
450        examined = examined + 1
460        IF examined > noofentries(subtable) THEN
             there = FALSE
           ELSE
            IF animal$(subtable,examined) = givenanimal$
            THEN found = TRUE
470      UNTIL found OR NOT(there)
480      IF found THEN PRINT "Animal's keeper is ";
                               keeper$(subtable, examined)
         ELSE PRINT "This animal is not in the zoo."
490    ENDPROC
```

This example illustrates a simple case of a 'hierarchical' table-access method. We use one method (direct access in this case) to find the appropriate subtable in which a given key could be found and then proceed to search for the given key in that subtable. In the above example we used linear search in the subtables, but in general any of the methods discussed could be used for organising and accessing the information within a subtable. In fact a subtable might itself be subdivided into further hierarchies of subtables.

Such hierarchical methods are extremely important when a

complete table is too large to be held in main memory. The subtables can be held on disk file, and only when a program has selected a particular subtable would that subtable be copied into main memory.

6.7 Open hash tables

The method of the previous section suffers from the disadvantage of breaking down as soon as one of the subtables is full. It is also rather uneconomical in terms of the amount of memory space used. It is surely unrealistic in the zoo-keeper example to allocate the same amount of space for animals whose names begin with X, Q or Z as for those whose names begin with B, say.

An open hash table provides a widely used method for dealing with the situation where we cannot define a function that converts each key into a unique value. The method makes more flexible use of available storage space than does the method described in the previous section.

An open hash table consists of a single table similar to that used in the direct access method. The range of values produced by the access function (or 'hash function') corresponds to the range of the subscripts for the table, but we accept the possibility that several keys may result in the same hash function value.

We describe first the simplest form of access mechanism for an open hash table. To find the location in which to insert the entry containing a given key, the hash value for that key is calculated and the entry is inserted in the first empty location from that point onwards. To find the entry in the table containing a given key, we evaluate the hash function and conduct a linear search in the table from that point onwards. The table is treated as being circular, i.e., if a search reaches the end of the table, the search carries on from the start of the table.

As a simple example, let each entry consist of a single integer and let us illustrate the process of inserting a sequence of these integers in a hash table, 'table'. We define the hash function value for a given key as:

h(key) = key MOD 10   (i.e. the last digit in the integer)

In general, the use of a hash function of the form 'key MOD n' is known as division hashing. Remember that this is an unrealistically small table used merely to introduce the technique. The point of the method is to speed up access to a large table using an access function that may map different keys into the same value, without the need to allocate a separate table for each possible access function value. We can use the 0 values that are inserted initially in all BASIC array locations to recognise 'empty' locations.

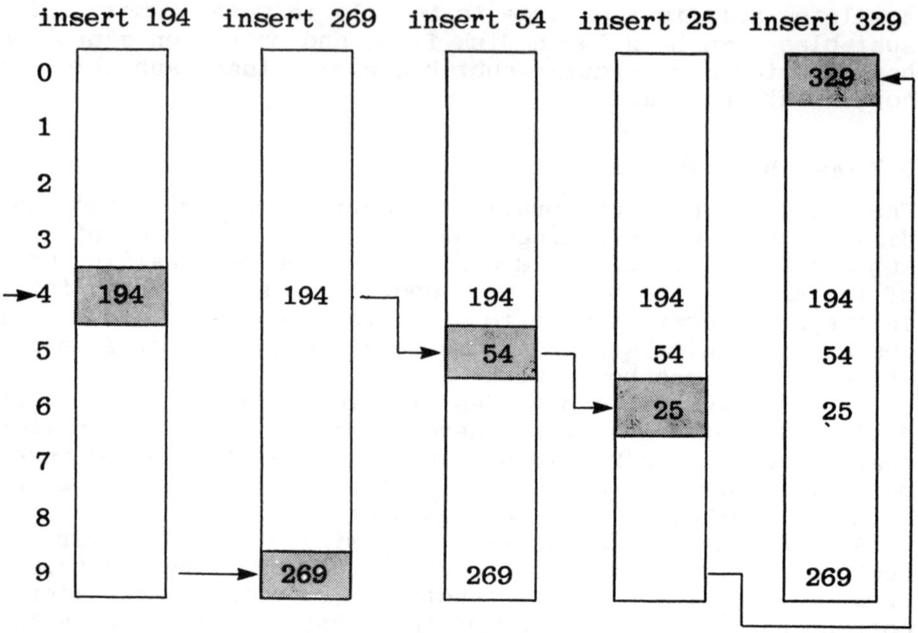

As a general rule, when inserting a new value in any table, we should check that it is not already there, and when searching for a given key in a table we should cater for the possibility that it is not there. These two processes are easily combined for our open hash table:

```
 10   DIM table(9)
          :
110   INPUT givenkey
120   probe = givenkey MOD 10 : there=TRUE : found=FALSE
130   REPEAT
140     IF table(probe) = givenkey THEN found = TRUE
        ELSE IF table(probe) = 0 THEN there = FALSE
        ELSE probe = (probe + 1) MOD 10
150   UNTIL NOT(there) OR found
160   IF found THEN PRINT "Given key is already there."
      ELSE   table(probe) = givenkey :
             PRINT "Key has been inserted in table."
```

Say, in the zoo-keeper example, we wish to allow for up to 26 animals, but we may have more than one beginning with the same letter. We can use the same table as was used for direct access:

```
10   DIM animal$(25), keeper$(25)
```

This time we organise it as an open hash table. The same

search algorithm can be used to find an empty slot in which to insert a new animal, or to find the slot containing a given animal. The following procedure carries out the search process required:

```
500   DEF PROCsearchfor(givenanimal$)
510   LOCAL probe, found, there
520     probe = ASC(LEFT$(givenanimal$,1)) - ASC("a")
530     found = FALSE : there = TRUE
540     REPEAT
550       IF animal$(probe) = givenanimal$ THEN
            found = TRUE
          ELSE IF animal$(probe) = "" THEN
                there = FALSE
          ELSE probe = (probe+1) MOD 26
560     UNTIL found OR NOT(there)
570     requiredslot = probe : animalfound = found
580   ENDPROC
```

Each time this procedure is called, it transmits information out to where it was called via the two variables 'requiredslot' and 'animalfound'. A sequence of animal-keeper pairs could be inserted in the table with:

```
200   DEF PROCsetupzootable
210   LOCAL noofanimals,i, nextanimal$,nextkeeper$
220     READ noofanimals
230     FOR i = 1 TO noofanimals
240       READ nextanimal$, nextkeeper$
250       PROCsearchfor(nextanimal$)
260       IF animalfound THEN
            PRINT nextanimal$; " is there already."
          ELSE animal$(requiredslot)=nextanimal$ :
                 keeper$(requiredslot)=nextkeeper$
270     NEXT i
280   ENDPROC
```

To answer an inquiry about who looks after a particular animal, we could use:

```
400   DEF PROCfindkeeper(givenanimal$)
410     PROCsearchfor(givenanimal$)
420     IF animalfound THEN
          PRINT keeper$(requiredslot); " looks after ";
        ELSE PRINT "We don't keep ";
430     PRINT givenanimal$; "s."
440   ENDPROC
```

This is what the table would look like after inserting the sequence

coyote
fox
wolf
bear
warthog
antelope
ocelot
elephant
lion
zebra
yeti
buffalo
yak
cougar
bison

	animal$
0	antelope
1	bear
2	coyote
3	buffalo
4	elephant
5	fox
6	yak
7	cougar
8	bison
9	
10	
11	lion
12	
13	
14	ocelot
15	
16	
17	
18	
19	
20	
21	
22	wolf
23	warthog
24	yeti
25	zebra

The keeper information is omitted to aid clarity in the diagram.

Note the tendency for the names to bunch together in particular areas of the table. This can result in very long search lengths for some names. A simple approach like this would be even more likely to cause bunching in other application areas, for example in storing an interpreter variable table: programmers tend to invent names for their variables in some systematic way - x, y, z, a, b, c, root1, root2, root3, etc. We usually combine two approaches to solving this problem.

Firstly, we should attempt to define a hash function that results in as wide a spread of values as possible over the subscripts of the table. The function need not be particularly meaningful. We could, for example, select an arbitrary subset of the bit pattern representation of a key and transform this in any way we like to give a hash value.

Secondly we can modify the simple linear search used above to find a location in the table. In the first example considered above, we calculate an initial value for probe (p say) and proceed to examine locations p, p+1, p+2,..., all values being taken MOD 10. We could, in general, examine locations p, p+d(1), p+d(2),..., where d is some displacement function. The simplest such function is a linear one, d(i) = ki and in the above case we used k = 1. A value of k > 1 can give us a better spread of the information in the table and shorten search lengths. With k = 7 we would examine locations p, p+7, p+14, ..., (all MOD the size of the table).

Modifying the zoo-keeper example in this way produces:

Using k = 7 and inserting the same names as before

coyote
fox
wolf
bear
warthog
antelope
ocelot
elephant
lion
zebra
yeti
buffalo
yak
cougar
bison

	animal$
0	antelope
2	bear
3	warthog
4	elephant
5	fox
6	
7	
8	buffalo
9	cougar
10	
11	lion
12	yak
13	
14	ocelot
15	bison
16	
17	
18	
19	
20	
21	
22	wolf
23	
24	yeti
25	zebra

Search lengths up to 9 were necessary in the previous table, but here the longest search length involves only 3 comparisons.

Note that if n is the size of the table, then k and n must be coprime, otherwise not all the locations of the table will be available for any given hash value. Consider n=12 and k=4. For hash value 7, only locations 7, 11 and 3 are visited by the algorithm and only these locations are available for storing keys with hash value 7.

The theory tells us that for a table of size n containing m records, use of a linear displacement function results in an average search length of (1-r/2)/(1-r), where r = m/n. In order to obtain the best time/space trade-off, the table should not get more than 2/3 to 3/4 full.

Improved search times can be obtained by using non-linear

displacement functions, but we will not discuss this here.

Finally, note that in real-life implementations, greatest efficiency is achieved by using a table of size n, where n is a power of 2. Calculations MOD n can then be performed by ANDing with a computer word containing a sequence of bits all set to 1. The hash function can be calculated efficiently in a similar way. In data processing jargon, hashing is sometimes known as 'randomising' and is an example of an 'address generating' access method.

Exercises

1 Write a program that reads the stock list for the small department store described in an earlier exercise. The program should store the stock list in an open hash table using the stock numbers as keys. This table should then be used in repeatedly processing price enquiries.

2 Modify the French-English word translation program so that it uses an open hash table for storing the dictionary.

3 Use the procedures of Chapter 4, Section 4.1, to animate the process of building up an open hash table. In the strings manipulated in Chapter 4, the last three characters represented a stock number. A suitable hash function that would allow the table to fit on the screen could be calculated by:

```
VAL(RIGHT$(nextitem$,3)) MOD 20
```

This gives values in the range 0 to 19 and we would therefore use a table where locations were numbered 0 to 19. The table would be better displayed at the right of the screen, the value that is to enter the table being displayed with its hash value at the left of the screen. Use colour to highlight the locations of the table being examined during the search for an empty location.

6.8 Indexing and pointers

In this section we introduce the idea of storing and manipulating indirect references to the information being handled by a program. We describe two applications of this idea.

Indexed access to a table – introduction

Here we return to the idea of hierarchical access methods. Let us consider the problem of storing our animal records in a table which we shall divide into 26 subtables as before, one for the animals beginning with A, one for the animals beginning with B, and so on. As discussed above, this permits a two level access method, firstly to find the subtable in which the required entry lies, and then to search that subtable. Remember that this will in general require less effort than the search of a single large table. Here we shall make our division into subtables more flexible than it was before. For example, we might want to allow 4 locations for animals beginning with A, 7 locations for animals beginning with B, ... 2 locations for X, 4 for Y and 2 for Z. We allocate one large table in which the animal entries are to be stored:

```
DIM animal$(150), keeper(150)
```

We shall store information in an 'index table' which indicates where in the main table to find information about animals beginning with each letter.

```
DIM noofentries(25), index(25)
```

The intention is that, for example, 'noofentries(i)' and 'index(i)' should contain two integers, the first indicating how many animals beginning with the ith letter of the alphabet are stored, and the second indicating where in the main table the first animal beginning with the ith letter is stored. (Letters are numbered from 0 as before.) Entries for all animals beginning with a certain letter are to be stored in consecutive locations of the main table. For example:

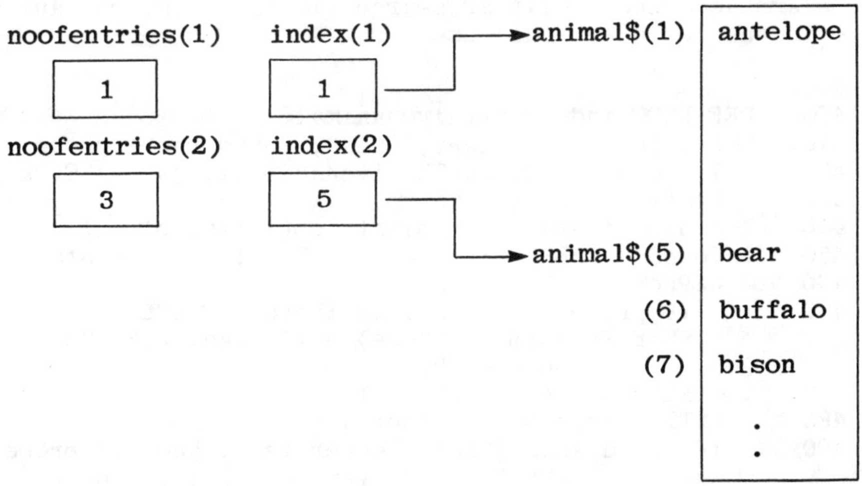

We can think of the entries in the index array as 'pointers' to information in the main table. One way of indicating to the program how large to make the subtables for each letter would be to supply these 26 sizes in a DATA statement:

```
DATA 4, 7, ..., 2, 4, 2
```

The next procedure sets up the table from DATA statements. Lines 220-260 initialise an empty table and the remainder of the procedure adds each animal to the appropriate subtable.

```
200    DEF PROCsetupzootable
210    LOCAL next,letter,size, i,entryno,location,
             nextanimal$,nextkeeper$
220      next = 1
230      FOR letter = 0 TO 25
240        noofentries(letter)=0 : index(letter)=next
250        READ size : next = next + size
260      NEXT letter
270      READ noofanimals
280      FOR i = 1 TO noofanimals
290        READ nextanimal$, nextkeeper$
300        letterno=ASC(LEFT$(nextanimal$,1))-ASC("a")
310        location=index(letterno)+noofentries(letterno)
320        noofentries(letterno)=noofentries(letterno)+1
330        animal$(location) = nextanimal$
340        keeper$(location) = nextkeeper$
350      NEXT i
360    ENDPROC
```

The index table is accessed directly using the first letter of an animal's name as a key and the subtables of the main table are accessed by linear search. To find a given animal name in the table we would use:

```
400    DEF PROCfindkeeper(givenanimal$)
410    LOCAL letterno, start,finish, found,there,probe
420      letterno = ASC(LEFT$(givenanimal$,1)) - ASC("a")
430      start = index(letterno)
440      finish = start + noofentries(letterno) - 1
450      found = FALSE  :  there = TRUE : probe = start
460      REPEAT
470        IF probe > finish THEN there = FALSE
           ELSE IF animal$(probe) = givenanimal$ THEN
                  found = TRUE
           ELSE probe = probe + 1
480      UNTIL found OR NOT(there)
490      IF found THEN PRINT "Keeper is "; keeper$(probe)
                  ELSE PRINT "Given name not found."
500    ENDPROC
```

Indexed sequential access

In the above example, the keys used to access the table were the animal names, and the main table in which the keys were stored was to a certain extent ordered on these keys. Whenever the main table is ordered on the keys, access to the main table can be easily accomplished via an index. In the above example, entries in the index table were found by direct access, but in general the distribution of the keys will not permit this. It would be silly to have index entries for animals beginning with A, B, C, ..., Z if we only have animals beginning with B and C, say. In such cases some of the keys themselves could be stored in the index table. For example:

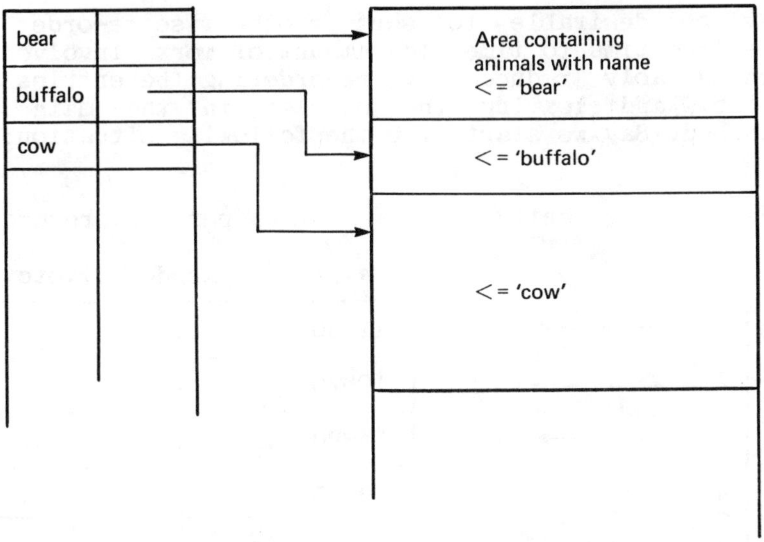

In these situations, entries in the index table could be found by linear search or binary search.

If the number of records involved is very large, resulting in a large index, an index to the index can be used, resulting in a three level access method.

In data processing applications where the records are usually held on disk, sequential files with indexes constitute the most common form of addressing. This is because most data processing applications involve a mixture of random access to a file (e.g. find the entry for a given employee) and sequential access to the file (e.g. print out the names of all employees in alphabetical order). For random access the index is used and for sequential access the main file itself can be scanned in order. These techniques are therefore known as 'indexed sequential access' methods.

Sorting an index table

Another area in which use of an index table is advantageous is in sorting when each table entry is large, perhaps spanning a number of parallel arrays. For example:

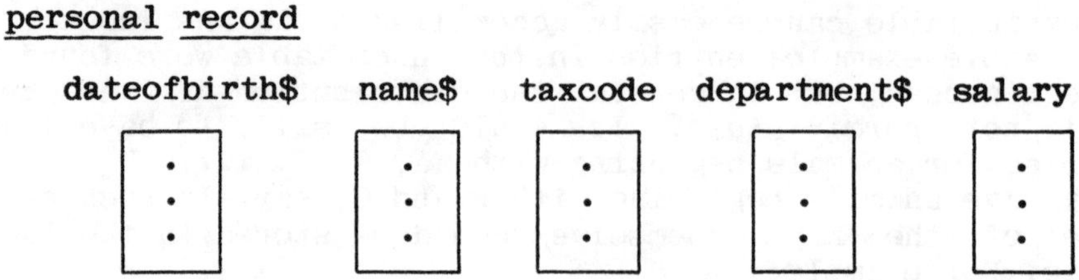

It may be desirable to sort or otherwise re-order these entries from time to time. The amount of work involved can be considerably reduced by re-ordering the entries in an index table and leaving the entries in the main table undisturbed. Say we start with the following situation:

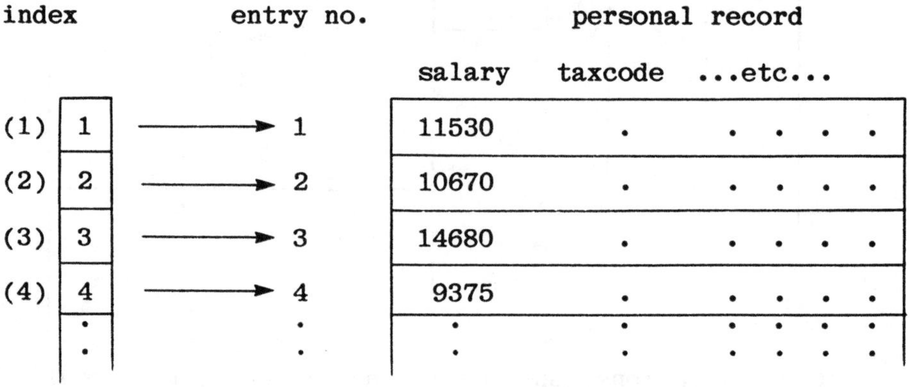

and we wanted to sort the entries into increasing order of salary. We can move the numbers or pointers in the index table until 'index(1)' contains the entry number for the entry with the lowest salary, 'index(2)' contains the entry number for the entry with the next lowest salary etc.

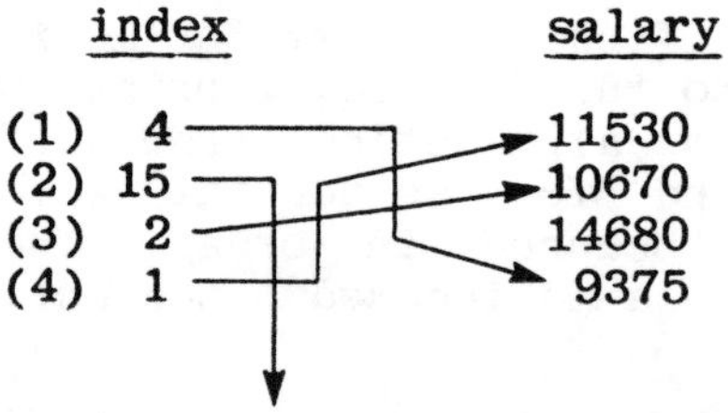

Here is a program that uses a simple exchange sort to sort the same stock list as was used in Section 6.3. In this case, we rearrange only the items in the index array to indicate the new ordering. You should refer back to the previous exchange sort and note the differences. Here, whenever we want to refer to the stock number for item i, we need to use:

```
stockno(index(i))
```

and to swap items i and j in the ordering, we need only move the contents of 'index(i)' and 'index(j)'.

```
 10   DIM stockno(100), price(100), index(100)
 20   PROCsetupstocktable
 30   PROCsortstocktable(noofitemsinstock)
 40   PROCoutputstocktable
 50   END

200   DEF PROCsetupstocktable
210   LOCAL i
220     READ noofitemsinstock
230     FOR i = 1 TO noofitemsinstock
240       READ stockno(i), price(i)
250       index(i) = i
260     NEXT i
270   ENDPROC

400   DEF PROCsortstocktable(n)
410   LOCAL i
420     FOR i = 1 TO n-1
430       PROCfindsmallestentryfrom(i)
440       PROCswop(i, posnsmallest)
450     NEXT i
460   ENDPROC

500   DEF PROCfindsmallestentryfrom(i)
510     LOCAL next
520     posnsmallest = i
530     FOR next = i+1 TO n
540       IF stockno(index(next))
            < stockno(index(posnsmallest))
          THEN posnsmallest = next
550     NEXT next
560   ENDPROC

600   DEF PROCswop(i, j)
610     LOCAL temp
620     temp = index(i)
630     index(i) = index(j)
640     index(j) = temp
650   ENDPROC

700   DEF PROCoutputstocktable
710   LOCAL i
720     FOR i = 1 TO noofitemsinstock
730       PRINT stockno(index(i)), price(index(i))
740     NEXT i
750   ENDPROC
```

Exercises

1 Set up two parallel arrays containing the French-English dictionary used earlier. Now initialise two index tables each of which should contain pointers to all the locations in the dictionary. The entries in the first index table should be sorted so that they point to entries in alphabetical order of English words. The second table should then be sorted on the French words. Check that the program now works by using the index tables to print out the dictionary once with the English words in order and again with the French words in order.

2 Use the index tables created by the last exercise in a program that translates a given word from French into English or from English into French. The program should use binary search in the appropriate index table.

6.9 Adventure games - an example of the use of pointers

An interesting possible use of indexing techniques is an adventure game. These games were originally developed on a mainframe computer and despite the fact that they are dialogue games, using no graphics facilities, they have become very popular.

In an adventure game the player 'moves' from one geographical state to another. When in a particular state a transition to another state is only possible by moving in a predetermined direction. For example, the transitions for an extremely simple nine-state game are shown by arrows in the 'map':

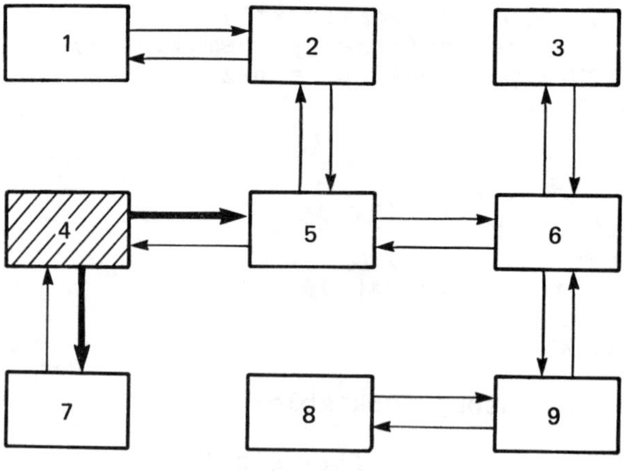

'Geographical' states 1 - 9 and possible transitions

Both the allowed directions and movement through the states can be controlled by a two dimensional array of indices or pointers. We could represent these by using rows of four elements. Each item in a row represents a possible transition path in the directions N,E,S, or W, say.

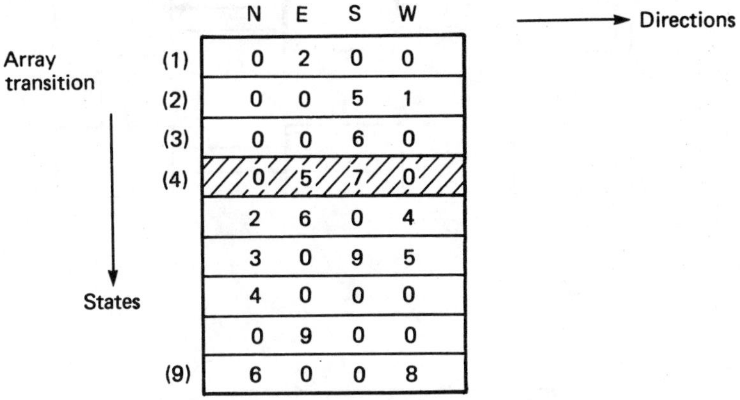

Transitions stored as pointers in a two-dimensional array

We could 'move' through these states by using the following structure. This structure or something equivalent forms the kernel of all adventure game programs.

```
10    PROCsetupdatastructures
20    position = 3
30    REPEAT
40      INPUT direction$
50      dir = INSTR("NESW", direction$)
60      IF transition(dir, position) = 0 THEN
             PRINT "can't move"
        ELSE position = transition(dir, position)
70    UNTIL FALSE
```

The important statement is the one that follows the ELSE. If we started with 'position' equal to 1 and typed the sequence E,S,N,W, we would 'move' from state 1 to states 2 and 5 back to state 1.

The player of the game must explore and attempt to construct his own map for the game.

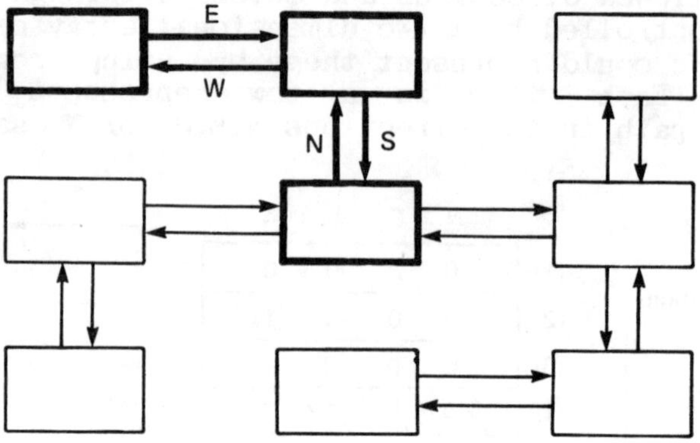

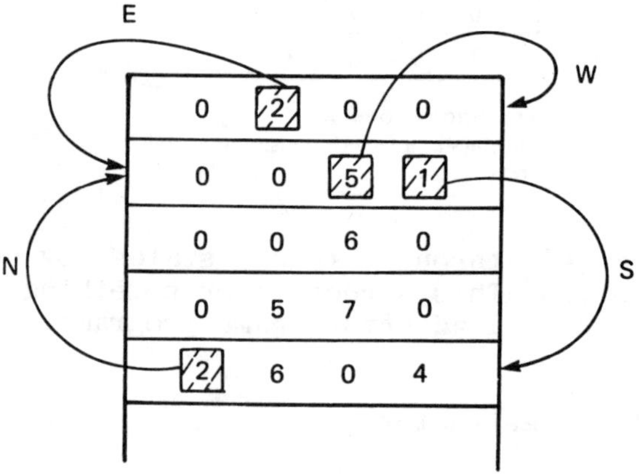

'Travelling through' the states in response to the sequence E, S, N, W.

Now another array is needed to store a description of each place so that the player/computer dialogue can be set in a particular environment, say:

```
description$(1)    in a shrubbery
            (2)    in a conservatory
            (3)    outside a gloomy house
            (4)    in a dark tunnel
            (5)    in a library
            (6)    in a dingy hallway
            (7)    in a smuggler's cave
            (8)    in a wizard's lair
            (9)    in a dark passage
```

The kernel can then be enhanced to include indexing to this array.

```
60    IF transition(dir, position) = 0 THEN
          PRINT "can't move"
      ELSE position = transition(dir, position):
          PRINT "You are now "; description$(position)
```

Now the point of the game is to reach a particular destination or goal. The instructions telling the player which state he is in needs to be part of a procedure that checks to see if the goal state has been reached.

```
20    position = 3 : goalachieved = FALSE
30    REPEAT
40      INPUT direction$
50      dir = INSTR("NESW", direction$)
60      IF transition(dir, position) = 0 THEN
             PRINT "can't move"
        ELSE position = transition(dir, position) :
             PROCcheckgoalreached
70    UNTIL goalachieved
```

So far so good, but it still isn't a very interesting game. The game is made more difficult by making a transition conditional on factors other than direction, such as possession of a particular object and avoiding various pitfalls. For example a lamp may be required to pass through a 'dark' state or a weapon may be required to deal with a state containing an enemy. Failure to cope with these pitfalls by non-possession of the requisite object or not taking the appropriate action with the object finishes the game.

```
30    REPEAT
        .
        .
        .
50    UNTIL goalachieved OR dead
60    IF goalachieved THEN PRINT "well done!"
      ELSE PRINT "hard luck"
```

The objects and the initial states that they appear in can be stored in two parallel arrays.

```
    object$ (1)  lamp          objectpostn (1)  5
            (2)  emerald                   (2)  7
            (3)  sword                     (3)  6
            (4)  axe                       (4)  7
            (5)  ogre                      (5)  4
            (6)  serpent                   (6)  9
```

Additional commands might now be included for 'getting' or 'dropping' objects, position code 0 being used to indicate that the player is carrying an object. The validity of a move might now be checked by calling a procedure such as:

```
100   DEF PROCcheckcanmove
110     IF transition(direction, dir) = 0 THEN
            PRINT "can't move" : ENDPROC
120     IF position = 6 AND objectpostn(1) <>0 THEN
          PRINT "You have fallen into a bottomless pit":
          dead = TRUE : ENDPROC
                      .
                      .  more pitfall checks
                      .
130     position = transition(dir, position)
140   ENDPROC
```

The implication of the first pitfall check is that in state 4 you must possess the lamp. Further elaborations can easily be added so that a sufficient level of detail is achieved to produce an intriguing game. For example, the lamp may be required to be lit.

The initialisation for the string arrays and the numeric arrays can originate from DATA statements or more usually from a file. Another important point is that a well-written program structure can be imposed on alternative data. Changing the string initialisations (and the numeric initialisation if required) produces a completely different game. The data would be a simple example of a database.

Exercises

1 Design a map for a simple adventure game and implement this as a transition table in a complete program which moves from one state to another in response to commands N, S, E, W. The main loop should repeatedly call a procedure PROCobeycommand:

```
goalachieved = FALSE : dead = FALSE
REPEAT
   INPUT command$
   PROCobeycommand
UNTIL goalachieved OR dead
```

At each step, the program should either print a message indicating that the move is not allowed or print the number of the new state reached. Do not attempt to add any frills until you are sure that the basic transition process is working and the program is moving around the map as expected. At first there will be no statements in the program for changing 'goalachieved' or 'dead' and you will have to terminate the program with the ESCAPE key.

2 Now invent a verbal description for each state and set up a description array of strings. Use this to print a description of each state reached.

3 Make up a short list of objects, decide on their initial position and set up two parallel arrays containing a description and a position for each object. Implement a new command L (for look) which prints a list of objects that are at the current position.

4 Implement new commands G (for Get), D (for Drop) each of which is followed by an object name. The object name will have to be looked up in the object description array and the corresponding object position code changed appropriately. Implement a command I (for Inventory) which prints a list of objects currently held.

5 Decide on a goal for your game. For example the purpose could be to find one of the objects and transfer it to a particular place. PROCobeycommand can be extended to test whether the goal has been achieved and set the variable 'goalachieved' accordingly.

6 Add some pitfalls to your program and test for these in a move-making procedure setting 'dead' accordingly.

Chapter 7 **Introduction to recursion**

In computing, a recursive process is one that is 'described in terms of itself'. Recursion is viewed with suspicion by beginners - how on earth can an operation be defined in terms of itself? One of our students recently remarked that writing a recursive program seemed like an act of faith. However, once mastered, recursion is a powerful tool and should not be neglected. There are many programming problems where a recursive solution is elegant and easy to write and the non-recursive solution is difficult and tricky. Many human problem-solving activities are recursive in nature. For example, let us consider the problem of planning a route for walking through London from Trafalgar Square to the British Museum. One way of solving this problem might be to pick an intermediate point such as Covent Garden and break our original problem down into the problem of getting from Trafalgar Square to Covent Garden and from Covent Garden to the British Museum. A problem of navigation has been broken down into two easier subproblems, also of navigation.

This is the essence of recursion. The solution to a problem is described in terms of solutions to easier or smaller versions of the same problem. We could (rather fancifully) describe how to find a route between two points as:

```
100   DEF PROCfind_route_between(a, b)
110     IF getting from a to b is 'easy' (one street say)
        THEN PROCprint_route(a, b) : ENDPROC
120     n = a point midway between a and b
130     PROCfind_route_between(a, n)
140     PROCfind_route_between(n, b)
150   ENDPROC
```

We shall not expand this into a complete BASIC program. In order to do so we would need to store a street map of London, lists of landmarks and their locations, a definition of what we mean by an 'easy' problem and so on. However, this outline procedure describes a process with which we are all subconsciously familiar. It also exhibits the essential features of a recursive procedure.

When a procedure is called, the particular problem to be

considered is specified by means of its parameters:

```
PROCfind_route_between("Trafalgar Square", "British Museum")
```

The first thing the procedure does is to decide whether the problem represented by its parameters can be solved directly without breaking it down into further subproblems. If this can be done, no recursion takes place. This is essential, otherwise the process of breaking the problem down into subproblems would never stop.

Finally if the problem to be solved by the call of the procedure is not an easy one, it breaks it down into easier subproblems and requests the solution to each of these subproblems in turn. The solutions to the subproblems are requested by calling the same procedure, but with different parameters. You might find it easier to think of the subproblems being solved by different copies of the procedure, although it does not happen like this behind the scenes. This is the classic 'divide and conquer' approach to problem solving, so important in areas like Artificial Intelligence.

Learning to use recursion successfully means learning to recognise when a problem can be broken down into easier, or smaller, versions of itself and remembering to start a recursive procedure with a test that recognises when a given problem does not need to be further broken down. It is usually easier to write a recursive procedure without worrying in detail about what the exact sequence of operations will be when the procedure is called (an 'act of faith' if you like). Just remember the two basic ingredients - the stopping condition and the breakdown into easier subproblems.

It is of course interesting to understand what does happen when we call a recursive procedure. In fact, when a program does not work as intended, such an understanding is essential. Later, we shall explain in detail how recursive programs work, but first let us write some simple programs that use recursion.

7.1 Some easy recursive programs

Many of the programs presented in this section could very easily be written without recursion using simple loops. However, such 'inappropriate' use of recursion provides a useful introduction to the subject using problems with which we are familiar.

The first example simply prints the positive integers from 1 to n using a procedure that can be called by:

```
10   INPUT n
20   PROCprintupto(n)
30   END
```

We shall break down the process of printing the numbers up to n into the problem of printing the numbers up to n-1 followed by the use of a PRINT statement to print n. Of course if n = 0, then there are no values to be printed and this is the condition that we shall use to terminate the recursion.

```
100   DEF PROCprintupto(n)
110     IF n = 0 THEN ENDPROC
120     PROCprintupto(n-1)
130     PRINT n
140   ENDPROC
```

In the next section we shall discuss in detail what happens when this program is obeyed. For the time being we shall take on trust the fact that a recursive program works!

An interesting variation on this program is to change it so that it prints the integers up to n, but in reverse order. In this case, the breakdown into an easier subproblem gives

```
PRINT n
print numbers up to n-1 in reverse order.
```

The only change that needs to be made to the previous program is to switch lines 120 and 130.

```
100   DEF PROCprintupto(n)
110     IF n = 0 THEN ENDPROC
120     PRINT n
130     PROCprintupto(n-1)
140   ENDPROC
```

The above two programs are examples of what is sometimes called 'unary recursion' - a problem is broken down into one easier version of itself together with straightforward operations such as PRINT.

A simple example of 'binary recursion', where a problem is broken down into two simpler versions of itself, is provided by an alternative approach to printing the first n integers. We can define a procedure that prints the integers in a given range. For example,

```
PROCprintbetween(3,7)
```

will print the integers 3, 4, 5, 6, 7.

```
PROCprintbetween(4,4)
```

will print the single integer 4. This procedure could be used to print the positive integers up to n by calling

```
PROCprintbetween(1,n)
```

PROCprintbetween can be defined using binary recursion if we break down the problem of printing a given sequence into:

print the first half of the sequence
print the second half of the sequence

If only one value is to be printed, then this breakdown will not be needed.

```
 10   INPUT max
 20   PROCprintupto(max)
 30   END

100   DEF PROCprintupto(n)
110     PROCprintbetween(1, n)
120   ENDPROC

130   DEF PROCprintbetween(i, j)
140   LOCAL mid
150     IF i=j THEN PRINT i : ENDPROC
160     mid = (i+j) DIV 2
170     PROCprintbetween(i, mid)
180     PROCprintbetween(mid+1, j)
190   ENDPROC
```

Again, we leave a detailed study of what happens when this program is run until the next section. For the time being, note that it is vital when writing recursive programs that variables should be declared to be LOCAL wherever appropriate. The reasons for this are discussed in the next section.

The problem of printing the first n integers is, of course, a rather trivial problem. We finish this section with a simple recursive program that could not be so easily written without recursion. The problem we consider is that of printing a given positive integer in binary. For example,

```
PROCbinaryprint(5)
```

should display

```
101
```

and

```
PROCbinaryprint(179)
```

should display

10110011

The easiest way to convert an integer into binary is to keep dividing by 2 and collect all the remainders. The remainders represent the bits required, but they are generated in reverse order.

		remainders
2	179	
2	89	1
2	44	1
2	22	0
2	11	0
2	5	1
2	2	1
2	1	0
	0	1

remainders in reverse order give 10110011

One way of programming this process without recursion would be to store the remainders in an array and print them out only when the repeated division has terminated with zero. With recursion, the solution is considerably simpler. We break down the problem of printing the number n in binary:

```
print n DIV 2 in binary
PRINT ; n MOD 2;
```

where n MOD 2 is the last bit of the number.

```
 10   INPUT "Integer to be expressed in binary", int
 20   PROCbinaryprint(int)
 30   END

100   DEF PROCbinaryprint(n)
110     IF n<2 THEN PRINT ;n; : ENDPROC
120     PROCbinaryprint(n DIV 2)
130     PRINT ; n MOD 2;
140   ENDPROC
```

You might like to experiment with the effect of omitting some of the semicolons in the above program. Changing line 110 affects only the first bit of the number printed while changing line 130 affects all the other bits apart from the first one.

Another experiment worth trying is to replace the stopping condition at line 110 with

```
110     IF n=0 THEN ENDPROC
```

The program will then work correctly in all cases except when the original input value is 0. Taking no action on a zero parameter is correct if the case 'n=0' arises as a 'subproblem'. We do not want to print a leading zero at the start of a non-zero number. However, if the original number is zero, then this number must be printed. We must ensure that our procedure correctly handles the case where the stopping condition is true on the first call of the procedure as well as the case where it is true for a subproblem.

7.2 How it works

We start this section by introducing a model - the 'tree of procedure calls' - that will be valuable in understanding the behaviour of recursive programs. To introduce this model, we first look at a program that involves procedures, but no recursion. This program draws a simple house.

```
 10  height=600:width=1000
 20  MODE 4
 30  PROCdrawhouse
 40  k=GET : MODE 7
 50  END

 60  DEF PROCdrawhouse
 70    PROCdrawfront
 80    PROCdrawroof
 90  ENDPROC

100  DEF PROCdrawfront
110    PROCdrawbox(0,0,width,height)
120    PROCdrawwindows
130    PROCdrawdoor
140  ENDPROC

150  DEF PROCdrawwindows
160    LOCAL ww,wh
170    ww=2*width/10 : wh=height/3
180    PROCdrawbox(ww/2,wh,ww,wh)
190    PROCdrawbox(7*ww/2,wh,ww,wh)
200  ENDPROC

210  DEF PROCdrawdoor
220    PROCdrawbox(4*width/10,0,width/5,height*2/3)
230  ENDPROC
```

```
240   DEF PROCdrawbox(x,y,w,h)
250     MOVE x,y
260     PLOT 1,0,h:PLOT 1,w,0
270     PLOT 1,0,-h:PLOT 1,-w,0
280   ENDPROC

290   DEF PROCdrawroof
300     MOVE 0,height
310     PLOT 1,width/2,height/3
320     PLOT 1,width/2,-height/3
330   ENDPROC
```

The process of drawing a house is broken down into the process of drawing a 'front' and then drawing a roof. We can illustrate this by

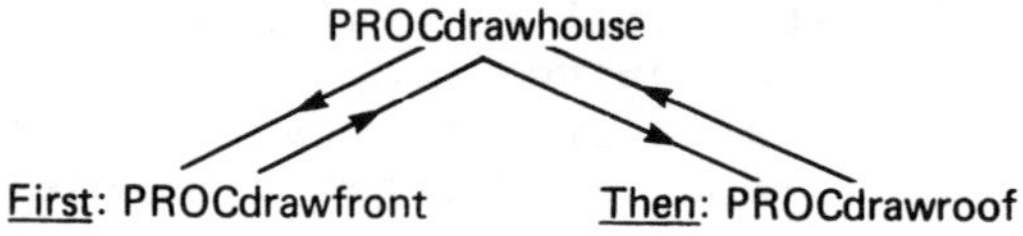

PROCdrawroof is defined in terms of primitive operations, MOVE and DRAW, but PROCdrawfront is broken down into further 'subproblems'.

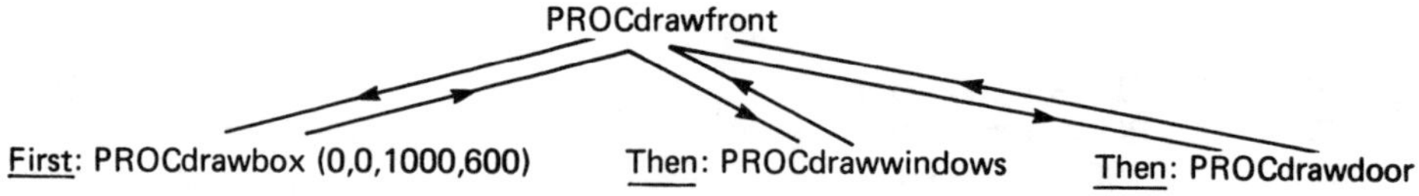

PROCdrawbox is primitive, but PROCdrawwindows and PROCdrawdoor are themselves defined in terms of other procedure calls. We can represent all this information as a complete 'tree of procedure calls' for the program, together with arrows representing the 'flow of control' through the program.

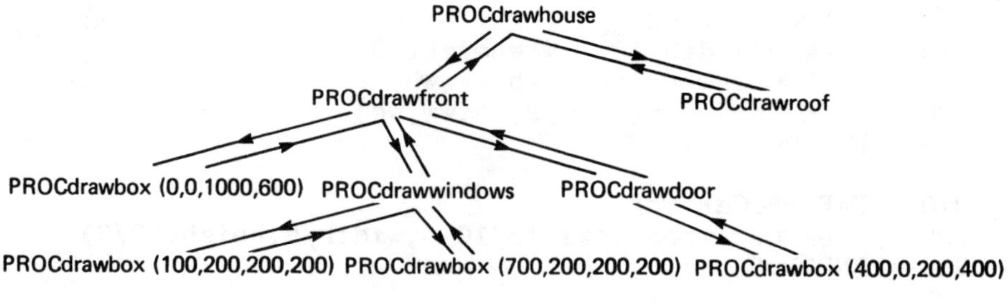

We shall often abbreviate such a diagram by using single lines in place of the double arrows and by omitting the word PROC.

Notice in this example that PROCdrawbox is obeyed on several different occasions with different sets of parameters. Each time it is used, this procedure behaves differently. However one call of PROCdrawbox is terminated before another is activated.

Now let us consider the behaviour of the first recursive program of the last section. We can illustrate the behaviour of this program for a call of

```
PROCprintupto(3)
```

by the following 'tree' of procedure calls.

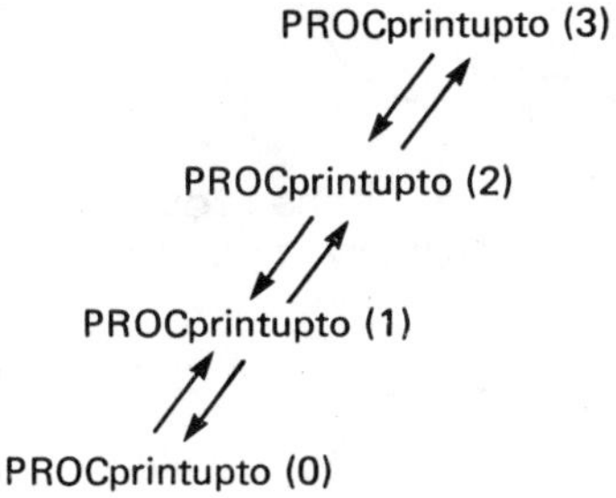

(The tree has only one branch at each level because we are using unary recursion.) Like PROCdrawbox, PROCprintupto is called at several points with a different parameter each time. The only difference is that successive calls of PROCprintupto take place <u>before</u> the previous call has finished. The easiest way to understand what is happening is to imagine a separate copy of the procedure being created each time it is called. Of course, such copying would be extremely wasteful of computer store (and time) and recursion is organised much more efficiently behind the scenes. Only the storage space for parameters and local variables need be copied when a procedure is called. However, in appreciating how a recursive procedure works, it is convenient to imagine the whole procedure being copied. We shall refer to these copies of a procedure as 'activations' of the procedure. We can expand the above tree of procedure calls in more detail:

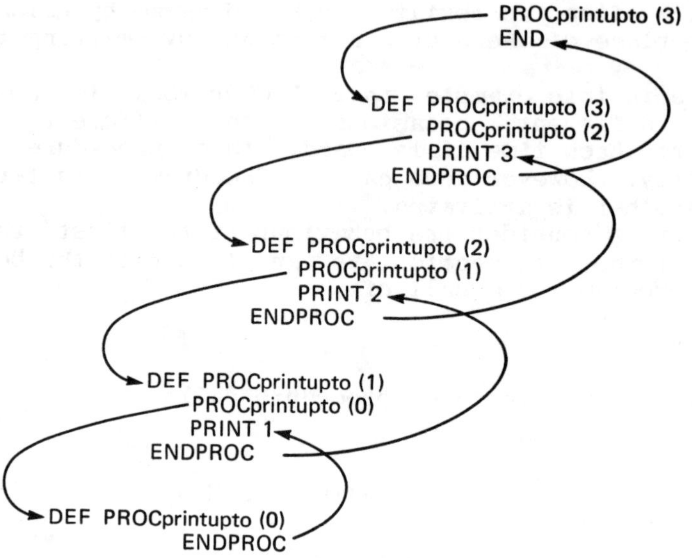

Now let us consider the behaviour of PROCprintbetween, the procedure that used binary recursion. In this program, a call of

```
PROCprintupto(5)
```

results in a call of

```
PROCprintbetween(1,5)
```

This executes the following:

```
mid = (1+5) DIV 2    i.e. mid = 3
PROCprintbetween(1,3)
PROCprintbetween(4,5)
```

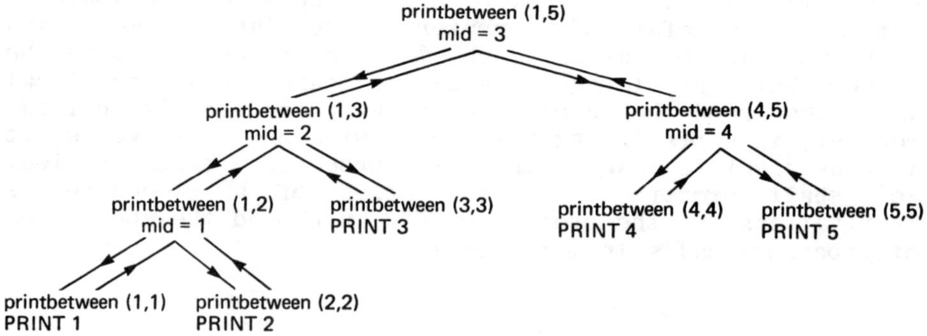

Each of the two recursive calls of PROCprintbetween behave in a similar way. You should now be able to follow the arrows through the tree and see exactly how the sequence of procedure calls results in the numbers being printed in the required order.

Note the importance of declaring 'mid' to be LOCAL to PROCprintbetween. This results in each recursive call of the procedure having its own private variable called 'mid'. Changing the value of this variable does not affect the current value of 'mid' in other activations or copies of the procedure. Thus, for example, when the activation PROCprintbetween(1,3) is terminated, control returns to PROCprintbetween(1,5) and the value of 'mid' in that procedure activation is still set to 3. The other procedure activations that have been obeyed since setting that value each used different storage locations for holding their LOCAL value for 'mid'. The value 'mid = 3' is needed in PROCprintbetween(1,5) for calculating the first parameter of the next recursive call (at line 180 of the program).

7.3 Towers of Hanoi

In this section we shall discuss the classic 'Towers of Hanoi' puzzle. The puzzle has been used as an illustration of recursion in the User Guide, but without explanation. The puzzle consists of three pegs mounted on a base together with a number of disks, all of different diameter. The disks have holes in them which allow them to be slipped on and off the pegs. The initial state is:

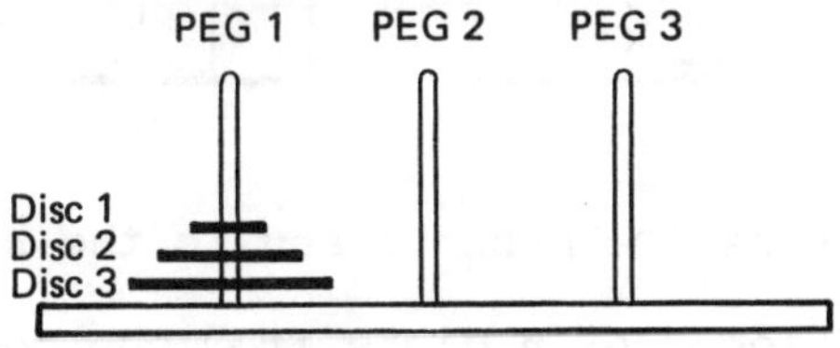

Towers of Hanoi puzzle

The problem is to find a sequence of moves that transfers the piles of disks from PEG1 to PEG2 subject to the following rules.

(1) Only one disk can be moved at a time.

(2) No disk can ever rest on a disk that is smaller than itself

PEG3 can be used during the transfer as a temporary resting place for disks. Here is a solution to the three disk problem.

```
Move DISK1 from PEG1 to PEG2
Move DISK2 from PEG1 to PEG3
Move DISK1 from PEG2 to PEG3
Move DISK3 from PEG1 to PEG2
Move DISK1 from PEG3 to PEG1
Move DISK2 from PEG3 to PEG2
Move DISK1 from PEG1 to PEG2
```

In order to produce a recursive procedure for printing a solution to the problem, we can reason as follows. At some stage during the solution, we must move DISK3 (the largest) from PEG1 to PEG2. In order to do this, all the other disks must be out of the way on PEG3. Thus, we must first solve the easier problem of transferring 2 disks to PEG3 (using PEG2 as the spare peg if necessary). While this subproblem is being solved, DISK3 can be treated as part of the fixed base. After this subproblem has been solved, and DISK3 has been moved to PEG2, we need to transfer the 2 disks on PEG3 to PEG2, DISK3 being treated as part of the base.

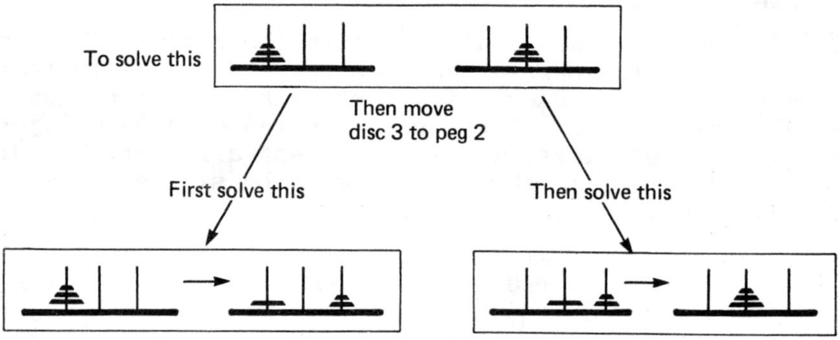

This breakdown can be generalised to the n-disk problem:

To transfer a tower of n disks from one peg to another peg given a spare peg:

First transfer a tower of n-1 disks from the 'from peg' to the spare peg using the 'to peg' as a spare.

Then move disk n to the 'to peg'.

Then transfer the tower of n-1 disks from the spare peg to the 'to peg' using the 'from peg' as a spare.

This can be implemented directly as a BASIC procedure.

```
100   DEF PROCtransfer(n,frompeg,topeg,sparepeg)
110     IF n=0 THEN ENDPROC
120     PROCtransfer(n-1,frompeg,sparepeg,topeg)
130     PRINT "Move DISK ";n; " from PEG ";frompeg;
              " to PEG ";topeg
140     PROCtransfer(n-1,sparepeg,topeg,frompeg)
150   ENDPROC
```

which can be called by:

```
10    INPUT"Number of disks",noofdisks
20    PROCtransfer(noofdisks,1,2,3)
30    END
```

We leave it as an exercise for the reader to draw the complete tree of procedure calls that takes place in the cases for n = 3 and n = 4.

7.4 Recursive patterns and curves

There are many complex patterns and curves that can easily be drawn recursively and recursion is a useful tool in computer graphics and computer generated art.

Recursive squares

The simplest recursive pattern is one in which a basic shape is drawn together with recursive copies of smaller versions of the complete pattern. For example, the next program creates a pattern of recursive squares. The pattern consists of a square, together with a recursive half-size copy of the complete pattern centered on each corner of the main square.

```
 10   INPUT "radius",r
 20   MODE 1
 30   PROCsquare(640,512,r)
 40   k=GET:MODE 7
 50   END

100   DEF PROCsquare(xc,yc,r)
110   IF r<10 THEN ENDPROC
120   LOCAL x1,x2,y1,y2
130     x1=xc-r:x2=xc+r
140     y1=yc-r:y2=yc+r
150     MOVE x1,y1
160     DRAW x1, y2 : DRAW x2,y2
170     DRAW x2,y1 : DRAW x1,y1
180     PROCsquare(x1,y1,r/2)
190     PROCsquare(x1,y2,r/2)
200     PROCsquare(x2,y2,r/2)
210     PROCsquare(x2,y1,r/2)
220    ENDPROC
```

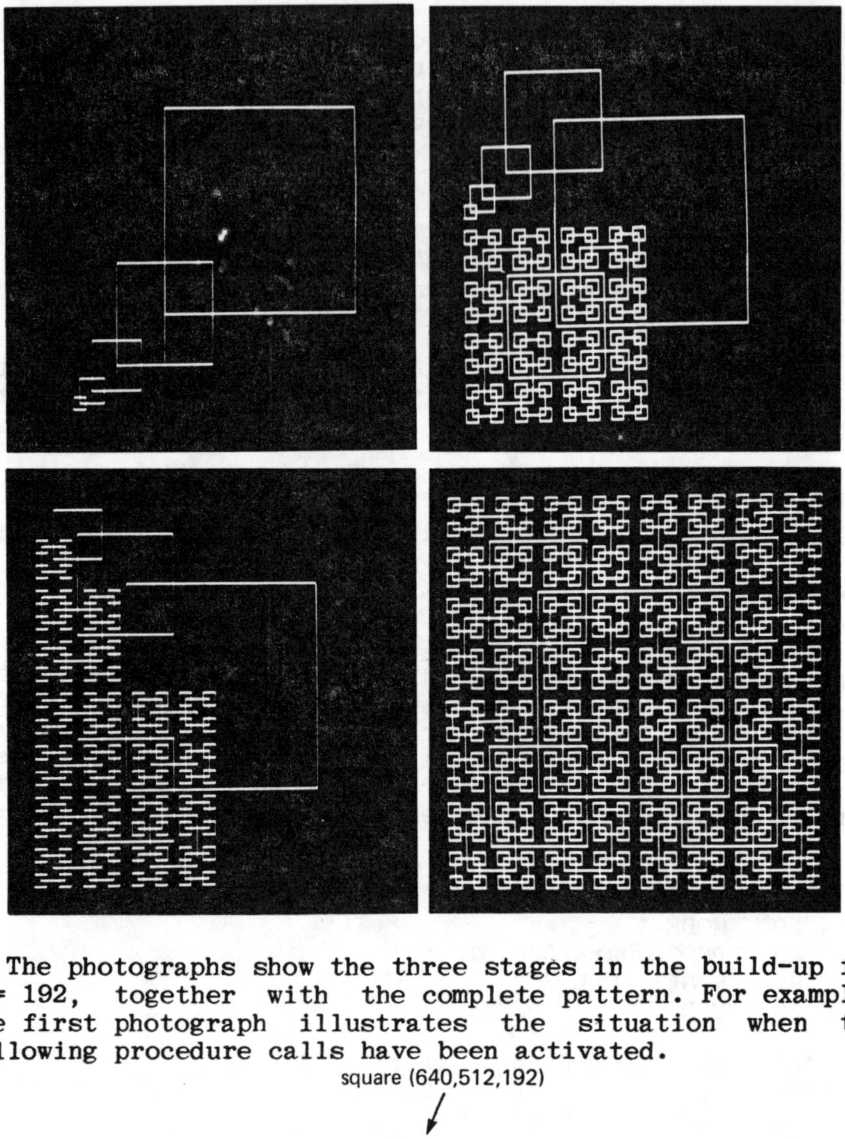

The photographs show the three stages in the build-up for r = 192, together with the complete pattern. For example, the first photograph illustrates the situation when the following procedure calls have been activated.

square (640,512,192)
↓
square (448,320,96)
↓
square (352,224,48)
↓
square (304,176,24)
↓
square (280,152,12)
↓
square (268,140,6)

The last procedure call triggers the stopping condition (r<10) and terminates without drawing a square.

At the stage reached in the second photograph, the tree of procedure calls that have been obeyed and terminated, together with the procedure calls that are still active, has the following shape. (The active procedure calls are down the right hand branch.)

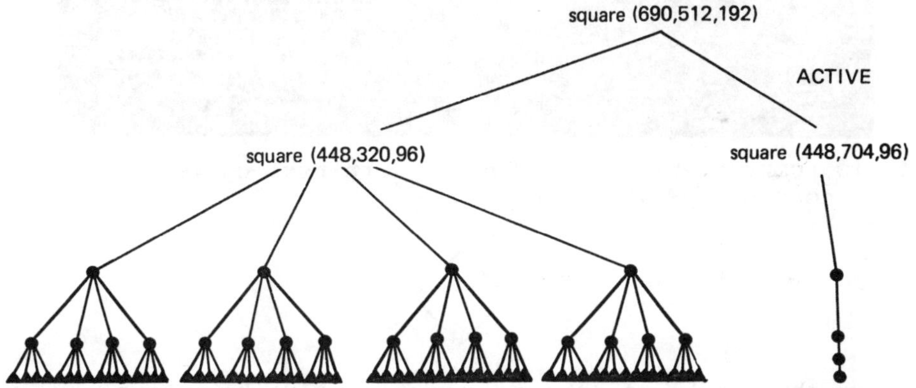

Space-filling curves

There is a large variety of patterns that come into the category of 'space filling curves'. These curves are such that they can usually be drawn as a single continuous line or curve in some well defined way. We shall illustrate the technique involved by using the so-called 'Sierpinski curves'.

The next set of photographs shows the Sierpinski curves of orders 1 to 4.

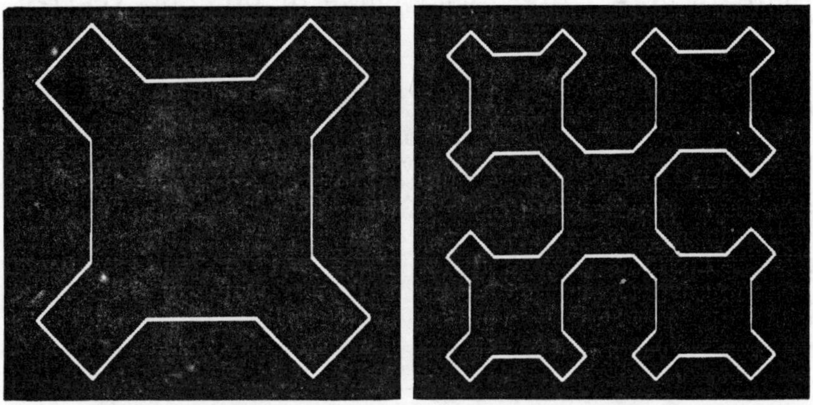

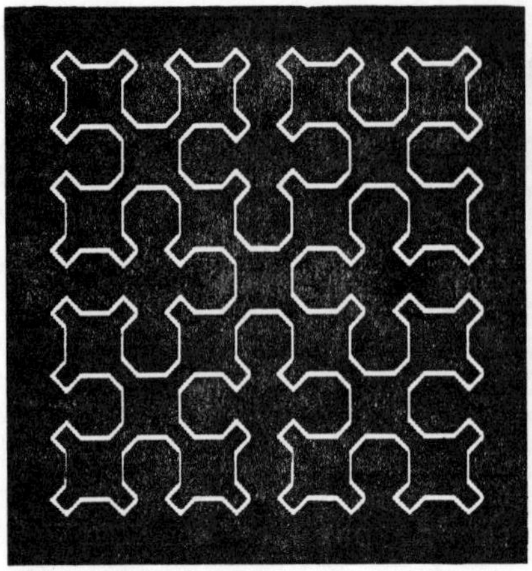

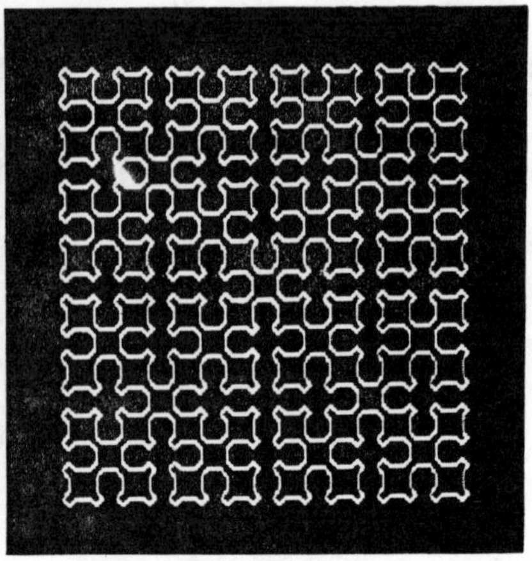

It is convenient to define a Sierpinski curve of order 0 which consists of a diamond:

Notice that each of these curves could be drawn as a continuous line, without lifting pencil from paper. We shall look at two ways of drawing these curves, where the second method draws the curve as a continuous line.

The first method is conceptually a little easier and for this approach, we must first recognise that the Sierpinski curve of order 1 consists of four order 0 curves 'joined' at the centre. Similarly the order 2 curve consists of four order 1 curves joined at the centre. In general, an order n curve consists of four order n-1 curves joined at the centre. Note that when four subcurves are joined, this involves deleting four diagonal lines from the subcurves and joining the subcurves with two horizontal and two vertical lines. This suggests the following outline for a recursive procedure to draw a Sierpinski curve of order n, centred at (x, y).

```
100   DEF PROCsierpinski(n, x, y)
110     IF n = 0 THEN draw a diamond
120     k = horizontal and vertical distance to
        the centres of the four subcurves
130     PROCsierpinski(n-1, x-k, y-k)
140     PROCsierpinski(n-1, x-k, y+k)
150     PROCsierpinski(n-1, x+k, y+k)
160     PROCsierpinski(n-1, x+k, y-k)
170   ENDPROC
```

In order to fill out this procedure, we need to examine the geometrical details fairly carefully. Any curve of order 1 or more consists of repeated copies of the same basic shape and we shall name the various dimensions of this basic shape as follows:

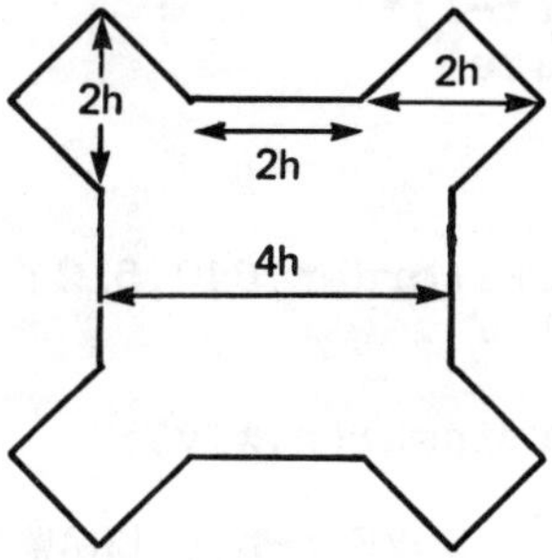

h is the smallest increment that will be required in our DRAW or MOVE statements. Thus the statements needed to draw a curve of order 0 (a diamond) centred at (x, y) are:

```
MOVE x-h, y
DRAW x, y+h : DRAW x+h, y
DRAW x, y-h : DRAW x-h, y
```

The distance from the centre of a curve of order n to the centre of one of its subcurves of order n-1 is 2^n*h. To convince yourself of this, you should mark the various distances on curves of different orders.

Finally the situation at the centre of a curve of order n, when the four subcurves of order n-1 have been drawn, can be illustrated as:

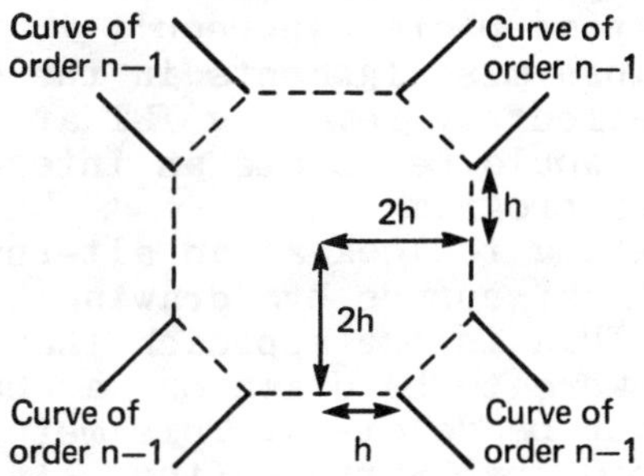

We need to delete the four dotted diagonal lines and draw the dotted vertical and horizontal lines. This can be easily accomplished by drawing round the dotted polygon using alternate PLOT 9 and PLOT 11 commands. These are relative plots, in the foreground and background colour respectively, which do not affect the last point visited on the line. Here is the complete program:

```
 10   INPUT"Order",order
 20   size=(2^order-1)*4+2
 30   h=INT(600/size)
 40   h2=h*2
 50   MODE 0

100   PROCsierpinski(order,640,512)
110   key=GET:MODE 7
120   END
130   DEF PROCsierpinski(n,x,y)
140   LOCAL k
150     IF n=0 THEN MOVE x-h,y:DRAW x,y+h:DRAW x+h,y:
          DRAW x,y-h:DRAW x-h,y:ENDPROC
160     k=2^n*h
170     PROCsierpinski(n-1,x-k,y-k)
180     PROCsierpinski(n-1,x-k,y+k)
190     PROCsierpinski(n-1,x+k,y+k)
200     PROCsierpinski(n-1,x+k,y-k)
210     MOVE x-h2,y-h
220     PLOT 9,0,h2 : PLOT 11,h,h
230     PLOT 9,h2,0 : PLOT 11,h,-h
240     PLOT 9,0,-h2 : PLOT 11,-h,-h
250     PLOT 9,-h2,0 : PLOT 11,-h,h
260   ENDPROC
```

Note the use of INT at line 30 which ensures that the increment, h, used in all the PLOTs is an integer. In programs that involve sequences of relative plots, it is always advisable to ensure that the increments used are integers as the graphics 'current point' is recorded internally as a pair of integer coordinates. Use of real increments in relative plots can result in an accumulation of errors that cause misalignments in the display produced. You can see this effect by removing INT at line 30. An even better alternative would be to use an integer variable (with a %) throughout the program.

It is interesting to look at an alternative approach to drawing the Sierpinski curves by drawing the curve as a continuous line. This is the approach that would have to be used if the curve were to be drawn on a hard copy device (where lines cannot be deleted). This method is based on an algorithm described by Wirth (the inventor of the programming language PASCAL).

We first observe that a curve of order n consists of four components connected at the corners - a left component, a top component, a right component and a bottom component:

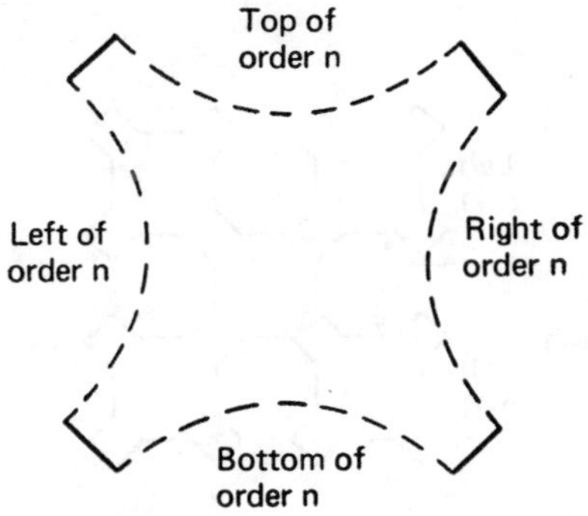

For example, in the case of the order 1 curve, we have:

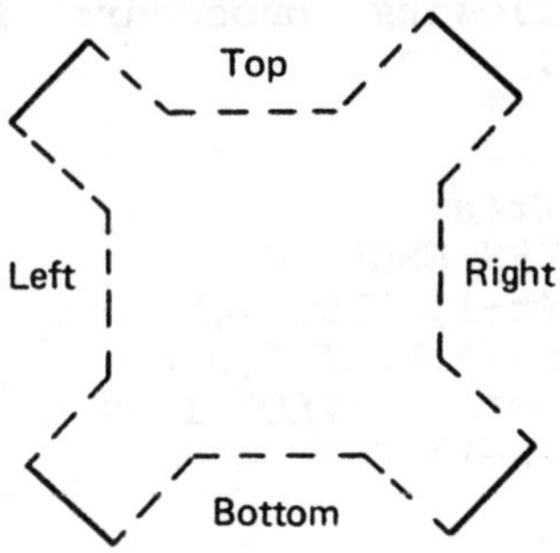

The procedure for drawing a Sierpinski curve of order n will be defined in terms of procedures for drawing its four components:

```
 90   DEF PROCsierpinski(n)
100     PROCleft(n):PLOT 1,h,h
110     PROCtop(n) :PLOT 1,h,-h
120     PROCright(n):PLOT 1,-h,-h
130     PROCbottom(n):PLOT 1,-h,h
140   ENDPROC
```

Now an order n <u>component</u> is made up of a sequence of order n-1 components joined in a well-defined way. For example, a left component of order n consists of:

a left component of order n-1
a diagonal line
a top component of order n-1
a vertical line
a bottom component of order n-1
a diagonal line
a left component of order n-1

For example, with n = 2,

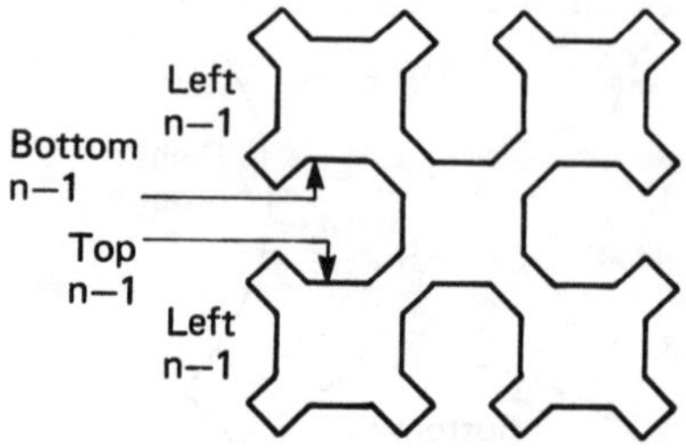

If n = 0, the components are empty - joining four empty components diagonally at the corners gives a diamond shape. this gives the following procedure for drawing a left component of order n.

```
150    DEF PROCleft(n)
160      IF n=0 THEN ENDPROC
170      PROCleft(n-1):PLOT 1,h,h
180      PROCtop(n-1):PLOT 1,0,h2
190      PROCbottom(n-1):PLOT 1,-h,h
200      PROCleft(n-1)
210    ENDPROC
```

A similar breakdown can be achieved for the top, right and bottom components and this gives the following complete program.

```
 10    MODE 0
 20    INPUT "Order ",order
 30    size=(2^order-1)*4+2
 40    h=INT(600/size):h2=h*2
 50    MOVE 300,200+h
 60    PROCsierpinski(order)
 70    K=GET:MODE7
 80    END

 90    DEF PROCsierpinski(n)
100      PROCleft(n):PLOT 1,h,h
110      PROCtop(n) :PLOT 1,h,-h
120      PROCright(n):PLOT 1,-h,-h
130      PROCbottom(n):PLOT 1,-h,h
140    ENDPROC
```

```
150   DEF PROCleft(n)
160     IF n=0 THEN ENDPROC
170     PROCleft(n-1):PLOT 1,h,h
180     PROCtop(n-1):PLOT 1,0,h2
190     PROCbottom(n-1):PLOT 1,-h,h
200     PROCleft(n-1)
210   ENDPROC

220   DEF PROCtop(n)
230     IF n=0 THEN ENDPROC
240     PROCtop(n-1):PLOT 1,h,-h
250     PROCright(n-1):PLOT 1,h2,0
260     PROCleft(n-1):PLOT 1,h,h
270     PROCtop(n-1)
280   ENDPROC

290   DEF PROCright(n)
300     IF n=0 THEN ENDPROC
310     PROCright(n-1):PLOT 1,-h,-h
320     PROCbottom(n-1):PLOT 1,0,-h2
330     PROCtop(n-1):PLOT 1,h,-h
340     PROCright(n-1)
350   ENDPROC

360   DEF PROCbottom(n)
370     IF n=0 THEN ENDPROC
380     PROCbottom(n-1):PLOT 1,-h,h
390     PROCleft(n-1):PLOT 1,-h2,0
400     PROCright(n-1):PLOT 1,-h,-h
410     PROCbottom(n-1)
420   ENDPROC
```

You should notice that there are two types of recursion involved in the last program. There is straightforward recursion where, for example, PROCleft calls PROCleft. There is also 'hidden' or 'mutual' recursion where, for example, PROCleft calls PROCtop which in turn calls PROCleft.

You should run both Sierpinski programs and observe the differences in their behaviour. Other well-known space filling curves are the 'C-curve' and the 'dragon curve'. Programs for drawing these curves are presented in 'Creative Graphics' published by Acornsoft.

Exercises

1 Animate a program for solving the 'Towers of Hanoi' puzzle. The program should display a picture of the pegs and disks, and, instead of printing a move, should move the appropriate disk in the display.

2 The family of patterns, of which the following is an example, can be described recursively.

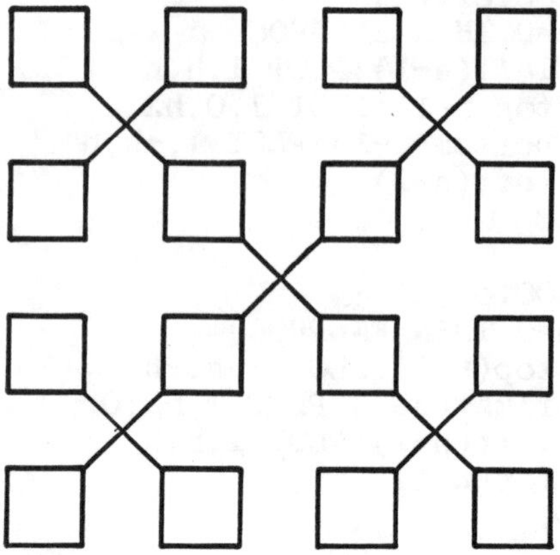

Write a program that generates patterns like this.

3 Write a program that generates patterns like those of the last exercise, but using diamonds instead of squares.

4 The next photographs show a family of curves (due to Wirth) called W-curves.

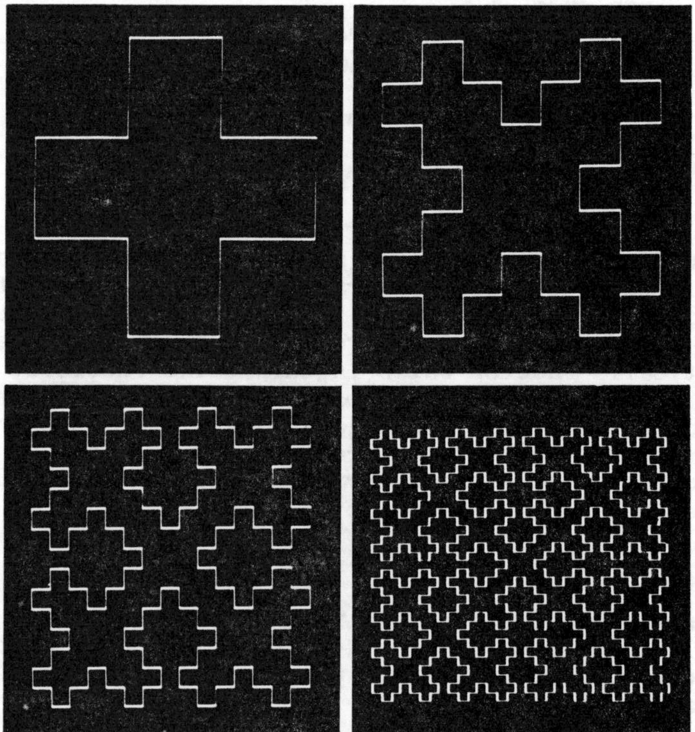

Write a program that draws a W-curve of order n as a continuous line.

7.5 Towers of Hanoi revisited - state space representation

Many non-numerical problems can be represented by a large (possibly infinite) set of 'problem states' together with a set of moves, or operators, each of which transforms one state into another. The definition of an operator may include restrictions on the states to which it can be applied.

For example, we could represent the complete set of 1-disk Tower of Hanoi states with a single triangle. There are three states in the 1 disk problem - the disk can be on one of three pegs. Each vertex of the triangle represents a state. The lines connecting vertices represent a possible move from one state to another.

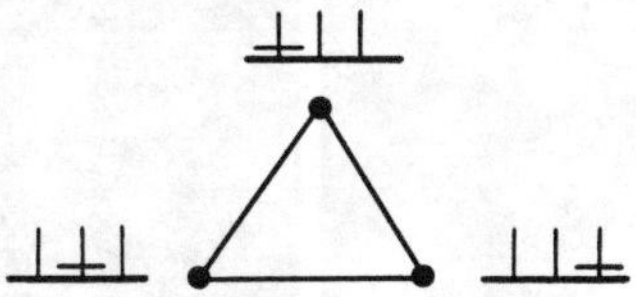

In the state space for the 2-disk problem we have three such triangles, one for each possible position of the larger disk. The three triangles are joined together by lines representing the three different ways of moving the larger disk from one peg to another.

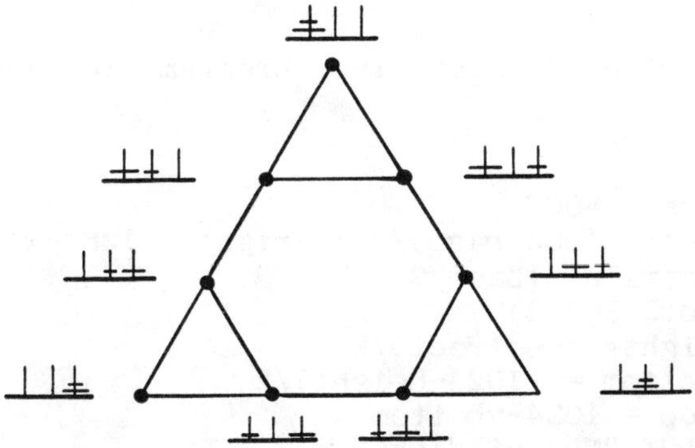

Similarly the 3-disk state-space diagram contains three 2-disk state-space diagrams. The block of photographs show the state space diagrams for the 3-, 4-, 5- and 6-disk problem.

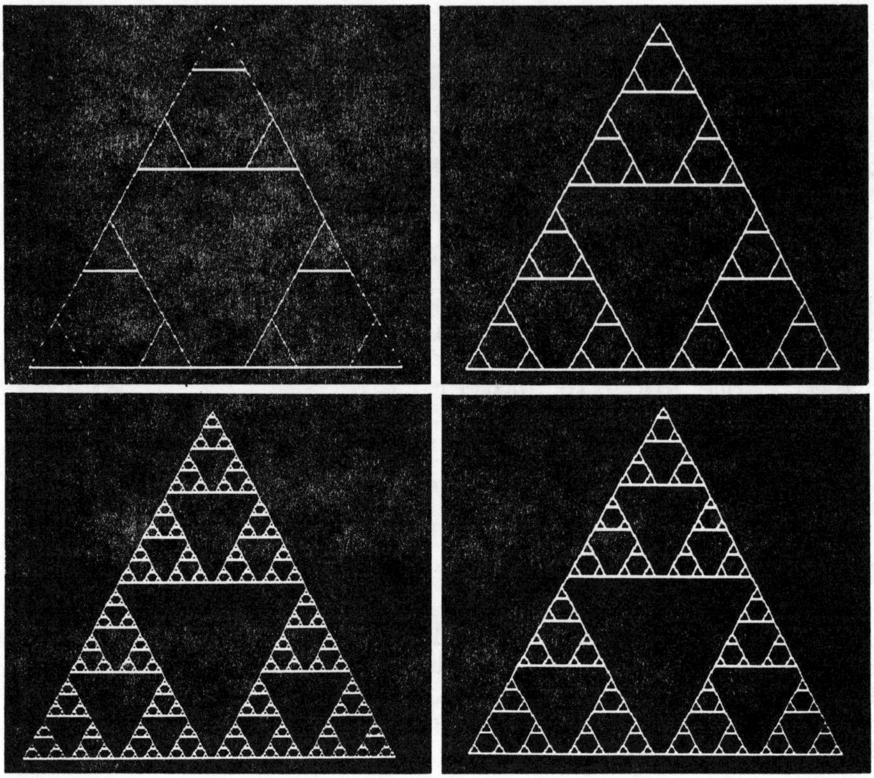

We can write a recursive program to generate these diagrams:

```
 10   base = 800
 30   xleft=(1280-base)/2 : xright = 1280-xleft
 40   xtop=xleft+base/2
 50   root3=SQR(3)
 60   height= base*root3/2
 65   ybottom = (1024-height)/2
 66   ytop = 1024-ybottom
 70   INPUT "No. of disks",n
 80   arclength=base/(2n-1)
 90   MODE 0
100   VDU 5
110   PROCdrawgraph(n,xleft,xright,ybottom,xtop,ytop)
120   k=GET:MODE 7:END
```

```
140   DEF PROCdrawgraph(n,x1,x2,y12,x3,y3)
150   LOCAL subside, subheight
160     IF n=0 THEN ENDPROC
170     subside = (2(n-1)-1)*arclength
180     subheight = root3*subside/2
190     PROCdrawgraph(n-1,x1,x1+subside,y12,x1+subside/2,
                        y12+subheight)
200     PROCdrawgraph(n-1,x2-subside,x2,y12,x2-subside/2,
                        y12+subheight)
210     PROCdrawgraph(n-1,x3-subside/2,x3+subside/2,
                        y3-subheight,x3,y3)
220     MOVE x1+subside,y12
230     DRAW x2-subside,y12
240     MOVE x1+subside/2,y12+subheight
250     DRAW x3-subside/2,y3-subheight
260     MOVE x2-subside/2,y12+subheight
270     DRAW x3+subside/2,y3-subheight
280   ENDPROC
```

7.6 Problems with recursion

In this section, we shall illustrate two problems that can arise when using recursion. To do this, we revisit the problem of colour filling a region that is defined by boundaries that have already been drawn on the screen. A non-recursive algorithm for accomplishing this was presented in Chapter 2.

Simple recursive colour fill - excessive recursive depth
Recall that the colour fill algorithm of Chapter 2 started from an arbitrary point in the region and worked outwards from that point to adjacent points, eventually visiting the whole region. We can very easily describe a recursive procedure for colour filling a 4-connected region:

```
200   DEF PROCfillfrom(x,y)
210     IF POINT(x,y)>0 THEN ENDPROC
220     PLOT 69,x,y
230     PROCfillfrom(x,y+4)
240     PROCfillfrom(x,y-4)
250     PROCfillfrom(x+4,y)
260     PROCfillfrom(x-4,y)
270   ENDPROC
```

This is certainly much shorter than the equivalent procedures in the program in Chapter 2. Now that we are familiar with recursion, the recursive version is also conceptually easier. If, however, you insert the above procedure in a program and run it, you will find that it will work only for very small regions. For larger regions, the program will terminate with the error message 'No room'. This is because a long sequence of recursive procedure calls has been entered and not yet terminated. To see how this happens, look at the following configuration of pixels.

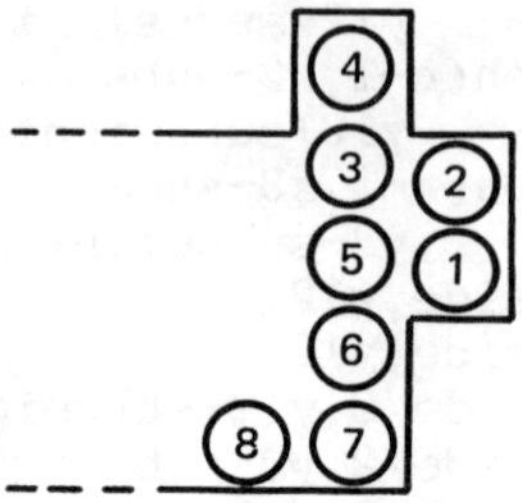

If we start the fill process by calling PROCfillfrom with parameters that specify pixel 1, then the following tree of procedure activations is created.

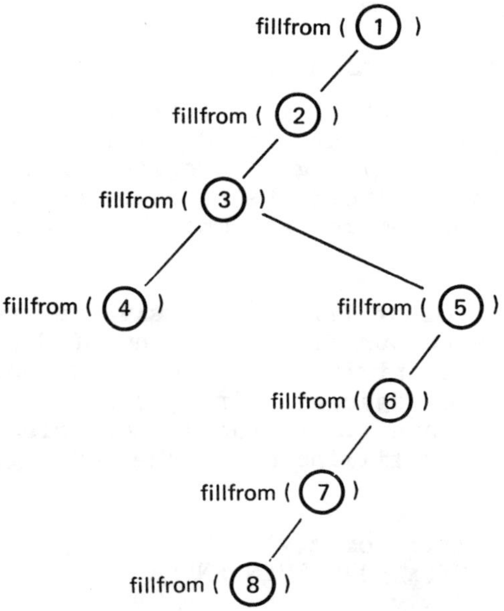

This process will continue, and as the pixels in the region are visited, the tree of procedure activations will get deeper and deeper. A procedure call will be terminated only when a dead end is encountered, for example at pixel 4. Each time a procedure is activated, storage space is used up for holding parameters, local variables and a record of where to return to when the procedure is terminated. This space is freed only when the procedure terminates. There is thus a limit to the depth to which the recursion can be extended, and for a region of any size the limit will soon be encountered. Notice also that, in this example, when a long chain of recursive calls is eventually terminated, most of the other recursive calls that then take place will be unnecessary and will terminate immediately. This redundancy is, however, necessary if the algorithm is to cater for a convoluted region. On a large processor with virtually unlimited storage space, the simple recursive algorithm might be usable, but on a micro, it is rather unsatisfactory.

The general point illustrated by this example is that recursion must not be allowed to proceed to any great depth.

Using horizontal fill - hidden loop nesting

As we have already seen in the last section the simple recursive approach to colour-fill leads to problems involving the depth of the recursion and the queue method introduced in Chapter 2 is obviously preferable. In this section an alternative recursive approach is examined. Although this also involves a common problem with recursion, this new problem can be easily overcome.

A common provision in graphics systems that operate with a raster scan display is a horizontal fill facility. Such a facility will typically be given the (x,y) coordinates of a point and will colour-fill pixels to the left and right of the given pixel as long as these pixels are in the background colour.

On the BBC micro, the first issue of the operating system (OS 0.1) did not provide such a facility, but this omission was rectified in later versions with a new set of PLOT instructions.

First of all, we present a BASIC procedure that implements a horizontal fill. At first, we shall not use the new PLOT commands and will implement the horizontal fill without them. Anyone who still has the first issue of the operating system will need to do it this way. The method can also be seen as an explanation of the version using the new PLOT facilities which are presented later.

```
300   DEF PROCfillalong(x,y)
310   LOCAL nextx
320     PROCdirectionfill(x,y,xstep)
330     rightx=nextx-xstep
340     PROCdirectionfill(x,y,-xstep)
350     leftx=nextx+xstep
360   ENDPROC

370   DEF PROCdirectionfill(x,y,dir)
380     nextx = x
390     REPEAT
400       PLOT 69,nextx,y
410       nextx=nextx+dir
420     UNTIL POINT(nextx,y)>0
430   ENDPROC
```

A call of PROCfillalong will first colour-fill to the right of the given pixel until a non-background point is encountered. The same thing is done to the left. Both scans are carried out using the subsidiary procedure PROCdirectionfill whose parameter 'dir' indicates the direction of the scan. As a result of calling PROCfillalong, the two non-local variables 'leftx' and 'rightx' are set to values indicating the extent of the strip that was filled. The value of 'xstep' will indicate the width of a pixel and this will depend on the mode being used. For example, in MODE 1, 'xstep=4'. We now present a recursive version of PROCfillfrom which could be used in place of previous versions of the same procedure, but which makes use of horizontal fill. The procedure will be given a point, and starts by filling the horizontal strips in which the point specified by its parameters lies. It then calls itself recursively to fill from each pixel above and below the strip that has just been filled. A first attempt at this procedure is:

```
200   DEF PROCfillfrom(x,y)
210   LOCAL leftx,rightx,scanx
220     IF POINT(x,y)>0 THEN ENDPROC
230     PROCfillalong(x,y)
240     FOR scanx = leftx TO rightx STEP xstep
250       PROCfillfrom(scanx,y+ystep)
260       PROCfillfrom(scanx,y-ystep)
270     NEXT scanx
280   ENDPROC
```

Note that 'ystep' is the height of a pixel. In MODE 1, 'ystep=4'. If we run our colour filling program with this version of PROCfillfrom, we again find that it will only work for small regions. With larger regions the program terminates with the message -'Too many FORs'. This usually means that too many FOR statements have been nested inside each other. A common cause of this error message is the omission of a NEXT statement. In our case, there are no explicitly nested FOR statements, but because the recursive procedure calls appear inside a FOR statement, any FOR statement entered during a recursive call behaves as if it were inside the outer FOR statement. The limit on the number of nested FOR statements is 10 and if the recursive depth goes beyond 10, as it will for a larger region, then the program will terminate. Unfortunately the only satisfactory solution is to replace the FOR loop with an equivalent GOTO loop:

```
200   DEF PROCfillfrom(x,y)
210   LOCAL leftx,rightx,scanx
220     IF POINT(x,y)>0 THEN ENDPROC
230     PROCfillalong(x,y)
240     scanx=leftx
250       PROCfillfrom(scanx,y+ystep)
260       PROCfillfrom(scanx,y-ystep)
270       scanx=scanx+xstep
280     IF scanx<=rightx GOTO 250
290   ENDPROC
```

The algorithm described above could be considerably improved. Notice that many of the recursive calls will be completely unnecessary. For example, once a line of pixels has been filled, the first recursive call of PROCfillfrom on the adjacent row will in most cases be sufficient and the remaining recursive calls will terminate immediately. Any additional recursive call from the adjacent row will only occasionally be necessary. For example, in the following situation:

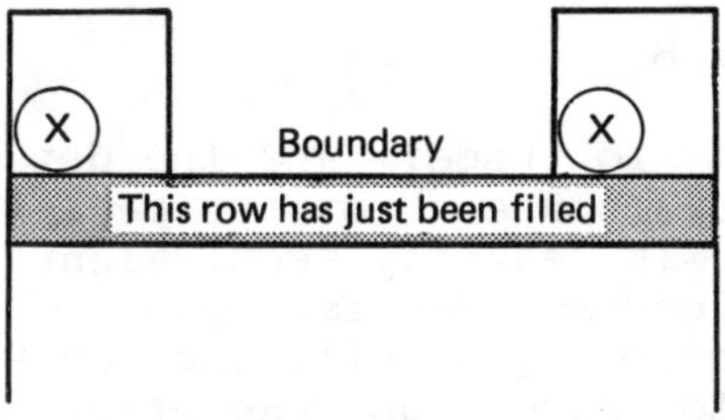

at least two recursive calls at pixels marked X are necessary on the row above the one that has just been filled, so as to initiate filling of the two concavities opening off the lower row. Similarly many recursive calls involve looking back at pixels in rows already visited and again this is only occasionally necessary.

An interesting adjustment to the program which will allow you to see which points are being visited for a second or third time, is to replace the line that recognises points that need not be filled by:

```
220   IF POINT(x, y) > 0 THEN PLOT 70, x, y : ENDPROC
```

This will invert the colour of any pixel that is already colour-filled and you will be able to observe the progress of the algorithm not only as it fills the background region, but also as it makes unnecessary recursive calls in areas that have already been filled. The improvements required to avoid this unnecessary work are fairly tricky and we will not go into them here.

Finally, here is an alternative version of PROCfillalong

that uses the PLOT 77 command for horizontal fill.

```
300   DEF PROCfillalong(x,y)
310     PLOT 77,x,y
320     X%=CPblock : Y%=CPblock DIV 256
330     A%=&0D : CALL &FFF1
340     leftx=(!CPblock AND 65535)
350     rightx=(!(CPblock+4) AND 65535)
360   ENDPROC
```

The PLOT 77 statement at line 310 scans left and right from the pixel specified by x and y until it reaches the last background point in both directions. A line is drawn between the two points reached. The rightmost point becomes the 'current graphics point' and the leftmost point becomes the previous graphics point. We now need to set 'leftx' to the x-coordinate of the previous graphics point and 'rightx' to the x-coordinate of the current graphics point. To do this we use the OSWORD call at lines 320 to 330. This uses a block of store declared at the start of the program by:

```
5   DIM CPblock 8
```

You do not need to understand the details of how OSWORD calls work in order to use this 'recipe'. The above version of PROCfillalong is exactly equivalent to that described earlier. It is of course much faster.

It is worth mentioning briefly another PLOT command that could be used to speed up execution of the loop in PROCfillfrom (lines 250 to 280). The statement

```
PLOT 92, x, y
```

searches pixels to the right of (x,y) for a background point and sets the last non-background point reached as the current graphics position. We leave the reader to think about how this could be used.

Finally, note that all recursive colour filling algorithms can run out of room for large or highly convoluted regions. The horizontal fill methods described here could all be reorganised to use a queue similar to that used in Chapter 2.

7.7 Divide and conquer - merge sorting

Yet another approach to sorting (a number of algorithms were introduced in the last chapter) is the merge sort algorithm, one of the most efficient sort algorithms available. This algorithm is tricky to implement without recursion. It illustrates one of the most important recursive approaches to a problem - that of divide and conquer. We sort the list by sorting each half and merging the two halves - merging is a fast process. Each half is sorted by dividing it into two and sorting each quarter. Each quarter is sorted by dividing it into two - in other words divide and conquer.

A program implementing a recursive merge sort, PROCmergesort, is now given.

```
  10   DIM number(100)
  20   INPUT "No. of items",noofitems
  30   FOR i=1 TO noofitems
  40     INPUT number(i)
  50   NEXT i
  60   PROCmergesort(noofitems)
  70   FOR i=1 TO noofitems
  80     PRINT number(i)
  90   NEXT i
  95   END

 100   DEF PROCmergesort(n)
 110     DIM aux(n)
 120     PROCsubsort(1,n)
 130   ENDPROC

 150   DEF PROCsubsort(i,j)
 160   LOCAL mid
 170   IF i>=j THEN ENDPROC
 190     mid=(i+j)DIV 2
 200     PROCsubsort(i,mid)
 210     PROCsubsort(mid+1,j)
 220     PROCmerge(i,mid,mid+1,j)
 230   ENDPROC

 250   DEF PROCmerge(begin1,end1,begin2,end2)
 260   LOCAL i,next,firstfinished,secondfinished
 270     FOR i=begin1 TO end1:aux(i)=number(i):NEXT i
 280     next = begin1
 290     firstfinished=FALSE : secondfinished=FALSE
 300     REPEAT
 310       IF aux(begin1)<number(begin2)
         THEN PROCtake1fromfirsthalf
         ELSE PROCtake1fromsecondhalf
 320       next=next+1
 330     UNTIL firstfinished OR secondfinished
 340     IF secondfinished THEN
           FOR i=next TO end2 : number(i)=aux(begin1) :
                                begin1 = begin1+1 : NEXT i
 350   ENDPROC
```

```
370   DEF PROCtake1fromfirsthalf
380     number(next)=aux(begin1)
390     IF begin1=end1 THEN
          firstfinished=TRUE
        ELSE begin1=begin1+1
400   ENDPROC

420   DEF PROCtake1fromsecondhalf
430     number(next)=number(begin2)
440     IF begin2=end2 THEN
          secondfinished=TRUE
        ELSE begin2=begin2+1
450   ENDPROC
```

PROCsubsort(i,j) sorts the list of elements from number(i) to number(j). Note that the recursion terminates on a call of subsort(i,j) where i = j, a list of one item is already sorted. In order to complete the above procedure, we need to define the procedure 'merge' which is used to combine the two separate <u>sorted</u> sequences in

```
    number(i) to number(mid)
and number(mid+1) to number(j)
```

into one sorted sequence in number(i) to number(j).

Merging two sublists that are already sorted is a fast operation although it is not easy to do in situ as required in the present context. We have defined:

```
PROCmerge(begin1, end1, begin2, end2)
```

which first copies the contents of number(begin1) to number(end1) into an auxiliary array 'aux' in locations aux(begin1) to aux(end1).

The procedure will then repeatedly select an item from one of our two subsequences and insert it into the next available location of the area that is to contain the merged sequence.

If the items of the first subsequence are exhausted then any remaining items in the second subsequence are in their correct positions. If the items in the second subsequence are exhausted, then any remaining items in the first subsequence must be copied from 'aux' into their new locations in 'number'. (Any items from the second subsequence that were previously there must already have been copied up into their new positions.)

The situation after one of the subsequences has been copied into the auxiliary array, but before merging starts, is illustrated in the next diagram.

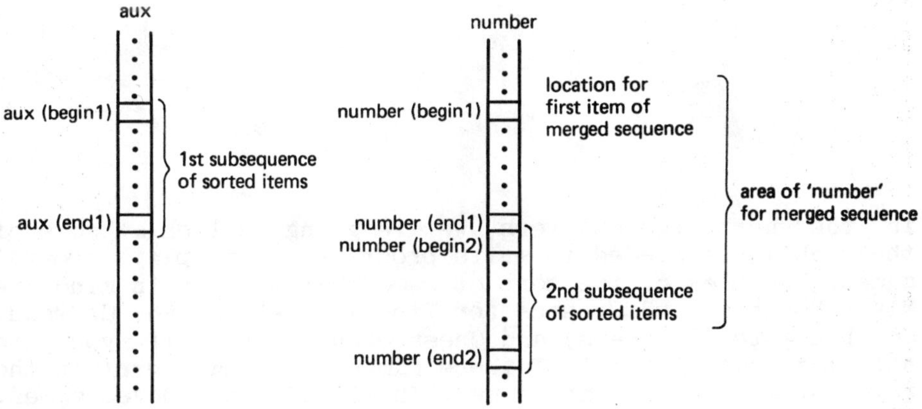

Exercises

1 Use the text animation procedures defined in Chapter 4, Section 4.1, to animate a merge sort. You will need to organise the display differently from the way it was organised for the other sort methods - display the two arrays involved, 'number' and 'aux' at either side of the screen.

2 The process of binary search presented in Chapter 6 (Section 6.4) can be described recursively. Do this, and write a recursive procedure to carry out a binary search on a suitable table.

3 The sorting method known as 'quicksort' can be described as follows:

To sort a table of n items:
Select a random entry (the first say)
Split the table into two sub-tables - the entries that should come before the selected entry and the entries that should come after the selected entry.
Sort each of the two sub-tables (recursively).
The two sub-tables with the selected entry in the middle give the final sorted table.

Write a recursive procedure that implements 'quicksort' on a table of numbers.

Chapter 8 **Board games and game trees**

In the next two chapters, we are going to look at some of the techniques needed to write programs that play 'board' games. Examples of the sort of game that we have in mind are NIM, Noughts and Crosses (or Tic-Tac-Toe), Kalah, Go-Moku, Go, Draughts (Checkers) and Chess. Don't worry if you are not familiar with all of these games - we shall explain the rules of any games that we use. In all of the above games, the outcome depends entirely on the skill of the two players involved. Both players have available exactly the same information and their choice of move is not influenced by the throw of a dice or the deal of a card. For the time being, we shall avoid consideration of games like Battleships and Cruisers where neither player can see the other's board or Backgammon where the throw of a dice affects the choice of moves available.

In Chapter 1, we presented the outline program structure needed for a program that plays a board game. In the next two chapters, we will look at techniques that can be used by such a program for choosing a good move.

In this chapter, we shall concentrate on rather trivial games. It may seem that these games are a long way removed from more intellectually demanding games like chess and draughts, but the techniques that we introduce by using these simple games are easily modified to deal with more difficult games. The modifications needed are discussed in the next chapter.

There are three main problem areas in programming games of the type that we are considering:

(a) Choosing a move:
In the next two chapters we shall devote a great deal of attention to the techniques that are available for writing procedures to choose good moves.

(b) Representing board positions and moves inside the computer:
For a given game, there may be several different ways of representing a board position inside a program. In our 'Last One Wins' program, a single integer was enough to represent the 'board'. In a more difficult game, there may be a choice of data structure representations for a board position. Different representations for the

Noughts and Crosses board were suggested at the end of Chapter 1.

(c) Displaying the board:
Producing elegant displays of board positions on the screen involves the use of graphics facilities that are extensively discussed elsewhere.

8.1 Game trees

Choosing a sensible move in a board game often involves exploring ahead from the current position in the game and considering the various sequences of moves and counter-moves that are available from the position. It will make our discussion of this process easier, if we introduce the idea of a 'game tree'. To do this, we use a variation of the game 'Last One Wins' (Chapter 1). In order to better illustrate a number of points we change the rules of the game as follows:

> Players now score a point for each counter removed during the course of a game. The player who makes the last move scores an additional two points. The aim of the game is to maximise the 'point difference' between oneself and one's opponent.

We shall call this version of the game 'Last One Wins - or does he?'.

There are a number pieces of information required to completely describe a position reached during the course of a game:

The number of counters left on the board;
Whose turn it is (player A or player B);
A's score so far;
B's score so far.

We shall represent a state of the game graphically by a box containing this information. For example:

4A21

represents a state of the game in which there are 4 counters left on the board, it is A's turn to play, A has scored 2 points so far and B has scored 1 point so far. A move can be represented by a line joining two such boxes and the sequence of moves played in a particular game starting with 7 counters (A starts) might be:

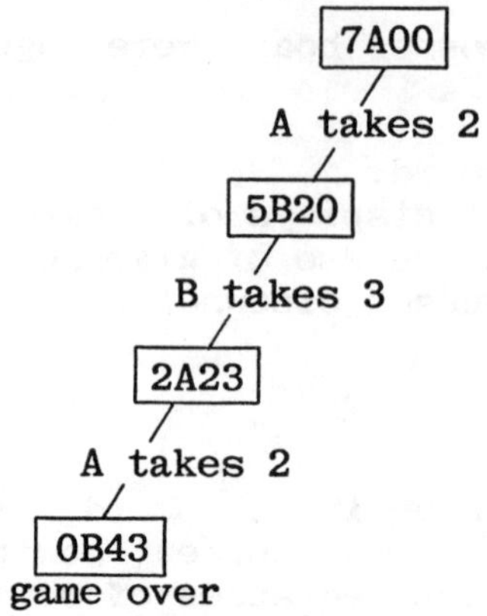

A scores 2 extra points and wins by +3

There is, of course, usually a choice of moves available in any one position and the complete set of possibilities available for the game with 5 counters (A starts) can be illustrated by the tree on the next page.

Any path starting at the 'root' of the tree (at the top) and moving down through the tree to a 'leaf' represents a particular sequence of moves making up one complete game that could be played. In this tree, there are represented 13 possible games. In terms of the tree, this means that there are 13 different leaves and 13 different pathways from root to leaf. The terminal positions or leaves in the tree are marked with the point difference for A and these values will be used later.

The boxes representing positions are often referred to as the 'nodes' of the game tree.

Exercises

1 The rules for 'Grundy's Game' are:

> Two players start with a pile of counters on the board between them. The first player divides the pile into two unequal piles. The players alternately do the same to one of the remaining piles. The player who first cannot play loses. (This happens when all the piles on the board contain 1 or 2 counters - a pile of two counters cannot be subdivided into two unequal piles.)

Draw a game tree for Grundy's Game starting with a pile of 7 counters.

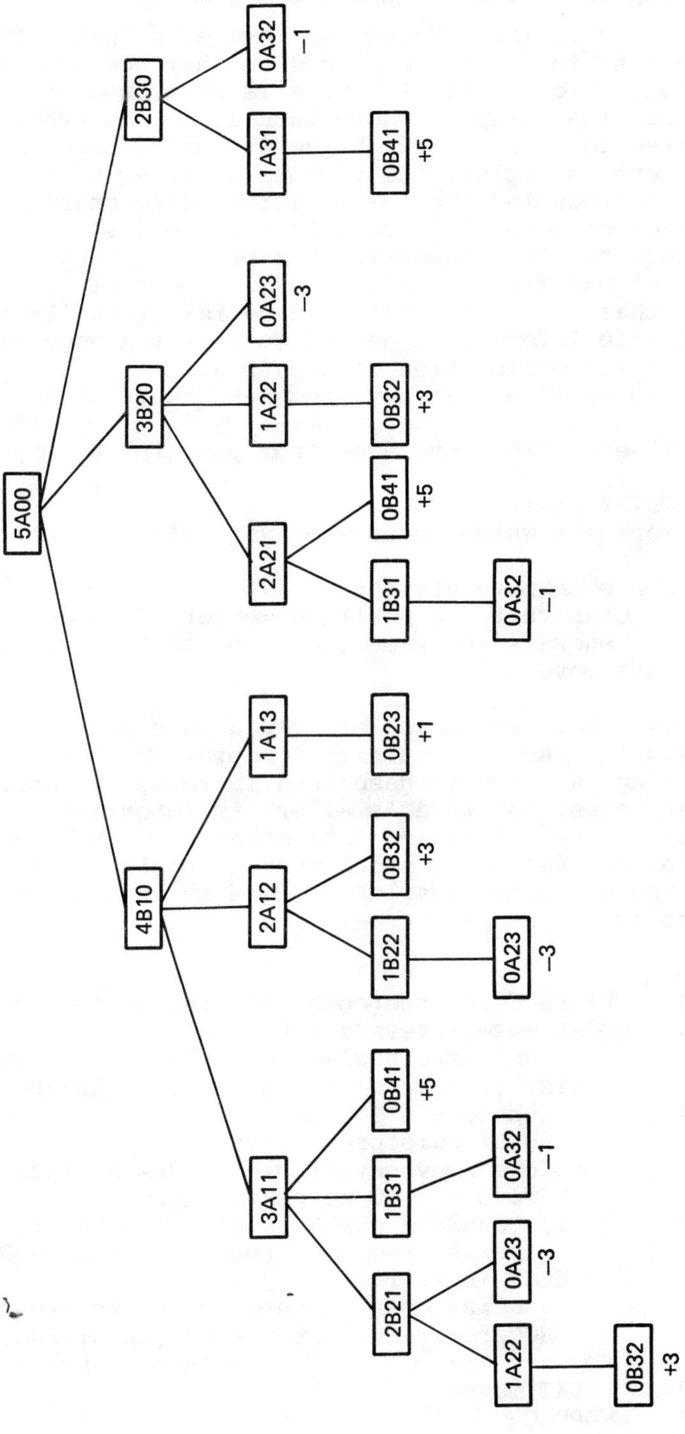
5A00
2B30
3B20
4B10
0A32
1A31
0B41
−1
+5
0A23
1A22
2A21
0B32
0B41
1B31
0A32
−3
+3
+5
−1
1A13
2A12
3A11
0B23
0B32
1B22
0A23
+1
+3
−3
0B41
1B31
2B21
0A32
0A23
1A22
0B32
+5
−1
−3
+3

8.2 Using recursion to generate a game tree

Our purpose in introducing the idea of a game tree is to enable us to write a procedure that decides, for a given position, which particular move is best from the point of view of the player whose turn it is. In order to use the game tree to help in its choice of moves, such a procedure will have to explore the various branches of the game tree. Before introducing the complication of comparing different sequences of possible moves, it will be instructive to write a procedure that generates and prints the entire game tree for 'Last One Wins - or does he?'. In fact we shall see later that this procedure can be fairly easily modified to collect the information needed to select a good move on the basis of its exploration of the tree.

We can outline what our procedure must do:

```
To generate the game tree from position P:

   Print position P.
   Work out which moves are available in P (if any).

   FOR each move available
      Construct the position we get if we make that move.
      Generate the game tree from this new position.
   NEXT move
```

The way that we have described this process immediately suggests the use of recursion (Chapter 7). In this case, generating a tree is described in terms of generating some smaller trees. The word 'smaller' is important - it is this aspect of our definition that makes sure that the recursive description eventually stops when a position is found in which no moves are available. Here is a recursive procedure for exploring the game tree.

```
100   DEF PROCgrowtree(counters, turn$, Ascore, Bscore)
110   LOCAL move,movesavailable,
            newturn$,newAscore,newBscore
120     PRINT ;counters; turn$; Ascore; Bscore
130     IF counters = 0 THEN
           PROCfinalscore : ENDPROC
140     PROCcheckmovesavailable   :REM defined as before.
150     FOR move = 1 TO movesavailable
160       IF turn$="A" THEN  newturn$ = "B" :
             newAscore=Ascore+move: newBscore=Bscore
          ELSE  newturn$ = "A" :
             newBscore=Bscore+move: newAscore=Ascore
170       PROCgrowtree(counters-move, newturn$,
                                  newAscore, newBscore)
180     NEXT move
190   ENDPROC
```

```
200   DEF PROCfinalscore
210     PRINT "Final Score: ";
220     IF turn$="A" THEN PRINT ;Ascore; " - "; Bscore+2
                     ELSE PRINT ;Ascore+2; " - "; Bscore
230   ENDPROC
```

The procedure takes some parameters that represent the position from which it is to generate the game tree. Note that the definition of PROCgrowtree reflects the outline and contains a call of itself.

In order to generate the tree for the game with 3 counters, A starts, we need to insert:

```
10   PROCgrowtree(3, "A", 0, 0)
20   END
```

A run of this program produced the following output:

```
3A00
2B10
1A11
0B21
Final score: 4 - 1
0A12
Final score: 1 - 4
1B20
0A21
Final score: 2 - 3
0B30
Final score: 5 - 0
```

The game tree for the game with 3 counters is:

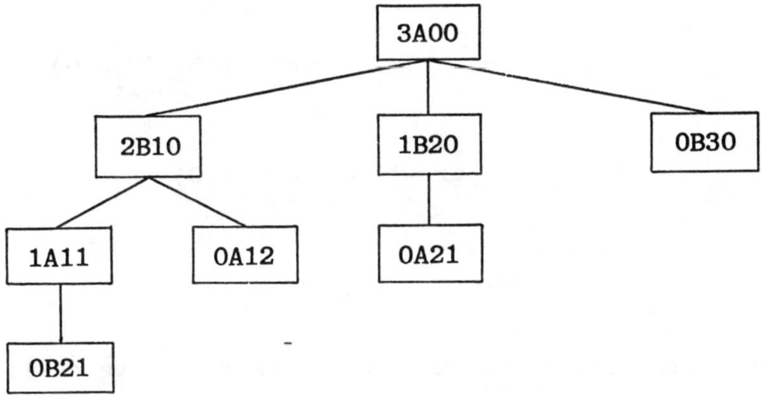

As we can see, our recursive procedure has generated and

printed all the nodes in the tree. We shall adjust the program so as to improve the layout of its output in a moment, but before doing this it will be instructive to look in some detail at how it works. The program starts by calling:

```
PROCgrowtree(3,"A",0,0)
```

We can think of this procedure call, together with its parameters, as representing the root of the game tree. In the course of the evaluation of this procedure call it sets move=1 and calls itself recursively (at line 170). We can represent the situation at this stage by:

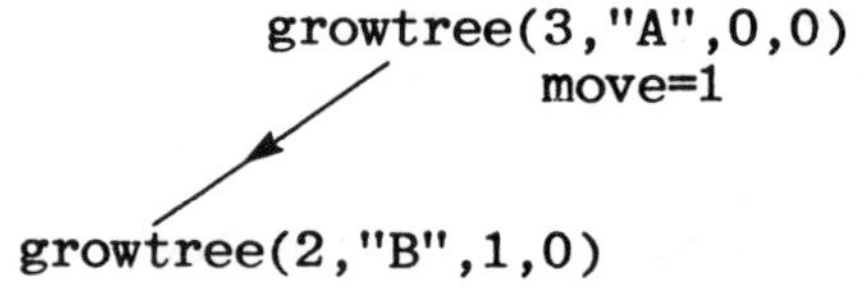

Because this new procedure call is entered before the previous one is exited, we now have two calls of the same procedure active at once, each with its own private set of parameters and each with its own private copies of its LOCAL variables. As we suggested in Chapter 7, you may find it easier to think in terms of two completely separate copies of the procedure, although of course it does not work like this behind the scenes. When the computer eventually exits from the second procedure call, it will carry on obeying the first where it left off, but that will not happen until the 'subtree' to be grown by the second procedure call has been completely generated. Having printed the values of its parameters, the second procedure call sets its local variable move=1 and calls PROCgrowtree recursively (at line 170). We can now picture the situation as:

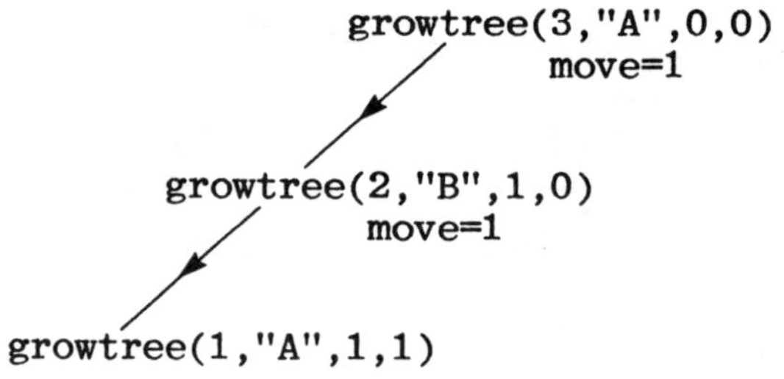

This procedure activation makes one more recursive call:

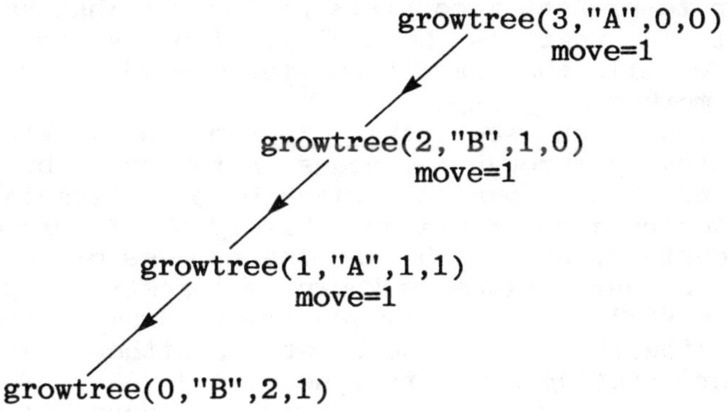

and on entry to this last call of the procedure the IF statement at line 130 is triggered. This outputs the final score for the current position and terminates the procedure call. The computer exits to the previous procedure call

```
growtree(1,"A",1,1)
```

and carries on from where it left off there (line 180). There are no more moves available in the position represented by that procedure activation and so the FOR loop terminates and that procedure activation is exited. The computer is now continuing its execution of the call

```
growtree(2,"B",1,0)
```

and again carries on at line 180. In this case, the FOR loop is executed for a second time with move=2 and this results in the procedure call

```
growtree(0,"A",1,2)
```

The new situation is illustrated in the following diagram:

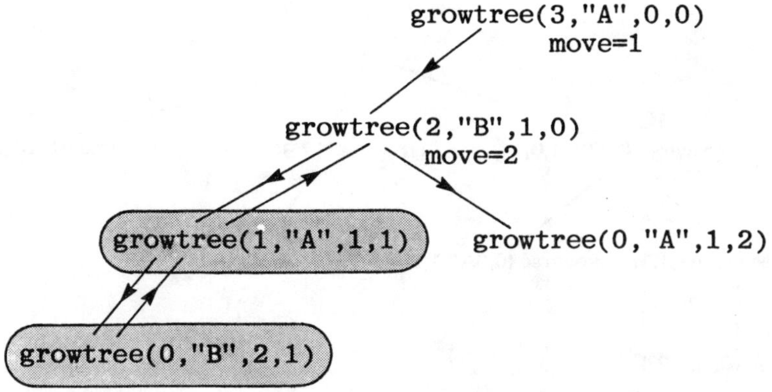

In order to present a complete picture of what has happened as well as what is happening, The diagram includes the procedure calls that have been terminated, but these are clearly marked.

As you can see, the program is working its way systematically through the nodes in the tree by proceeding as far as it can down one branch before retracing its steps and exploring another branch. This type of exploration is known 'depth-first search' and the process of going back and trying another branch is known as 'backtracking'. You will observe a similar effect if you try to draw a tree without lifting the pen off the paper and without retracing your steps more than is absolutely necessary.

The latest procedure activation represents another position in which the end of the game has been reached and after printing the final score for this position, the procedure call is terminated. The program retraces its steps to line 180 in the call

```
growtree(2,"B",1,0)
```

which also terminates as there are no more moves available in this position. This takes us back to line 180 in the procedure activation that started the whole process off. The FOR loop here is repeated with move=2 and this results in the call

```
growtree(1,"B",2,0)
```

which in turn calls

```
growtree(0,"A",2,1)
```

When the final score for this position has been printed, the program retraces its steps back through the last two procedure calls to the topmost procedure call in which the FOR loop is executed with move=3. This results in the situation illustrated in the next tree.

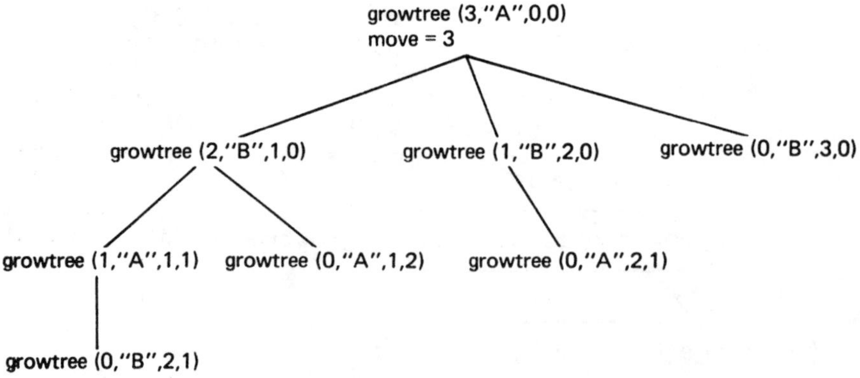

A final score is output for the last time and the two remaining procedure calls exit in turn.

You should now be able to see how the program keeps track of the structure of the game tree as it is being generated. If recursion were not available, the game positions generated and information about which moves have been tried in each position would have to be stored in some sort of data structure that would allow the program to retrace its steps when all the possibilities down one branch of the tree have been considered. The data structure that would be needed to do this is called a 'stack'. In a programming language that allows recursion, we do not need to create such a data structure - we can use the procedure entry and exit mechanisms to handle the 'bookkeeping' details needed to implement the backtracking process. (In fact the computer uses its own stack behind the scenes to keep track of recursive procedure calls.) When we use recursion, trying a move corresponds to calling a procedure - the resultant procedure activation and its parameters represent the new game position. Note the importance of the LOCAL declaration at the head of the procedure. Several procedure activations can be in existence at once, and each one needs its own private copy of information that is unique to that activation and the position that it represents.

One final point: if you try to use PROCgrowtree for more than 10 counters, it will fail with the error message 'Too many FORs'. There is a limit to the number of FOR's that can be 'nested' inside one another and when we call our procedure recursively it behaves as if the FOR loop obeyed in the recursive call were inside the FOR loop of the procedure that made the call. (This problem was discussed in Chapter 7.) There are over 1100 positions in the tree for the game starting with 11 counters, so you are unlikely to want to print them out. If you do want to use the procedure for 11 or more counters, you will have to replace the FOR-NEXT with an IF-GOTO loop or a REPEAT loop (REPEAT loops can be more deeply nested than FOR loops).

Now that we have seen how our tree generating program works, it is interesting to see if we can improve the layout of the output produced. One way of doing this is to make the output reflect the structure of the tree being explored by printing some extra spaces at the start of each line of output. The number of spaces printed before a position is proportional to the depth of the position in the game tree. The easiest way of doing this is to add an extra parameter to our recursive procedure. Remember that a call of the procedure represents a game position. Each time we call the procedure we shall supply an extra parameter that indicates the depth of the new position in the game tree. We need to make the following changes to our procedure:

```
100   DEF PROCgrowtree(counters, turn$,
                           Ascore, Bscore, depth)
110   LOCAL move,movesavailable,
                     newturn$,newAscore,newBscore
115     PRINT
120     PRINT TAB(4*depth);counters;turn$;Ascore;Bscore
130     IF counters = 0 THEN PROCfinalscore : ENDPROC
                  :
170       PROCgrowtree(counters-move, newturn$,
                      newAscore, newBscore, depth+1)
                  :
200   DEF PROCfinalscore
210     PRINT TAB(4*depth); "Final score: ";
                  :
```

Note that when an activation of the procedure tries a move by calling the procedure recursively, the depth of the new position created is one more than the current depth. Hence the need to supply depth+1 as a parameter to the recursive procedure call at line 170. When the procedure call corresponding to depth=depth+1 is exited, The old value of depth is restored. If the procedure is now called by

```
10   PROCgrowtree(3, "A", 0, 0, 0)
```

the output produced is

```
3A00
    2B10
        1A11
            0B21
            Final score: 4 - 1
        0A12
        Final score: 1 - 4
    1B20
        0A21
        Final score: 2 - 3
    0B30
    Final score: 5 - 0
```

The lines have been drawn to make it clear how the layout of the program output corresponds to the structure of the game tree. A rather interesting variation of the above program would be one that uses graphics statements to draw a complete game tree.

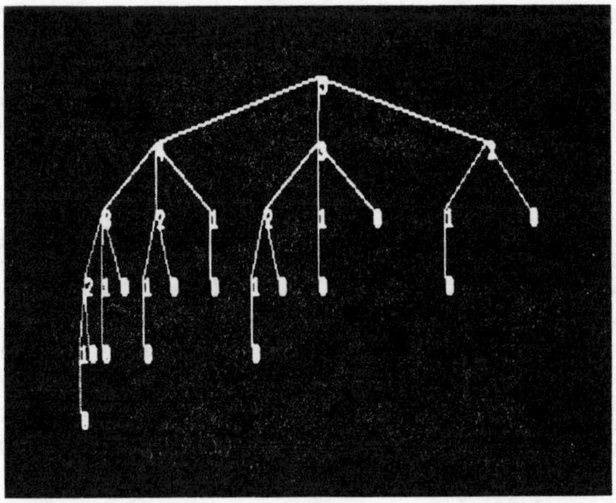

Here is the program that produced the photograph:

```
 10   INPUT "Counters", counters
 20   MODE 4
 30   MOVE 640,1000
 40   VDU 5
 50   PROCdrawtree(counters, 640,1000,1280)
 60   k=GET:MODE 7
 70   END

100   DEF PROCdrawtree(counters, x,y, width)
110   LOCAL move,movesavailable, newx, newy, newwidth
120     PRINT ;counters
130     IF counters=0 THEN  ENDPROC
140     PROCcheckmovesavailable
150     newwidth = INT(width/movesavailable)
160     newx = INT(x-width/2+newwidth/2)
170     newy = y-100
180     FOR move= 1 TO movesavailable
190       MOVE x,y : DRAW newx,newy
200       PROCdrawtree(counters-move,newx,newy,newwidth)
210       newx = newx + newwidth
220     NEXT move
230   ENDPROC

250   DEF PROCcheckmovesavailable
260     IF counters<3 THEN movesavailable = counters
       ELSE movesavailable = 3
270   ENDPROC
```

Exercises

1 Draw the game tree of procedure calls that takes place as a result of obeying the statement

```
PROCgrowtree(4,"A",0,0)
```

Make sure that you understand the order in which procedure activations are entered and exited.

8.3 Manipulating board positions during recursion

In the procedures written in the last section, a board position could be easily represented by a single integer. When PROCgrowtree was called recursively, it was given a value for a parameter ('counters') representing a new board position. When the recursive procedure call exits, that value for 'counters' disappears and the old value is now available for trying other moves.

More complicated data structures such as arrays cannot be passed as parameters in BBC BASIC and we need to find some other way of restoring a board position to the state it was in before a move was tried by a recursive call of the procedure. One way of doing this is to make the move by changing the board before calling the procedure recursively and then 'unmake' the move after the recursive procedure call has exited. This is illustrated in the following program that prints the tree for Grundy's Game.

If you wonder why we have used a REPEAT at line 350 instead of a FOR, try replacing the REPEAT with a FOR and refer back to page 267.

```
 10   DIM pile(20)
 20   pile(1) = 7              :REM  start with one pile
 30   PROCgrowtree("A", 1) :REM    of 7 counters.
 40   END

100   DEF PROCgrowtree(turn$, piles)
110   LOCAL p, pilestried, nextturn$
120     PRINT turn$;
130     FOR p=1 TO piles : PRINT ;pile(p); : NEXT
140     PRINT
150     IF turn$="A" THEN nextturn$="B"
                     ELSE nextturn$="A"
160     pilestried = 0
170     FOR p = 1 TO piles
180       IF pile(p)>2 THEN PROCtrysplits
190     NEXT p
200     IF pilestried=0 THEN
            PROCfinalresult :REM there were no moves.
210   ENDPROC
```

```
300   DEF PROCtrysplits
310   LOCAL posssplits, split
320     pilestried = pilestried+1
330     posssplits = INT((pile(p)-1)/2)
340     split = 0
350     REPEAT
360       split = split+1
370       pile(piles+1) = split
380       pile(p) = pile(p) - split
390       PROCgrowtree(nextturn$, piles+1)
400       pile(p) = pile(p) + split  :REM 'unmake' move.
410     UNTIL split=posssplits
420   ENDPROC

500   DEF PROCfinalresult
600     IF turn$ = "B" THEN PRINT "  A wins."
                       ELSE PRINT "  B wins."
700   ENDPROC
```

The program also exhibits some other interesting features that you should study. For example, the recursion is no longer quite so obvious - PROCgrowtree uses a subsidiary procedure, PROCtrysplits, to try different ways of splitting a given pile and it is this procedure that may call PROCgrowtree again. Also there is no explicit test at the head of PROCgrowtree to terminate the recursion - recursion terminates if there are no piles to be subdivided and this is not known until all the piles have been examined.

Exercises

1 Draw the tree of procedure calls that take place as a result of obeying the above program. Mark alongside each procedure call the state of the array 'pile' when the procedure is entered.

8.4 Minimaxing

We now need to introduce a criterion that can be used by a game playing program to decide on the best move in a given position. When a good human game player is presented with a board position in which he has to make a move, he usually considers some of the moves available, some of his opponents possible responses to these moves, some of his possible responses to his opponent's moves, and so on. In other words, he looks ahead and explores part of the game tree rooted at the current position. Human game players are very selective about which branches of the tree they explore - they have to be because of their slow processing speed and limited short term memory capabilities. A typical human player thinks about only one or two moves at each position in his lookahead, whereas a computer program usually explores a much bushier game tree:

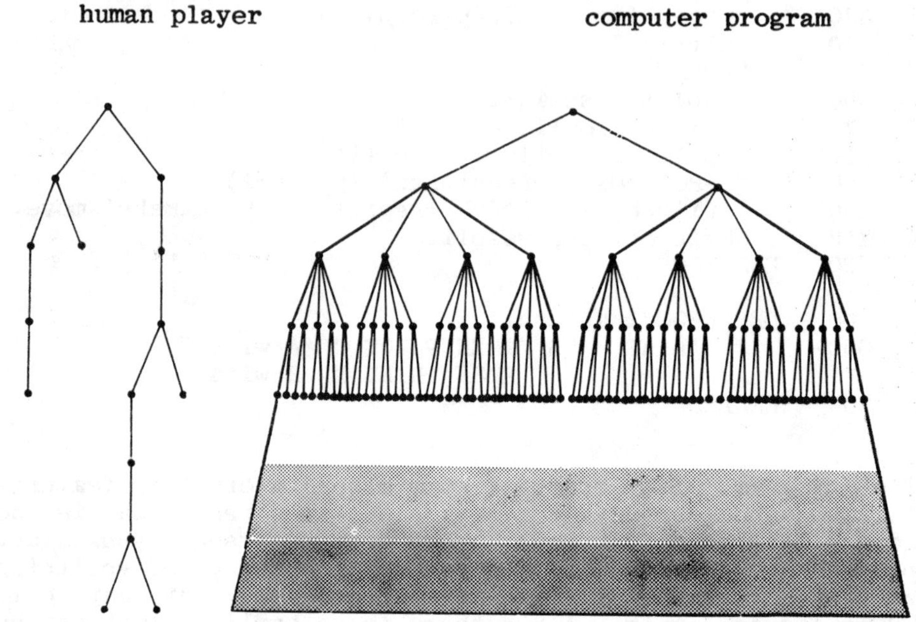

The better the human player, the better he is at recognising the promising branches of the tree that need exploration. This process of ignoring branches of the lookahead tree - 'tree pruning' - is very important for programs too, and will be discussed later, but for the time being we shall assume that a game playing program will explore the entire game tree in deciding on its move. Such a complete exploration is possible only for trivial games like 'Last One Wins - or does he?', but the programming techniques required for the partial exploration of a much larger tree are almost identical and will be discussed later.

Consider the problem of deciding on a move in the following situation.

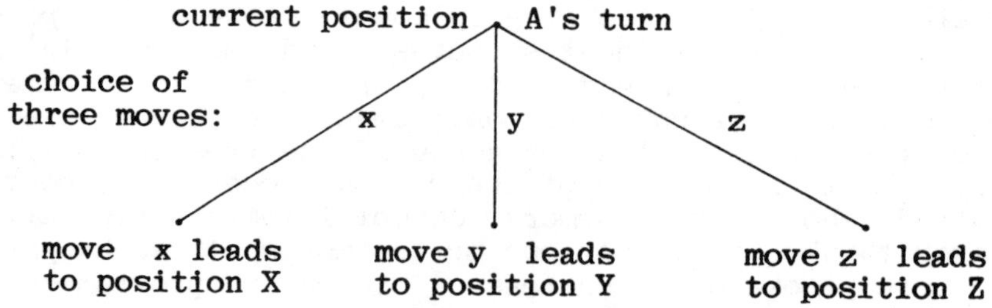

One way of making a choice of moves would be to give numerical values to positions X, Y and Z where the value assigned to a position indicates how good that position is from player A's point of view. A could then choose the position with the highest value. It is easy to assign such a value to a terminal position of a game tree. In a position where the game is over, we can compute a final score for the game. For example, in the tree for 'Last one Wins - or does he' each terminal position was given a value representing the point difference by which player A has won. A negative value means that player A has lost by that amount. In a game where the outcome must be just win, draw or lose, we could assign values +1, 0 or -1 to the terminal nodes of the tree. Thus if X, Y and Z were all terminal positions, we could easily give values to these positions for the purpose of comparing moves x, y and z. A problem arises when X, Y and Z are not terminal positions and player B now has a choice of moves in each of these positions. Let us extend the above tree to one more level. We assume that there are three moves available in each of positions X, Y and Z and that any one of these moves will terminate the game. We have assigned hypothetical final scores to each of the terminal positions.

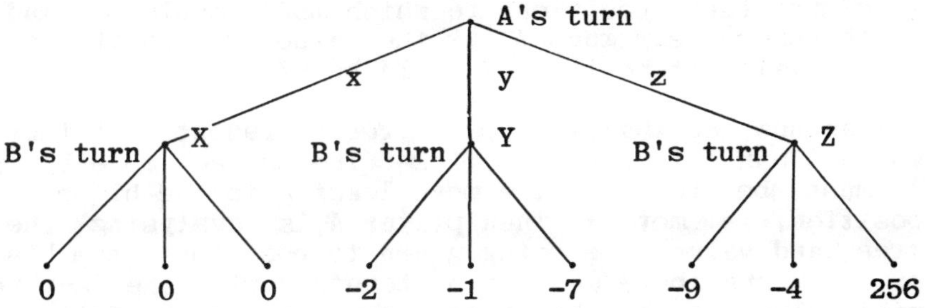

We assume that positive values represent a win for A (the higher the better) and negative values mean that A has lost. It is highly unlikely that an actual game would have such widely differing terminal values but we have chosen values that will emphasise the points that we wish to make. We must now decide how to evaluate the non-terminal positions X, Y and Z.

All three moves available in position X lead to scores of 0. Whatever move player B chooses in position X must inevitably lead to a draw, and there is no difficulty in deciding that position X should be given a value of 0.

The three moves available in position Y all lead to positions where A loses by varying amounts. It is clear that we can classify position Y as a losing position and assign it a negative value. We shall decide exactly what negative value it should be given when we have considered position Z.

In position Z, B has a choice of moves, one of which leads to a spectacular win for player A. In evaluating position Z, player A must decide what likelihood there is of achieving this spectacular win. After player A has made a move control of the outcome will pass to player B and, in order to decide on the value of position Z, A must make some assumption about how player B will choose his move. If A assumes that B is making completely random moves, then he might decide that the value of position Z is the average of the values of the three positions that B might move to. This would be a reasonable assumption in a game where B's move is determined by the throw of a dice, but in games of the type that we are dealing with both players have exactly the same information available and both players have a completely free choice of move. Under these circumstances, experienced board game players know that the only safe assumption is that one's opponent will choose his best move in any position. In our imaginary game, this means that player A assumes that if player B is presented with position Z then B will make his best move, ie. the move leading to the lowest possible value from A's point of view. Under this assumption, the value of Z is the minimum of the values of the three positions to which moves could be made. We therefore say that Z has the value -9. (In the same way, the value of position Y would be -7.)

We can now see that this part-tree represents a situation in which A can only win by a fluke. The correct move by player A must be to make the move leading to the highest valued position, ie. move x. When player A is analysing the game tree and values are being given to positions from his point of view, the above assumption together with the fact that A will always choose his best move gives us the following two rules:

(a) The value of a position at which it is A's turn is the <u>maximum</u> of the values of positions to which moves are available.

(b) The value of a position at which it is B's turn is the <u>minimum</u> of the values of positions to which moves are available.

You should now examine the game tree for 'Last one Wins - or does he' and attempt to apply these rules in order to give values to the non-terminal nodes. You should find that you can do this provided that you work backwards from the terminal nodes. For obvious reasons this process is known as 'minimaxing'. In the next tree we have done this and all the non-terminal nodes have been given values, including the node at the root of the tree.

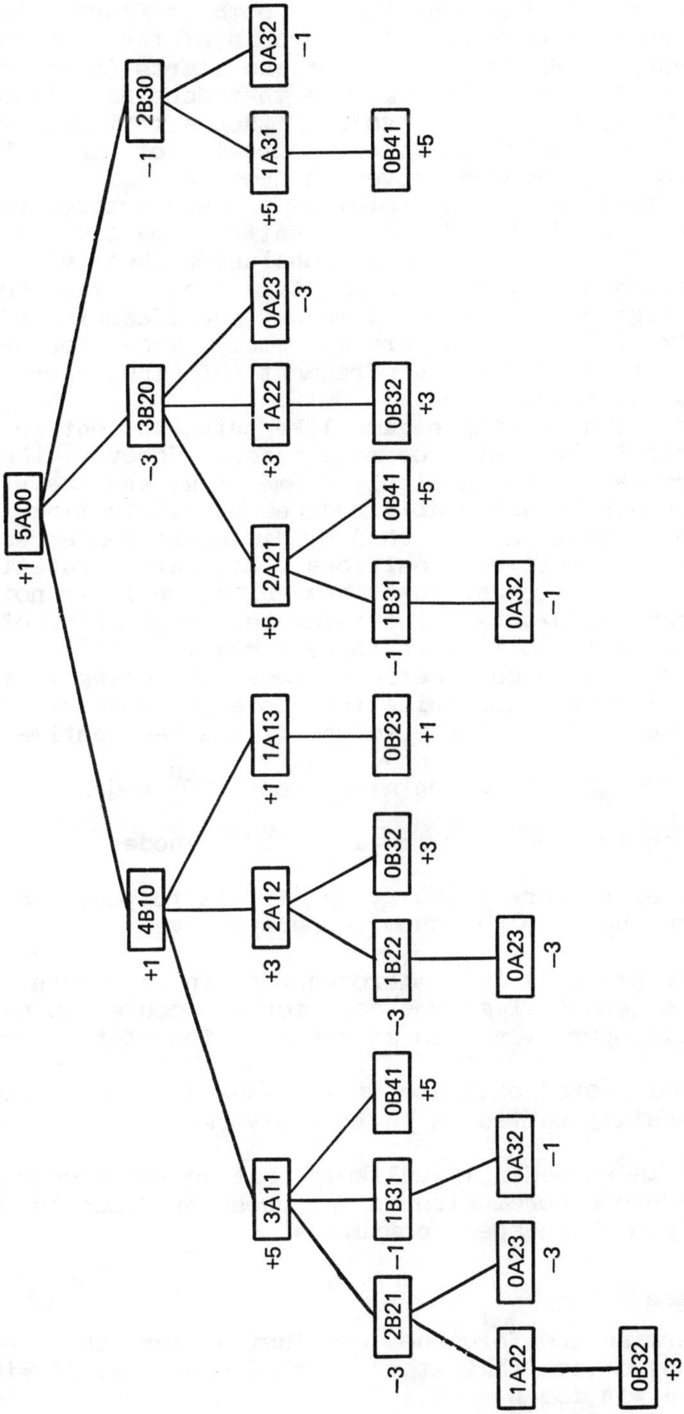
5A00 +1
4B10 +1
3B20 −3
2B30 −1
3A11 +5
2A12 +3
1A13 +1
2A21 +5
1A22 +3
0A23 −3
1A31 +5
0A32 −1
2B21 −3
1B31 −1
0B41 +5
1B22 −3
0B32 +3
0B23 +1
1B31 −1
0B41 +5
0B32 +3
0B41 +5
0A23 −3
1A22 +3
0A32 −1
0A23 −3
0A32 −1
0B32 +3

The value that has been assigned to the position at which the game starts tells us that if both players always make their best moves, then the outcome of the game is bound to be a score of +1 for the player who starts (A in this case). If player B ever chooses a move that does not lead to the position with minimum value, then A will improve on this score. You should convince yourself of this by trying different sequences of moves in the tree.

The fact that the minimax process determines a unique value for the root node of the entire game tree is sometimes referred to as the 'Foregone Conclusion Theorem'. In theory, the outcome of any game of the type that we are considering is a foregone conclusion. However, the trees for all but the most trivial of games are extremely large. For example, on the next page we have a fragment of the game tree for noughts and crosses.

Even with a simple game like this, the entire game tree could easily be a mile or more across. However, the noughts and crosses board is highly symmetrical and the size of the tree could be considerably reduced by eliminating duplicate positions that are reached by different sequences of moves and by eliminating positions that are rotations and reflections of other positions (although it is not easy for a program to do this). The foregone conclusion of noughts and crosses is well known to be a draw.

If we move to more serious games like draughts and chess, the problem of determining the 'foregone conclusion' becomes many orders of magnitude worse. It has been estimated that

The draughts tree contains about 10^{40} nodes.

The chess tree contains about 10^{120} nodes.

If these numbers mean very little to you, the following facts may help to put them in perspective.

There are only 10^{16} microseconds in a century and it takes about 1 microsecond for a computer to carry out a simple operation such as the addition of two numbers.

Cosmologists estimate that there are about 10^{80} elementary particles in the universe.

Thus it is exceedingly unlikely that we shall ever know what the foregone conclusion is for chess or draughts, even with the help of high-speed computers.

Exercises

1 Determine the foregone conclusion for the version of Grundy's Game that starts with 7 counters. (A win for A = +1, a win for B = -1.)

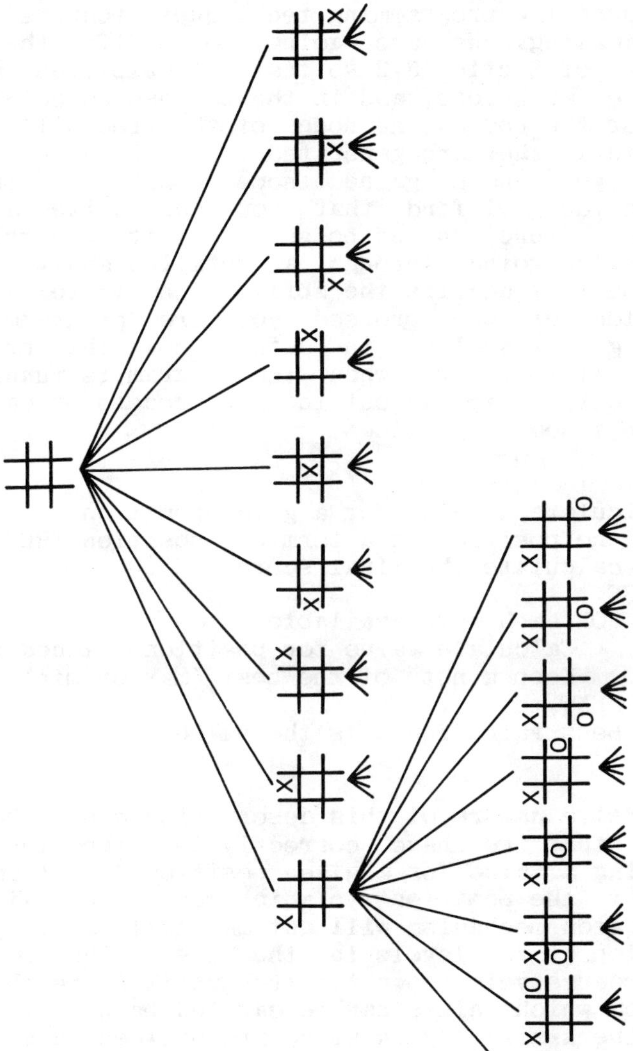

8.5 A recursive function for minimaxing

Despite the remarks made at the end of the last section, the process of minimaxing still plays an important role in programs that play more difficult games like draughts and chess. Before modifying our analysis to deal with such games, we shall use the game 'Last One Wins - or does he?' to introduce the programming techniques required to carry out minimaxing. We are going to modify the procedure 'growtree' of Section 8.2 so that it explores the entire game tree as before, and in the process calculates minimax values for the nodes. The nodes of the tree will no longer be printed as they are generated.

Once you have gained some confidence in handling recursion you will find that you can write a recursive procedure or function and be sure that it is correct without subsequently going through a detailed analysis of how it works. You must acquire the ability to write a recursive description of the process you are programming without attempting to visualise in detail how the procedure or function will behave when the program is running. In the present context, we can outline the process of calculating a value for a node as follows:

```
To calculate a value for a given position:
   IF the position is a terminal position THEN
      calculate the final score
   ELSE
      FOR each move available
         Calculate value for position reached by move
         Keep a note of the best (max or min) value found
      NEXT move
      Best value found is the value required.
```

The recursive nature of this description should be obvious. Provided that we have correctly described the process of calculating a value for a given position in terms of the values of the positions to which moves are available, then the recursion mechanism will automatically apply our correct description at all levels in the tree. The program will search recursively down the tree until it reaches terminal nodes from which values can be carried back up the tree.

Note the similarity in structure between this description of the minimax process and the procedure 'growtree' programmed in Section 8.2. In this case, it is convenient to define a function rather than a procedure, the value produced by a function call being the minimax value for a node. Conversion of the above outline description into a recursive Basic function is fairly straightforward:

```
100   DEF FNminimaxval(counters, turn$, Ascore, Bscore)
110   LOCAL move, movesavailable, newturn$,
            newAscore, newBscore, bestsofar, nextval
120     IF counters = 0 THEN = FNfinalscore
130     PROCcheckmovesavailable
140     IF turn$="A" THEN bestsofar = -100
                     ELSE bestsofar = +100
150     FOR move = 1 TO movesavailable
160       IF turn$="A" THEN  newturn$ = "B"  :
             newAscore=Ascore+move: newBscore=Bscore
          ELSE  newturn$ = "A"  :
             newBscore=Bscore+move: newAscore=Ascore
170       nextval = FNminimaxval(counters-move,
                        newturn$, newAscore, newBscore)
180       IF turn$="A" THEN
               bestsofar=FNmax(bestsofar,nextval)
          ELSE bestsofar=FNmin(bestsofar,nextval)
190     NEXT move
200   = bestsofar

300   DEF FNfinalscore
310     IF turn$="A" THEN = Ascore-(Bscore+2)
                     ELSE = (Ascore+2)-Bscore

400   DEF FNmax(old,new)
410     IF new<old THEN =old
                   ELSE =new

420   DEF FNmin(old,new)
430     IF new>old THEN =old
                   ELSE =new
```

As was the case with the procedure 'growtree', an activation of the above function represents a node in the game tree. The nodes are examined in exactly the same order as they were by 'growtree'. Instead of printing the node represented by the parameters of a function activation, the minimax value calculated by a call of the function is returned as the result of that function call. The value returned by a recursive call of the function is immediately examined by the function activation that made the call (line 180).

In order to discover the 'foregone conclusion' of the game with 3 counters (A starts), we could call our function as follows:

```
10   PRINT "3 counters - foregone conclusion:" ;
20   PRINT ; FNminimaxval(3, "A", 0, 0)
30   END
```

This prints the minimax value of the initial position in the game starting with 3 counters. The tree of function calls produced during a run of this program is:

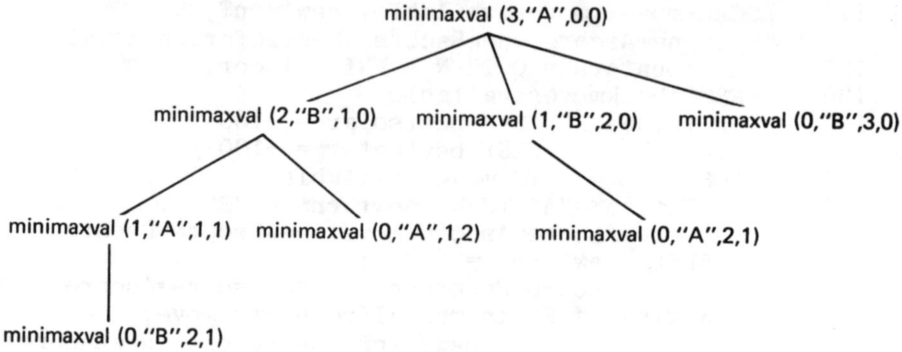

This tree of function calls is generated in the same way as the tree of procedure calls discussed in detail in Section 8.2. You should annotate each function call in the tree with the minimax value that is the eventual result of that call.

8.6 Mutually recursive functions for minimaxing

The purpose of a call of PROCgrowtree was simply to print a representation of a node of the game tree. The operations carried out by FNminimaxval depend to a much greater extent on the question of whose turn it is. For this reason, the above function looks very cumbersome because of the repeated need to examine the value of the parameter 'turn$' in order to decide whether the current function activation represents a position at which it is A's turn (maximising) or B's turn (minimising). We can produce a considerably more elegant program for minimaxing if we define two <u>mutually recursive</u> functions. One function, FNmaxval, will be used to calculate the minimax value of a node at which it is player A's turn and the other, FNminval, will be used to calculate the minimax value of a node at which it is player B's turn. FNmaxval will try each move available in a position and must use FNminval to evaluate the position reached by each move. In a similar way, FNminval uses FNmaxval.

```
100   DEF FNmaxval(counters, Ascore, Bscore)
120   LOCAL move, movesavailable, maxsofar, nextval
130     IF counters = 0 THEN = Ascore-(Bscore+2)
140     PROCcheckmovesavailable
150     maxsofar = -100
160     FOR move = 1 TO movesavailable
170       nextval = FNminval(counters-move,
                                Ascore+move, Bscore)
180       maxsofar=FNmax(maxsofar,nextval)
190     NEXT move
200   = maxsofar
```

```
300    DEF FNminval(counters, Ascore, Bscore)
320    LOCAL move, movesavailable, minsofar, nextval
330      IF counters = 0 THEN = (Ascore+2)-Bscore
340      PROCcheckmovesavailable
350      minsofar = +100
360      FOR move = 1 TO movesavailable
370        nextval = FNmaxval(counters-move,
                                   Ascore, Bscore+move)
380        minsofar=FNmin(minsofar,nextval)
390      NEXT move
400    = minsofar

500    DEF FNmax(old,new)
510      IF new<old THEN =old
                    ELSE =new

520    DEF FNmin(old,new)
530      IF new>old THEN =old
                    ELSE =new
```

Note that the parameter 'turn$' is no longer needed. To print the 'foregone conclusion' of the game starting with 4 counters we now need:

```
10    PRINT "4 counters - foregone conclusion:";
20    PRINT ; FNmaxval(4, 0, 0)
30    END
```

The tree of function calls resulting from a run of this program is:

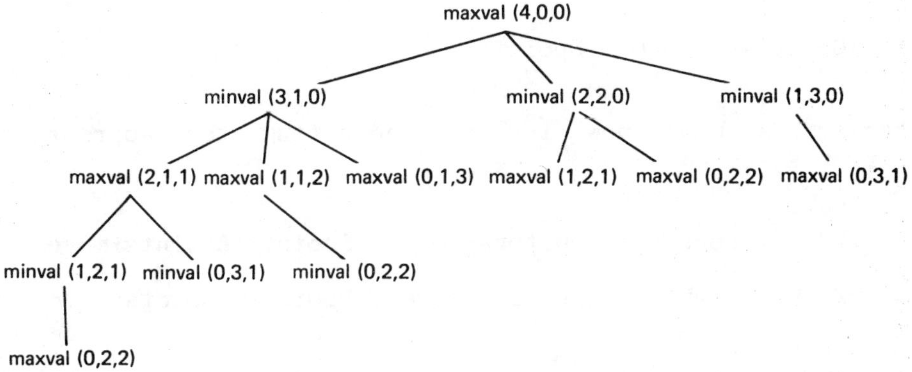

The nodes of the game tree are examined in the same order as before, but activations of FNmaxval represent positions at which it is A's turn and activations of FNminval represent positions at which it is B's turn.

We have mentioned before that our emphasis in the book is on clarity of presentation of ideas. There are various ways in which the above program could be changed so as to reduce the amount of work that it has to do. For example, we could replace the two parameters 'Ascore' and 'Bscore' by a single parameter 'Asnetscore' whose value is the difference between A's score and B's score. Other more subtle improvements could be made, but only at the cost of obscuring the way that the function works.

Finally, note that none of the above minimaxing functions, as presented, will work for more than ten counters (see page 267 for a discussion of the reasons for this).

Exercises

1 Write functions FNminval and FNmaxval for calculating the minimax values of positions in Grundy's Game.

2 If you are familiar with any other 'simple' board games, such as NIM, do the same for them.

8.7 Choosing a move in a 'small' game

Before studying the problem of choosing a move in a more difficult game, we shall finish our study of 'small' games by examining a number of ways in which a program can be made to choose its move in such a game.

The program at the end of Chapter 1 is easily modified to play 'Last One Wins - or does he?'. We need two variables 'Apoints' and 'Bpoints' initialised to zero at the start of PROCplaygame:

```
105 Apoints = 0 : Bpoints = 0
```

Making a move now involves adjusting the appropriate player's score:

```
750      counters=counters-move : Apoints=Apoints+move
         :
         :
920      counters=counters-move : Bpoints=Bpoints+move
```

and the program must now announce the final score at the end of the game:

```
610     IF turn$="A" THEN Bpoints = Bpoints+2
                      ELSE Apoints = Apoints+2
611     PRINT "Final Score -  ME:"; Apoints
612     PRINT "               YOU:"; Bpoints
```

The techniques introduced in this section can now be described by reprogramming PROCplayerA in various ways.

Exhaustive lookahead with minimaxing

When presented with a position, the program can use the minimax functions defined in Section 8.6 to carry out an exhaustive lookahead along all possible sequences of moves from the current position. The result of this lookahead will be to obtain a value for each of the positions that can be reached by a legal move from the current position. The program should then choose the move leading to the position with the highest value. The following version of PROCplayerA does this.

```
 700   DEF PROCplayerA
 710   LOCAL move
 720     move = FNbestmove
 730     PRINT "I take "; move; " counters."
 740     counters=counters-move : Apoints=Apoints+move
 750     turn$ = "B"
 760   ENDPROC

1100   DEF FNbestmove
1110   LOCAL move,movesavailable,nextval,max,bestmovesofar
1120     PROCcheckmovesavailable
1130     max = -10
1140     FOR move = 1 TO movesavailable
1150        nextval = FNminval(counters-move,
                                 Apoints+move, Bpoints)
1160        IF nextval>max THEN
               max = nextval : bestmovesofar = move
1170     NEXT move
1180   = bestmovesofar
```

FNmaxval and FNminval will have to be renumbered from 1200 onwards. You should notice the similarity between FNbestmove and FNmaxval. The difference is that FNmaxval is used to find the value of the best position to which moves are available, whereas in the above context we wish to find the move that leads to the best position.

Decision tables

In small games like Noughts and Crosses or 'Last One Wins', the number of different positions that might be encountered by a program is small enough for a program to store a table containing a list of possible positions together with the recommended move for each position.

In the case of 'Last One Wins - or does he?', positions such as:

7 A 0 0 (the start of a game with 7 counters)

7 A 2 1

7 A 5 3

are all different in the sense that the scores are different in each position. However the move recommended by a minimax lookahead will be the same in each case. Once a sequence of moves has been irrevocably made, there is nothing a player can do to change the points scored so far. All he can do is to optimise subsequent scoring from his point of view. Thus the best move for the player whose turn it is depends only on the number of counters left on the board. The following table lists the best move (in the minimax sense) for various positions:

counters left	best move: no. of counters to be taken
1	1
2	2
3	3
4	3
5	1
6	2
7	3
8	3
9	3
10	any move

We could construct a table like this by hand for a game that we wish to program, but it would be more sensible to use a program to do it for us. Ways of using the minimax function previously written to automatically construct a decision table are discussed shortly. Whether we have constructed the above list by hand or automatically, our program can use it as a decision table as follows:

```
  5   DIM tablemove(10)
  6   PROCsetuptable
        .
        .
 50   DEF PROCsetuptable
 51   LOCAL c
 52     FOR c = 1 TO 10
 53       READ tablemove(c)
 54     NEXT c
 55   ENDPROC
 56   DATA 1, 2, 3, 3, 1, 2, 3, 3, 3, 3
        :
700   DEF PROCplayerA
710     move = tablemove(counters)
720     PRINT "I take "; move; " counters."
730     counters = counters-move : Apoints = Apoints+move
740     turn$ = "B"
750   ENDPROC
```

In 'Last One Wins - or does he?', a game position to be looked up in the decision table consists of a single integer. The decision table can thus be represented by an array containing the recommended moves, a board position being used as a subscript to access the table. In a game with more complicated board positions, each board position together with its corresponding recommended move would have to be stored in the table. Table access techniques of the type discussed in Chapter 6 would then have to be used to find a given position in the table.

Whenever a decision table is being constructed for a game, spectacular savings in space requirements for the table can often be made by careful use of the fact that the decisions in the table will confine the game to a subtree of the main game tree. The diagram on the next page shows the first three levels of the game tree for Noughts and Crosses in which we have treated symmetrical positions as being identical. (As we have already mentioned, it is not easy for a program to recognise such symmetries.) If the program starts and the entry in the decision table for the initial position recommends playing in the centre, then the program will always do this and there is clearly no possibility that the program will ever have to make a move in any of the marked positions that are at depth two down the branches reached by the other possible initial moves. These positions can be left out of the decision table. Note that we cannot leave out all the positions down these branches of the tree. For example, if the program's opponent starts, then he might make any one of the three initial moves and thus all three possible positions at depth one have to be stored.

The next two trees illustrate, for a hypothetical game, the overall effect that we get if one of the two players always chooses his best move (in the minimax sense).

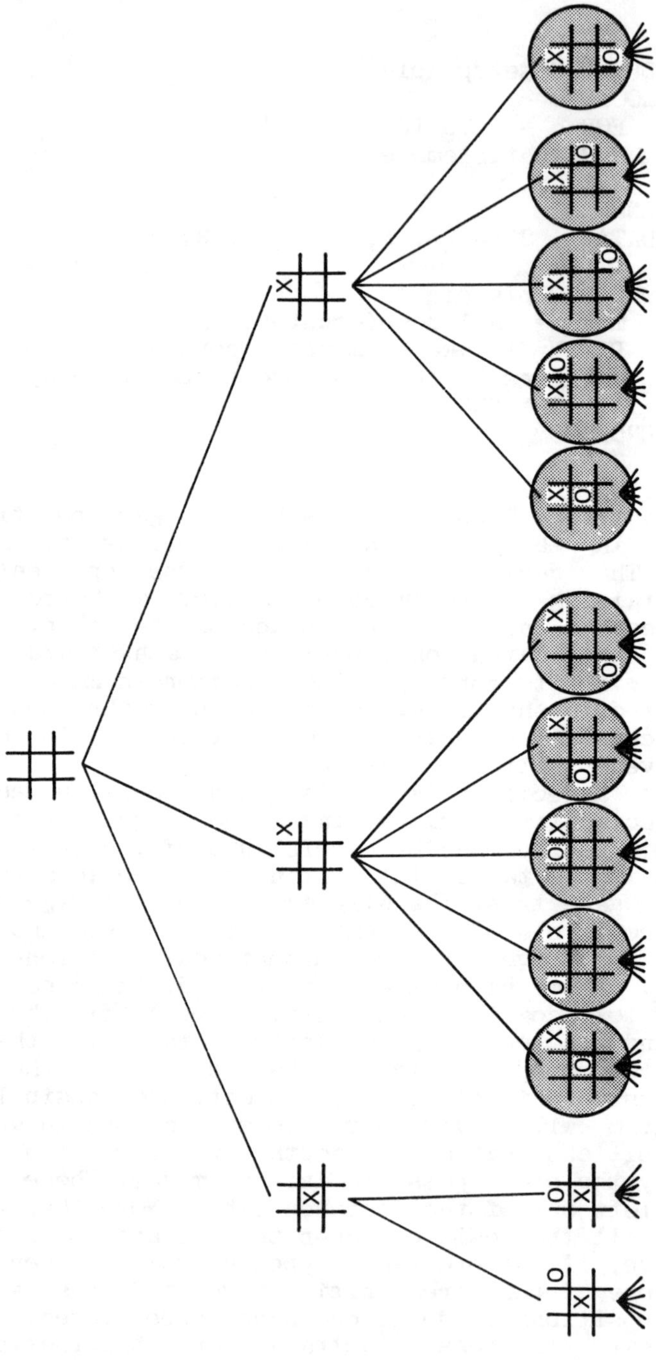

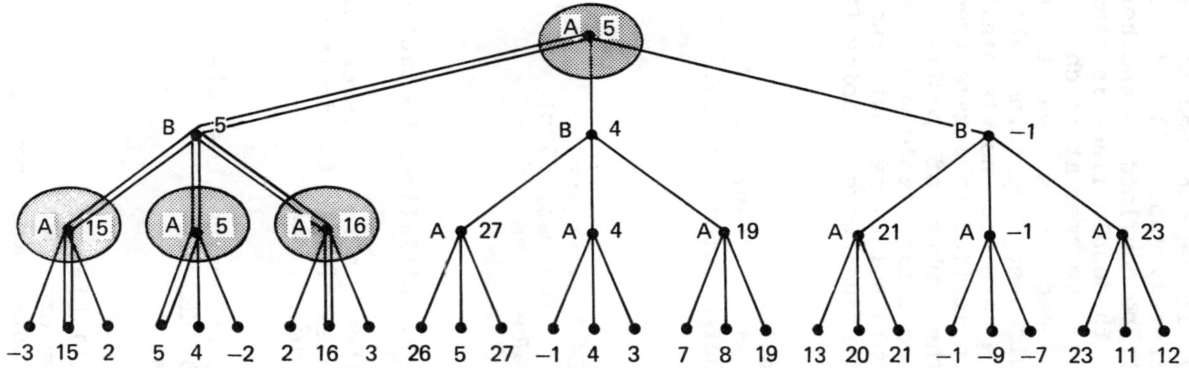

Best strategy subtree for player A

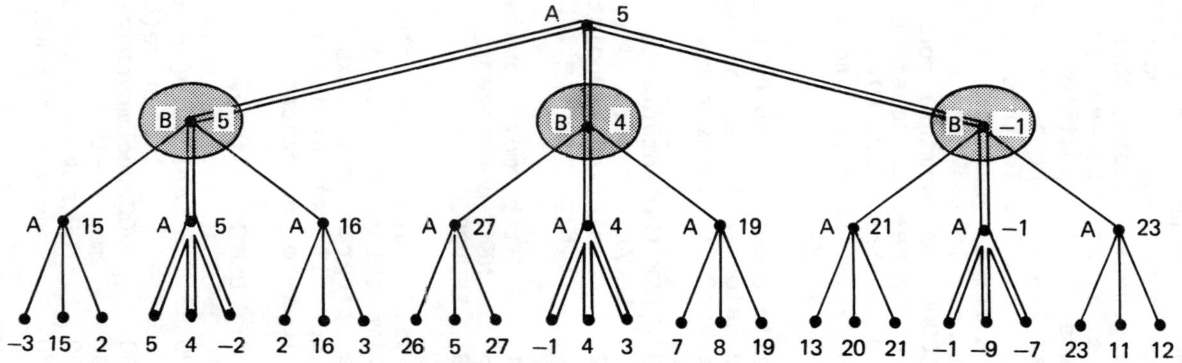

Best strategy subtree for player B

Best strategy subtrees for a hypothetical game

Note that although the minimax values have been calculated on the assumption that both players always make their best moves, we cannot rely on the program's opponent doing this. We must allow the possibility that the program's opponent will make a non-optimal move when it is his turn. If the program starts then play will be confined to one subtree (sometimes called a 'best strategy subtree') and if its opponent starts, then play will be confined to another subtree. These subtrees are marked with double lines in the diagrams. Only positions in these subtrees at which the program has to make a move (shaded) need be stored in a decision table. In this case we would need 7 decision table entries for a game in which there are 13 non-terminal positions. If the same analysis were applied to a game tree with 10000 non-terminal positions, the number of positions that would need to be stored in the decision table would be reduced to about 200. Clearly, we could not carry out such an analysis manually and we now introduce ways of doing it automatically.

Automatic construction of a decision table

The decision table that we constructed for 'Last One Wins - or does he?' could have been constructed automatically:

```
50    DEF PROCsetuptable
51    LOCAL counters
52      Apoints=0 : Bpoints=0
53      FOR counters = 1 TO 9 :REM 10 wont work
                                  (Too many FORs)
54        tablemove(counters) = FNbestmove
55      NEXT counters
56    ENDPROC
```

This will take rather a long time to initialise the tables each time the program is used.

The program will exhibit rather more interesting behaviour if we initialise all the entries in the decision table to zero and extend FNbestmove as follows:

```
1100   DEF FNbestmove
1110   LOCAL move,movesavailable,max,nextval,bestvalsofar
1120     IF tablemove(counters)>0 THEN
             = tablemove(counters)
1130     PROCcheckmovesavailable
1140     max = -10
1150     FOR move = 1 TO movesavailable
1160       nextval = FNminval(counters-move,
                             Apoints+move, Bpoints)
1170       IF nextval>max THEN
              max = nextval : bestmovesofar = move
1180     NEXT move
1190     tablemove(counters) = bestmovesofar
1195   = bestmovesofar
```

We must also revert to using the version of PROCplayerA that called FNbestmove. Each time FNbestmove is called, the decision table is examined and, if an entry has previously been inserted for the given number of counters, then that entry determines the best move. If no entry has yet been inserted, FNbestmove carries on and calculates the best move by carrying out a minimax analysis. Before this move is returned as a result of the function, it is inserted in the decision table for future use. This version of FNbestmove can now be used by PROCplayerA. Now consider what happens if we use the following loop to control the execution of our game-playing program.

```
10   REPEAT
11      PROCplaygame
13      INPUT "Another go (Y/N)", reply$
14   UNTIL reply$="N"
```

If we run the program and play several games during one run, then the program will gradually fill in entries in its decision table. For example, the first time the program has to choose a move with 10 counters on the board, it will take a long time to analyse the situation, but the next time, its response will be instantaneous - we have implemented a fairly primitive form of 'learning'. Furthermore, we are only inserting entries in the decision table for positions that are encountered during actual games. This, together with the effect discussed in the last section, would reduce the storage space required for a decision table in a game with more complicated board positions.

Another possibility that we shall not program in detail is some form of 'learning by trial and error'. We could set up a decision table in which each position has associated with it a set of values that determine the probabilities with which each move is to be selected. For a position that has not been encountered before, the probabilities for the moves available would all be equal. Thus the program would start by selecting completely random moves. During the course of a game the program would keep a record of the positions encountered and the moves selected. At the end of the game, if the program wins, then the probabilities of making all the moves recorded can be increased slightly; if the program loses, the probabilities for the moves made can be decreased slightly. The adjustments made must not more than slight: winning a game does not mean that all the moves made were good. Over a period, the performance of the program will gradually improve.

If we are experimenting with the 'learning' techniques discussed in this section, then it can be very frustrating if we have painstakingly improved the program's performance during a RUN and then have to start from scratch again the next day. For this reason, a useful option in such a program would be the ability to output a decision table to a file and to read the table from the file at the start of the next run.

Playing by rule

For simple games, it is often possible to define a rule or rules that can be used to select a good move without exhaustive exploration of the game tree.

In the game 'Last One Wins' used at the end of Chapter 1, there is a very simple rule that can be used to find a winning move if there is one available:

> Try to make a move that leaves a multiple of 4 counters on the board. (If no such move is available, then you are in a losing position.)

In Noughts and Crosses, we might use a sequence of rules that are to be applied in turn until a move is found. For example,

> If there is a winning move, make it.
> If the opponent has a winning move, block it.
> If the centre is empty, play there.
> Make a random move.

This Noughts and Crosses strategy does not always select the best move and draws attention to the fact that a set of rules need not be optimal. In fact, it would be quite easy to define a set of simple rules for choosing a move in Chess, but the resulting program would play a very poor game.

Exercises

1 Extend your Noughts and Crosses program so that it chooses a move by using a set of simple rules like those outlined above.

Chapter 9 Difficult board games – the beginnings of Artificial Intelligence

In the last chapter, the games that we used as examples were all fairly easy games with moderately sized game trees. In this chapter, we are going to introduce the methods that are needed for programming more difficult games. We shall demonstrate these methods by using an ancient game called Kalah. Kalah is somewhat easier than Chess and Draughts, but is still very much more intellectually demanding than any of the games that have been used so far. It is ideal for experimentation with game playing techniques.

9.1 The game Kalah

We now present the rules for Kalah and suggest that you familiarise yourself with these rules by finding someone who will play a few games with you. (You can mark out a board on a sheet of paper and use coins or counters for stones.)

The Rules of Kalah

Kalah Originated as a desert game played by two people using stones and holes made in the sand. We can imagine the game to be played on a rectangular board:

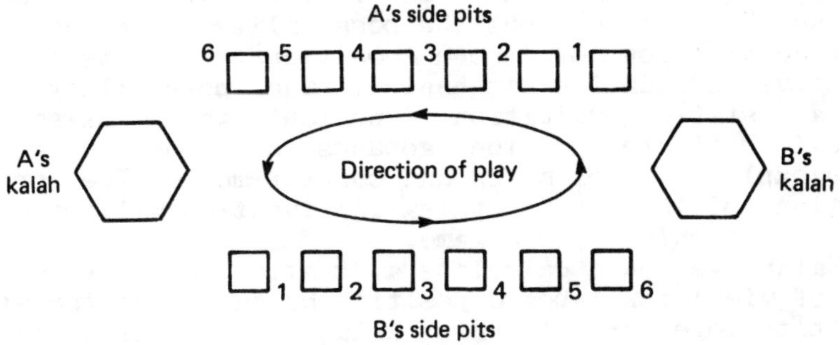

In front of him, each player has six pits numbered 1 to 6 (called his 'side' pits). To the right of his side pits, each player has a special pit called a 'kalah'. Initially, all the side pits contain an equal number of stones. A move consists of taking the stones from one of one's own side pits and distributing them anti-clockwise one by one into the other pits including one's own kalah but not the opponent's. There are two rules:

(a) Players make moves alternately except when the last stone of a pile that a player moves lands in his own kalah. That player then makes another move.

(b) If the last stone of a pile that a player is moving lands in an empty pit on his own side, that stone along with any stones in the pit opposite are placed in that player's kalah.

The game ends when the player whose turn it is cannot make a move (ie. all his side pits are empty). Each person's score is the number of stones in his kalah plus the number (if any) in his side pits. The player with the highest score is the winner.

For a good beginner's game, start with 2 or 3 stones in each side pit. Starting with 6 stones in each pit results in quite a difficult game.

9.2 Static evaluation functions

If you have run the recursive procedures for exploring the 'Last One Wins - or does he?' game tree for positions with 9 or 10 counters, you will have discovered that, even for a trivial game like this, the computer takes a fairly long time to do an exhaustive exploration of the game tree. For games like Kalah, Draughts or Chess, exhaustive exploration of the game tree is completely impossible.

The first possible alternative that we consider is to make a program select a move by carrying out a one-level lookahead from its current position. In order to compare the moves available in a given position, we need some way of comparing the new positions reached by the available moves. Since we have ruled out the possibility of an exhaustive minimax evaluation of these positions, we need some alternative evaluation mechanism. One possibility is to define a 'static evaluation function' which makes some numerical estimate of the goodness of a position without further exploration of moves and counter-moves. The precise definition of the static evaluation function will of course depend on the rules of the game.

In Kalah, we could calculate a static value (from A's point of view) for a board position by adding up the stones in A's pits together with his kalah and subtracting the stones in B's pits and kalah. This simple function could be improved upon, but it will suffice for our present purposes.

The next diagram illustrates the process of choosing a move by using a one-level lookahead together with a static evaluation function.

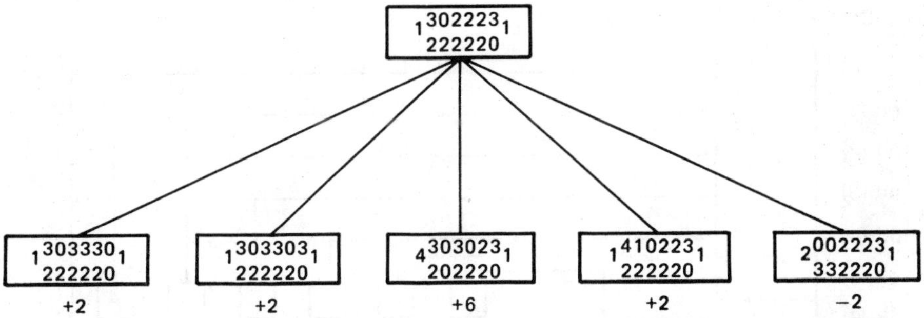

The program will try each move available, apply its static evaluation function to each position reached and choose the move that leads to the position with the best static value.

9.3 An introductory Kalah program

Before discussing improvements to the simple approach described in the last section, we shall write a complete Kalah program that uses a one-level lookahead to choose its moves.

We use as our framework the procedure PROCplaygame defined in Chapter 1. Before filling in the details by writing the other procedures required, we must decide how to represent a Kalah board in our program. There are various possibilities available. One that immediately suggests itself is a 7x2 array of integers where each integer represents the number of stones in one of the pits. Another possibility would be to pack a board position into two numeric variables and represent the number of stones in one pit by one hexadecimal digit. Such a representation would not be very convenient from the point of view of making moves, but it might be useful if we ever wanted to store large numbers of board positions in a table and needed to economise on storage space.

We shall in fact represent the Kalah board using a one-dimensional array of 14 locations numbered 0 to 13:

```
5   DIM pit(13)
```

Although this does not reflect the two-sided structure of the board, it is an extremely convenient representation in which to manipulate moves. For the purpose of making moves, the Kalah board is circular, and moving round the board corresponds to increasing the subscript of our one-dimensional array. We can use the MOD operator to make sure that the subscript goes back to zero if we reach 13:

```
pitno = (pitno + 1) MOD 14
```

The representation chosen is illustrated:

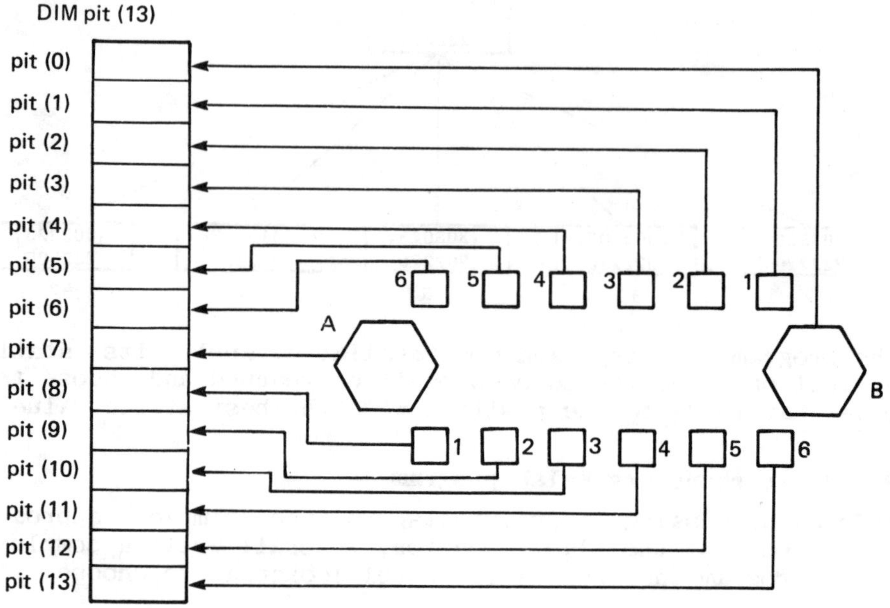

We first define a procedure for displaying a board position that is represented in this way. For the time being we simply print the number of stones in a pit as a number on the screen. Whenever a move has been made, this procedure will be used to display a completely new representation of the board. We leave as an exercise the use of character graphics to produce a more realistic display of the board.

```
205   DEF PROCdisplayboard
210   LOCAL p
215     @% = &0303
220     PRINT:PRINT:PRINT "    (6)(5)(4)(3)(2)(1)"
225     PRINT TAB(3);
230     FOR p = 6 TO 1 STEP -1 : PRINT pit(p); : NEXT p
235     PRINT
240     PRINT pit(7); TAB(21); pit(0)
245     PRINT TAB(3);
250     FOR p = 8 TO 13 : PRINT pit(p); : NEXT p
255     PRINT : PRINT "    (1)(2)(3)(4)(5)(6)" : PRINT
260     @% = &0A0A
265   ENDPROC
```

The board would be initialised by the following procedure:

```
300    DEF PROCsetupboard
310    LOCAL p, stones
320      INPUT "How many stones per pit", stones
330      FOR p = 1 TO 6
340        pit(p) = stones
350      NEXT p
360      FOR p = 8 TO 13
370        pit(p) = stones
380      NEXT p
390      pit(0) = 0 : pit(7) = 0
400      INPUT "Do you want to start", reply$
410      IF LEFT$(reply$,1) = "Y" THEN  turn$="B"
                                   ELSE  turn$="A"
420    ENDPROC
```

The next two procedures are straightforward:

```
500    DEF PROCtestgameover
510    LOCAL moves, start, p
520      IF turn$="A" THEN start = 1
                      ELSE start = 8
530      moves = 0
540      FOR p = start TO start+5
550        IF pit(p) > 0 THEN moves = moves+1
560      NEXT p
570      gameover = (moves=0)
580    ENDPROC

700    DEF PROCannouncewinner
710    LOCAL Apoints, Bpoints, p
720      Apoints = pit(7)   :  Bpoints = pit(0)
730      FOR p=1 TO  6 : Apoints=Apoints+pit(p) : NEXT
740      FOR p=8 TO 13 : Bpoints=Bpoints+pit(p) : NEXT

750      IF Apoints>Bpoints THEN  PRINT "I win!"
         ELSE IF Bpoints>Apoints THEN  PRINT "You win!"
              ELSE  PRINT "Its a draw."

760      PRINT "Final score -  ME:"; Apoints
770      PRINT                    YOU:"; Bpoints
780    ENDPROC
```

There are a number of useful relationships that we can take advantage of in manipulating board positions. For example, if 'k' is the location of one player's kalah (k=0 or k=7), then '7-k' gives the location of the other player's kalah; if 'p' is the location of one of the pits then '14-p' is the location of the opposite pit.

We now define the procedures for inputting and making the program's opponent's moves.

```
 900    DEF PROCplayerB
 910    LOCAL pitno
 920      PROCinputmove
 930      PROCmakeBmove(7+pitno)
 940    ENDPROC

1000    DEF PROCinputmove
1010      PRINT "Your move, which pit do you play from";
1020      INPUT pitno
1030      IF FNlegalBmove(pitno) THEN  ENDPROC

1040      REPEAT
1050        PRINT "Illegal Move."
1060          INPUT "Try again:" pitno
1070      UNTIL FNlegalBmove(pitno)
1080    ENDPROC

1100    DEF FNlegalBmove(p)
1110      IF p<0 OR p>7 THEN =FALSE
1120      IF pit(7+p)<=0 THEN =FALSE
1130    =TRUE
```

It is slightly more convenient to define two different procedures for making moves, one for player A and one for player B. The two procedures will be almost identical, but defining them separately eliminates some testing. The move-making procedures must decide whose turn it is next, setting the value of 'turn$' accordingly.

```
1200    DEF PROCmakeAmove(p)
1210    LOCAL lastpit
1220      PROCmovestones(p,0)
1230      IF lastpit<7 AND pit(lastpit)=1 THEN
             capture = pit(14-lastpit) :
             pit(14-lastpit) = 0 : pit(lastpit) = 0 :
             pit(7) = pit(7)+capture+1
          ELSE capture = -1 :REM signifies no capture
1240      IF lastpit = 7 THEN turn$="A" ELSE turn$="B"
1250    ENDPROC

1400    DEF PROCmakeBmove(p)
1410    LOCAL lastpit
1420      PROCmovestones(p,7)
1430      IF lastpit>7 AND pit(lastpit)=1 THEN
             capture = pit(14-lastpit) :
             pit(14-lastpit) = 0 : pit(lastpit) = 0 :
             pit(0) = pit(0)+capture+1
          ELSE capture = -1
1440      IF lastpit = 0 THEN turn$="B" ELSE turn$="A"
1450    ENDPROC
```

```
1600    DEF PROCmovestones(p, oppkalah)
1610    LOCAL s
1620      s = pit(p) : pit(p) = 0
1630      REPEAT
1640         p = (p+1) MOD 14
1650         IF p<>oppkalah THEN pit(p)=pit(p)+1 : s=s-1
1660      UNTIL s=0
1670      lastpit = p
1680    ENDPROC
```

We now define the procedures that carry out the one-level lookahead from a position at which it is the program's turn to play.

```
1800    DEF PROCplayerA
1810    LOCAL move
1820      move = FNbestmove
1830      PRINT "I move from pit "; move
1840      PROCmakeAmove(move)
1850    ENDPROC

2000    DEF FNbestmove
2010    LOCAL p, maxsofar, bestmove
2020      maxsofar = -100
2030      FOR p = 1 TO 6
2040         IF pit(p)>0 THEN PROCtryAmove
2050      NEXT p
2060    =bestmove

2200    DEF PROCtryAmove
2210    LOCAL stones, v, capture
2220      stones = pit(p)
2230      PROCmakeAmove(p)
2240      v = FNstaticval
2250      IF v>maxsofar THEN  maxsofar=v : bestmove=p
2260      PROCmoveback(p, stones, capture, 0)
2270    ENDPROC
```

Note the need to move the stones back to their original positions each time a move has been tried. This is done by PROCmoveback which needs to be told at which pit the move started, how many stones were in the pit before the move and how many stones, if any, were captured. At the moment, this procedure is used only for undoing a move by player A, but we shall shortly use it for undoing a move by B and it will be convenient if we give the procedure a 4th parameter telling it the location of the opponent's kalah.

```
2400    DEF PROCmoveback(p, s, capt, oppkalah)
2410      pit(p) = pit(p) + s
2420      REPEAT
2430        p = (p+1) MOD 14
2440        IF p<>oppkalah THEN
                pit(p) = pit(p) - 1 : s = s-1
2450      UNTIL s=0
2460      IF capt>-1 THEN
             pit(p)=pit(p)+1 : pit(14-p)=pit(14-p)+capt :
             pit(7-oppkalah) = pit(7-oppkalah)-capt-1
2470    ENDPROC
```

Finally, we define FNstaticval which is straightforward:

```
2600    DEF FNstaticval
2610    LOCAL p, points
2620      points = pit(7) - pit(0)
2630      FOR p = 1 TO  6 : points=points+pit(p) : NEXT
2640      FOR p = 8 TO 13 : points=points-pit(p) : NEXT
2650    = points
```

The program that we have defined so far plays an extremely poor game of Kalah. You will find that it is quite easily beaten. In the next few sections we shall look at ways of improving the program's performance. We shall do this by redefining FNbestmove and PROCtryAmove in various ways, leaving the rest of the program unchanged.

Exercises

1 Change FNbestmove so that it considers moves in reverse order, ie. using:

```
FOR p = 6 TO 1 STEP -1
```

Why does this improve the program's performance for games starting with two or three counters?

2 Try to improve the program's performance by defining an improved static evaluation function. For example, if a large pile of stones builds up in pit 6, then these eventually have to be distributed into one's opponent's pits. The program could be discouraged from doing this by making the static evaluation function give less credit for stones in pit 6. The credit given for stones in other pits could be varied in the same sort of way.

3 Modify the Kalah program so that it does not display a fresh copy of the board each time a move is made. It should instead use the TAB function to update the

existing display, changing the numbers already on the screen in the same order as the pits are changed while making a move. Use time delays so that the numbers do not change too quickly. If you are familiar with the use of Teletext colour and large character facilities in MODE 7, you could make use of these to enhance the display.

9.4 Looking further ahead in non-trivial games

In the last section, we saw how a simple static evaluation function could be used by a program for evaluating and comparing positions. The program that we produced did not play very well. Its performance could be improved by defining a better static evaluation function, but you will find that the extent to which it can be improved is limited. This is because it is difficult for a static evaluation function to take account of the possible sequences of moves and counter-moves that are available in the position being evaluated. The availability of certain moves can make the true value of a position very different from the value obtained by a static evaluation function. For example, the program might apply a static evaluation to a position in which its opponent was about to make a spectacular capture. In such circumstances, the value obtained will clearly be misleading.

We have already decided that exhaustive exploration of the game tree is out of the question, but a possible compromise way of evaluating a position is to look ahead in the game tree as far as time and space allow, perform a static evaluation of the positions reached, and minimax with these values in order to obtain a value for the starting position. A static value is calculated only after a sequence of moves and counter-moves has been tried. The value obtained by minimaxing with static values obtained in this way will hopefully be a better estimate of the value of the initial position than would have been obtained by using the static evaluation function alone. The minimax value of a position is the static value of some position that can be reached from the first position by a 'likely' sequence of moves and counter-moves.

One way of limiting the extent of the lookahead would be to impose some bound on the depth of the subtree that is to be explored by the program.

This is illustrated in the next diagram for a hypothetical game. The root of the subtree is a position at which the program has to decide on a move. To do this we have to obtain values for each of the three positions to which moves are available. These values are obtained by looking ahead to a further depth of 2 and minimaxing with the static values of the positions reached. Thus the program chooses a move by carrying a lookahead with an overall depth of 3.

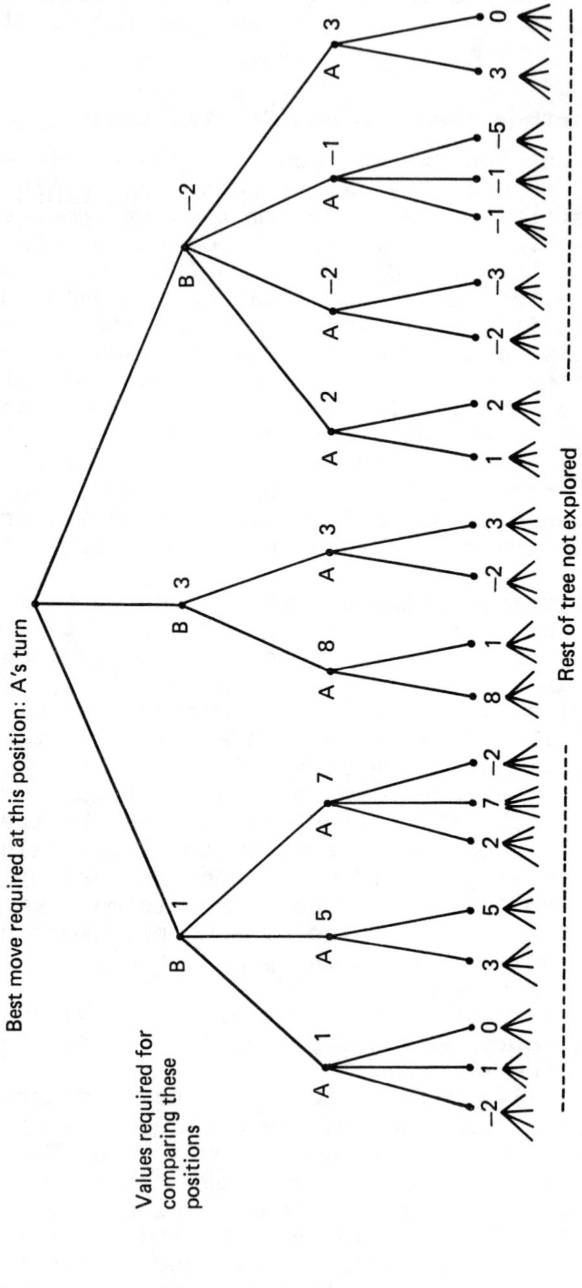
Best move required at this position: A's turn
Values required for comparing these positions
Rest of tree not explored

The structure of the procedures required to carry out a minimax lookahead of the type just described will be essentially the same as the structure of the procedures that carried out an exhaustive minimax lookahead for 'Last One Wins - or does he?'. We shall write two functions, FNminval for obtaining the value of a position at which it is B's turn and FNmaxval for a position at which it is A's turn.

In 'Last One Wins - or does he?', lookahead was terminated when a terminal position of the game was reached. In this case, lookahead will be terminated if a 'depth bound' is reached (or earlier if a terminal position of the game is reached). Each of our two minimax functions needs to be given a depth parameter that can be used to test whether or not to terminate the lookahead.

Before we define FNminval and FNmaxval, let us define a modified version of PROCtryAmove that can be used by FNbestmove.

```
2200   DEF PROCtryAmove
2210   LOCAL stones, v, capture, turn$
2220     stones = pit(p)
2230     PROCmakeAmove(p)
2240     IF turn$="B" THEN v=FNminval(1)
                      ELSE  v=FNmaxval(1)
2250     IF v>maxsofar THEN  maxsofar=v : bestmove=p
2260     PROCmoveback(p, stones, capture, 0)
2270   ENDPROC
```

There are two points to note here. We have made use of the fact that PROCmakeAmove sets 'turn$' to indicate whose turn it is in the new position created. This information is used to decide whether we use FNminval or FNmaxval to evaluate the new position. The parameter, 1, given to FNminval or FNmaxval indicates that the position to be evaluated is at depth 1 from the position at which a move has to be made. We shall assume in what follows that a variable 'maxdepth' has been set to an appropriate value, say:

```
   6   maxdepth = 2
```

FNminval and FNmaxval are defined as:

```
3000   DEF FNminval(depth)
3010   LOCAL minsofar, p
3020     IF depth=maxdepth THEN =FNstaticval
3030     minsofar=100
3040     FOR p = 8 TO 13
3050        IF pit(p)>0 THEN PROCtestBmove
3060     NEXT p
3070   IF minsofar<100 THEN =minsofar  ELSE =FNstaticval
```

```
3100   DEF PROCtestBmove
3110   LOCAL stones, v, capture, turn$
3120     stones = pit(p)
3130     PROCmakeBmove(p)
3140     IF turn$="A" THEN v=FNmaxval(depth+1)
                      ELSE v=FNminval(depth+1)
3150     IF v<minsofar THEN minsofar=v
3160     PROCmoveback(p,stones,capture,7)
3170   ENDPROC

3200   DEF FNmaxval(depth)
3210   LOCAL maxsofar, p
3220     IF depth=maxdepth THEN =FNstaticval
3230     maxsofar=100
3240     FOR p = 1 TO 6
3250        IF pit(p)>0 THEN PROCtestAmove
3260     NEXT p
3270   IF maxsofar>-100 THEN =maxsofar  ELSE =FNstaticval

3300   DEF PROCtestAmove
3310   LOCAL stones, v, capture, turn$
3320     stones = pit(p)
3330     PROCmakeAmove(p)
3340     IF turn$="B" THEN v=FNminval(depth+1)
                      ELSE v=FNmaxval(depth+1)
3350     IF v>maxsofar THEN maxsofar=v
3360     PROCmoveback(p,stones,capture,0)
3370   ENDPROC
```

Our two minimax evaluation functions, together with their two subsidiary procedures PROCtestBmove and PROCtestAmove, look rather more complicated than their counterparts for 'Last One Wins - or does he?'. However, you should be able to see that they work in essentially the same way. An activation of FNminval tests its depth and terminates if 'maxdepth' has been reached. If the maximum depth has not been reached then FNminval tries each pit in turn and, if a move is available from that pit, it is made (by PROCtestBmove) and the resulting position is evaluated by calling FNmaxval or FNminval recursively with the depth parameter increased by 1 (line 3140). Each move that is tried is always undone by PROCmoveback.

There is a possibility that FNminval will be called for a position in which no moves are available. If this happens, then all the pits will be examined (line 3050) with no moves being tried and no recursion taking place. This possibility is covered by the IF-statement at line 3070. If 'minsofar' has not been set as a result of trying a move, this means that no moves are available and the position must be evaluated by FNstaticval.

FNmaxval and its subsidiary procedure PROCtestAmove are identical in structure to FNminval and PROCtestBmove. You will notice that PROCtestAmove is the same as PROCtryAmove except that PROCtryAmove records 'bestmove' as well as 'maxsofar'. PROCtryAmove could have been used instead of PROCtestAmove, but we have used two different procedures to draw attention to the different contexts in which they are used.

If you run this version of the program, you will find that, with 'maxdepth' set to 3, it can take 30 seconds or more to choose a move. With 'maxdepth' set to 4, it can take five or six times as long. We will be looking at ways of improving these times in the next section. However, even with 'maxdepth' set as low as 2, the performance of the program is considerably better than that of the version that used only a one-level lookahead. It now tries not to leave stones where they can be captured on the next move and it can spot situations where gaining an extra turn gives it an immediate capture move (for example, moving from pit 5 at the start of the game).

Now that we have presented the structure of our minimax lookahead procedures, it will be fairly easy to make various improvements to these procedures.

For example, the main test as to whether the lookahead should terminate appears at the head of FNminval and FNmaxval. This test can be easily modified if we wish to alter the conditions for terminating the lookahead. Stopping at a fixed depth and carrying out a static evaluation is almost as arbitrary as stopping at level one. A position at our maximum depth might be part of a capture-recapture sequence along which the static values fluctuate wildly. For this reason most game-playing programs use a variable-depth lookahead. They attempt to terminate the lookahead in 'stable' situations, even if this means looking ahead further than the maximum depth along some branches of the tree.

In our Kalah program, we might decide to terminate the lookahead only if <u>both</u> the maximum depth has been reached <u>and</u> the last move was <u>not</u> a capture. We can arrange this by changing the test at the head of each of FNminval and FNmaxval as:

```
3020   IF depth>=maxdepth AND capture<=0  THEN =FNstaticval

3220   IF depth>=maxdepth AND capture<=0  THEN =FNstaticval
```

Here, the structure of a typical lookahead tree for Kalah using this more flexible stopping rule is compared with that of a tree in which the lookahead stops at a fixed depth bound.

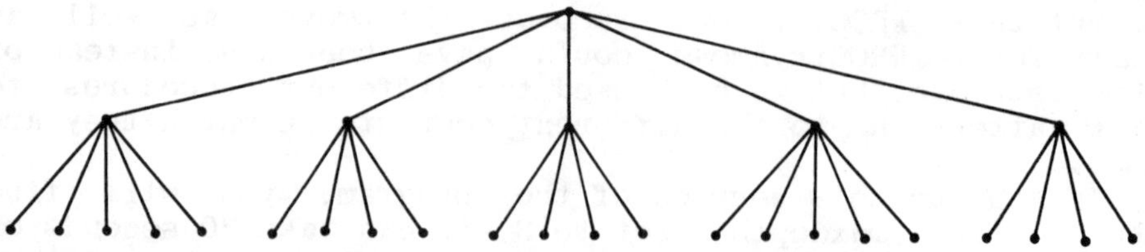

Typical structure of tree explored with maxdepth = 2

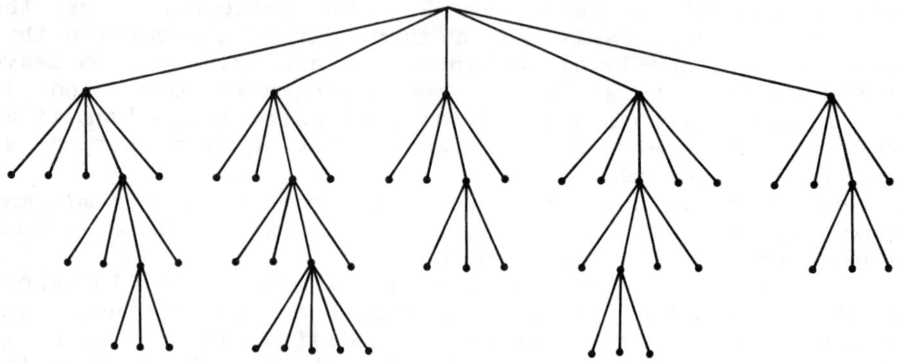

Typical structure of search tree explored with maxdepth = 2
and capture-recapture sequences being explored further

It might be necessary in some games to impose a second maximum depth bound beyond which this exploration of unstable sequences has to stop. We could do this by adding a second stopping test at the head of our minimaxing functions, for example:

```
3025   IF depth=2*maxdepth THEN =FNstaticval

3225   IF depth=2*maxdepth THEN =FNstaticval
```

Exercises

1 A game-playing program often allows the user to ask the computer for help. Change the program so that the user can ask it to recommend a move. To do this you will have to extend the definition of PROCinputmove so that it uses a new function, FNbestBmove.

2 Alter PROCplayerA so that it times the call of FNbestmove and reports the exact time taken by the program to choose its move. This alteration will be useful in the next exercise, and later for comparing the effectiveness of

various tree-pruning techniques.

3 In some applications, the speed of execution of part of a program may be critical, for example in processing real-time data or in animation. In such circumstances the programmer may be justified in attempting to speed up execution of the relevant sections of program by shortening variable, function and procedure names, by using '%' variables where possible, and even using GOTO and GOSUB statements where appropriate. By using such tricks, see if you can increase the speed at which the program selects a move. Note that there is no point in attempting to speed up procedures such as PROCplaygame, PROCsetupboard, PROCdisplayboard, etc. Procedures that are obeyed only once per game or once per move are hardly critical. Concentrate on FNminval, FNmaxval and any functions and procedures used by them. Obtain some timings for the fast program and compare these with the timings for the original version. Are the time savings worth the decrease in readability of the program?

Note that on the BBC computer, BASIC programs are normally interpreted when we RUN them. In Chapter 10, we discuss the difference between an interpreter and a compiler. Perhaps we should state here that if our game-playing program were being compiled before being run, then changes like those described above would have little or no effect on the execution time of the program.

9.5 Tree pruning

We have now described the overall approach that is used by programs that play board games like Chess, Draughts and Kalah. We shall devote the remainder of this chapter to techniques for improving the structure of the lookahead tree explored by such programs when choosing a move.

It is an fact of life that difficult games have very 'bushy' game trees. For example, Chess has an average of about 30 moves available in each position. Each time we go down one level in the Chess tree we find that there are 30 times as many positions as there were at the previous level. We say that the 'branching factor' of the Chess tree is 30.

If a Chess program looks two moves ahead it could examine 1+30+900 positions in the process. An 'obvious' way of improving the quality of the program's play is to make it look further ahead when deciding on its move. If the program were to look 4 moves ahead, it could examine 1+30+900+27000+810000 positions which would take nearly 900 times as long.

In our Kalah playing program, looking 3 moves ahead can take half a minute or more. As the program stands, increasing 'maxdepth' would make it unusable.

Increasing the depth of a program's lookahead would be

quite impossible without the help of 'tree-pruning' techniques. These allow the program to ignore certain branches of its lookahead tree and use the time saved to explore other branches more deeply.

Alpha beta pruning - an introduction

No game-playing program can afford not to use the technique known as 'alpha-beta pruning'.

Some of the pruning methods that we mention later involve a risk that the program will ignore a move that is superficially bad but which would have turned to be the best move available. For example, moves in Chess that that sacrifice material in exchange for a superior position can be missed as a result of over enthusiastic tree pruning.

There is no such risk associated with alpha-beta pruning. Exactly the same move will be chosen by the program whether or not the technique is used. If it is used, it can result in spectacular reductions in the number of positions examined during a lookahead.

We introduce alpha-beta pruning by considering two very simple examples of its use. In the next diagram, we illustrate a depth 2 lookahead from the Kalah position at the root of the subtree. For convenience we shall refer to the 4 positions at depth 1 as positions P, Q, R and S. We assume that a program is conducting a minimax search from left to right as we have drawn the tree.

Position P is considered first. After the program has considered all the moves available in position P, the value of 'minsofar' is known to be +2 and this value is returned to the level above as the final value for position P. At this stage 'maxsofar' at the root of the tree is +2.

The program now examines position Q. The first move considered in position Q leads to a position with a static value of 0 and, when this position has been examined, 'minsofar' for position Q is 0. The 'minsofar' value at position Q can only get smaller and we can see at this stage that, even if we consider all the other moves available in position Q, the final value of position Q must be less than or equal to 0 which is in turn less than the value of 'maxsofar' at the root of the tree. Whatever the final value of position Q, it cannot possibly be greater than the current value of 'maxsofar' at the root. The value obtained for position Q can therefore have no effect on the value obtained for the position at the root or on the move chosen at the root. It would thus be a waste of time considering the other moves that are available in position Q. This is an example of an 'alpha cut-off'. (We shall see where the term 'alpha' comes from in a moment.)

A similar thing happens in positions R and S. As soon as the value of 'minsofar' becomes less than or equal to the value of 'maxsofar' at the position immediately above, an alpha cut-off takes place and the program can stop trying moves at the current position.

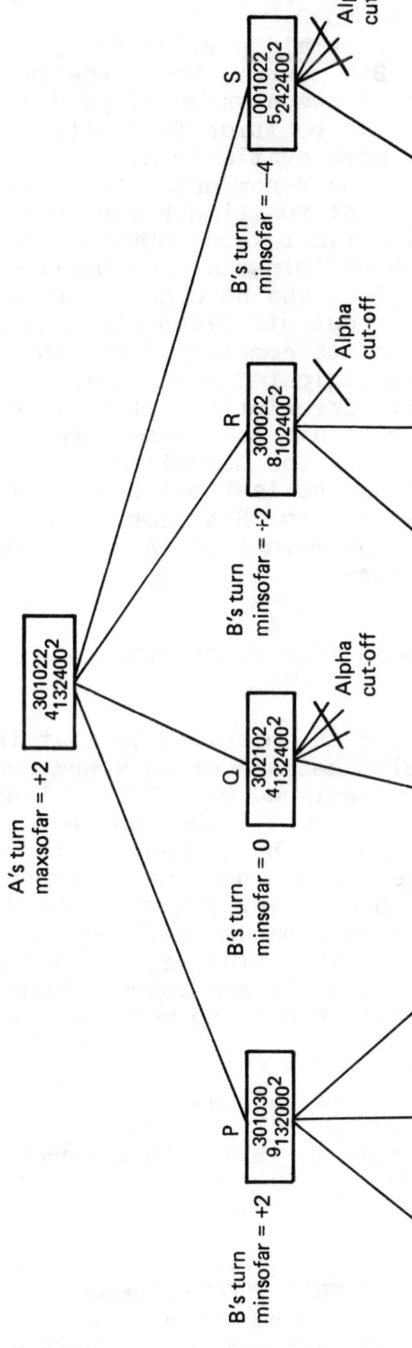
A's turn
maxsofar = +2
301022
4 132400 2
B's turn
minsofar = +2
P
301030
9 132000 2
301030
9 042000 2
+8
301000
9 103100 6
+2
301000
9 130100 6
+2
B's turn
minsofar = 0
Q
302102
4 132400 2
302102
4 042400 2
0
Alpha
cut-off
B's turn
minsofar = +2
R
300022
8 102400 2
300022
8 002400 3
+6
300002
8 100500 5
+2
Alpha
cut-off
B's turn
minsofar = –4
S
001022
5 242400 2
001022
5 053400 2
–4
Alpha
cut-off

In order to see a simple example of a 'beta cut-off', we have to examine a lookahead of depth 3 or more. The diagram on the next page illustrates part of a fixed depth lookahead tree with 'maxdepth' set to 3.

During its attempt to obtain a value for position T (at which it is player B's turn) the program explores the subtree shown. Position U has a value of +4 and this becomes the value of 'minsofar' at position T. Position V is then examined and the first move available at position V leads to a value of +6. Position V now has a 'maxsofar' of +6 and considering other values at position V can only cause this value to get bigger. The final value obtained for position V cannot affect the value of 'minsofar' at position T above. A beta cut-off takes place and no other moves at position V need be tried. A similar cut-off takes place at position W.

Alpha-beta pruning in its complete form is rather more general than has been indicated here. Before we complicate matters by giving a full description, it will be useful to implement the method as it has been described so far.

We start by considering the so-called alpha cut-off that occurred at position Q in the last but one diagram. This is a position at which it is B's turn to play and it is evaluated by FNminval. The main loop in this function tries each possible move in turn:

```
3040      FOR p = 8 TO 13
3050        IF pit(p)>0 THEN PROCtestBmove
3060      NEXT p
```

We now have to cater for the possibility that this loop has to terminate prematurely (because of an alpha cut-off) and it must therefore be replaced by a REPEAT loop. (No GOTOs jumping out of FOR-loops please!) The loop terminates either because all possible moves have been tried or because 'minsofar' has become less than or equal to the current 'maxsofar' value of a node above. This 'maxsofar' value must be passed into FNminval as a parameter. Because this value comes from a position at which it is A's turn, it has traditionally been called an 'alpha value' (hence the term 'alpha cut-off'). FNminval has to be modified as follows:

```
3000    DEF FNminval(depth, alpha)
3010    LOCAL minsofar, p
3020      IF depth=maxdepth THEN =FNstaticval
3030      minsofar=100
3040      p = 7
3050      REPEAT
3060        p = p+1
3070        IF pit(p)>0 THEN PROCtestBmove
3080      UNTIL p=13  OR  minsofar<=alpha
3090    IF minsofar<100 THEN =minsofar  ELSE =FNstaticval
```

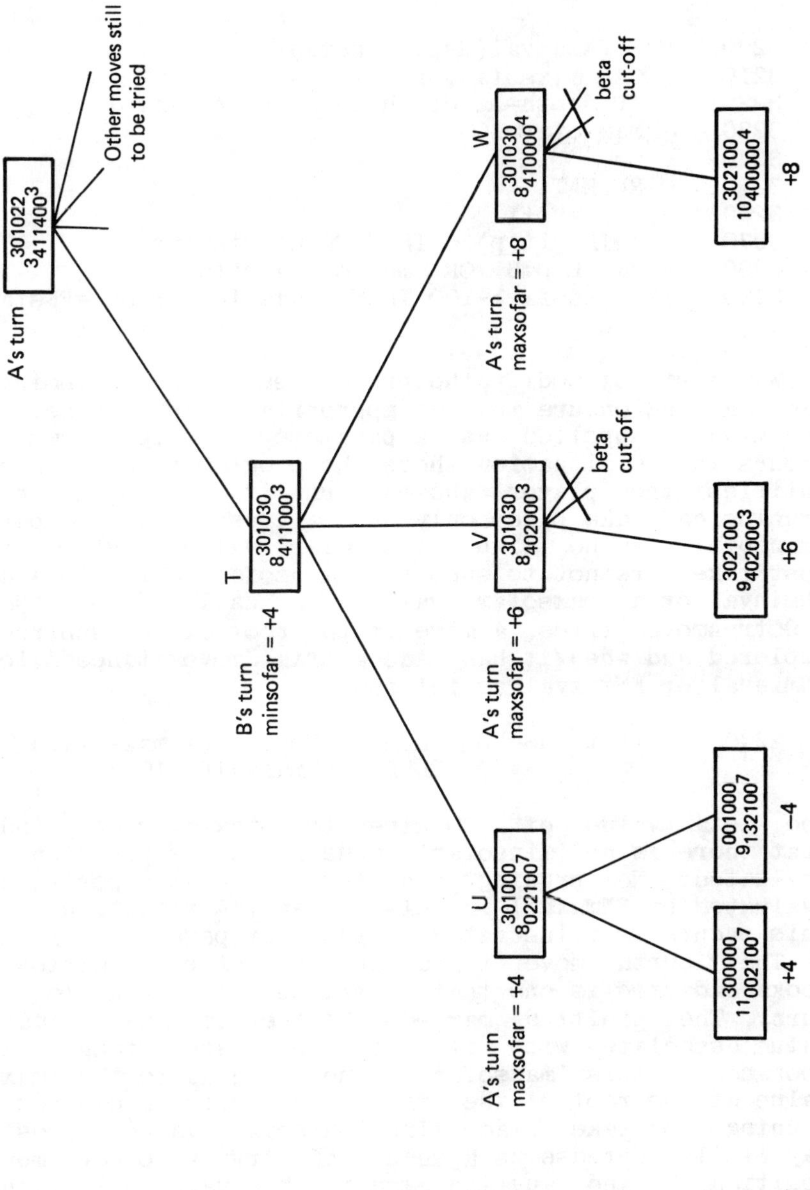

A's turn
301022 3411400 3
Other moves still to be tried
T
B's turn
minsofar = +4
301030 8411000 3
U
A's turn
maxsofar = +4
301000 8022100 7
V
A's turn
maxsofar = +6
301030 8402000 3
W
A's turn
maxsofar = +8
301030 8410000 4
beta cut-off
beta cut-off
300000 11002100 7
+4
001000 91321007
–4
302100 9402000 3
+6
302100 10400000 4
+8

The variable-depth alteration could of course be included at line 3020.

A similar alteration can be made to FNmaxval to allow for the possibility of a beta cut-off, where beta is the 'minsofar' value of a position above at which it is B's turn.

```
3200    DEF FNmaxval(depth, beta)
3210    LOCAL maxsofar, p
3220      IF depth=maxdepth THEN =FNstaticval
3230      maxsofar=100
3240      p=0
3250      REPEAT
3260        p = p+1
3270        IF pit(p)>0 THEN PROCtestAmove
3280      UNTIL p=6  OR  maxsofar>=beta
3290    IF maxsofar>-100 THEN =maxsofar  ELSE =FNstaticval
```

We must now modify the procedures that call FNminval and FNmaxval and ensure that an appropriate alpha or beta value is always supplied as a parameter. A slight complication occurs in the situation where the program tries a move that entitles the player whose turn it is to another turn. Pruning can take place only as a result of comparing a 'minsofar' value with a 'maxsofar' value or vice versa. We must take care not to supply a 'minsofar' value to a call of FNminval or a 'maxsofar' value to a call of of FNmaxval. PROCtryAmove tries a move at the root of the subtree being explored and when it has made a trial move it needs to call FNminval or FNmaxval as follows:

```
2240      IF turn$="B" THEN v=FNminval(1,maxsofar)
                       ELSE v=FNmaxval(1,100)
```

The beta value of 100 given to FNmaxval simply indicates that there is no 'minsofar' value above the position to be evaluated. No pruning can take place at a position to be evaluated by FNmaxval in this context. A situation in which this occurs is illustrated on the next page.

The fourth move tried at the start position of the lookahead tree is one that entitles player A to another turn. The position marked 'X' therefore has a 'maxsofar' value associated with it. At the stage reached in the lookahead, this 'maxsofar' value is equal to the 'maxsofar' value at the root of the tree, but this does not cause pruning to take place. The 'maxsofar' value at position X may easily increase as a result of trying other moves at position X and any increase in this value will eventually cause a change in the 'maxsofar' value at the root of the tree.

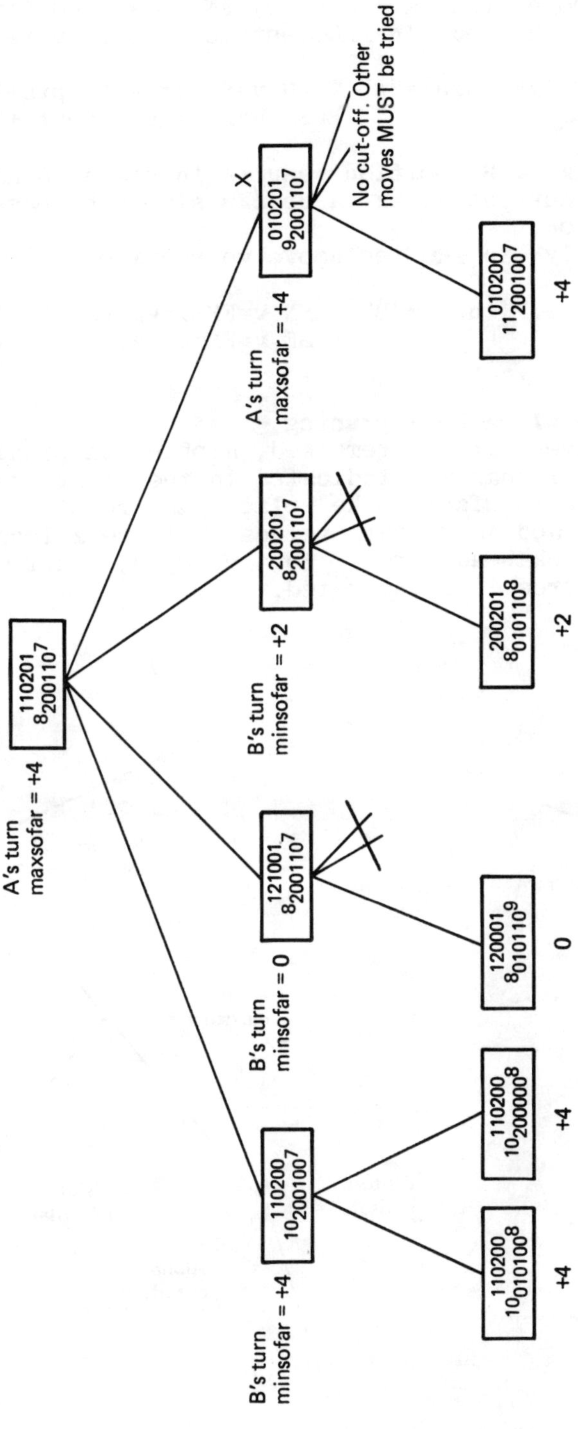
A's turn
maxsofar = +4
110201
8 200110 7
B's turn
minsofar = +4
110200
10 200100 7
110200
10 010100 8
+4
110200
10 200000 8
+4
B's turn
minsofar = 0
121001
8 200110 7
120001
8 010110 9
0
B's turn
minsofar = +2
200201
8 200110 7
200201
8 010110 8
+2
A's turn
maxsofar = +4
X
010201
9 200110 7
010200
11 200100 7
+4
No cut-off. Other
moves MUST be tried

The two subsidiary procedures, PROCtestBmove and PROCtestAmove, that are used by FNminval and FNmaxval, also need to be changed. In PROCtestBmove we require

```
3140      IF turn$="A" THEN v=FNmaxval(depth+1, minsofar)
                       ELSE v=FNminval(depth+1, alpha)
```

If a move at a B-position results in player B having another turn, the current alpha value can simply be passed on to the new position.

Similarly, in PROCtestAmove we require

```
3340      IF turn$="B" THEN v=FNminval(depth+1, maxsofar)
                       ELSE v=FNmaxval(depth+1, beta)
```

Full scale alpha-beta pruning

As we have already remarked, alpha-beta pruning is rather more general than was indicated in the last section. Cut-offs can in fact take place as result of comparing 'minsofar' and 'maxsofar' values that are a long way apart in the lookahead tree. For example, part of a 4-level lookahead tree is illustrated:

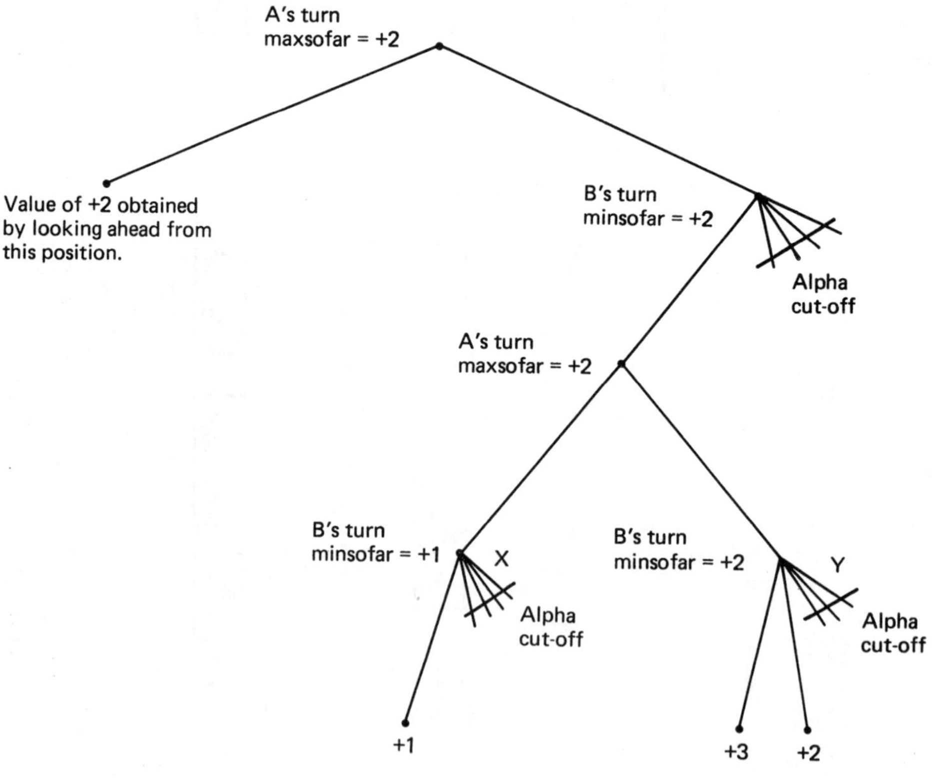

We assume that the left-hand branch of this tree has already been explored and that, as a result, the position at the top of the tree has a 'maxsofar' value of +2. If the program now explores the right-hand branch of the tree, it will encounter position X. The first move tried at position X gives X a 'minsofar' value of +1. We do not yet have a 'maxsofar' value for the position immediately above X, but the position at the root of the tree, three moves above X, does have a 'maxsofar' value of +2. Because the 'minsofar' value at X can only decrease, the final value of X cannot possibly affect the 'maxsofar' value (or the move chosen) at the root of the tree. The 'maxsofar' value from a position three moves above X can be used as an alpha value for pruning at position X.

In general, the alpha value for a position is defined as the maximum of all the 'maxsofar' values above that position in the lookahead tree. Similarly, the beta value of a position is the minimum of all the 'minsofar' values above that position.

To implement full scale alpha-beta pruning, each of our minimax functions must now have both an alpha and a beta parameter. For example, FNminval needs an alpha value so that it can test for alpha cut-offs. It also needs a beta value that can be compared with its own 'minsofar' value before an up-to-date beta value is passed on down the tree. FNmaxval needs both parameters for similar reasons.

The final versions of the relevant functions and procedures are:

```
2200   DEF PROCtryAmove
2210   LOCAL stones, v, capture, turn$
2220     stones = pit(p)
2230     PROCmakeAmove(p)
2240     IF turn$="B" THEN  v=FNminval(1, maxsofar, 100)
                      ELSE  v=FNmaxval(1, maxsofar, 100)
2250     IF v>maxsofar THEN  maxsofar=v : bestmove=p
2260     PROCmoveback(p, stones, capture, 0)
2270   ENDPROC
3000   DEF FNminval(depth, alpha, beta)
                   :   as before
                   .

3100   DEF PROCtestBmove
3110   LOCAL stones, v, capture, turn$
3120     stones = pit(p)
3130     PROCmakeBmove(p)
3140     IF turn$="A" THEN v=FNmaxval(depth+1, alpha, beta)
                      ELSE v=FNminval(depth+1, alpha, beta)
3150     IF v<minsofar THEN minsofar=v
3155     IF minsofar<beta THEN beta=minsofar
3160     PROCmoveback(p,stones,capture,7)
3170   ENDPROC
```

```
3200   DEF FNmaxval(depth, alpha, beta)
           :  as before

3300   DEF PROCtestAmove
3310   LOCAL stones, v, capture, turn$
3320     stones = pit(p)
3330     PROCmakeAmove(p)
3340     IF turn$="B" THEN v=FNminval(depth+1,alpha,beta)
                      ELSE v=FNmaxval(depth+1,alpha,beta)
3350     IF v>maxsofar THEN maxsofar=v
3355     IF maxsofar>alpha THEN alpha=maxsofar
3360     PROCmoveback(p,stones,capture,0)
3370   ENDPROC
```

Exercises

1 Use the timing version of PROCplayerA, suggested earlier, to test the effectiveness of the alpha-beta pruning techniques that have been described.

2 Alter the two minimaxing functions defined for 'Last One Wins - or does he?' so that they use alpha-beta pruning. Arrange for the number of positions examined during a minimax search to be counted by the program. To do this, remember that each position is examined by a call of FNminval or FNmaxval. We therefore need the statement

```
count = count+1
```

at the start of each function. 'count' (not a LOCAL variable) is set to zero before the start of the search. Compare the number of positions examined by the program during a minimax search from various starting positions

(a) without alpha-beta pruning,

(b) with alpha-beta pruning,

(c) with alpha-beta pruning, but with moves being considered in the reverse order, ie. in the order 3,2,1, at each position.

Increasing the effectiveness of alpha-beta pruning

The effectiveness of alpha-beta pruning is highly dependent on the order in which moves are considered in each position in the lookahead. For example, if we use alpha-beta pruning in exploring the 'Last One Wins - or does he?' tree, the amount of pruning that takes place is considerably greater if we reverse the order in which the program considers the moves available.

If we look back at the diagram used to introduce alpha-beta pruning, we can see that pruning took place at position Q because the program had already tried a much better move to position P. If position P had had a much lower value, then 'maxsofar' at the root of the tree would have been lower and no pruning could have taken place at Q. Alpha-pruning can be further enhanced by looking first at a good move for player B in the position at which pruning is going to take place. For example, pruning would have taken place earlier at position R if the second move had been considered first.

In the next diagram, pruning took place at position V because the best move for player B at position T had already been tried. (Remember that high values are good for A, low values are good for B.) Thus pruning can take place only if a good move has already been tried at a position higher up the tree.

When fully effective, alpha-beta pruning reduces the branching factor of the lookahead tree explored to about the square root of its original value. For example, the number of positions in a Chess lookahead tree of depth 4 could, in theory, be reduced from over 800 000 to under 2000.

The only way that such spectacular pruning could be achieved would be if, at each position in the lookahead tree, the first move tried by the program were in fact the move that turned out to be best for the player whose turn it was at that position. Unfortunately, this information is not available until after the lookahead has been carried out!

Because of the large potential savings from alpha-beta pruning, it is important that, when evaluating a position, some attempt should be made to order the moves from the point of view of the player whose turn it is in that position. Any extra work involved in doing this will hopefully be offset by extra pruning.

One possibility would be to decide that capture moves tend to be good moves for the player whose turn it is. We could replace the single loop in each of FNbestmove, FNminval and FNmaxval, by two consecutive loops. In the first loop the program would try only the capture moves, and in the second it would try the other moves. This involves extra work in recognising the capture moves, but the extra work could be more than justified by enhanced alpha-beta pruning.

Many game playing programs order the moves in a position by carrying out a preliminary lookahead from <u>each</u> position encountered in the main lookahead tree. This preliminary lookahead might typically be of depth one or two. The moves available at a position are ordered on the basis of this preliminary lookahead and this ordering is used in considering moves for the main lookahead. It would be sensible if the work done generating new board positions during a preliminary lookahead was not repeated in the main lookahead. To avoid this, it would be necessary to copy and store all the positions generated during a preliminary lookahead so that they could be examined later in the main lookahead.

The process of ordering moves at each position before continuing with a lookahead is often referred to as 'plausibility analysis'. The program attempts, usually on fairly superficial evidence, to decide which of the moves appear most plausible.

Other tree pruning techniques

In a game like chess with an average branching factor of 30, even with effective alpha-beta pruning, exploring a lookahead tree of any reasonable depth is impossible without further pruning. In the last section, we introduced the idea of a plausibility analysis for ordering the moves in a position before continuing the lookahead. This was done with the aim of increasing the amount of alpha-beta pruning that takes place.

Once a plausibility analysis has been done at a position, the results of the analysis can be used to implement further pruning. The program could be made to examine only the 'n' most plausible moves when continuing the main lookahead from that position. The value chosen for 'n' will determine how drastic the pruning is. One possibility is to give 'n' a fixed value at the start of the program. A more common arrangement is for the value of 'n' to decrease as the depth of the lookahead increases.

A plausibility analysis is usually fairly superficial. It must be stressed that pruning on the basis of such superficial evidence carries the risk that the program will eliminate a move from consideration when in fact a more detailed analysis would have shown that move to be a good one.

There is no such risk attached to alpha-beta pruning. The result of a lookahead with alpha-beta pruning will be exactly the same as if alpha-beta pruning had not been used.

Exercises

1 It was suggested earlier that improved alpha-beta pruning might be obtained if capture moves were considered first at each position in the lookahead. A capture can be recognised by making the move and examining the value of the variable 'capture', but this involves moving the pieces back if that move is not to be explored immediately. You could alternatively try to define an arithmetic test for recognising a capture move without actually making it. Implement and evaluate this modification. Two factors will be of interest: the number of positions examined in deciding on a move and the time taken to decide on a move. It will be interesting to see if fewer positions are examined than with the previous

version of the program. However, this increased pruning will be of only theoretical interest if the time saved by increased pruning does not compensate for the extra time taken to recognise capture moves.

2 If you succeeded earlier in defining an improved static evaluation function, then incorporate this in the final program. (If the function is too complicated, you may find that the program is slowed down by an unacceptable amount.)

3 Alter the program so that it keeps a complete record of the moves made during the course of a game and gives the user the option of seeing the game played through again after it is over. You will need to number the moves and use two parallel arrays to record whose turn it was at each move alongside the number of the pit from which the move was made.

Chapter 10 Language processors – a LOGO interpreter

When a computer is designed, it is organised so that it will respond to instructions in a very primitive programming language known as machine code. A machine code instruction consists of a bit pattern (Appendix 2) and, when such an instruction is obeyed, it is sent (as a pattern of electrical impulses) to a circuit in the computer which decodes the instruction and activates other circuits to carry out the the fundamental operation represented by the bit pattern. Such instructions may cause the machine to perform an arithmetic operation between two operands, or it may cause the transfer of a unit of information from one part of the machine to the other. A machine code program consists of a sequence of such bit patterns which are sent one after the other from the memory, in which the program resides, to the control unit to be decoded and obeyed.

Programming in machine code is extremely tedious and error prone, and before a computer can be easily programmed it has to be provided with software that enables it to be programmed in higher level languages.

For a particular machine a variety of languages may be available. Some languages are general purpose and some are problem oriented. The current lingua franca of microcomputers is BASIC and this is supposed to be a general purpose high level language.

A high level language is designed with two aims in mind. First of all it should be machine independent and this is true, to a greater or lesser extent, of languages such as BASIC, PASCAL, FORTRAN and COBOL. BBC BASIC is a new language incorporating significant extensions to 'standard' BASIC and is thus machine dependent, but it could be said that the designers are attempting to set a new standard. The other aim of a high level language is that it should buffer the user from having to know anything about how the machine works, and, should supply him with the tools that enable him to implement his algorithms with ease. Whether this is achieved with standard BASIC is perhaps a matter for some discussion that we will not go into here.

Programming in low level languages is still sometimes necessary and so that we do not have to write in actual machine code, the lowest level language that is used for practical programming is assembly code. Assembly code is a mnemonic version of machine code that uses characters and words rather than bit patterns. Programming may be necessary in assembly code when access is required to a machine facility that is not available through BASIC, or when high program running speed is essential. For example, many of the arcade games sold for your BBC micro are written in assembly language (although they are translated into machine code before being sold). The program that translates assembly code into machine code is called an assembler.

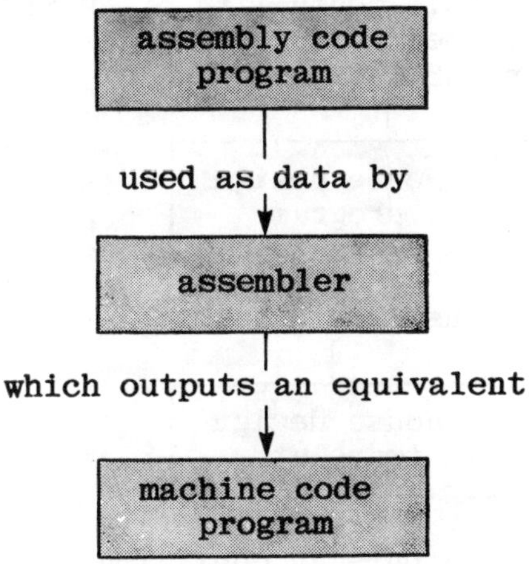

BASIC is either compiled or interpreted (the difference is explained fully later in the chapter).

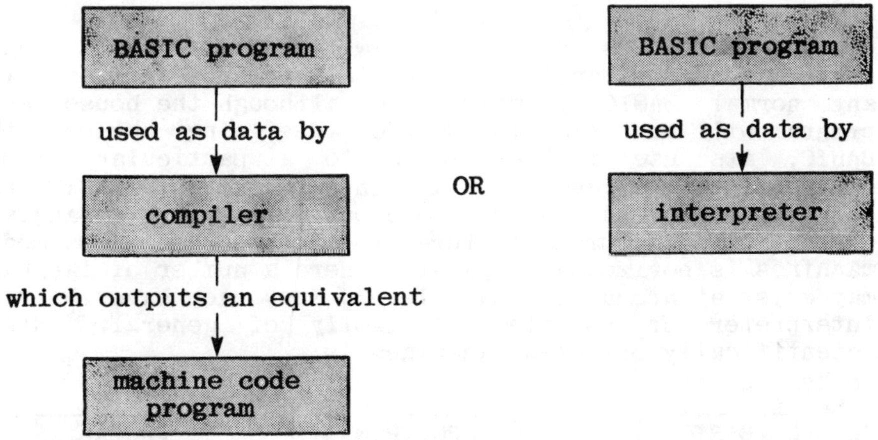

Superimposed on this basic language scheme of a single high level language and an assembly language we may have 'vertical' and 'horizontal' expansion. Vertical expansion means having a higher level language than BASIC or one that is more problem oriented. Say, for example, we wished to have a house design graphics package to be used by architects. The architect is only interested in house design and does not want to be concerned with all the tedious details involved in programming graphics in BASIC. Rather than writing long programs containing BASIC constructs controlling PLOT statements, he wishes to write such things as:

```
drawfrontelevation(wallfinish, doorstyle, windowstyle)
```

He does not need the full generality of BASIC and uses a specific problem oriented language or package. This may well be itself written in BASIC.

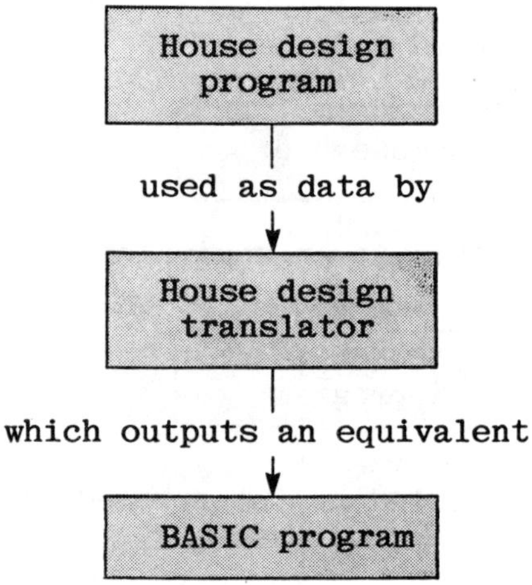

The house design translator will output a BASIC program that can then be handled by the BASIC interpreter just like any normal BASIC program. Now although the house design program will be easier to use (for designing houses) than BASIC, its use is restricted to a particular problem environment. The generality and the tedium of BASIC have been traded for an easier to use but more specific language.

The other common feature of language systems on modern machines is horizontal expansion. Here a number of languages may exist at around the same level. They each have their own interpreter or compiler. A family of general purpose scientifically oriented languages is:

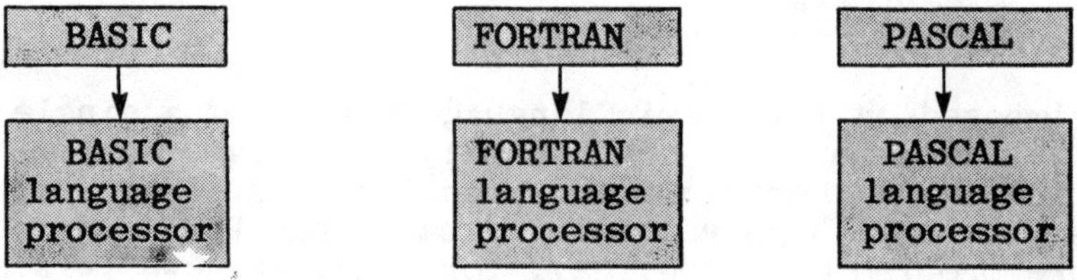

These different languages exist because, although they all offer a common subset of programming constructs, user preference has caused a proliferation.

Other languages exist 'horizontally' because they are not general purpose but are meant for particular applications. For example, LISP for list processing and artificial intelligence and COBOL for commercial data processing. Here the programming constructs are designed for the problem environment in which the language is used.

In this chapter we shall be looking at how you can design language processors in BASIC that will accept commands in another language and arrange for the computer to obey these commands.

10.1 Language processors - an illustrative example

A language processor that enables a computer to be programmed in a new programming language can take one of two forms. A program in the new language may be stored in the computer and 'interpreted' by an 'interpreter' which scans the program being interpreted and carries out the operations indicated by the instructions being scanned. Alternatively, the language processor may take the form of a translation program that translates a program in the new language into an equivalent program, in a language that the computer can handle already. If the language into which programs are translated is machine code the translation program is called a 'compiler', otherwise it is called a translator.

We shall demonstrate the difference between these two approaches by writing both an interpreter and a translator for a rather trivial 'programming language' that we shall call SKETCH. The symbols in this language are the letters N, S, E and W and a 'program' in this language consists of a single line containing a sequence of these symbols in any order. This defines the 'syntax' of the language. We must also define the meaning or 'semantics' of programs in our language. We shall say that a program represents an instruction to draw a line, starting in the centre of the screen, where the letter N indicates that the line should be extended by four units 'North', E indicates that the line should be extended by four units 'East' and so on. Thus, for example, the program:

```
NNNNEEEESSSSWWWW
```

will draw a small square; and:

```
NENENENENENENENE
```

will draw a short diagonal line.

An interpreter for SKETCH

First we shall write, in BASIC, an interpreter for SKETCH programs. The interpreter will accept as input a SKETCH program and will carry out the operations specified by the sequence of symbols constituting the SKETCH program.

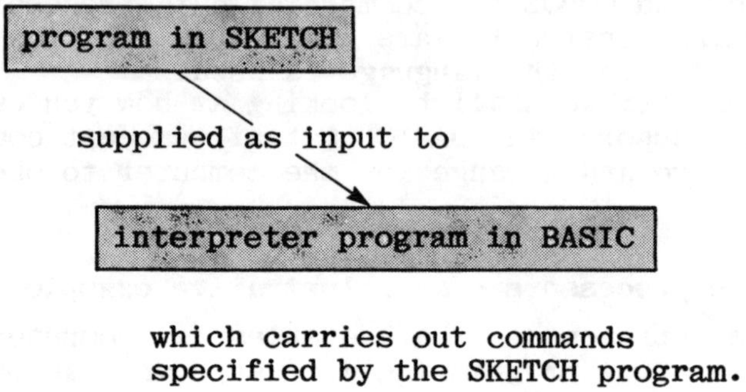

The main loop in the interpreter program will have the form:

```
REPEAT
  PROCprocesscommand
UNTIL end of program encountered
```

We shall store the program to be interpreted in a string and the interpreter will maintain an integer variable 'next' indicating the point reached so far in the SKETCH program. The complete program is:

```
 10   INPUT LINE program$
 20   MODE 4
 30   MOVE 640, 512
 40   length=LEN(program$)
 50   next=1
 60   REPEAT
 70     command$=MID$(program$,next,1)
 80     next=next+1
 90     PROCprocesscommand
100   UNTIL next>length
110   END

120   DEF PROCprocesscommand
130    IF command$="N" THEN PLOT 1, 0 ,8
140    IF command$="E" THEN PLOT 1, 8, 0
150    IF command$="S" THEN PLOT 1, 0,-8
160    IF command$="W" THEN PLOT 1,-8, 0
170   ENDPROC
```

PROCprocesscommand examines the next symbol in the input 'program' and interprets it immediately by drawing a short line in the direction indicated by the symbol. In order to execute a program using an interpreter, it is the interpreter that must be obeyed. The main characteristic of an interpreter is that each instruction in the program being interpreted is analysed and the operation specified by the analysed instruction is carried out immediately.

At the risk of obscuring the ideas presented above, it is interesting to note that the BASIC system on the BBC computer is an interpreter. The BASIC programs typed in by the user are stored in random access memory (RAM). A user's BASIC program is not stored completely in character form - the BASIC keywords are stored as integer codes, or 'tokens' as they are sometimes called. This economises on program storage space and also speeds up recognition of the keywords while the program is being interpreted. The interpreter is a largish machine code program permanently stored in 'read only memory' (ROM) and when the user types RUN, it is this interpreter that is obeyed. Thus when the SKETCH interpreter presented above is RUN, this interpreter is itself being interpreted by the BASIC interpreter! If you find this complication confusing, you can simplify matters by ignoring the existence of the BASIC interpreter and imagine your BBC micro as a 'black box' that can obey BASIC programs.

A translator for SKETCH

In this section, we shall write a BASIC program that will translate a SKETCH program into an equivalent BASIC program. Note that there are three programs involved in this process, apart from the BASIC interpreter. The program that carries out the translation process is called the translator. The program that is being translated is usually called the 'source program' and the program being output by the translator is called the 'object program'.

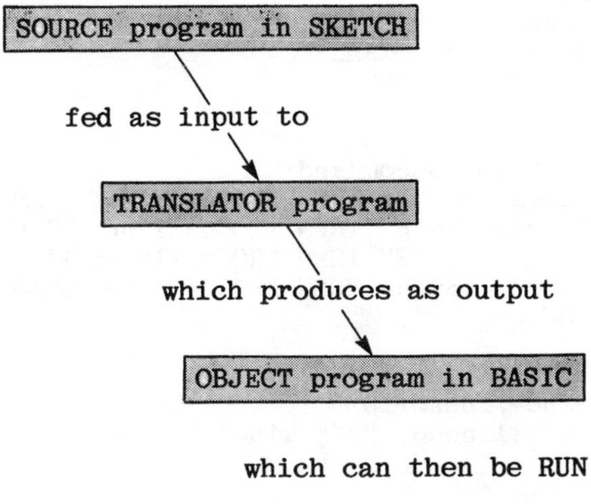

We now have the problem of deciding where to put the translated version of the SKETCH program as it is generated by the translator. Clearly this program must be stored somewhere if it is eventually to be RUN. For the moment, we shall ignore this problem and shall simply assume that we want the translated program displayed on the screen. It will be quite an easy task to divert this output to a cassette or disc file by using the *SPOOL facility.

Part of the task carried out by a translator is very similar to that carried out by an interpreter. Both programs have to carry out an analysis of the input or source program and recognise the instructions contained in the source program. The differences between an interpreter and a translator manifest themselves only after this syntax analysis has been carried out. Once a particular instruction in the source program has been recognised, an interpreter will carry out the instruction immediately whereas a translator outputs one or more object program instructions that are equivalent in meaning to the source program instruction just analysed. For this reason the main loop in our translator is identical to the main loop in our interpreter. Instead of switching to MODE 1 and moving to the centre of the screen, the translator must output instructions to carry out these operations. It must also arrange to number the subsequent lines in the object program that it outputs. Finally, each command in the source program causes an equivalent PLOT statement to be output. Each output PLOT statement is numbered and the variable 'lineno' is used to keep count of these line numbers.

```
 10   INPUT LINE program$
 20   PRINT "10 MODE 4"
 30   PRINT "20 MOVE 640, 512"
 40   lineno = 20
 50   length=LEN(program$) : next=1
 60   REPEAT
 70     command$=MID$(program$,next,1) : next=next+1
 90     PROCprocesscommand
100   UNTIL next>length
110   END

120   DEF PROCprocesscommand
130     IF command$="N" THEN PROCoutline("PLOT 1, 0, 8")
140     IF command$="E" THEN PROCoutline("PLOT 1, 8, 0")
150     IF command$="S" THEN PROCoutline("PLOT 1, 0,-8")
160     IF command$="W" THEN PROCoutline("PLOT 1,-8, 0")
170   ENDPROC

200   DEF PROCoutline(line$)
210     lineno=lineno+10
220     PRINT ;lineno; " "; line$
230   ENDPROC
```

Here PROCprocesscommand examines the next symbol in the input program and 'translates' it into a PLOT statement for drawing a line in the appropriate direction. If we run the SKETCH translator and input, for example,

```
NNNNEEEE
```

then the translator will display the object program.

```
 10   MODE 1
 20   MOVE 640, 512
 30   PLOT 1, 4, 0
 40   PLOT 1, 4, 0
 50   PLOT 1, 4, 0
 60   PLOT 1, 4, 0
 70   PLOT 1, 0, 4
 80   PLOT 1, 0, 4
 90   PLOT 1, 0, 4
100   PLOT 1, 0, 4
```

In order to run the program, it must somehow be RUN by the BASIC system. A translator would normally build up the object program in a file or in a separate area of the computer store. A simple way of outputting our object program to a file is to leave our translator exactly as it is and issue a *SPOOL command before running the translator. This diverts a copy of every character that subsequently appears on the screen to a named file, and, the BASIC program in that file can subsequently be loaded using the *EXEC command the complete sequence would be:

```
> *SPOOL "Program"
> RUN
? NNNNEEEE
      .
      .
object program appears on screen
  (and in file)
      .
      .
> *SPOOL
> NEW
> *EXEC "Program"
> RUN
```

The second *SPOOL command closes the file. This sequence of actions is extremely cumbersome and you may well wonder if there is ever any point in using a translator (or compiler) instead of an interpreter. The answer lies in the fact that once we have gone through the above process, we can run the object program as often as we like. In the case of SKETCH this is not much of an advantage but for a more realistic and complex language, a translator or compiler could have considerable advantages.

The process of syntax analysis carried out by a language processor (an interpreter or a compiler) can be very time consuming if the source language is of any complexity and the source program is of any length. For a source program that is to be obeyed many times, it is advantageous to analyse it once and for all and then run the translated version whenever required. If a compiler is available for the source language, then the object program is in machine code and would be handled directly by the computer hardware. When using an interpreter, every time a program is run it is re-analysed.

A second advantage of the use of a translator or compiler concerns the the memory requirement. Using an interpreter, both the source program and the interpreter have to be in memory at the same time. In the case of a translator, it can usually be arranged for the source program to be supplied from a file, a small fragment at a time and during the translation phase only the translator program needs to occupy space. The object program is output to a file as it is generated. During the execution phase of the object program, the translator is no longer required and only the object program needs to occupy space in memory. These considerations are very important when large programs are handled and no doubt you have already encountered space problems in your experience with the BBC micro.

10.2 A simple LOGO interpreter

Most of the remainder of this chapter will be devoted to a case study - developing a translator for a real language - LOGO. This will be used to illustrate the techniques involved in writing a language processor.

Writing a translator or a compiler requires similar techniques. This is because all types of language processors share the need to analyse the structure of the source program.

An introduction to LOGO

The programming language LOGO is widely used for introducing young children to the ideas involved in computer programming. LOGO was originally conceived as a language for controlling a 'turtle graphics system'. A turtle is a small wheeled vehicle containing a pen that can be raised or lowered. A LOGO program contains commands that control the actions of the turtle and make it draw a picture. The turtle system is usually replaced by a graphics screen on which the pictures are drawn, but the behaviour of a LOGO program is still explained in terms of an imaginary turtle moving about the screen drawing a picture.

The basic LOGO interpreter usually operates on a line by

line basis. A line of instructions is typed by the user and that line is interpreted immediately by the system, the current picture being extended if appropriate. The turtle always starts in the centre of a blank screen facing the top of the screen.

We begin by introducing a number of simple commands. The following commands each consist of just a single word.

command	effect
PENDOWN	press pen down onto paper (i.e. switch on the plot)
PENUP	lift pen off the paper (i.e. switch off the plot)
CLEARSCREEN	clear the screen and move the turtle to its start position

The following commands each need to be followed by a single numeric parameter.

command	effect
FORWARD	move the turtle forward a specified distance
BACK	move the turtle back a specified distance
LEFT	Turn the turtle anti-clockwise through a specified number of degrees.
RIGHT	Turn the turtle clockwise through a specified number of degrees

Thus the following sequence of LOGO commands will draw a square.

```
PENDOWN
FORWARD 100
LEFT 90
FORWARD 100
LEFT 90
FORWARD 100
LEFT 90
FORWARD 100
```

This LOGO program could be typed one statement to a line, as above, each line being interpreted as it is typed. Alternatively, several statements can be included on a single line, for example:

```
PENDOWN   FORWARD 100
LEFT 90   FORWARD 100
LEFT 90   FORWARD 100
LEFT 90   FORWARD 100
```

or

```
PENDOWN   FORWARD 100  LEFT 90  FORWARD 100
LEFT 90   FORWARD 100  LEFT 90  FORWARD 100
```

Note that there is no statement separator. This small subset of LOGO statements will suffice for introductory purposes and we shall write a simple interpreter to handle these statements. In later sections, we shall introduce LOGO loops and procedures and show how the interpreter can be extended to handle such constructs. For the time being, we also assume that the numeric parameters for our simple statements can only be numeric constants.

Lexical analysis

Most computer programming languages have a more elaborate syntax than the simple language SKETCH that was used in the preceding sections. Before we move on to the problem of 'syntax analysis', we first look at another problem that must be considered - that of 'lexical analysis.

A computer program is usually presented to the computer as a string of characters. The syntax (or grammar), on the other hand, is usually defined in terms of 'symbols' where a symbol may consist of more than one character. A language processor must analyse the sequence of characters with which it is presented and must break it up into the separate symbols to which the syntax analysis will be applied. The purpose of lexical analysis is to do this, generally ignoring spaces (these are used arbitrarily by a programmer for layout). In the case of the BBC BASIC interpreter, reserved words (FOR, PRINT, etc.) are compressed by lexical analysis into single numeric codes, but we will not do this in the LOGO interpreter. In our LOGO interpreter, lexical analysis will be carried out by PROCgetnextsymbol which will be called whenever the interpreter is ready to examine the next symbol in the LOGO program being interpreted. It will scan through the characters from the point reached so far until a complete symbol has been found and will extract that symbol in the form of a string. A symbol may be a word like PENUP or FORWARD, it may be a number such as 100 or it may be a single character symbol such as '[' or ']' or ':'. (We shall see what square brackets and colons are used for in later sections.) The largest unit handled by our simple interpreter will be a line, each line being interpreted when it has been typed.

The line of LOGO program currently being interpreted will always be held in a variable 'line$'. A variable 'linep' (short for line pointer) will indicate the position in the line at which the search for the next symbol should start. We shall always ensure that a line is terminated by a recognisable symbol by adding such a symbol to each line before it is processed by the interpreter. The symbol we shall use for this purpose is the single character '!'. Here is the definition of PROCgetnextsymbol.

```
100   DEF PROCgetnextsymbol
110     LOCAL j
120     IF MID$(line$,linep,1)=" " THEN
           REPEAT : linep=linep+1 :
           UNTIL MID$(line$,linep,1)<>" "
130     IF INSTR("[!]:",MID$(line$,linep,1)) THEN
           symbol$=MID$(line$,linep,1) :
           linep=linep+1 : ENDPROC
140     j=linep
150     REPEAT
160       j=j+1
170     UNTIL INSTR("[!]: ",MID$(line$,j,1))
180     symbol$=MID$(line$,linep,j-linep)
190     linep=j
200   ENDPROC
```

Note that the rules concerning separation of symbols are built into this procedure, for example, at line 170.

Syntax analysis

We shall not adopt a very formal or mathematical approach to syntax analysis. There are whole text books on syntax definition and syntax analysis. In Chapter 5, a brief presentation of a notation for the precise definition of the syntax of music rhythms was given. Similar notation can be used for the precise definition of the syntax of a programming language, but we shall not do this here. Instead, we move straight to syntax analysis and adopt the pragmatic (and effective) approach of writing a procedure to handle each construction in the language.

An introductory LOGO interpreter

An interpreter that handles the set of simple LOGO statements that have been described is now presented. A text window of four lines at the bottom of the screen is used for displaying the input lines of the program and any error messages. The remainder of the screen constitutes the graphics area for the turtle.

```
  10 MODE 4
  20 PROCinitialise
  30 REPEAT
  40   PROCprocessline
  50 UNTIL FALSE
  60 END
       :
       :
 300 DEF PROCinitialise
 310   VDU 24,0;128;1279;1023;
 320   VDU 28,0,31,39,28
 330   PROCclearscreen
 340 ENDPROC

 360 DEF PROCclearscreen
 370   CLG
 380   x=642 : y=578 : MOVE x,y
 400   xdir=0 : ydir=1 : angle=90 : penup=TRUE
 430 ENDPROC

 500 DEF PROCprocessline
 510   PROCgetline("Line: ")
 520   linep=1 : PROCgetnextsymbol
 530   PROCprocessgroup("!")
 540 ENDPROC

 550 DEF PROCgetline(prompt$)
 560   REPEAT : PRINT prompt$; : INPUT LINE ""line$
 570   UNTIL line$<>""
 580   line$=line$+"!"
 590 ENDPROC

 600 DEF PROCprocessgroup(terminator$)
 610   failed=FALSE
 620   REPEAT
 630     PROCprocesscommand
 640     PROCgetnextsymbol
 650   UNTIL symbol$=terminator$ OR failed
 660 ENDPROC

 700 DEF PROCprocesscommand
 710   IF symbol$="PENDOWN" THEN penup=FALSE:ENDPROC
 720   IF symbol$="PENUP"   THEN penup=TRUE :ENDPROC
 730   IF symbol$="CLEARSCREEN" THEN
         PROCclearscreen:ENDPROC
 740   IF symbol$="FORWARD" THEN PROCforward:ENDPROC
 750   IF symbol$="BACK"    THEN PROCback   :ENDPROC
 760   IF symbol$="LEFT"    THEN PROCleft   :ENDPROC
 770   IF symbol$="RIGHT"   THEN PROCright  :ENDPROC
 780   PROCfail(1)
 790 ENDPROC
```

```
 900    DEF PROCforward
 910    LOCAL d
 920      d=FNgetvalue
 930      IF failed THEN ENDPROC
 940      x=x+d*xdir
 950      y=y+d*ydir
 960      IF penup THEN MOVE x,y ELSE DRAW x,y
 970    ENDPROC

1000    DEF PROCback
1010    LOCAL d
1020      d=FNgetvalue
1030      IF failed THEN ENDPROC
1040      x=x-d*xdir
1050      y=y-d*ydir
1060      IF penup THEN MOVE x,y ELSE DRAW x,y
1070    ENDPROC

1100    DEF PROCleft
1110    LOCAL a
1120      a=FNgetvalue
1130      IF failed THEN ENDPROC
1140      angle=(angle+a)MOD 360
1150      xdir=COS(RAD(angle))
1160      ydir=SIN(RAD(angle))
1170    ENDPROC

1200    DEF PROCright
1210    LOCAL a
1220      a=FNgetvalue
1230      IF failed THEN ENDPROC
1240      angle=(angle-a)MOD 360
1250      xdir=COS(RAD(angle))
1260      ydir=SIN(RAD(angle))
1270    ENDPROC

1300    DEF FNgetvalue
1310      PROCgetnextsymbol
1320      value=VAL(symbol$)
1330      IF value=0 THEN PROCfail(2)
1340    =value

1400    DEF PROCfail(errorno)
1410      PRINT"Error ";errorno
1420      PRINT LEFT$(line$,LEN(line$)-1)'TAB(linep-2);""
1430      failed=TRUE
1440    ENDPROC
```

Although the main unit handled by our interpreter is a line (PROCprocessline), we have defined PROCprocessline in terms of a separate procedure for processing a 'group' of statements, PROCprocessgroup. This procedure takes a parameter indicating the symbol that is expected to terminate the group. For the time being, a group of statements is just a line of statements, but it will be convenient to have a separate procedure PROCprocessgroup when we come to interpret LOGO REPEAT loops, where it will be necessary to repeatedly process a group of statements up to a loop terminator.

Error handling

It is appropriate at this point to make a few remarks about the problem of 'error handling'. What should the interpreter do if it encounters a symbol that it does not recognise or does not expect? Clearly an error message should be displayed and our procedure PROCerror displays an error number indicating the type of error encountered.

Error 1 : Unrecognised symbol at the start of a statement

Error 2 : Illegal parameter

The line containing the error is displayed with a marker in the next line pointing to the symbol that caused the problem.

Once an error message has been displayed, our interpreter simply sets a logical variable 'errorfound' to TRUE and this causes interpretation of the current line to be abandoned. It would be rather risky for the interpreter to attempt to continue execution of the line after an error has been detected, as there is no way of knowing which of many possible events caused the error. For example, a symbol may have been misspelt, a symbol may have been omitted, or an extra symbol may have been typed.

A translator or compiler will often attempt to continue its syntax analysis after an error has been encountered with a view to finding all the errors in the program in one go. Whether or not this is useful will depend on how good the translator's 'error recovery' system is. The translator must make some assumption about the likely cause of the error and continue the syntax analysis process on the basis of that assumption. An interpreter cannot easily do this.

10.3 Interpreting loops

We now extend our subset of LOGO to include simple loops. A LOGO loop takes the form

```
REPEAT number_of_times [ ...any number of statements... ]
```

For example, we can abbreviate the instructions for drawing a square to

```
PENDOWN   REPEAT 4 [ FORWARD 100   LEFT 90]
```

Here are two more examples:

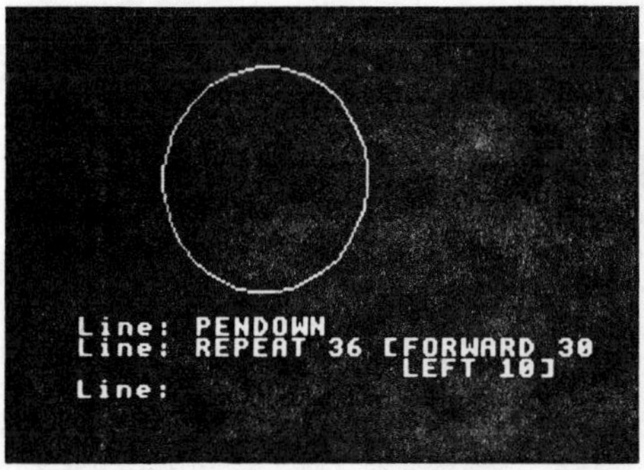

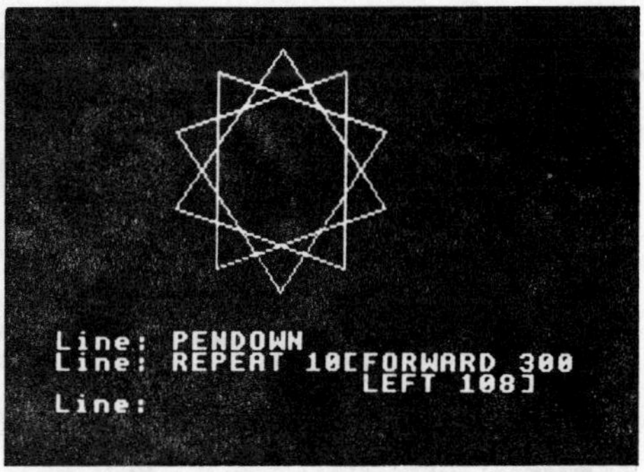

(These photographs, and the others displayed in this chapter, were obtained using the LOGO interpreter that is developed in this chapter.) To deal with such a construction, we must extend PROCprocesscommand to recognise the word REPEAT and take appropriate action.

```
772   IF symbol$="REPEAT"  THEN PROCrepeat :ENDPROC
```

To process the loop, the interpreter must evaluate the repeat count, check for the symbol '[', record the point reached in the current line and then repeatedly obey the following group of statements up to the symbol ']' setting 'linep' to point to the start of this group each time round. If an error occurs, execution of the loop should be abandoned.

```
1500   DEF PROCrepeat
1510     LOCAL start,no,loop
1520     no=FNgetvalue
1530     IF failed THEN ENDPROC
1540     PROCgetnextsymbol
1550     IF symbol$<>"[" THEN PROCfail(3)
1560     start=linep:loop=0
1570     REPEAT
1580       loop=loop+1
1590       linep=start
1600       PROCgetnextsymbol
1610       PROCprocessgroup("]")
1620     UNTIL loop=no OR failed
1630   ENDPROC
```

Note that there is hidden recursion here: PROCprocessline calls PROCprocessgroup which may call PROCrepeat which calls

PROCprocessgroup.

The above alterations will also handle loops within loops such as

```
REPEAT 4 [ REPEAT 4 [DRAW 100  LEFT 90]   RIGHT 90]
```

which draws a pattern of four squares (a 'window pane' pattern). Here are two more examples:

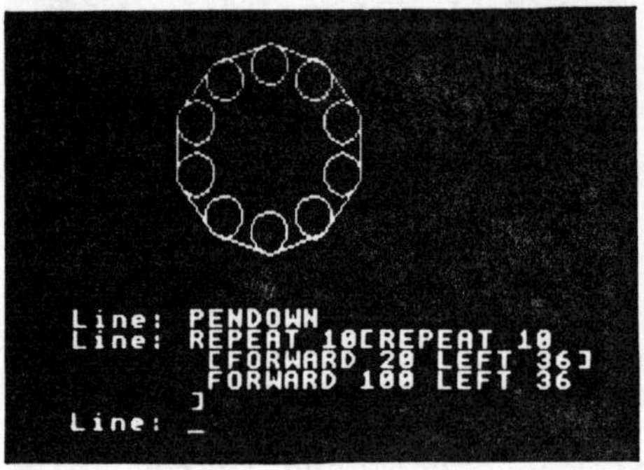

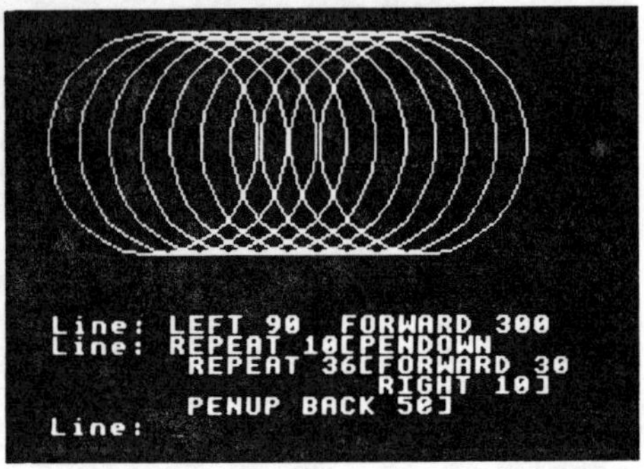

Such constructs will cause further recursion in the interpreter. PROCprocessgroup calls PROCrepeat which calls PROCprocessgroup which calls PROCrepeat which calls PROCprocessgroup. Note that the use of LOCAL in these procedures is essential (see Chapter 7). The activation of PROCrepeat for the inner loop must have its own local variable for recording information about the loop, so as not to destroy the corresponding information for the outer loop.

10.4 Defining and interpreting simple LOGO procedures

A LOGO procedure definition is started by a line containing the word TO followed by the name of the procedure. For example

```
TO DRAWSQUARE
   PENDOWN
   REPEAT 4 [FORWARD 100   LEFT 90]
END
```

This definition will be stored by the LOGO system and the LOGO programmer can subsequently type lines such as

```
DRAWSQUARE
DRAWSQUARE   RIGHT 90   DRAWSQUARE
REPEAT 4 [DRAWSQUARE   RIGHT 90]
```

which draws the 'window pane' pattern. Here is another call

of DRAWSQUARE and the pattern produced:

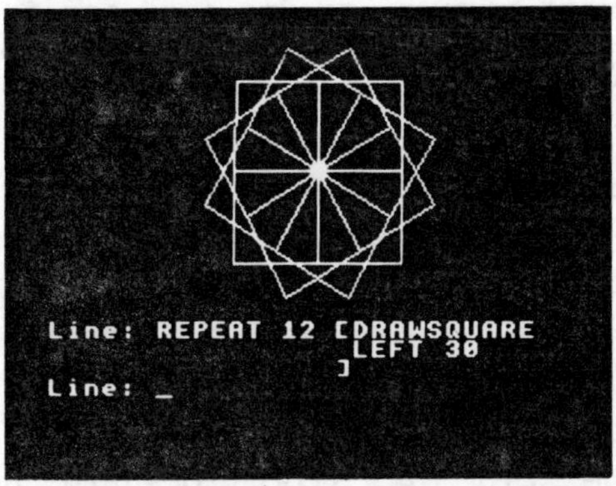

In order to implement such a facility, we require to use some form of look-up table in which a procedure name can be stored together with its definition. Whenever the system is processing a command that starts with a symbol that is not one of the LOGO primitive symbols, then that symbol must be looked up in the table. If it is found there, the procedure definition associated with the symbol must be returned and obeyed. If it is not found then the system must report an unrecognised symbol as before.

For the purposes of illustration, we shall use simple linear search for finding procedure names in our table. Associated with each procedure name will be two 'index entries' that point to the start and finish of the procedure definition in an array of strings that contains the lines of all the procedures stored. For example, the next diagram shows the state of the table when it contains two simple procedure definitions.

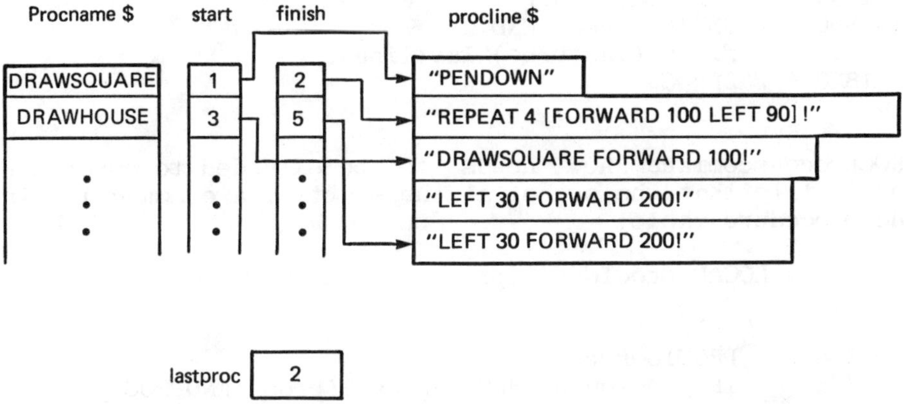

Because DRAWHOUSE appears in slot 2 of 'procname$, this means that 'start(2)' and 'finish(2)' indicate the position in 'procline$' of the first and last lines of the definition of DRAWHOUSE. These arrays are declared and initialised by:

```
304 DIM procname$(10),start(10),finish(10),procline$(100)
         :
306   lastproc=0: lastline=0
```

We now need to arrange for a procedure definition to be added to the above table when a procedure heading is encountered. We insist that the TO heading for the definition of a procedure appears by itself on a line and it is therefore appropriate to alter PROCprocessline so that it can recognise the start of a LOGO procedure definition and act accordingly:

```
530      IF symbol$="TO" THEN PROCdefineproc
                         ELSE PROCprocessgroup("!")
```

PROCdefineproc will read the rest of the procedure definition a line at a time and add it to the above data structure:

```
1700   DEF PROCdefineproc
1710     PROCgetnextsymbol
1720     lastproc=lastproc+1
1730     procname$(lastproc)=symbol$
1740     start(lastproc)=lastline+1
1750     PROCgetline("TO line: ")
1760     REPEAT
1770       lastline=lastline+1
1780       procline$(lastline) = line$
1790       PROCgetline("TO line: ")
1800     UNTIL line$="END!"
1810     finish(lastproc)=lastline
1820   ENDPROC
```

PROCprocesscommand now needs to be extended to cover the possibility that the symbol at the start of a command is in the procedure table:

```
705   LOCAL procfound, proc
         :
774     PROClookup
776     IF procfound THEN PROCcall(proc):ENDPROC
```

Finally, PROClookup and PROCcallproc are defined:

```
1900   DEF PROClookup
1910     IF lastproc=0 THEN procfound=FALSE : ENDPROC
1920     proc=0
1930     REPEAT
1940       proc=proc+1
1950       procfound = procname$(proc)=symbol$
1960     UNTIL procfound OR proc=lastproc
1970   ENDPROC

2000   DEF PROCcall(proc)
2010   LOCAL line$,linep,count
2020     count=start(proc)
2030     REPEAT
2040       line$=procline$(count)
2050       linep=1 : PROCgetnextsymbol
2060       PROCprocessgroup("!")
2070       count = count+1
2080     UNTIL count>finish(proc) OR failed
2090   ENDPROC
```

The declaration of LOCAL variables 'line$' and 'nextp' in PROCcall is absolutely essential. The new variables with these names are used for holding successive lines of the LOGO procedure as they are being interpreted. The previous variables with these names are restored when PROCcall terminates and interpretation can then continue on the line that contained the LOGO procedure call. You will also find that, for similar reasons, the LOCAL declaration at line 705 is essential if one LOGO procedure is to be allowed to call another.

10.5 Parameters and variables

In this section we shall demonstrate how our interpreter can be extended to handle procedure parameters. A parameter is simply a local variable that is given a value when a procedure is called and similar techniques to those described here could be used to extend our LOGO interpreter to handle variables of all kinds.

Here is an example of a LOGO procedure to draw a rectangle whose length and width are specified as parameters. The turtle ends up in the same position and pointing the same way as it was when it started.

```
TO DRAWRECTANGLE  :LENGTH  :WIDTH
    PENDOWN
    FORWARD :LENGTH   LEFT 90
    FORWARD :WIDTH    LEFT 90
    FORWARD :LENGTH   LEFT 90
    FORWARD :WIDTH    LEFT 90
END
```

Note that a LOGO variable or parameter name is always preceded by a colon. This procedure could be called by, for example,

```
DRAWRECTANGLE 200  100
RIGHT 90   DRAWRECTANGLE 100 75
RIGHT 90   PENUP   FORWARD 100
DRAWRECTANGLE 200 50
```

or:

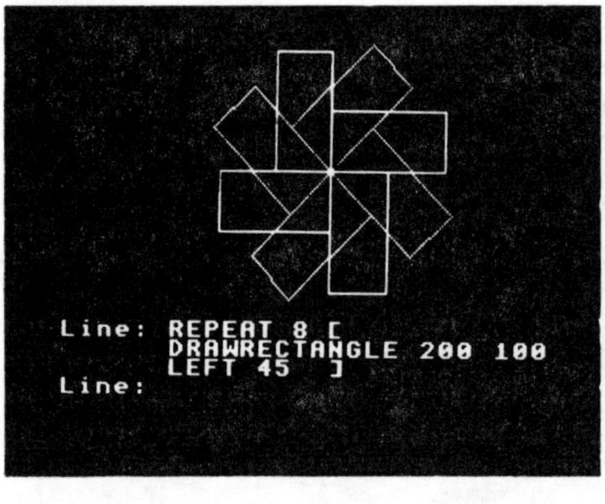

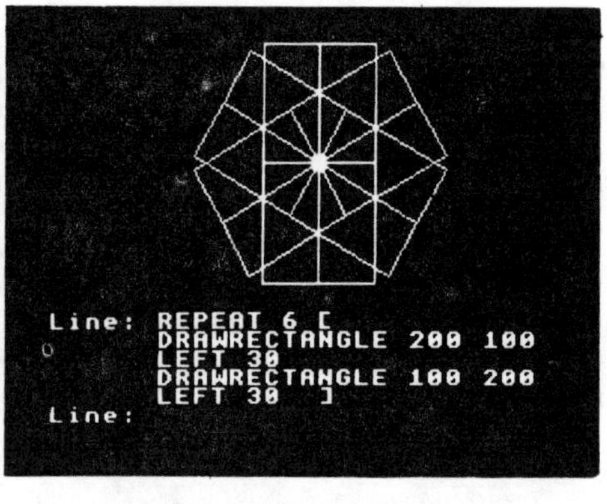

There are two aspects to the problem of handling parameters. Firstly, additional information has to be stored in the procedure table described earlier, so that when a procedure is called, the interpreter knows how many parameters to expect after the procedure name, each time it is used. Secondly, when a procedure is called, the value supplied for each parameter must be associated with the name of the parameter so that when the name is encountered in a statement being obeyed, its current value can be obtained. To handle the first problem, we extend our procedure table to include the number of parameters each procedure takes together with an index pointer to an array that contains the parameter names. The arrays 'start', 'finish' and 'procline$' are set up as before. We need the additional statements:

```
305 DIM params(10), paramstart(10), paramname$(30)
307  lastpn = 0
```

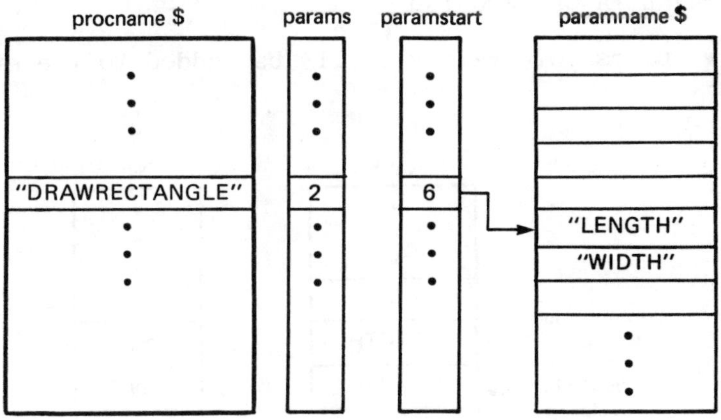

When a procedure definition is processed, the heading must be analysed in more detail, in case it includes parameters. the alterations to PROCdefineproc to add parameter information to the procedure table are as follows.

```
1735    PROCgetparamnames
                 .
                 .
2200    DEF PROCgetparamnames
2210      params(lastproc)=0
2220      PROCgetnextsymbol
2230      IF symbol$<>":" THEN ENDPROC
2240      paramstart(lastproc)=lastpn+1
2250      REPEAT
2260        params(lastproc)=params(lastproc)+1
2270        PROCgetnextsymbol
2280        lastpn=lastpn+1
2290        paramname$(lastpn)=symbol$
2300        PROCgetnextsymbol
2310      UNTIL symbol$<>":"
2320    ENDPROC
```

When a procedure call is processed and the procedure name is found in the table, the extra information is used to determine how many parameter values to search for. These values must then be paired with the corresponding parameter names. For this purpose, we will use a parameter or variable value table, or 'stack' as it is more usually called. This stack will consist of two parallel arrays containing parameter (or variable) names and corresponding values. A variable 'stackp' points to the last entry in the table. When a procedure is called, for example, by:

```
DRAWRECTANGLE 200 100
```

two new pairs of values will be added to the stack as follows:

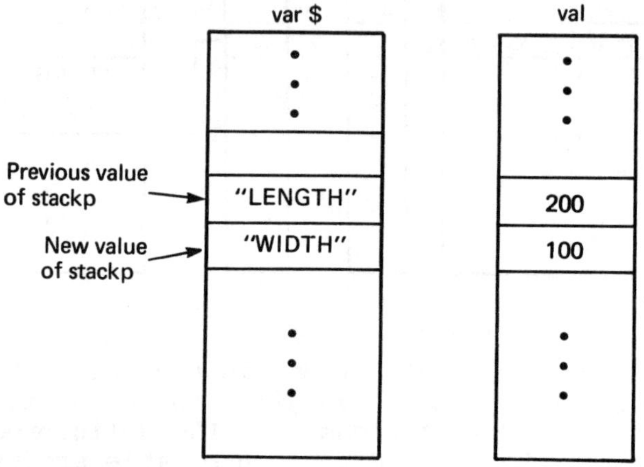

The stack is initialised by:

```
303 DIM var$(100), val(100)
          :
308   stackp = 0
```

PROCcallproc must be extended to add this information to the variable stack.

```
2005      PROCgetparamvals:IF failed THEN ENDPROC
                  :
2400    DEF PROCgetparamvals
2410    LOCAL pn,nextpn,v
2420      IF params(proc)=0 THEN ENDPROC
2430      pn=paramstart(proc)
2440      nextpn=pn+params(proc)
2450      REPEAT
2460        v=FNgetvalue
2470        stackp=stackp+1
2480        var$(stackp)=paramname$(pn) : val(stackp)=v
2490        pn=pn+1
2500      UNTIL pn=nextpn OR failed
2510    ENDPROC
```

Note the position of line 2005 within PROCcall. The LOGO parameter values must be obtained from the line of LOGO that contains the procedure call being obeyed. Only when this has been done can the LOCAL versions of 'line$' and 'nextp' be declared. When a procedure call terminates, the parameter information can be removed from the stack as follows:

```
2085    stackp=stackp-params(proc)
                             :REM clears parameters from stack
```

When the procedure is being obeyed, the above table can now be used to look up a named value encountered while a line of the procedure is being interpreted. When a name is being searched for in the variable stack, we must search through the stack in reverse order. We want to find the most recent occurrence of the variable whose name has been encountered. There may be two currently active procedure calls, each with a parameter of the same name and, when that name is encountered, it is the value supplied with the most recent procedure activation that must be used. FNgetvalue needs to be extended.

```
1315    IF symbol$=":" THEN =FNvarvalue
                 :
2600    DEF FNvarvalue
2610    LOCAL varfound,sp
2620      PROCgetnextsymbol
2630      IF stackp=0 THEN PROCfail(5): =0
2640      sp=stackp+1 : varfound=FALSE
2650      REPEAT
2660        sp=sp-1
2670        varfound = var$(sp)=symbol$
2680      UNTIL varfound OR sp=1
2690      IF varfound THEN =val(sp)
2700      PROCfail(5)
2710    =0
```

Exercises

1 Arrange for our LOGO interpreter to output meaningful error messages instead of error numbers.

2 In our LOGO interpreter, the only expressions that can be used for representing parameter values are single integer constants or single variable names. Extend the interpreter so that it will accept expressions involving + and -. The easiest way to do this is to insist that an expression is always enclosed in round brackets. If this restriction is not imposed, you will have to restructure

the way in which the interpreter calls PROCgetnextsymbol.

3 A LOGO IF statement has the form

```
IF condition THEN [...list of statements...]
```

where a 'condition' is an expression involving =, <, >, etc. Extend the interpreter to handle IF statements. You may again prefer to insist that expressions (conditions) are always enclosed in round brackets and you could restrict the operators permitted in a condition.

4 The LOGO STOP statement has the same effect as an ENDPROC statement in BASIC. Implement this. You should now find that your interpreter can handle recursive procedures such as:

```
TO SPIRALRECTANGLES :LENGTH :WIDTH
  IF (:WIDTH<4) THEN [STOP]
  DRAWRECTANGLE :LENGTH :WIDTH
  LEFT 10
  SPIRALRECTANGLES (:LENGTH-4) (:WIDTH-4)
END
```

10.6 A program compacter

In this final section on language processors, we present an extremely useful utility program that can be used to process the BASIC programs that you write. The program compacts BASIC programs and this is useful for two reasons. Firstly throughout this book we have been fairly extravagant with our use of long variable names, extra spaces, remarks and the insertion of redundant program features such as the control variable after NEXT. All of these devices contribute towards the readability of a program and this is extremely important when developing a program of any complexity or indeed when writing a book on programming techniques. However, because BASIC is an interpreted language, all these features occupy extra storage space. This may mean that there is not enough user memory space (or RAM) available for the program, its variables and arrays and the screen memory needed to run the program in a high resolution graphics mode such as MODE 0.

We can, however, adopt the strategy of developing the program in a low resolution mode such as MODE 4 and eventually run the program in a high resolution mode by compacting it. Once the program development is complete and the program is ready for regular use, the readable version has served its purpose and we can remove all the redundant spaces shorten our variable names and so on. Of course this strategy is not guaranteed to work - a program may still be too long after compaction.

Depending on the style of programming that you adopt a compacted program will occupy some fraction of the storage space occupied by the uncompacted version. Programs in this book can be compacted by around 50 per cent so you can see that the savings are worthwhile. For example the f(x,y) hidden line removal algorithm in Chapter 3 (Section 3.5) must be compacted before it can be run in MODE 0. Another incidental advantage in using compacted programs is that the loading time is also reduced in the same proportion. A disadvantage with compacted programs is that they are by definition not amenable to further development and you should always keep a copy of the uncompacted version in case further development is necessary.

The second reason for presenting a program compacter in this chapter is that it gives further insight into the way in which BASIC programs are represented in store. The next diagram illustrates the line by line organisation of a BASIC program which is normally stored by the computer in memory locations &E00 onwards (in a cassette based system).

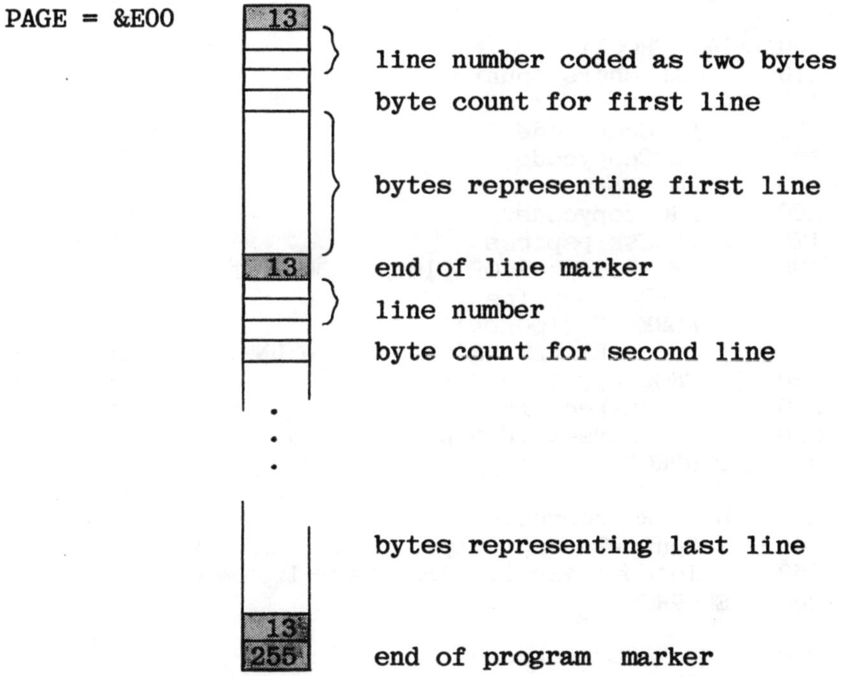

Within a line, each BASIC keyword is represented as a single one-byte code or 'token'. For example REM is coded as 244 or &F4. NEXT is coded as &ED. Apart from keywords, (and a special coded representation for labels) each character in a user's program is stored as the corresponding ASCII code.

The above information should enable you to understand our explanation (below) of how the compacter program works. The program to be compacted should be loaded with PAGE set to its normal value (PAGE = &E00 for a cassette system). The compacter itself must be loaded with

PAGE = &5000

and run with PAGE set to this value. When the compacter has been run, change PAGE back to &E00 to use the compacted program.

```
 10  putp=&E00:lookp=&E00
 20  DIM var$(100)
 30  lastvar=-1
 40  PROCcopycode
 50  REPEAT
 60    PROCline
 70  UNTIL ?lookp=255
 80  PROCcopycode
 90  END

100  DEF PROCline
110  LOCAL chars,countp
120    chars=0
130    PROCcopycode
140    PROCcopycode
150    countp=putp
160    PROCcopycode
170    PROCskipspaces
180    IF ?lookp=42 OR ?lookp=&DC THEN
         PROCcopyline
       ELSE IF ?lookp<>13 THEN
             REPEAT:PROCcheckcode:UNTIL ?lookp=13
190    PROCcopycode
200    ?countp=chars
210    IF chars=4 THEN putp=putp-4
220  ENDPROC

230  DEF PROCcopycode
240    ?putp=?lookp:putp=putp+1
250    lookp=lookp+1:chars=chars+1
260  ENDPROC

270  DEF PROCcheckcode
280    IF ?lookp=32 THEN lookp=lookp+1:ENDPROC
290    IF ?lookp=34 THEN PROCcopystring:ENDPROC
300    IF ?lookp=&F4 THEN PROCrem:ENDPROC
310    IF (?lookp>64 AND ?lookp<91) OR
         (?lookp>96 AND ?lookp<123) OR ?lookp=95
       THEN PROCvariable:ENDPROC
```

```
320     IF ?lookp>47 AND ?lookp<58 THEN
          PROCnumber:ENDPROC
330     IF ?lookp=38 THEN PROChex:ENDPROC
340     IF ?lookp=&ED THEN PROCnext:ENDPROC
350     IF ?lookp=141 THEN
          PROCcopycode:PROCcopycode:PROCcopycode:
          ENDPROC
          :REM 141 is code that precedes a label.
360     IF ?lookp=42 AND (?(putp-1)=58 OR
          ?(putp-1)=&8B OR ?(putp-1)=&8C)
        THEN PROCcopyline:ENDPROC
370     PROCcopycode
380   ENDPROC

390   DEF PROCcopystring
400     REPEAT
410       PROCcopycode
420     UNTIL ?lookp=34
430     PROCcopycode
440   ENDPROC

450   DEF PROCrem
460     REPEAT
470       lookp=lookp+1
480     UNTIL ?lookp=13
490   ENDPROC

500   DEF PROCvariable
510   LOCAL name$,position
520     name$=""
530     REPEAT
540       IF FNvarchar THEN
            name$=name$+CHR$(?lookp):lookp=lookp+1
550     UNTIL NOT FNvarchar
560     IF LEN(name$)=1 AND
         ASC(name$)>64 AND ASC(name$)<91
        THEN PROCputvar(name$):ENDPROC
570     position=FNlookup
580     newname$=FNmakename(position)
590     PROCputvar(newname$)
600     PRINT name$;TAB(20);newname$
610   ENDPROC

620   DEF PROCputvar(n$)
630   LOCAL i
640     FOR i=1 TO LEN(n$)
650       ?putp=ASC(MID$(n$,i,1))
660       putp=putp+1:chars=chars+1
670     NEXT i
680     PROCskipspaces
690     IF FNvarchar THEN
          ?putp=32:putp=putp+1:chars=chars+1
700   ENDPROC
```

```
710   DEF FNlookup
720   LOCAL i
730     i=-1
740     REPEAT
750       i=i+1
760       found=(var$(i)=name$)
770     UNTIL found OR i>lastvar
780     IF found THEN =i
790     lastvar=lastvar+1
800     var$(lastvar)=name$
810   =lastvar

820   DEF FNmakename(no)
830     letter$=CHR$(no MOD 26 + 97)
840     IF no<26 THEN =letter$
850   =letter$+CHR$(no DIV 26 + 96)

860   DEF PROChex
870   LOCAL hexchar,ch
880     PROCcopycode
890     REPEAT
900       ch=?lookp
910       hexchar=(ch>47 AND ch<58) OR (ch>64 AND ch<71)
920       IF hexchar THEN PROCcopycode
930     UNTIL NOT hexchar
940   ENDPROC

950   DEF PROCnext
960     PROCcopycode
970     PROCskipspaces
980     REPEAT
990       IF ?lookp=44 THEN
            ?putp=58:putp=putp+1:?putp=237:putp=putp+1:
            lookp=lookp+1:chars=chars+2:PROCskipspaces
1000      REPEAT
1010        IF FNvarchar THEN lookp=lookp+1
1020      UNTIL NOT FNvarchar
1030      PROCskipspaces
1040    UNTIL ?lookp<>44
1050  ENDPROC

1060  DEF FNvarchar
1070  LOCAL ch
1080    ch=?lookp
1090  =(ch>64 AND ch<91) OR (ch>96 AND ch<123) OR
       (ch>47 AND ch<58) OR ch=95

1100  DEF PROCskipspaces
1110    REPEAT
1120      IF ?lookp=32 THEN lookp=lookp+1
1130    UNTIL ?lookp<>32
1140  ENDPROC
```

```
1150   DEF PROCcopyline
1160     REPEAT
1170       PROCcopycode
1180     UNTIL ?lookp=13
1190   ENDPROC

1200   DEF PROCnumber
1210     PROCcopynumber
1220     PROCskipspaces
1230     IF FNvarchar THEN
           ?putp=32:putp=putp+1:chars=chars+1
1240   ENDPROC

1250   DEF PROCcopynumber
1260     REPEAT
1270       PROCcopycode
1280     UNTIL ?lookp<48 OR ?lookp>57
1290   ENDPROC
```

The compacter operates with two addresses 'lookp' and 'putp'. 'lookp'contains the address of the next byte in the uncompacted program and 'putp' contains the address for the next byte in the compacted program. These pointers both start at &E00, but they will soon get out of step as spaces, REMs and blank lines are eliminated, and variable names are shortened.

Note the special cases that have to be checked for by PROCcheckcode. We will deal with the handling of variables (line 310) in a moment. A space in the source program is simply ignored. There are a number of other special cases that also have to be dealt with.

Characters between quotation marks must be copied exactly as they stand (including spaces) or the behaviour of the compacted program could change. If the character code for a quotation mark (34) is encountered, then PROCcopystring is called. This copies characters from the source program to the object program until the next question mark is encountered.

If the word REM (token &F4) is encountered, the rest of the line in the source program is skipped by PROCrem. Decimal numbers and hex numbers are copied character for character (PROCnumber and PROChex). Any variable after the word NEXT (token &ED) is omitted (PROCnext).

A label is stored in a program in a special coded form (code 141 followed by two bytes) which has to be copied (line 350).

Operating system commands (statements starting with a *) or DATA statements (token &DC) cause the rest of the current line in the source program to be copied (lines 180 and 360).

Variable names are replaced with shortened names as they are encountered. This is done by PROCvariable (called at line 310). Clearly, if the same name is encountered at several points in the source program, it must always be replaced by the same shortened name in the object program. This is achieved by building up a table of the variable names encountered in the source program. A name is added to the table only if it is not already there (see FNlookup). The position of a name in this table determines the shortened name to be used (see FNmakename). The first 26 entries in the table are given the single letter names 'a', 'b', 'c', ..., 'z'. The remainder are given the names 'aa', 'ba', 'ca', ..., 'za', 'ab', 'bb', 'cb', ... Single capital letter variable names are left unaltered - some of these, such as X%, Y%, A%, P% and so on, have special significance in some programs.

Here is an example of a compacted program (the hidden line removal algorithm of Chapter 3, Section 3.5).

```
 10INPUTa,b,c,d
 20PROCe(a,b,c)
 30MODE0:VDU29,640;512;
 32PROCf
 40FORg=360TO-360STEP-20
 50PROCh(g,-360,FNi(g,-360)):MOVEj,k
 55l=(640+j)DIVm:n=k
 60FORo=-340TO360STEP20
 70PROCh(g,o,FNi(g,o)):PROCp
 80NEXT
 90NEXT
100q=GET:MODE7:END
110DEFFNi(r,s)=100*(COS(RAD(r))+COS(RAD(s)))
120DEFPROCh(r,s,t)
130LOCALu,v,w
140PROCx(r,s,t)
150PROCy(u,v,w,d)
160ENDPROC
300DEFPROCf
310LOCALz
320m=2:aa=1279DIVm
330DIMba(aa),ca(aa)
340FORz=0TOaa
350ba(z)=512:ca(z)=-512
360NEXT
370ENDPROC
400DEFPROCp
410LOCALda,ea,fa,z
420da=(j+640)DIVm
430IFda=lTHENPROCga(da,k)
440ea=(k-n)/(da-l)
450fa=n
460FORz=lTOda
470fa=fa+ea
480PROCga(z,fa)
490NEXT
```

```
500l=da:n=k
510ENDPROC
520DEFPROCga(z,s)
530LOCALr:r=z*m-640
535IFz<0ORz>aaTHENMOVEr,s:ENDPROC
540IFz<0ORz>aaTHENMOVEr,s:ENDPROC
550IFs<ca(z)ANDs>ba(z)THENMOVEr,s:ENDPROC
560IFs<ba(z)THENba(z)=s
570IFs>ca(z)THENca(z)=s
580DRAWr,s
590ENDPROC
700DEFPROCe(a,b,c)
710LOCALha,ia,ja,ka
720ha=SIN(RAD(b)):ia=COS(RAD(b))
730ja=SIN(RAD(c)):ka=COS(RAD(c))
740la=-ha:ma=ia
750na=-ia*ka:oa=-ha*ka
760pa=ja
770qa=-ia*ja:ra=-ha*ja
780sa=-ka:ta=a
790ENDPROC
800DEFPROCx(r,s,t)
810u=la*r+ma*s
820v=na*r+oa*s+pa*t
830w=qa*r+ra*s+sa*t+a
840ENDPROC
850DEFPROCy(u,v,w,d)
860j=d*u/w
870k=d*v/w
880ENDPROC
```

It is interesting to note that the compacted program could not be typed in the form in which it appears here. Extra spaces would have to be inserted between variable names and keywords so that the system could distinguish them. However, a keyword is stored as a single recognisable token and these spaces can be omitted in the internal version of a program.

Exercises

1 Try applying the compacter to itself! First load the compacter with PAGE=&E00. Then set PAGE=&5000, load the compacter again and run it. Set PAGE=&E00 and you should find a compacted compacter.

2 The compacter runs rather slowly. This is partly due to the complexity of the task that it has to carry out, but its operation on a large source program could be speeded up by using a more efficient table look-up method. Do this.

3 A further saving in program size could be made by joining consecutive lines of program into a single line (with extra colons inserted). Each time two consecutive lines are joined, three further bytes of memory space are saved. Note the following points:

(a) Any line that includes IF statements must not be joined onto the next line.

(b) Any line starting with DEF must not be joined onto the previous line.

(c) Any line referred to by a label elsewhere in the program must not be joined onto the previous line. Your program will need to build up a list of labels by doing a preliminary scan through the source program.

4 Our LOGO interpreter was not written with efficiency of storage use in mind. Devise a scheme for storing LOGO programs that is similar to that used for storing BASIC programs. For example, invent single one-byte codes for the LOGO keywords and store these in place of the keywords.

Appendix 1 Summary of mode and colour facilities

Text facilities available in different modes

mode	colours available	characters per line	lines
0	2	80	32
1	4	40	32
2	16	20	32
3	2	80	25
4	2	40	32
5	4	20	32
6	2	40	25
7	Teletext display	40	25

Graphics facilities available in different modes

mode	colours available	graphics resolution
0	2	640 x 256
1	4	320 x 256
2	16	160 x 256
4	2	320 x 256
5	4	160 x 256

Note that there no graphics facilities in modes 3, 6 and 7.

Memory requirements for different modes

mode	memory requirements
0	20K
1	20K
2	20K
3	16K
4	10K
5	10K
6	8K
7	1K

Overall colour range

There are sixteen actual colours available (on the Model A or B). These colours are numbered from 0 to 15.

Actual colour numbers and corresponding colours

colour number	colour name
0	black
1	red
2	green
3	yellow
4	blue
5	magenta
6	cyan
7	white
8	flashing black-white
9	flashing red-cyan
10	flashing green-magenta
11	flashing yellow-blue
12	flashing blue-yellow
13	flashing magenta-green
14	flashing cyan-red
15	flashing white-black

Colour codes in different modes

In each mode colours are referred to by code numbers from 0 upwards (using COLOUR for text colour and GCOL for graphics colour). The background colour is set by adding 128 to the required code number. The code numbers for a mode can be made to refer to any combination of actual colours (using VDU 19). There is an initial or default setting for each mode which specifies the colour that you get if you do not use VDU 19.

2 colour mode (MODES 0,3,4,6)

colour code numbers		default actual colours	
foreground	background	colour	number
0	128	black	0
1	129	white	7

4 colour mode (MODES 1 and 5)

colour code numbers		default actual colours	
foreground	background	colour	number
0	128	black	0
1	129	red	1
2	130	yellow	3
3	131	white	7

In the 16 colour mode (MODE 2) the colour codes are initially set to the corresponding actual colour numbers.

Appendix 2 Bits, bytes and hex

For the majority of straightforward programming applications, the user of the BBC micro need not concern himself with the details of how things like numbers and strings are represented inside his computer, but for some advanced applications a more detailed knowledge of the internal representation of information is required.

Bits

All information stored in a modern digital computer is held in the form of 'binary digits'. In this context, the word 'binary' means 'having two possible values', and a binary digit can thus be set to one of two possible values. We usually abbreviate the term binary digit to 'bit'.

When we write a bit on paper, we represent its two possible values as 0 or 1. Inside a computer, a bit might be represented by a magnetic field lying in one of two possible directions, or by an electronic voltage that can be positive or negative. The programmer, however, need not concern himself with the practicalities of representing a bit electronically or magnetically. When he needs to think in terms of the binary representation of information, he can think entirely in terms of ones and zeros.

With one bit, we can represent only two possible values, 0 or 1, and in fact some of the information in our BBC computer is coded using only one bit. For example, in MODE 4, one bit is used to code the colour of each pixel on the screen. Each pixel can be one of two colours, colour 0 or colour 1.

Bit patterns

Bits are usually organised into groups or 'patterns'. With a group of two bits, each bit can one of two values giving 2x2 possible different patterns.

first bit	second bit	bit pattern
0	0	00
0	1	01
1	0	10
1	1	11

A two-bit pattern is used to code the colour of each pixel on the screen in a four colour mode such as MODE 5.

With three bits, there are 2x2x2 possible different patterns and so on:

no. of bits in pattern	example	no. of possible different patterns
1	0	2
2	10	4 = 2x2
3	011	8 = 2x2x2
4	1010	16 = 2x2x2x2
5	10100	32 = 2x2x2x2x2
6	011010	64 = 2x2x2x2x2x2
7	1101001	128 = 2x2x2x2x2x2x2
8	11000101	256 = 2x2x2x2x2x2x2x2

Bit numbering

The bits in a bit pattern are usually referred to by numbering them from zero upwards from right to left, bit0, bit1, bit2 and so on.

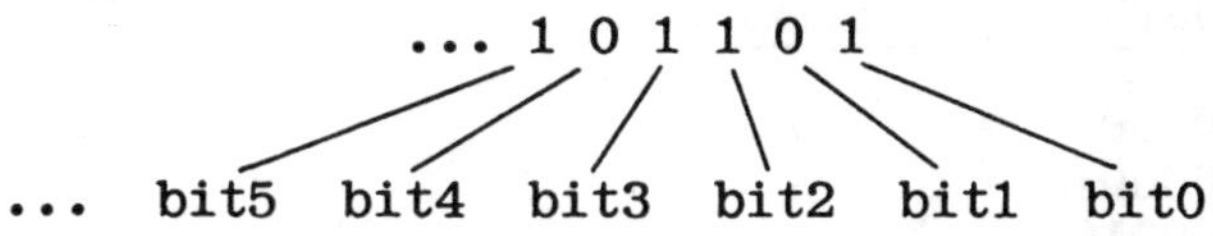

Bytes

A group of 8 bits is called a 'byte'. One 'word' on your BBC micro contains one byte or one 8-bit pattern. The entire store that is accessible to the user consists of 16,384 words or bytes on a Model A and 32,768 words or bytes on a Model B. We usually quote storage capacity in 'K' where:

1K = 1024 $(1024 = 2^{10})$

Because we are working on a binary system, everything is organised behind the scenes in powers of 2. Thus we say that a Model A has 16K bytes of store, i.e. 16*1024 bytes or 16*1024*8 bits.

8-bit integers

When we use a group of decimal digits to represent a non-negative integer, each digit has a weight that is a different power of 10. For example, with 5-digits:

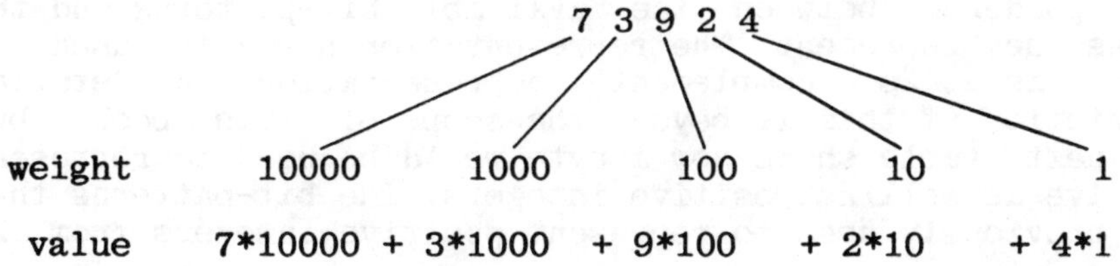

When we use a bit-pattern to represent a non-negative integer, only two values are available for each digit, so we give each digit a weight that is a power of 2. For example, with a 6-bit pattern we might have:

```
                        1 0 1 1 0 1

weight   2*2*2*2*2  2*2*2*2    2*2*2      2*2        2         1
               =32      =16       =8       =4

 value         1*32  + 0*16    + 1*8    + 1*4     + 0*2     + 1*1

            =  45 in decimal
```

When we use a full byte to represent an integer in this way, we have:

binary		decimal
00000000	=	0
00000001	=	1
00000010	=	2
00000011	=	3
:		:
01111110	=	126
01111111	=	127
10000000	=	128
:		:
11111110	=	254
11111111	=	255

We saw earlier that there are 256 different 8-bit patterns and they can be used in this way to represent integers in the range 0 to 255. Because it contributes least weight to an integer, the rightmost bit, bit0, is usually called the least significant bit and the leftmost bit is called the most significant.

8-bit positive and negative integers

If we want to use bytes to represent both positive and negative integers, we have to define a different correspondence between the available bit-patterns and the values they represent. The representation normally used is known as '2s complement' representation. A detailed description of this is beyond the scope of this book, but the next table shows how a byte would be used to represent negative as well as positive integers. The bit-patterns that were previously used to represent positive integers from 128 up to 255 are now used in the same order as before to represent the negative integers from -128 up to -1. In particular, -1 is represented by a bit-pattern that consists entirely of ones. This representation for negative numbers may seem rather strange, but it has many advantages when the computer is doing calculations that involve positive and negative numbers.

binary		decimal
10000000	=	-128
10000001	=	-127
10000010	=	-126
:		:
11111110	=	-2
11111111	=	-1
00000000	=	0
00000001	=	1
00000010	=	2
:		:
01111110	=	126
01111111	=	127

Note that you cannot tell by looking at a bit-pattern what sort of information it is being used to represent. This is determined by the context in which it is used and by the way it is processed by the circuits of the computer. For example, the same bit pattern might be used in different contexts to represent an integer or a character code.

Hexadecimal notation

When we are working with bit-patterns, it becomes very tedious having to write long sequences of ones and zeros when we want to specify a particular bit-pattern. We could abbreviate a byte by writing it as the equivalent positive decimal number, such as 179, but it is not at all obvious if we write 179 that we are talking about the bit-pattern 10110011. When we want to abbreviate a bit-pattern in a way that is not too far removed from its binary form, it is usual to write it in 'hexadecimal' notation (or hex for short). The bit-pattern is first divided into groups of four bits. There are 16 possible different patterns of four bits and each of these possible patterns can be represented by a single 'hexadecimal digit' as follows:

4-bit pattern	hexadecimal digit	4-bit pattern	hexadecimal digit
0000	0	1000	8
0001	1	1001	9
0010	2	1010	A
0011	3	1011	B
0100	4	1100	C
0101	5	1101	D
0110	6	1110	E
0111	7	1111	F

We can thus write the bit-pattern 10100011 in hex as A3:

```
10100011
A   3
```

In BBC BASIC, we can write numbers in a program in hex if we precede the number by the symbol '&'. Thus we write &B3. Here are some other examples of bytes and the corresponding hex and decimal numbers:

byte	hex	decimal
00011111	&1F	31
00101110	&2E	46
01101001	&69	105
11111111	&FF	255

Note that &69 is quite different from decimal 69 which would be represented by the bit-pattern:

01000101 = &85

Because one hexadecimal digit corresponds to four binary digits, it is easy to visualize the bit-pattern corresponding to a hexadecimal number (provided that we are familiar with the sixteen patterns that correspond to the sixteen hex digits). Thus, for example, &B7 is easily visualized as:

```
  &B7
11010111
```

and &FA is easily visualized as:

```
  &FA
11111010
```

32-bit numbers

A numeric variable in BASIC occupies four computer words which contain four bytes or 32 bits. A number stored in such a variable is coded as a pattern of 32 bits. The way in which a 32-bit pattern is used to represent positive and negative integers is a simple extension of the 8-bit 2s complement representation introduced earlier. Note in particular that -1 is represented by a pattern of 32 ones. Details of how real numbers are coded as bit-patterns are beyond the scope of this book.

Logical operations on bit-patterns

The various logical plotting modes selected by GCOL (Chapter 2) use logical operations on bit-patterns when plotting new information on the screen. For this reason alone, some knowledge of these operations is necessary. The logical operators AND, OR, EOR and NOT treat the values to which they are applied as bit-patterns and operate on the individual bits of those patterns. A detailed knowledge of how these operations work is occasionally useful in advanced programming applications.

When a logical operation is applied to a bit-pattern or to a pair of bit-patterns, the individual bits are handled separately in creating the resultant bit-pattern. AND, OR and EOR are each applied to a pair of bit-patterns of the same length and the result is another bit-pattern of the same length. NOT is applied to a single bit-pattern and the result is another bit-pattern of the same length. We shall illustrate the behaviour of the logical operations on bytes, but they will behave in exactly the same way on shorter or longer bit-patterns.

AND

Each bit in the new pattern is the result of 'anding' the two bits in the same position in the two given bit-patterns according to the following table:

bit1	bit2	bit1 AND bit2
0	0	0
0	1	0
1	0	0
1	1	1

Thus, for example:

```
          byte1        10110100
          byte2        01100101

  byte1 AND byte2      00100100
```

OR

Each bit in the new pattern is the result of 'oring' the two bits in the same position in the given bit-patterns according to the following table:

bit1	bit2	bit1 OR bit2
0	0	0
0	1	1
1	0	1
1	1	1

Thus, for example:

byte1	10110100
byte2	01100101
byte1 OR byte2	11110101

EOR

Each bit in the new pattern is the result of 'exclusive oring' the two bits in the same position in the given bit-patterns according to the following table:

bit1	bit2	bit1 EOR bit2
0	0	0
0	1	1
1	0	1
1	1	0

The name of the operator derives from the fact that it 'excludes' the case where both bits to which it is applied are 1. Thus, for example:

byte1	10110100
byte2	01100101
byte1 EOR byte2	11010001

NOT

Each bit in the new bit-pattern is the result of 'negating' the same bit in the given bit-pattern. NOT produces the 'logical inverse' of the given bit-pattern by changing 0s to 1s and 1s to 0s.

bit	NOT bit
0	1
1	0

Thus, for example:

byte	10110100
NOT byte	01001011

Representation of TRUE and FALSE

In BBC BASIC, the value TRUE is represented by a bit-pattern containing nothing but ones and FALSE is represented by a bit-pattern containing nothing but zeros. When these values are stored in numeric variables, they look like the numeric values -1 and 0.

Appendix 3 Characters, ASCII codes, control codes and Teletext codes

ASCII codes

A character is stored inside the computer as an integer that occupies 8 bits or one byte. There is an internationally agreed standard set of codes for the commonly used characters. These are the ASCII codes (American Standard Code for Information Interchange). The next table contains a list of the common visible characters together with their ASCII codes in decimal and hex.

ASCII characters and their codes

decimal code	hex code	char	decimal code	hex code	char	decimal code	hex code	char
32	&20		64	&40	@	96	&60	•
33	&21	!	65	&41	A	97	&61	a
34	&22	"	66	&42	B	98	&62	b
35	&23	#	67	&43	C	99	&63	c
36	&24	$	68	&44	D	100	&64	d
37	&25	%	69	&45	E	101	&65	e
38	&26	&	70	&46	F	102	&66	f
39	&27	'	71	&47	G	103	&67	g
40	&28	(	72	&48	H	104	&68	h
41	&29	)	73	&49	I	105	&69	i
42	&2A	*	74	&4A	J	106	&6A	j
43	&2B	+	75	&4B	K	107	&6B	k
44	&2C	,	76	&4C	L	108	&6C	l
45	&2D	-	77	&4D	M	109	&6D	m
46	&2E	.	78	&4E	N	110	&6E	n
47	&2F	/	79	&4F	O	111	&6F	o
48	&30	0	80	&50	P	112	&70	p
49	&31	1	81	&51	Q	113	&71	q
50	&32	2	82	&52	R	114	&72	r
51	&33	3	83	&53	S	115	&73	s
52	&34	4	84	&54	T	116	&74	t
53	&35	5	85	&55	U	117	&75	u
54	&36	6	86	&56	V	118	&76	v
55	&37	7	87	&57	W	119	&77	w
56	&38	8	88	&58	X	120	&78	x
57	&39	9	89	&59	Y	121	&79	y
58	&3A	:	90	&5A	Z	122	&7A	z
59	&3B	;	91	&5B	[	123	&7B	{
60	&3C	<	92	&5C	\	124	&7C	¦
61	&3D	=	93	&5D	]	125	&7D	}
62	&3E	>	94	&5E	^	126	&7E	~
63	&3F	?	95	&5F	_			

Control codes

A number of the 256 available character codes are reserved for special purposes on the BBC computer. Sending one of these codes to the display hardware by using a PRINT or a VDU statement has a special effect. These codes are usually referred to as 'VDU drivers'. Note that some of the codes must always be followed by a fixed number of additional codes or 'parameters'. If these are omitted, the next few characters printed will be taken as the missing parameters.

Summary of VDU codes

decimal	hex	parameters	effect
0	0	0	Does nothing
1	1	1	Send a character to printer only
2	2	0	Switch on printer output
3	3	0	Switch off printer output
4	4	0	Separate text and graphics cursors
5	5	0	Join text and graphics cursors
6	6	0	Enable VDU drivers
7	7	0	Beep
8	8	0	Move cursor back one space
9	9	0	Move cursor forward one space
10	&A	0	Move cursor down one line
11	&B	0	Move cursor up one line
12	&C	0	CLS (clear text screen)
13	&D	0	Move cursor to start of current line
14	&E	0	Page mode on
15	&F	0	Page mode off
16	&10	0	CLG (clear graphics screen)
17	&11	1	COLOUR c
18	&12	2	GCOL 1,c
19	&13	5	New actual colour for colour number
20	&14	0	Restore default actual colours
21	&15	0	Disable VDU drivers
22	&16	1	MODE m
23	&17	9	Create user-defined character shape
24	&18	8	Define graphics window
25	&19	5	PLOT k,x,y (2 bytes for x, 2 for y)
26	&1A	0	Restore default windows
27	&1B	0	Does nothing
28	&1C	4	Define text window
29	&1D	4	Define graphics origin
30	&1E	0	Move text cursor to top left
31	&1F	2	MOVE x,y
127	&7F	0	Backspace and delete

These codes can also be sent from the keyboard by typing a CONTROL character - hold down the CTRL key and type the character. For example, codes 1 to 26 correspond to CONTROL-A to CONTROL-Z.

Teletext control codes

In Teletext mode (MODE 7), a number of special effects can by switched on and off by displaying special control codes. Remember that one of these control codes appears as a space on the screen and that its effect lasts only for the current screen line.

Teletext control codes for MODE 7

code	controls	effect
129	colour	text characters in red
130	colour	text characters in green
131	colour	text characters in yellow
132	colour	text characters in blue
133	colour	text characters in magenta
134	colour	text characters in cyan
135	colour	text characters in white
136	flash	set flashing on current line
137	flash	clear flashing on current line
140	char. ht.	single height characters
141	char. ht.	double height characters
145	graphics	graphics characters in red
146	graphics	graphics characters in green
147	graphics	graphics characters in yellow
148	graphics	graphics characters in blue
149	graphics	graphics characters in magenta
150	graphics	graphics characters in cyan
151	graphics	graphics characters in white
152	special	supress display (hide)
153	special	normal graphics (not separated)
154	special	separated graphics
156	colour	reset background colour to black
157	colour	background colour = current foreground

Teletext graphics characters

The Teletext (MODE 7) graphics characters consist of 2x3 patterns of foreground and background colour. There are two numeric codes for each of the graphics character shapes. After a line of text has been switched to graphics mode by one of the graphics codes in the previous table, the ASCII characters with codes 32 to 63 and 95 to 126 are displayed as graphics characters. (The codes from 64 to 94 are displayed as normal ASCII characters, i.e. numeric digits and capital letters.)

These ASCII codes provide a convenient way of printing a string of graphics characters. A PRINT statement in a program can contain a string of the corresponding ASCII characters, and, providing an appropriate code precedes them on the output line, they will be displayed as graphics characters.

The graphics shapes that replace the normal ASCII characters are given in the next table. Note that there is no lower code for a solid block of foreground colour.

Graphics characters that replace the normal ASCII characters

decimal code	hex code	ASCII char.	graphics char.	decimal code	hex code	ASCII char.	graphics char.
				95	&5F	_	
32	&20	space		96	&60	•	
33	&21	!		97	&61	a	
34	&22	"		98	&62	b	
35	&23	#		99	&63	c	
36	&24	$		100	&64	d	
37	&25	%		101	&65	e	
38	&26	&		102	&66	f	
39	&27	'		103	&67	g	
40	&28	(		104	&68	h	
41	&29	)		105	&69	i	
42	&2A	*		106	&6A	j	
43	&2B	+		107	&6B	k	
44	&2C	,		108	&6C	l	
45	&2D	–		109	&6D	m	
46	&2E	.		110	&6E	n	
47	&2F	/		111	&6F	o	
48	&30	0		112	&70	p	
49	&31	1		113	&71	q	
50	&32	2		114	&72	r	
51	&33	3		115	&73	s	
52	&34	4		116	&74	t	
53	&35	5		117	&75	u	
54	&36	6		118	&76	v	
55	&37	7		119	&77	w	
56	&38	8		120	&78	x	
57	&39	9		121	&79	y	
58	&3A	:		122	&7A	z	
59	&3B	;		123	&7B	{	
60	&3C	<		124	&7C	¦	
61	&3D	=		125	&7D	}	
62	&3E	>		126	&7E	~	
63	&3F	?					

The other codes for graphics characters are 160 to 191 and 224 to 255. To print graphics characters using these codes, the VDU statement can be used, or CHR$ can be used to construct a string containing graphics codes. The advantage of these higher codes is that the order in which the codes correspond to the graphics shapes is more systematic. A program (or programmer) can more easily calculate a code for a given shape. We label the six cells in a graphics character as follows:

bit0	bit1
bit2	bit3
bit4	bit6

These numberings correspond to the bits in the one byte character code as follows:

1	0	1	0	0	0	0	0
bit7	bit6	bit5	bit4	bit3	bit2	bit1	bit0

In the higher codes for graphics characters, bit5 and bit7 are always set to 1. The remaining bits are set to 1 for foreground colour and to 0 for background colour in the corresponding cell. Thus, given the bit values that specify a shape, the code for the required character can be calculated by

$$\text{bit0} + \text{bit1}*2 + \text{bit2}*4 + \text{bit3}*8 + \text{bit4}*16 + \text{bit6}*64 + 32 + 128$$

There is no such simple expression for calculating the lower codes.

Appendix 4 Matrix notation and multiplication

In Chapter 3 we have made use of matrix notation in linear transforms. We say that a point (x,y) transforms to a point (xt,yt):

$$xt = ax + by$$
$$yt = cx + dy$$

Given that all our transformations are of this form we can say that the transform T can be represented by the matrix:

$$\begin{bmatrix} a & c \\ b & d \end{bmatrix}$$

Now using matrix notation to represent the above operation we rewrite the equations in the form:

$$(xt, yt) = (x, y) \begin{bmatrix} a & c \\ b & d \end{bmatrix}$$

On the right hand side we are multiplying a row matrix (representing a single point in two-dimensional space) by a 2x2 matrix. The equation specified in the matrix notation is identical in every respect to the non-matrix form of the equation. To obtain xt from the matrix form we multiply the row matrix (x,y) by the first column:

$$xt = (x, y) \begin{bmatrix} a & . \\ b & . \end{bmatrix}$$

$$= ax + by$$

and to obtain yt from the matrix form we multiply the row vector by the second column:

$$yt = (x, y) \begin{bmatrix} . & c \\ . & d \end{bmatrix}$$
$$= cx + dy$$

The other context in which we used matrix multiplication was to concatenate transforms together.

$$T = T1*T2$$
$$= \begin{bmatrix} a & c \\ b & d \end{bmatrix} \begin{bmatrix} e & g \\ f & h \end{bmatrix}$$

$$= \begin{bmatrix} (ae + cf) & (ag + ch) \\ (be + df) & (bg + dh) \end{bmatrix}$$

$$= \begin{bmatrix} p & r \\ q & s \end{bmatrix}$$

p is formed by taking the sum of the products of the entries in the first row of T1 with the first column in T2. q is formed by taking the sum of the products of the entries in the second row in T1 with the first column in T2. Inspecting the other two entries r and s will show how these are similarly derived. In the general case:

$$C = A*B$$

each entry Cij of the product is the sum of the products of the entries of the ith row of A with the corresponding entries of the jth column of B. We could easily write a procedure to multiply two 3x3 matrices together and this follows. In Chapter 3 we multiplied matrices together manually.

```
100    DEF PROCmatmult
110      FOR i = 1 TO 3
120        FOR j = 1 TO 3
130          INPUT A(i,j)
140        NEXT j
150      NEXT i

160      FOR i = 1 TO 3
170        FOR j = 1 TO 3
180          INPUT B(i,j)
190        NEXT i
200      NEXT j

210      FOR i = 1 TO 3
220        FOR j = 1 TO 3
230          sum = 0
240          FOR k = 1 TO 3
250            sum = sum + A(i,k)*B(k,j)
260          NEXT k
270        C(i,j) = sum
280        NEXT j
290      NEXT i
300    ENDPROC
```

Here we have used the usual convention when handling matrices - the first subscript is the row number, the second subscript is the column number (not to be confused with the convention for handling screen coordinates). Note that the each matrix must be typed in row-wise.

Appendix 5 The viewing transformation

The viewing transformation, V, transforms points in the world coordinate system into the eye coordinate system:

(xe, ye, ze, 1) = (xw, yw, zw, 1)V

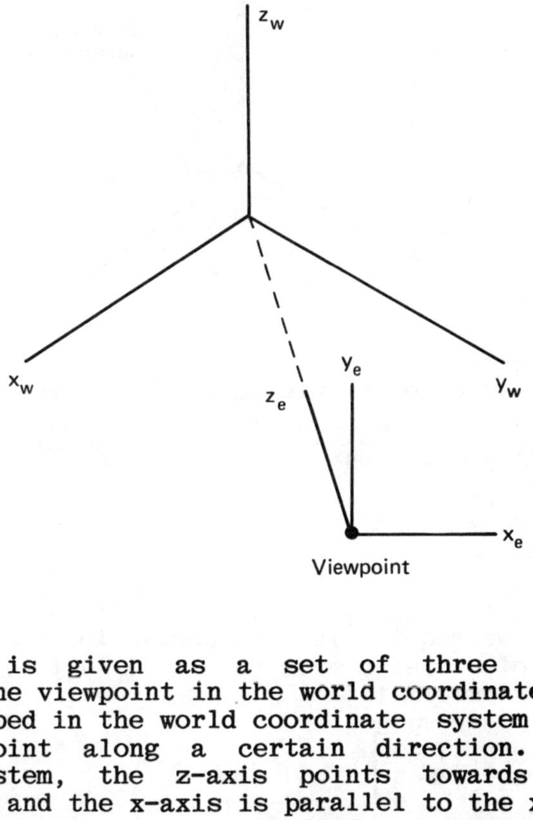

A viewpoint is given as a set of three coordinates specifying the viewpoint in the world coordinate system. An object described in the world coordinate system is viewed from this point along a certain direction. In the eye coordinate system, the z-axis points towards the world system origin and the x-axis is parallel to the x-y plane of the world system. It is standard to adopt a left-handed convention for the eye coordinate system. In the eye coordinate system the x and y-axes match the axes of the display system and the ze direction is away from the viewpoint (into the display screen). World coordinates are normally right handed systems so that in the computation of a net transformation matrix for the viewing transformation we would include a conversion to a left-handed system.

We can now specify the net transformation matrix as a series of translations and rotations that take us from the world coordinate system into the eye coordinate system, given a particular viewpoint. These steps will be given as separate transformation matrices and the net transformation matrix resulting from the product will simply be stated. If you are unhappy with the derivation you can of course skip it and accept the final result - the net transformation matrix required for a viewing transformation.

Now the viewing transformation is best specified using spherical instead of cartesian coordinates. We specify a viewpoint in spherical coordinates by giving a distance from the origin (rho) and two angles (theta and phi).

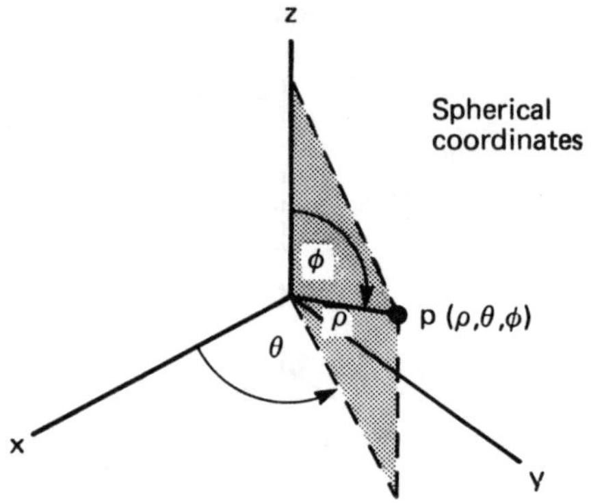

These are related to the viewpoint's cartesian coordinates as follows:

$$Tx = \rho \sin\phi \cos\theta$$
$$Ty = \rho \sin\phi \sin\theta$$
$$Tz = \rho \cos\phi$$

Another fact we require in this derivation is that to change the <u>origin</u> of a system from (0, 0, 0, 1) to (Tx, Ty, Tz, 1) we use the transformation:

$$\begin{bmatrix} 1 & 0 & 0 & 0 \\ 0 & 1 & 0 & 0 \\ 0 & 0 & 1 & 0 \\ -Tx & -Ty & -Tz & 1 \end{bmatrix}$$

Note that this is the <u>inverse</u> of the transformation that would take a point from (0, 0, 0, 1) to (Tx, Ty, Tz, 1).

The four transformations required to take the object from a world coordinate system into an eye coordinate system are:

(1) Translate the world coordinate system to (Tx, Ty, Tz), the position of the viewpoint. All three axes remain

parallel to their counterparts in the world system.

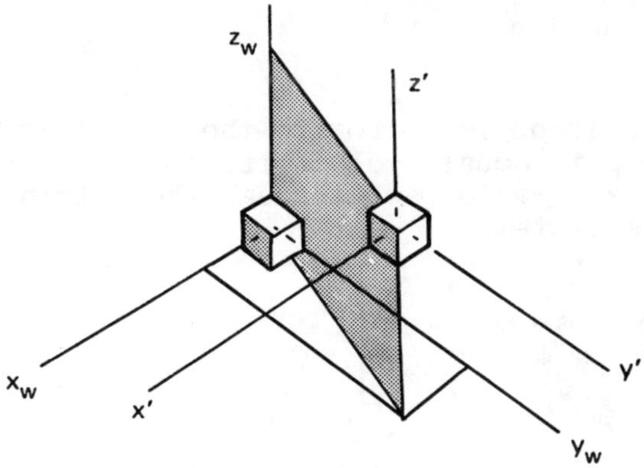

The cube in the diagram is not an object that is being transformed, but is intended to enhance an interpretation of the axes. Using spherical coordinate values for Tx, Ty, and Tz the transformation is:

$$T1 = \begin{bmatrix} 1 & 0 & 0 & 0 \\ 0 & 1 & 0 & 0 \\ 0 & 0 & 1 & 0 \\ -\rho\cos\theta\sin\phi & -\rho\sin\theta\sin\phi & -\rho\cos\phi & 1 \end{bmatrix}$$

(2) The next step is to rotate the coordinate system through (90 degrees - theta) in a clockwise direction about the z'-axis. The rotation matrices defined in Chapter 3 were for counter-clockwise rotation relative to a coordinate system. The transformation matrix for a clockwise rotation of the coordinate system is the same as that for a counter-clockwise rotation of a point relative to the coordinate system. The x''-axis is now normal to the plane containing rho.

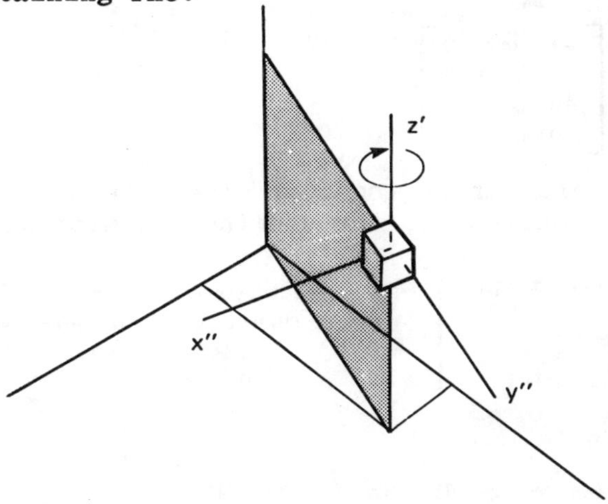

$$T2 = \begin{bmatrix} \sin\theta & \cos\theta & 0 & 0 \\ -\cos\theta & \sin\theta & 0 & 0 \\ 0 & 0 & 1 & 0 \\ 0 & 0 & 0 & 1 \end{bmatrix}$$

(3) The next step is to rotate the coordinate system (180 degrees - phi) counter-clockwise about the x'-axis. This makes the z'''-axis pass through the origin of the world coordinate system.

$$T3 = \begin{bmatrix} 1 & 0 & 0 & 0 \\ 0 & -\cos\phi & -\sin\phi & 0 \\ 0 & \sin\phi & -\cos\phi & 0 \\ 0 & 0 & 0 & 1 \end{bmatrix}$$

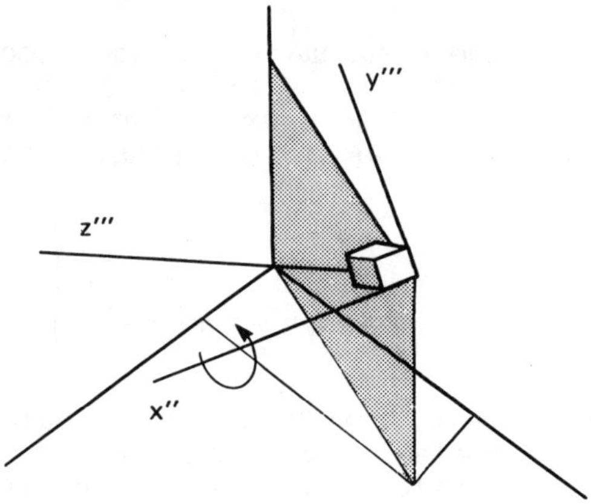

(4) Finally we convert to a left-handed system as described above.

$$T4 = \begin{bmatrix} -1 & 0 & 0 & 0 \\ 0 & 1 & 0 & 0 \\ 0 & 0 & 1 & 0 \\ 0 & 0 & 0 & 1 \end{bmatrix}$$

Multiplying these together gives the net transformation matrix required for the viewing transformation.

$$V = T1*T2*T3*T4 = \begin{bmatrix} -\sin\theta & -\cos\theta\cos\phi & -\cos\theta\sin\phi & 0 \\ \cos\theta & -\sin\theta\cos\phi & -\sin\theta\sin\phi & 0 \\ 0 & \sin\phi & -\cos\phi & 0 \\ 0 & 0 & \rho & 1 \end{bmatrix}$$

where

$$(xe \quad ye \quad ze \quad 1) = (xw \quad yw \quad zw \quad 1)*V$$

Index